XHTML 1.0 Web Development Sourcebook

XHTML 1.0 Web Development Sourcebook

Building Better Sites and Applications

Ian S. Graham

Wiley Computer Publishing

John Wiley & Sons, Inc.

NEW YORK · CHICHESTER · WEINHEIM · BRISBANE · SINGAPORE · TORONTO

Publisher: Robert Ipsen

Editor: Cary Sullivan

Assistant Editor: Christina Berry

Managing Editor: Marnie Wielage

Text Design & Composition: North Market Street Graphics

Designations used by companies to distinguish their products are often claimed as trademarks. In all instances where John Wiley & Sons, Inc., is aware of a claim, the product names appear in initial capital or ALL CAPITAL LETTERS. Readers, however, should contact the appropriate companies for more complete information regarding trademarks and registration.

This book is printed on acid-free paper. ♾

This publication is designed to provide accurate and authoritative information in regard to the subject matter covered. It is sold with the understanding that the publisher is not engaged in professional services. If professional advice or other expert assistance is required, the services of a competent professional person should be sought.

Library of Congress Cataloging-In-Publication Data:

Graham, Ian S., 1955–
    XHTML 1.0 Web development sourcebook: building better sites and applications / Ian S. Graham.
      p. cm.
    "Wiley Computer Publishing."
    ISBN 0-471-37486-5 (paper/website: alk. paper)
    1. XHTML (Document markup language)   I. Title.
QA76.76.H94 G73345 2000
005.7'2—dc21
                                      00-043325

Printed in the United States of America.

10 9 8 7 6 5 4 3 2 1

Contents

Acknowledgments

Every book is written based on things that the writer learns or has grown through experience to understand. In my case, much of this learning and growth has been due to the many friends and colleagues with whom I have talked, argued, and worked over the past seven years. Many people have contributed in this way, but a few helped directly in the preparation of this book and warrant specific mention here. In particular, Marc Lalonde and Sian Meikle graciously edited Chapters 1 through 5 and were always willing to talk over Web design or site management issues. In the same vein, Lidio Presutti edited Chapter 9 and suggested some useful clarifications and improvements. Laurie Harrison carefully edited Section 4.4 and turned a rambling section into a much improved, literate summary. Nancy Sicchia contributed some wonderful figures for Chapters 4 and 6, and Jay Moonah contributed humor (always needed!) and provided some useful overall feedback. Allen Forsyth helped me set up some Java testing tools, and Norman Wilson wrote the code for the original *listen* program (Appendix C). Jutta Treviranus simply let me write when I needed to, knowing that my real work would get done. To them and all the others who provided input or feedback on material used in previous books (John Bradley, Michael Lee, Håkon Lie, Chris Lilley, Kelly Peters, Liam Quin, Steve Rapaport, and others), I offer my profound thanks.

On a more personal side, my friend Tad Homer-Dixon helped me retain my sanity—as I was finishing this book, so was he finishing his own, and we commiserated with each other as deadlines were missed and as our failing bodies seemed to fail us at our hour of need. And as for the last aspect, I must especially thank my physiotherapists Carl Gale and Scott Whitmore, who literally kept my body working when I thought it was truly going to collapse under the strain. So, remember all you computer programmers or writers—sitting and typing for 12 hours a day is bad for you! Go for a walk! Stretch! And *listen* to your body when it starts to hurt!

But first, above all others, I must thank my wife, Ann, for her love, patience, editing skills, coffee, snacks, occasional gin and tonics (but not while writing), and pointed reminders that sitting in my chair for 18 hours straight really *will* kill me! My thanks and love can never be sufficient.

Introduction and Book Outline

Building Web sites used to be easy—slap up a few Web pages, add in a few links, and you were done. Indeed, this was essentially the "Web design" model during the first few years of the Web's existence. Indeed, initially the only differences were that the number of pages got larger, good graphic and page designers helped make the pages look better, and large sites started to use software tools to help manage the deployment and maintenance of pages, or to allow simple interactive queries of online databases.

However, in the past few years, the job has rapidly become far more complex. There are many technical reasons why this is so, but the driving forces can be boiled down to two main points:

1. Today's Web sites are technically far more complicated and are often Web front ends to complicated back-end software applications and/or databases.

2. As Web sites have become business-critical services, as opposed to one-off marketing ploys, more care is needed to control and understand the costs of ongoing maintenance and updates (it's simply too expensive to start from scratch every time).

Thus, building a Web site is now a lot more than slapping up a few pages, and it has become a craft that requires a good technical understanding of the Web plus sophisticated skills in project planning and management. Today's Web developers, therefore, need to clearly understand the technical functions and roles of the various Web technologies (not just HTML and a bit of JavaScript), so that they can appropriately understand how to use these tools when designing complex applications. Moreover, because developers must often work with large teams to accomplish these goals, and need to develop maintainable, scalable sites and applications, they need to know how to carefully define such projects and manage their development. The goal of this book is to help you learn and understand these features, by providing a solid review of the technical model for the Web, along with a sound analysis of the ways in which Web projects can be technically defined and managed.

About the Book and the Intended Audience

This book is intended for Web developers who want to learn new technical and management skills so that they can jump to the next level of Web project development. Thus, this book outlines the technical details of the main Web technologies and explains how they are related to each other and how they are best used. For example, what is XML and why should I care? What are the advantages and disadvantages of using JavaScript? How do markup, URLs, JavaScript, CGI programs, servlets, HTTP, and MIME work, and how do they work together? What do I need to know about Internet networking to make my site perform properly?

Second, this book looks at the organizational and management problems associated with planning and implementing a Web site. Thus, the book examines how to work with clients to set reasonable page design and performance requirements, describes models for site layout and implementation, and looks at approaches for designing a site or Web application, and for managing the site's development.

Chapters 1 through 3 review markup, formatting, and document scripting. After reading these chapters, you will have a sound understanding of HTML, XHTML, XML, CSS, XSL, JavaScript, and the DOM. If you don't know these acronyms now, don't worry—they are explained in these chapters and are reviewed briefly in the next section of this Preface. If you want the hard-core details about XHTML and CSS, then I recommend you purchase the *XHTML 1.0 Language and Design Sourcebook* (Wiley, 2000), the companion book to this one. Indeed, these books were designed to be complementary—the *XHTML 1.0 Language and Design Sourcebook* provides details on how to use XHTML and CSS to design well-crafted Web pages, and this book explains how to hook all the pages together to create a large-scale application.

Chapter 4 switches gears and talks about the high-level technical task of designing Web documents and setting requirements for such designs. This is in part a tips-and-tricks chapter (e.g., how to measure browser performance, how to optimize markup designs, how to create component based designs), but it's also a chapter that describes how to set technical requirements for page designs of an upcoming project.

Chapter 5 steps back from the local scale of the individual pages and discusses global issues associated with designing entire Web sites. In particular, it is helpful to know some well-defined models for how sites can be built; this chapter provides and explains many such models and uses actual Web site pages to illustrate the different approaches. This chapter also provides some design and implementation tips to help you understand common design issues and to avoid common design mistakes.

Chapter 6 returns to the management and implementation question and looks at the process of managing a site's design, implementation, and ongoing maintenance. This chapter touches on some technical issues, but it primarily focuses on the big-picture questions: How do you define the scope for the project? How do you mock up a design? How do you go from a prototype to an implemented application?

Chapters 7 through 11 return to technical issues. Chapter 7 provides a concise overview of Internet networking, and helps explain how components such as the domain name systems, firewalls, and security play an important role when you physically implement a Web site. Chapter 8 reviews the syntax of URLs and describes the many different types of URLs in use on the Web. Chapter 9 goes on to explain how the HTTP protocol works and how data is sent between Web clients and servers. This is essential knowledge for anyone involved in building complex Web applications. Chapter 10 looks at the ways in which Web servers can be customized to provide the application services and, in particular, looks at the *common gateway interface* (CGI) mechanisms that define how data gets passed between a Web server to back-end software applications. Chapter 11 then reviews some simple CGI-based examples to illustrate how this works.

Finally, Chapter 12 discusses the types of tools you need to use when managing a Web site or when developing Web applications. This is partly a technical chapter, but mostly it is a guide to how to define your technical problems and how to choose wisely the tools you need for implementing your project.

Review of the Web Model

Understanding how the whole Web works requires a good appreciation of how the key components fit together. Although these issues are discussed in detail in the rest of this book, a quick summary is found in this section—a figurative illustration of these components and the relationships between them is found in Figure P.1. The user's tool is the Web client (typically a *browser* and sometimes called a *user agent*), which retrieves data from Web (or other) servers using the HTTP (or other) protocol. The Web client is the component that understands and displays markup documents and that can run script programs that interact with the document to provide for dynamic content. This is the component that understands the HTML data it receives and that can use style sheet documents to control how it actually displays the content. Also, the browser understands Uniform Resource Locators (*URLs*) and can use them to locate and communicate with URL-specified resources, using the communications mechanism (or *protocol*) specified in the URL. One of the most important protocols is *HyperText Transfer Protocol (HTTP)*—most Web servers use this protocol and are called *HTTP* or *Web servers*. Using a Web server's *CGI* (or other, similar mechanisms), users can access other resources on the Web server, such as databases.

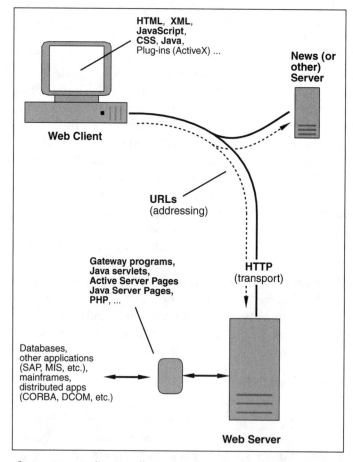

Figure P.1 A diagram illustrating the essential components of the World Wide Web and of a World Wide Web application. See the text for a discussion of this figure.

The next few paragraphs describe each of these key components in a little more detail.

The HyperText Markup Language (HTML, and its successor language, XHTML). The markup language with which most World Wide Web hypertext documents are written, which allows you to create hypertext links, fill-in forms, and so on. Writing good documents involves both technical issues (proper construction of the document) and design issues (ensuring the information content is clearly presented to the user). These issues are discussed in detail in the *XHTML 1.0 Language and Design Sourcebook,* the companion book to this one. Documents can contain hypertext links that reference, using *URLs,* other resources on the Internet. They can also contain *document scripts* that allow for local interaction between the user, the browser, and the marked-up document.

Uniform Resource Locators (URLs). The way in which Web resources are named or addressed. If you want to reference a resource on the Internet, you specify its URL.

Document script programs. Typically written in the *JavaScript* programming language (although other languages are supported by some browsers); can be included with marked-up documents. They allow for dynamic interaction with the document markup and formatting [using the *Document Object Model* (DOM) interfaces].

The Cascading Style Sheets (CSS) language. Can control page layout and formatting of HTML, XHTML, or XML documents. This language can define how a document should be formatted and displayed by the browser or when printed. This language is discussed in detail in the *XHTML 1.0 Language and Design Sourcebook,* the companion book to this one. Document script programs can dynamically changes CSS formatting characteristics using the DOM programming interfaces.

The eXtensible Markup Language (XML). A tool for creating markup languages of your own and a mechanism for delivering custom data to browsers, or for storing and processing such data on a server. There is also a special language, called *eXtensible Stylesheet Language Transformation* (XSLT), designed for transforming incoming XML documents into other XML documents more useful to the browser or other applications.

The Document Object Model (DOM). Defines a generic programming interface that lets programs dynamically interact with markup (e.g., HTML or XML) content and with CSS formatting properties attached to such documents. Thus, a JavaScript program on a browser can use the DOM interface to dynamically change the information on a page or the way a page looks.

The HyperText Transfer Protocol (HTTP). The tool used on the Internet to move data between Web clients (e.g., a browser) and a Web server. This communication goes in both directions—clients send data to servers, and servers send data to clients. The Internet supports many other protocols, such as the File Transfer Protocol [FTP (for simple files transfers)], the Simple Mail Transfer Protocol [SMTP (for sending e-mail messages)], and others. Resources available using these different protocols can be referenced using appropriate URLs.

Gateway programs. Java servlets and other technologies let a Web server connect to back-end software lying on the same machine as the server. This effectively provides a tunnel through the server to back-end software, and it is what lets you turn a Web browser into the front end for a sophisticated Web application. Gateway access can be implemented through the so-called CGI, through Java servlets, through parsed document scripts [e.g., Active Server Pages (ASP) or PHP], or through using special modules that are built into the server. These back-end components may then use software tools such as Common Object Request Broker Architecture (CORBA) or Distributed Component Object Model (DCOM) to connect to other processes running on other computers.

Book Notation

Note that the shorthand notation *X/HTML* refers to *both* the HTML and XHTML languages (the languages are largely the same—Chapter 2 explains the similarities and differences). In this book, X/HTML element and attribute names are generally given in boldface normal font, for example, **div** or **align**="left". Similarly, the names of URL schemes are given in a boldface lowercase text, as in the phrase ". . . and with **ftp** or **http** URLs . . ." On the other hand, cascading style sheet property names and values are given in a monospace font, as in ". . . the `text-align` property can take the value `left` to mean. . . ." This helps distinguish the X/HTML markup from CSS mechanisms, and it should make reading the text easier.

A monospace font is always used for explicit examples of markup or JavaScript code, as in "the start tag `<div class="foo">` denotes the start of a **div** element . . ." or "A new window can be opened using the `window.open()` method of the . . ." Sometimes, this text is italicized for emphasis, or to note values that need to be set by the author. In general, this usage should be obvious (or, in the case of figures, explained in the figure caption).

Program, directory, and file names are often given in an italicized normal font to make them stand out from the text and to reduce confusion (e.g., "the file *test.html* is found in . . ."). However, this is not always the case, and in many situations, the names are given in a regular nonitalicized font to make the text easier to read.

URL references are written using the standard text font, again, sometimes in italics to make them stand out. However, to make the text shorter and easier to read, the http:// portion has been omitted from all **http** URLs. Most browsers (in particular, Netscape Navigator and Internet Explorer) assume that strings typed into the Location (Netscape) or Address (Microsoft) windows are **http** URLs, if no other protocol is specified. With some other browsers, you will need to explicitly add the http:// portion. And, of course, you *always* need to add the http:// when you use a URL as an **href** value in a document or as the value of some other attribute.

The Companion Web Site

www.utoronto.ca/ian/books/
www.wiley.com/compbooks/graham/

For those of you familiar with previous books by this author, much of the utility of the book is found at the book's supporting Web site. This site provides all the example documents used in this book, plus additional information such as reference lists, appendixes, and sample documents that help illustrate newer points. So, if you want the example HTML documents or JavaScript programs, or if you want to download the source code for *backtalk.c, listen.c,* or *monitor.c,* just visit the Web site—it's all there waiting for you. Of particular interest will be the online References pages, which provide, in hypertext format, all of the URL references included in this book. You'll also find the following book appendixes:

   Appendix A: Character Sets, Character Encoding, and Document Character Sets

   Appendix B: Multipurpose Internet Mail Extensions (MIME)

   Appendix C: Monitoring HTTP Transactions

   Appendix D: HTTP Methods and Header Fields Reference

   Appendix E: Syntax for Server Side Includes

Download a Copy of the Web Site!

www.utoronto.ca/ian/books/
xhtml2/download.html

Moreover, the entire Web site content is available as a downloadable archive, so that you can easily download it and install it on your computer's hard disk, giving you a local copy of all these resources. Simply access the URL just mentioned and follow the links from there—the file is not big and will download in a few minutes even over a slow modem. In this sense, the Web site is similar to, but better than, a CD-ROM—it's cheaper and more up to date!

The Companion Book: The *XHTML 1.0 Language and Design Sourcebook*

www.utoronto.ca/ian/books/xhtml1/

Of course, every Web designer will also want to know the nitty-gritty details of X/HTML, CSS, and Web page design. These topics are covered in detail in the *XHTML 1.0 Language and Design Sourcebook,* the companion book to this one. The *XHTML 1.0 Language and Design Sourcebook* is a complete guide to Web design using HTML 4.01, XHTML 1.0, and CSS. Designed to teach you the how and why of technical Web design, the first 20 chapters provide progressively more details of these languages and of page design, with particular emphasis on universal, cross-browser approaches. These chapters also discuss the differences between HTML and the newer XHTML language, and they describe how to easily build XHTML documents that work well in both worlds. Finally, the last two chapters provide detailed, concise references to the HTML and CSS languages. It's just what the doctor ordered when trying to figure out how an element or attribute (or CSS property value) can be used.

CHAPTER 1

Markup and Layout Review: HTML and CSS

Topics/Concepts Covered: Introduction to markup; introduction to HTML; parsing markup; style sheets and rendering control

This chapter introduces the basics of text markup: what it is, how it works, and how software processes marked-up data. The intent here is to introduce essential ideas without going into too many details. If you understand the concepts behind markup parsing, the construction of parse trees (how the computer internally represents a document), and style sheet–based control of the rendering of marked-up text, you will probably want to just glance through this chapter and move on to Chapter 2. If these ideas are a bit new, then this short chapter will quickly get you up to speed.

A markup language is a tool for describing the meaning of, and/or the relationship between different parts of a document. In general, such a language consists of instructions, embedded in the text of a document, that divide the document into parts and assign meaning to those parts. For example, the following document:

> **[start_paragraph]** My **[begin_boldface]** Frozen Albatross **[end_boldface]** is too frozen to eat. What am I going to do? **[end_paragraph]**

consists of *text* (the phrases "My Frozen Albatross is too frozen to eat. What am I going to do?") and *markup* (the text inside the brackets) that defines the parts of the document: a paragraph containing text, some of which should be rendered in boldface. The strings **[start_paragraph]**, **[begin_boldface]**, and so

on (highlighted in boldface for emphasis) would be defined as part of the markup language. In general, a markup language has rules for how the special strings (often called *tags*) are written, and defines a set of such tags (such as the ones in the preceding example) that provide the desired description of a document's content.

There are two conceptual approaches to markup: *physical* and *semantic*. With physical markup, the tags indicate how the text should look when displayed: The [**begin_boldface**] and [**end_boldface**] tags shown previously are examples. This approach is good if the text is only being printed, but bad if printing is not the only goal. Suppose, for example, the preceding document is displayed by a device (such as a text-to-speech converter) incapable of rendering text in boldface. In this case, the physical markup tags are useless— "boldface" has no meaning to a text-to-speech converter!

With *semantic* markup, tags define the meaning or structure behind the text, not how it is supposed to look. In the previous example, the tags [**start_paragraph**] and [**end_paragraph**] are good examples of semantic markup. These tags mark the beginning and end of a paragraph—a logical unit of the document that could reasonably be displayed in a number of different ways.

A particular advantage of semantically marked-up documents is that the document content, or data, can often be used in ways not originally considered when the document was written. For example, if a document contains all the information of a purchase order, then software can extract this information and render it on a computer screen, print it on paper, or read it into an order processor and automatically process the purchase. Thus, marked-up data is not just useful for word processing—it can also be an important component of data processing and machine-to-machine communication.

Note how this latter paragraph expands upon the traditional idea of a document: Whereas most people think of a document as something that might be read by a person, software is not nearly so restricted. Indeed, as far as software is concerned, a document is anything that can be marked up—a novel, a purchase order, a spreadsheet, or even the content of a database. Indeed, it is this ability to mark up just about any type of data that makes markup languages so powerful, and a key component of Web-based applications. Chapter 2 will deal with this more general functionality of markup. The rest of this chapter will discuss HTML as an example of a markup language.

1.1 The HyperText Markup Language

The *HyperText Markup Language* (HTML) is a simple markup language designed for distributing information over the Web. In terms of the semantic/physical markup models just described, HTML is best thought of as an "impure" semantic language: It contains many purely semantic markup components (paragraphs, headings, divisions, block quotations, etc.), but also some components (boldface font, italic font, text color) specific to how things should look.

We can illustrate the general principles of markup using the simple HTML document shown in Figure 1.1. The focus here is on the underlying concepts of markup syntax and document *parsability* (i.e., the ability of software to reliably handle the document's data). The details of the HTML language itself are found in the companion book, *XHTML 1.0 Language and Design Sourcebook.*

In HTML, markup tags are just strings of text enclosed by a less than and greater than sign (< . . . >). There are two main types of tags, called *start* and *end* tags, which denote the start and end points of marked-up regions. For example, in Figure 1.1 the text

```
<h2> 1.2 An Example HTML Document </h2>
```

has the tag `<h2>` to mark the start of a level 2 heading, and the tag `</h2>` to mark the end of the heading: The text (and possibly other markup) between the two tags is called the *content.* Note how the forward slash indicates an end tag.

Tags and their content are also called markup *elements.* Thus, the markup

```
<h2> 1.2 An Example HTML Document </h2>
```

is an **h2** element, consisting of the start tag, the enclosed text, and the end tag. Elements like this are also called *containers,* since they *contain* the text that makes up the heading.

Some elements, instead of being containers, are *empty.* This is the case for elements that do not contain (i.e., affect) the document text. (Note: The HTML specification defines the element names that are part of the language, and also defines which elements are and are not "empty.") Because they are empty, such elements do not have end tags. In HTML, they are written using just a start tag: It is up to the software processing the document to understand that the tag corresponds to an empty element and that it does not have an end tag. For example, the **img** (inline image) element is empty (an inline image clearly does not "contain" any text), and appears only as a start tag, as shown in Figure 1.1:

```
<img src="weird-icon.gif" height="110" width="110"
     alt="Weird Icon -- just for show" align="right" >
```

This **img** element also illustrates element *attributes*—tools for defining properties or special information about the element. For example, this ele-

```
<HTML>
  <head>
    <title>An Example HTML Document</title>
    <link rel="stylesheet" href="ex-stylesheet.css">
  </head>
  <body>
    <div class="section">
      <h2> 1.2 An Example HTML Document </h2>
        <p>XHTML, and its predecessor language HTML, are just
        markup languages designed for use on the Web. They both use
        tags that are written using regular printable characters.
        Indeed, the two languages are nearly identical--
        <a href="chapter2.html">Chapter 2</a>
        looks at them, and their differences, in more detail.
        </p>
        <img src="weird-icon.gif" height="110" width="110"
            alt="Weird Icon -- just for show" align="right">
        <p>
        To illustrate how these languages work, we will start with
        a simple example HTML (not XHTML) document, shown in Figure
        ... omitted content ...
        example as an XHTML document to help highlight the differences
        between HTML and XHTML.
        </p>
        <DIV CLASS="tip">
          <h3> TIP: Differences between XHTML and HTML </h3>
          <p> The rules for writing correct XHTML and HTML documents
              are slightly different, and are outlined in more
          ... omitted content ...
          treated as HTML.
        </div>
    </div>
  </body>
</html>
```

Figure 1.1 A simple HTML document. The text indentation helps illustrate how the elements are nested one within another. The italicized lines of the form *... omitted content ...* indicate text content that was omitted from this figure to save space. The original document is available from the book's supporting Web site.

ment has five attributes (**src**, **height**, **width**, **alt**, and **align**) that are assigned specific values. The meanings of these attributes, like the meanings of the elements themselves, are defined in the language specification. Indeed, the language specification defines the names and types of each element along with the attributes supported by it.

In HTML, tag (and attribute) names are *case insensitive*. Thus the tag <HTML> that begins the document is paired with the tag </html> that ends it, while the tag <DIV CLASS="tip"> is paired against the end tag </div>.

1.1.1 Syntax and Structured Markup

The preceding paragraphs described the *syntax* rules for writing the markup tags. Another important structural rule states that elements must always be *nested* one inside the other. Consequently, markup like

```
<em> <h2> em and h2 overlap -- this is illegal markup! </em> </h2>
```

is illegal, since the **em** and **h2** elements do not nest, but instead overlap. Nesting is a fundamental requirement of all markup languages, not just HTML. We will see why this is so important in the next section.

Additional structural rules can be imposed by the *grammar* specific to each language. For example, the HTML grammar defines the names (e.g., **h1**, **body**, etc.) of the markup elements, the attributes they can have, and the allowed nestings of those elements (e.g., **h1** can be inside **body** but not vice versa). These rules state that an HTML document must have an **html** element that in turn contains one **head** and one **body** element, and that the **head** and **body** can, in turn, only contain certain other elements, but cannot contain other **head** or **body** elements. It is these grammar rules that define the basic structure of every HTML document:

```
<html>
  <head>
  ... head-content elements
  </head>
  <body>
  ... body-content elements
  </body>
</html>
```

Again, the companion book (*XHTML 1.0 Language and Design Sourcebook*) goes into the details of HTML, should you want more information on this language.

1.1.2 Parsable Documents

When software reads a document containing markup, it converts the data and markup into a form understandable to and usable by the software. If this cannot be done reliably, the software is left in a quandary. It can either attempt to do its best (which will yield unpredictable results, as different software will likely attempt this differently) or it can choose to simply stop processing the data and signal an error. Neither is acceptable, and one of the goals of writing marked-up documents is to ensure that the conversion process can proceed reliably.

The process by which software reads the document and markup is called *parsing;* a document that can be successfully parsed and converted into a form suitable to software is said to be *parsable.* After a parser has successfully analyzed a document, it has effectively created a software representation of the document called a *parse tree.* This is just a way of representing the data content of a document in a form easy for software to process.

1.2 The HTML Processor

With Web browsers, HTML documents are parsed and processed using the browser's *HTML processor.* This processor understands the syntax rules for HTML, as well as the names and special grammatical rules for all the tags defined in the language. Using this hardwired knowledge, an HTML processor can take an HTML document, parse it into a well-understood form, and do useful things with it. Indeed, because of the way HTML tags are written, the HTML processor must be hardwired with the names and grammatical rules for each markup element in order to be able to parse a document. The reasons why are explained in the following text.

Figure 1.2 illustrates the parse tree corresponding to the HTML document in Figure 1.1. Note how the nested structure of the document (**html** element containing a **head** and a **body**, etc.) is transformed into a tree, with elements lower down "contained" within the element one level up. When creating the tree, the parser must be able to unambiguously determine where an element begins and ends so that it knows the bounds of the container. This is why the language needs start and stop tags, and why elements cannot overlap. Indeed, if elements overlap, then they are not contained one within another, and the structure cannot be turned into a tree.

However, an HTML parser must know more than this. In particular, the parser *must* know ahead of time that some elements (like **img**) are empty, and don't have an end tag—otherwise the parser would keep looking for an ending `</img>` tag, never find it, and assume the document was in error. Also, the rules of HTML allow some end tags to be omitted—for example, `</p>` end tags are optional—so the parser must know that these are optional, and must be able to infer the location of missing end tags. Looking at Figure 1.1, you will notice that the last paragraph in the document (beginning: `<p> The rules for writing ...`) does not end with a `</p>`. An HTML parser knows that this tag is optional and will "automatically" insert the end where appropriate when it converts the text into a parse tree. This explains why an HTML processor must know most of the rules of HTML in order to parse an HTML document.

Note that this also means that you cannot add arbitrary markup tags to an HTML document, since the HTML parser will not know how to process

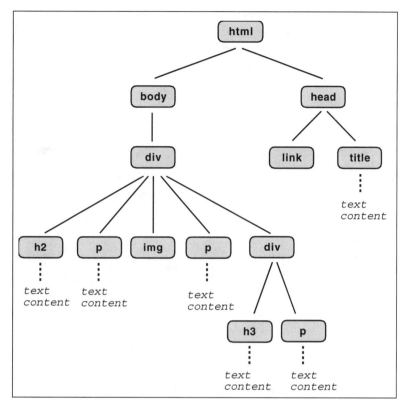

Figure 1.2 The element "parse tree" associated with the document listed in Figure 1.1. This is the way the software sees the document and its content.

them. For example, if a document contains the "custom" tag `<biggles href="http://www.biggles.com">` the HTML parser will have no way of knowing if it needs to look for an end tag (`</biggles>`), and thus cannot reliably process documents containing this new element.

This lack of extensibility is one of the main weaknesses of HTML. As we will see in the next chapter, the new eXtensible Markup Language (XML) changes the markup authoring rules somewhat to make custom tags possible.

1.2.1 Page Rendering

Once a document is successfully parsed, the parser is finished: It has done its job, which was to create an in-memory data structure corresponding to the document. However, to *display* the document, the software needs to do more work, and needs additional information—namely, instructions explaining how to render the different parts of the document, such as headings, paragraphs, quotations, emphasized text, and so on.

In general, a browser's HTML processor is equipped with rendering software (for drawing information to the display) and with default rules for how the rendering engine should format the text inside the various HTML elements. Figure 1.3 shows some example "default" renderings of the HTML document listed in Figure 1.1. The default renderings by the three graphical browsers (Internet Explorer, Netscape Navigator, and Opera) are largely the

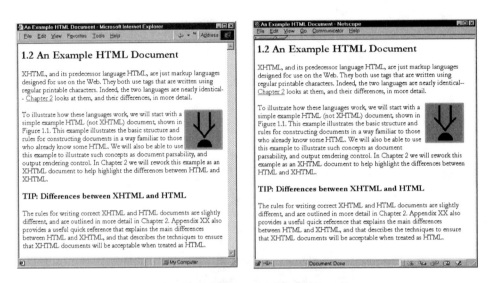

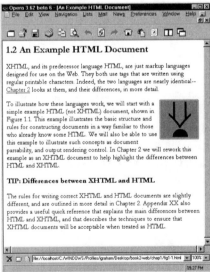

Figure 1.3 Rendering, by Internet Explorer 5 (upper left), Netscape Navigator 4 (upper right), and Opera 3.6 browsers, of the HTML document listed in Figure 1.1, in this case with style sheet support turned off. This demonstrates the "default" rendering of HTML markup by these browsers.

same. This is so because the companies developed these browsers by imitating each other's default formatting rules, so that pages would display as similarly as possible.

Indeed, up until Navigator 4 and Internet Explorer 4, the only way you could control the rendering on the page was by using HTML tags (such as **font**, **basefont**, etc.) that specified special formatting properties for the document. However, as described earlier, this mixing of physical markup tags with semantic ones is generally a bad idea, as it makes the language both more complicated and more difficult to reuse in other ways (for example, if displaying a document using a "voice synthesized" browser). It is thus useful to separate the formatting rules from the markup itself, and to use a separate language for describing the formatting rules. Such a language is called a *style sheet language*. We discuss this approach in Section 1.3.

1.2.2 Processed and Interactive Markup

When rendering an HTML document, a browser does more than simply process and render text. In many cases it must also invoke special functions associated with the element or defined by the attributes for that element. For example, when the browser processes and renders an anchor element such as

```
<a href="http://www.foo.org">linked text</a>
```

it must render the text appropriately (typically blue, with an underline), but it must also configure the software so that it detects whenever the mouse passes over the link (changing the icon from a text selection icon to a pointer icon). Also, if the user clicks the mouse over the link, the software must detect this "event," and must invoke the software that takes the **href** attribute value, retrieves the associated resource, and loads the new page into view.

Similarly, the browser must know that an **img** element represents an inline image (and that the browser must retrieve the referenced image and display it in the window), that an **input** element represents a user input mechanism of some sort (as defined by the **type** attribute), and so on.

This reflects two aspects of the HTML processor—its ability to allow interaction with the markup (via "events") and its ability to use markup (such as **img** elements) as instructions to special-purpose rendering software (such as a tool for displaying image files). With HTML browsers, this information is also hardwired into the HTML processor. Thus, once an HTML document has been parsed, the rendering engine knows that the empty **img** element references an image, and knows how to retrieve the referenced resource and replace the **img** element (on the rendered page) with the image. Similarly, the rendering engine knows that the "empty" **input** element corresponds to an input mechanism of some sort, and arranges for the appropriate mechanism (text box, checkbox, etc.) to be added to the display. It also registers this component with the form-processing software, so that the browser properly processes data entered by the user.

Note that this again makes it difficult to add tags to the HTML language. This is because you not only have to tell the parser how to parse the new element, you also need to hardwire the HTML processor to know how to render and/or process the information provided by the new element.

In a sense, the **embed** element is a work-around for this markup-related problem. **Embed** essentially assigns a "blank box" on the display to some external piece of code (referenced by the **embed** element) and lets this external code draw whatever it wants to in this box, based on parameters passed to it via the **embed** element attributes.

1.3 Advanced Rendering Model

The modern approach to display rendering is to separate the parsing of the document from the actual rendering, and to have a second resource specify how the markup should be displayed. This second resource is called a *style sheet*, and is typically written in a second language called a *style sheet language.*

It is important to note that style sheets only work if the marked-up document can be accurately parsed—that is, if the placement of the elements follows the rules of the language. Technically, the process works as follows:

1. The browser reads the document and parses it.

2. The browser reads a designated style sheet document and interprets the different formatting rules.

3. The browser visits each element "node" in the document parse tree. At each node in the tree (i.e., at each element) the browser determines the appropriate formatting rules for that node, as specified by the style sheet, and "attaches" those formatting rules to the node. This process continues until all nodes of the tree have been processed.

4. The rendering software accesses the text content and formatting rules stored in this tree, and renders the content of each node according to the formatting instructions.

This functionality is illustrated in Figure 1.4, which shows how the rendering software takes the parse tree and the style sheet document and then applies the style sheet document rules to each node of the tree when it renders the content to the display.

To a Web site author or site manager, this approach has several advantages over tag-based (e.g., **font**, **basefont**, etc.) formatting:

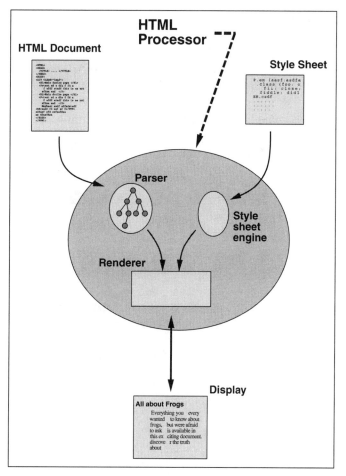

Figure 1.4 Example of a browser processing model, in which an HTML document and a style sheet are combined to produce the displayed page.

- The documents are simpler to write (and maintain), because they do not need to contain lots of formatting-specific markup tags.

- Different style sheets can be written for different rendering systems, so that pages do not have to be rewritten for different devices (PC, Palm Pilot, cell phone) or browsers (Internet Explorer, Lynx, Braille, spoken word).

- The page look and feel can be "refreshed" by changing the style sheet, without changing the markup.

- A style sheet can be shared among many documents, so that changing one style sheet can "refresh" any number of pages.

1.3.1 CSS: Cascading Style Sheets

The latest versions of most browsers, including those from Netscape, Microsoft, and Opera Software, support a style sheet language known as *Cascading Style Sheets* (CSS). Using CSS, an author can define, in a resource separate from the HTML document, how specific HTML elements should be formatted, positioned, and displayed. Then, when the HTML document is rendered, the browser adjusts the layout according to the rules in the style sheet.

Figure 1.5 shows the rendering of the document listed in Figure 1.1, but

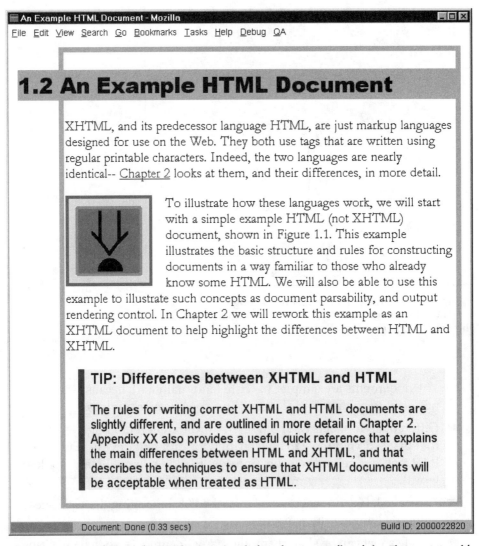

Figure 1.5 Rendering (by Navigator 6) of the document listed in Figure 1.1 with rendering controlled by style sheet rules shown in Figure 1.6. Note how the style sheet affects the layout and typography of the page.

with a style sheet to control some aspects of the rendering. The actual style sheet is referenced from this document via the **link** element:

```
<link rel="stylesheet" href="ex-stylesheet.css" >
```

Figure 1.6 shows the content of the style sheet document *ex-stylesheet.css*. The style sheet consists of rules, each of which defines formatting information specific to an element or a group of elements. For example, the first rule applies to the **body** element; it sets the default font family and text color for the document (the **body** and all elements inside it) and also sets the default background color. The second rule states that **div** elements with attribute **class**="section" are set to have left and right margins that are 5 percent of the available width (here, the inner width of the browser window). The third rule states that **h2** elements that are *inside* **div** elements with attribute **class**="section" should use the "Arial Black" font and should have a background of color #99ccff.

This book does not go into the details of CSS, other than to discuss some strategies for working within the limitations of current browsers' support for this language. CSS is discussed in detail in several other books, including *XHTML 1.0 Language and Design Sourcebook,* the companion book to this one. Other CSS books are listed in the references section at the end of this chapter.

```
body { font-family: garamond, "times new roman", serif;
       font-size: 1.4em;
       background-color: white;
       color: black; }
img   { float: left; padding: 0.5em;
       border: solid gray 5px;
       margin: 0 1em 0 0 ;
       background-color: #ccffff; }
div.section    { margin-left: 10%;
                 margin-right: 1%;
                 padding-left: 2px;
                 border: 8px solid #99ccff;}
div.section h2 { margin-left: -12%;
                 font-family: "arial black", arial, sans-serif;
                 background-color: #99ccff; }
div.tip        { font-family: arial, helvetica, sans-serif;
                 font-size: 0.9em;
                 margin-left: 3%;
                 margin-right: 3%;
                 background-color: #ffffcc;
                 border-left: red solid;
                 border-left-width: 10px;
                 padding-left: 10px; }
```

Figure 1.6   The CSS rules in the file *ex-stylesheet.css* that produce the rendering shown in Figure 1.5.

1.4 Advanced Page Processing Model

The rendering model presented in Section 1.3 is essentially a static one that describes how an HTML document is rendered using rules defined in a style sheet but does not allow for any change in the rendering once the document is displayed. In general, it is felt that such functionality should be the responsibility of tools separate from the markup or style sheet languages. Indeed, newer browsers support programming interfaces that let script programs interact with the document structure and rendering processes. These mechanisms, traditionally called *dynamic HTML,* are discussed in Chapter 3.

More importantly, there is nothing in the markup/style sheet model that explains how the renderer knows that some markup needs to be specially handled, such as the special handling required of **img** and **form** elements, as described in Section 1.2.1.

At present, much of this functionality is hardwired into the HTML processor. For example, the processor (which encompasses most of the components shown in Figure 1.4) knows that **img** elements refer to external image files, and knows how to reference code that downloads and draws images to the display. Similarly, the processor understands the special nature of **input**, **select**, and other **form** elements, and is designed to understand (and apply) the special logic that glues together all the elements inside a **form**.

To make Web applications more portable and extensible, the Web needs a way of separating these "functional definitions" from the processing engine, in the same way a style sheet separates the rendering specification from it. In this "ideal" model, a Web page-based application would have three parts:

■ A marked-up document

■ A rendering style sheet

■ A specification for how the markup should be attached to the processing software

In particular, this approach is critical for XML-based browser applications, as discussed in Chapter 2, since XML markup elements have no predefined functionality attached to them. The World Wide Web consortium is leading the effort to develop tools for defining functional implementations for markup elements. Some of the results of these efforts are discussed in Chapter 3.

1.5 References

HTML RESOURCES AND SPECIFICATIONS

www.w3.org/MarkUp/   HTML standards overview

www.w3.org/TR/html4/   HTML 4.01 Specification

developer.netscape.com/docs/ manuals/htmlguid/index.htm	HTML in Navigator
developer.netscape.com/docs/manuals/ htmlguid/tags_complete.html	Navigator HTML history
msdn.microsoft.com/workshop/author/ html/reference/elements.asp	HTML in Internet Explorer

CSS RESOURCES AND SPECIFICATIONS

www.w3.org/Style/CSS/	CSS standards overview
www.w3.org/TR/REC-CSS1	CSS Level 1 specification
www.w3.org/TR/REC-CSS2/	CSS Level 2 specification
webreview.com/pub/guides/style/style.html	CSS compatibility charts
css.nu/pointers/bugs.html	Browser CSS bugs list
developer.netscape.com/support/bugs/ known/css.html	Navigator 4.x bugs
www.css.nu/	General CSS information

SOME TECHNICAL HTML AND CSS BOOKS

XHTML 1.0 Language and Design Sourcebook, by Ian Graham, John Wiley & Sons (2000)—The companion book to this one, this is a good, detailed book on HTML, XHTML (see Chapter 2!), and CSS as tools for designing Web pages.

HTML: The Definitive Guide, by Chuck Musciano, Bill Kennedy, and Mike Loukides (ed.), O'Reilly and Associates (1998)—Another good technical book focusing on the details of HTML 4.0.

Cascading Style Sheets, Second Edition: Designing for the Web, by Hakon Wium Lie, Bert Bos, and Robert Caillau, Addison-Wesley (1999)—This is a very complete book on the technical details of CSS Level 2, by the editors of the language specification.

Cascading Style Sheets: The Definitive Guide, by Eric Meyer, O'Reilly and Associates (2000)—A good, detailed description of CSS as implemented in current browsers, by the author of the Webreview CSS compatibility charts (webreview.com/pub/guides/style/style.html).

XML: The eXtensible Markup Language

Topics/Concepts Covered: Introduction to XML; Review of XHTML, MathML, SMIL, and other XML dialects; Distributing XML data over the Web; Browsers and XML; Nonbrowser uses for XML

Chapter 1 introduced the basic ideas behind markup languages and software processing of marked-up text, using HyperText Markup Language (HTML) as a markup language example. It also pointed out some of the problems found with HTML, namely that it is difficult to:

- Extend HTML (i.e., by adding new markup tags) and have these new features understood by existing HTML processors (the software that processes the HTML markup).

- Write software that processes HTML documents incorporating extensions or additions.

The chapter also alluded to the fact that HTML is not the only type of data people (including Web application designers) now want to distribute over the Web. Indeed, one of the outcomes of the rapid growth of the Web was the desire of many groups to deliver their own types of data (mathematics, literary text, multimedia, spreadsheets, and so on) in a manner as easy as with HTML. Some tried to do this by adding "application-specific" tags to the HTML language—but the issues mentioned earlier made this a problematic approach, particularly if the intention was to use these new tags in a Web browser. Alternatively, some tried creating (and using) their own markup languages, designed specifically for their own data. But the existing mechanism for doing so [a language called Standard Generalized Markup Language (SGML), discussed in Section 2.1] was not designed to work on the Web, and was found to be inadequate for this purpose.

A consensus soon developed that a new approach was needed that would allow for the same ease of use as HTML, but also increased flexibility and reliability. This new approach was the *eXtensible Markup Language* (XML), which is rapidly becoming a core technology of Web-based applications. Indeed, many Web applications—ranging from Microsoft push channels to Real Player multimedia files—already use XML to encode data. Consequently, every true Web professional must understand what XML is, how it works, and how it fits into the overall design of Web-based applications. The goal of this chapter (and parts of the next one) is to explain these issues.

This chapter provides a brief overview of XML, and explains how the new Web technologies are being built around the XML model. It also briefly describes how the most recent Web browsers use XML (as opposed to HTML) data (these issues are discussed in more technical detail in Chapter 3). Last, the chapter briefly outlines how XML is being used outside the browser—namely by Web site or content management systems, or by business-to-business e-commerce systems.

To understand how and why this happened, it helps to revisit the HTML language and the HTML family tree. This interesting yet brief historical tour helps explain what went right—and what went wrong—with HTML and how the move to XML came about. This review is found in Section 2.1.

Please note, however, that this chapter presents only a review of XML—the language is itself a large topic that deserves a book all to itself. There are several good books available on the XML language (including my own, *The XML Specification Guide*), as well as many Web sites. Some books and Web sites I have found particularly useful are listed in the references section at the end of this (and the next) chapter.

2.1 A Brief History of HTML

The syntax and definition of HTML didn't come out of the blue. Indeed, the formal rules for HTML are defined using another exceedingly complex language called the *Standard Generalized Markup Language* (SGML). Developed in the 1980s, SGML is an International Organization for Standardization (ISO) standard for defining markup languages. That is, SGML is really a *metalanguage* for defining different markup language rules. Indeed, at the time SGML was the only standard appropriate for defining a language like HTML, and was the obvious choice for doing so.

SGML lets you define the syntax rules (i.e., how tags can be written, surrounded by angle brackets) and grammar (e.g., that the language has **item** and **list** elements, and that **item** elements can appear inside a **list** element but not vice versa) for a markup language. SGML also supports a number of features originally designed to make authoring easier. One such feature lets you omit (under certain conditions) end tags when the end of an element can be inferred from the context. For example, if a **p** element supports this optional end tag feature (as it does in HTML), then the markup

```
<p> ...... <p> paragraph text </p>
```

is perfectly fine; it is up to the SGML software to automatically add in the missing `</p>` end tag

```
<p> ...... </p><p> paragraph text </p>
```

and end the paragraph at the right place.

All the SGML rules for a specific markup language are defined in a resource called a *Document Type Declaration* (DTD). That is, the DTD defines the names of the elements, the attributes each type of element supports, and the grammar for the elements (e.g., where the elements are allowed, whether an element is empty, and, if it is not empty, whether the end tag is optional). Every SGML-based language, such as HTML, DocBook (designed for technical documentation), and Text Encoding Initiative (TEI, designed for marking up literary text) has its own SGML DTD defining the language rules. Figure 2.1 shows an extract of the DTD for the HTML 4.0 language. This book does not discuss DTDs in any detail—the purpose of Figure 2.1 is to show what the DTD content looks like and to illustrate how it is quite different (and far more complex) than the HTML markup itself.

With SGML, every document has two fundamental parts: the document itself (the tags and content) and the DTD that defines the language rules used in that document. Indeed, the SGML processing model assumes that documents and DTDs are always found together. This is because SGML software needs to know the information in the DTD (i.e., which elements are empty, which have optional end tags) in order to parse the markup content. Since this information is only available from the DTD, an SGML document is largely useless without it. We can see this need in the HTML model—recall that the parser processing HTML needed to know that **img** elements were empty (and did not have an end tag) and that **p** element end tags were optional (and could be inferred in some way). Thus you can think of an HTML parser/processor as being able to process HTML only because it has hardwired knowledge of the DTD for HTML.

There were several proposals to distribute SGMLized data (other than HTML) via the Web. However, this did not happen for a variety of reasons, including:

```
<!--================== Text Markup ==============================-->

<!-- following defines an entity, formctrl, that represents
     the list of FORM input elements -->

<!ENTITY % formctrl "INPUT | SELECT | TEXTAREA | LABEL | BUTTON">

<!-- % inline covers all inline and other text-level elements -->

<!ENTITY % inline
    "#PCDATA | %fontstyle; | %phrase; | %special; | %formctrl;">

<!- The following ELEMENT declaration says that SUB or SUP
    elements can contain any elements defined by the
    above %inline definition. The ATTRIBUTE declaration
    lists the attributes the element can have. -->

<!ELEMENT (SUB|SUP) - - (%inline;)* -- subscript, superscript -->
<!ATTLIST (SUB|SUP)
  %attrs;                      -- %coreattrs, %il8n, %events --
  >

<!-- The following defines the "BR" element to be 'EMPTY' (no
     end tag is needed -->

<!ELEMENT BR - O EMPTY         -- forced line break -->
<!ATTLIST BR
  %coreattrs;                  -- id, class, style, title --
  >

<!--=================== HTML content models ====================-->
<!--
    HTML has two basic content models:

        %inline; character level elements and text strings
        %block; block-like elements e.g., paragraphs and lists
-->
```

Figure 2.1   An extract of the DTD for HTML 4.0. The full DTD is available as part of the HTML 4.0 specification (www.w3.org/TR/html401/) or via this book's supporting Web site.

The inability to process a document without the DTD.   One of the lessons of HTML is that marked-up data (i.e., HTML) is useful even without a DTD. With SGML, a document is largely unusable without the DTD.

The inflexibility of DTDs.   DTDs are complex and not easy to reuse or modify. Moreover, with SGML it is well nigh impossible to mix one document (with one DTD) with another document (using another DTD) or to expand upon the syntax of a given DTD (e.g., by adding new elements).

The complexity of SGML itself. SGML is a tremendously rich language, with many complex (some might say cryptic) features. That means it can be very difficult to write software that can reliably process SGML data, since such software has to allow for all those features!

Indeed, it was soon realized that the Web needed a "lightweight" version of SGML that would work without DTDs and that was easy to design programs for. That is, it needed a language with syntax rules that allowed documents to be processed reliably without a DTD and that were simple enough that software for processing documents would be easy to write.

2.1.1 The Birth of XML

Once the SGML community recognized these requirements, a group of Web and SGML experts was formed to develop a new SGML-like language for the Web. The end result of this process was the *eXtensible Markup Language* (XML). Like SGML, XML is a tool for defining other markup languages, and, like SGML, it can use DTDs to define language-specific grammatical rules. However, unlike SGML, it imposes strict rules on the syntax rules for all languages—and these rules make documents usable even if the DTD is not present.

NOTE Formally, XML was designed to be consistent with the formalism of SGML. This meant that existing SGML software could process XML data (provided it came with a DTD).

Some of those rules are:

1. *Element and attribute names are case sensitive.* Thus, the tags `<PARA>` and `<para>` are the start tags for distinctly different elements. This is unlike HTML or many other SGML languages, where the names are case insensitive (i.e., `<DIV>` is the same as `<div>`).

2. *Every start tag must have an end tag.* That is, if **para** is nonempty, then it must always have an end tag, as in `<para> content </para>`. You can never leave off an end tag in XML.

3. *Empty elements are written using empty-element tags.* Empty elements (ones that never have end tags) are written using a special tag that has a slash character just before the ending angle bracket, as in `<break class="special" />`. This identifies, right in the markup, that that element is empty.

4. *Element attributes must always be assigned values, and these values must always be quoted.* The previous tag illustrated a correct attribute value assignment: `class="special"`. The quotes can be either double (as in the example) or single (e.g., `<break class='special' />`). This is different

from the HTML syntax rules, where some attributes take no value and some values don't need to be quoted.

The first rule was introduced to simplify the language and to allow for internationalized (e.g., Cyrillic or Chinese tag names) tagging schemes. Items two through four simply make the markup easier to process by removing all ambiguity—all start tags have end tags, all empty-element tags are clearly identified, and all attribute values are quoted. These requirements, combined with a few others, lead to an essential characteristic of XML:

An XML document can be parsed without a DTD.

That is, an arbitrary XML document (such as the one in Figure 2.2) can always be processed and converted into a parse tree (as in Figure 2.3), and can then be processed unambiguously by software, independent of any DTD. XML documents that are parsable in this way are said to be *well formed.*

An example of such a document is shown in Figure 2.2. This simple document illustrates the basic structure of an XML document. Note how each XML document begins with an XML declaration (`<?xml version="1.0" encoding="UTF-8" ?>`), which designates the document as being XML and gives the character encoding used to store the characters (character encodings are discussed in more detail in Appendix A on this book's companion Web site). The remainder consists of a single markup element (**menu**), called the *document element*, which in turn contains all other markup.

```
<?xml version="1.0" encoding="UTF-8" ?>

<menu date="12nov1998">
  <rname>Liam's Chowder House and Grill</rname>
    <item type="appetizer" >
      <desc>Warmed leek salad, coated with a balsamic vinegar and
            goat cheese dressing</desc>
      <price units="usd">6.95</price>
      <graphic gtype="gif"
               src="http://www.goodfood.com/menu/leek-salad.gif" />
    </item>
    <!-- Following Item is tasty! -->
    <item type="appetizer" >
      <desc>Prosciutto ham with melon</desc>
      <price units="usd">7.95</price>
      <graphic gtype="jpeg"
               src="http://www.goodfood.com/menu/ham-melon.jpeg" />
    </item>
  </menu>
```

Figure 2.2 A simple XML document illustrating an XML declaration, start tags, end tags, empty-element tags, and attributes. The parsed tree structure corresponding to this document is illustrated in Figure 2.3.

Figure 2.3 shows the parse tree corresponding to Figure 2.2. Because all end tags are present, and because all empty elements are marked using empty element tags, this parse tree is always well defined.

NOTE Formally, you can also write an empty element using start and end tags, with no data between the tags, as in `<myTag value="foobie"></myTag>`. However, this is not a wise choice, as it leaves open the notion that **myTag** is simply empty by choice, and that it is OK to actually add content between the tags.

Like SGML, XML also supports DTDs for defining specific language rules—the difference is that, with XML, this DTD is often not needed. A document that is well formed (i.e., whose tags are all written correctly), and that also satisfies the rules in a DTD, is said to be *valid.* However, it is very rare that documents distributed over the Web are distributed with DTDs. Instead, document authors typically use DTDs only when creating documents, since the DTD lets them ensure that the documents are created according to the established rules. The documents are then distributed without the DTD.

We won't go into the details of DTDs or other aspects of XML. If you want to find out more, there are many useful books and Web sites providing addi-

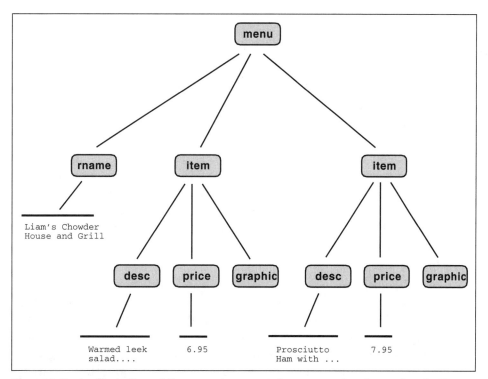

Figure 2.3 An illustration of the parse tree created on processing the markup in Figure 2.2. Note how the tree structure has a single root node—the *document element.*

tional information. My book, *The XML Specification Guide* (co-authored with Liam Quin) is one choice that, of course, I highly recommend!

Please also note that XML is still an evolving language, and some central issues, such as a special language for linking between XML documents, an XML language for describing document *schemas* (syntax and grammar rules), and others, are still in the works. The World Wide Web Consortium's XML Web site (www.w3.org/XML/) has information on all these ongoing efforts, while the references at the end of this chapter provide links to the current language standards. We briefly discuss one such standard (the XML *namespace* specification) in Section 2.2.2.

2.2 The Many XML Languages

Once the XML specification was established, there was a flourishing of XML language and software development. On the language side, various XML languages were (and continue to be) specified, each targeted at a specific purpose or function—which, of course, was exactly the intention of XML. In particular, the World Wide Web Consortium led the way in developing several generic languages that satisfied commonly expressed needs of the Web community. Some of these languages are:

The Mathematical Markup Language (MathML). MathML can describe mathematical equations in a form suitable for rendering on a display or for communicating the meaning of an expression suitable for use by mathematical analysis software. MathML is now supported by a number of applications. The MathML information Web site (listed in the references at the end of this chapter) lists many of the applications that support MathML.

Synchronized Multimedia Integration Language (SMIL). SMIL is designed to allow authoring of simple, TV-like multimedia presentations, composed of streaming audio, streaming video, images, text, or any other media type. Many common Web browser media player plug-ins support SMIL. The SMIL information Web site (listed in the references at the end of this chapter) lists many of the applications that support SMIL.

Scalable Vector Graphics (SVG). SVG is an XML language for describing two-dimensional graphics, including vector graphic shapes, images, and text. By letting software interact with the XML, such graphics can be made interactive. Several browser plugins and graphics production tools now support the SVG format. The SVG Web site (listed in the references at the end of this chapter) lists many of the applications that support SVG.

The Resource Description Framework (RDF).   RDF is a graphical language for expressing *metadata* about resources. RDF was designed to support a wide variety of metadata structures, including sitemaps, content ratings schemes, channel definitions (for "push" data), search engine data collections, digital library collections, and distributed authoring. XML is used as the interchange syntax for RDF—that is, graphical RDF statements are encoded in XML for distribution on the Web.

Extensible Stylesheet Language (XSL).   XSL is a language for expressing style sheet instructions. It consists of two parts: an XML language for specifying formatting details [called Extensible Stylesheet Language-Flow Objects (XSL-FO), analogous to Cascading Style Sheets (CSS)] and a language for transforming XML documents [called XSL Transformations (XSLT)]. This latter language can take a given document and transform it into another having a different structure and different tags. XSLT is often used by software processing XML data, such as databases or document management systems—there are several software packages that support XSLT. Also, the Internet Explorer 5 browser supports a version of XSLT that lets this browser display XML data. We will discuss XSLT in Chapter 3.

XML-based HyperText Markup Language (XHTML).   This is a reexpression of the HTML language to make it consistent with the strictness and syntax requirements of XML. This is discussed in more detail in Section 2.2.1.

Various other organizations have also developed XML dialects for other purposes or tasks. Some examples are the Bean Markup Language (BML) used for describing the architecture of a software application made up of Java Beans; the XML User interface Language (XUL) used by the Mozilla/Navigator 6 browser to specify the layout and functional components of the browser's user interface; VoiceXML, a language for creating audio dialogs that feature synthesized speech; Simple Object Access Protocol (SOAP), a Microsoft endeavor aimed at using XML and HyperText Transfer Protocol (HTTP) for invoking remote programs via the Web; User Interface Markup Language (UIML), a language for defining user interfaces; Wireless Markup Language (WML), a language for defining user interfaces for wireless devices such as cell phones; and literally dozens more. The XML references at the end of this chapter provide links to sites discussing these and other XML dialects.

2.2.1 XHTML: A Reworking of HTML

As mentioned in the previous section, XHTML is a reworking of the rules of HTML to make the language consistent with the XML syntax rules. Thus,

XHTML defines the same elements and attributes as HTML, but only changes the ways these elements and attributes can be written. To show what this means in practice, Figure 2.4 illustrates the HTML page from the previous chapter (Figure 1.1) "transformed" into XHTML. The differences between the two are shown in boldface: in general, these differences are subtle. The rest of this section briefly explains these differences and why they are needed.

```
<html xmlns="http://www.w3.org/1999/xhtml">
 <head>
  <title>An Example HTML Document</title>
  <link rel="stylesheet" href="ex-stylesheet.css" />
 </head>
 <body>
  <div class="section">
   <h2> 1.2 An Example XHTML Document </h2>
    <p>XHTML, and its predecessor language HTML, are just
    markup languages designed for use on the Web. They both use
    tags that are written using regular printable characters.
    Indeed, the two languages are nearly identical--
    <a href="chapter2.html">Chapter 2</a>
    looks at them, and their differences, in more detail.
    </p>
    <img src="weird-icon.gif" height="110" width="110"
       alt="Weird Icon -- just for show" align="right" />
    <p>
    To illustrate how these languages work, we will start with
    a simple example HTML (not XHTML) document, shown in Figure
    ... omitted content ...
    example as an XHTML document to help highlight the differences
    between HTML and XHTML.
    </p>
    <div class="tip">
     <h3> TIP: Differences between XHTML and HTML </h3>
     <p> The rules for writing correct XHTML and HTML documents
       are slightly different, and are outlined in more
     ... omitted content ...
     treated as HTML.
     </p>
    </div>
   </div>
  </body></html>
```

Figure 2.4 The HTML document listed in Figure 1.1, reworked to be XHTML. The differences from Figure 1.1 are shown in boldface. Note in particular the conversion of all uppercase tag names to lowercase and the added "/" character at the end of the **link** and **img** empty-element tags. The heading element was also changed to make it correct—this is now XHTML.

Figure 2.4 illustrates several basic features of all XHTML documents. The first thing to note is that all the markup elements use the same names as in HTML, and that the basic structure of the documents is essentially the same. Indeed, most of the structural rules of HTML carry over to XHTML. The main differences are:

All element and attribute names must be given in lower case.   This means that you cannot write the start tag for the **html** element as <HTML>—you must use lowercase letters. This is required by the rules of XML, which do not treat uppercase and lowercase letters as the same (unlike HTML, which is not case sensitive). Thus, when HTML documents are converted to XHTML, all tag and attribute names must be switched to lowercase. Notice in Figure 2.2 how the string <DIV CLASS="tip"> was converted to lowercase to make this document correct XHTML.

All empty elements must be written using XML's special empty-element tags.   In XML, empty-element tags must be written with a forward slash character (/) at the end of the tag, just before the ending greater than character. Thus, the link element in Figure 2.2 is written as

```
<link rel="stylesheet" href="ex-stylesheet.css" />
```

and the **img** element (later in the document) also has an added slash. When HTML documents are converted to XHTML, all empty elements must have this character added at the end of the tag. Note that it is best to have a space character before the slash, as this makes processing of the data easier for some software packages.

All end tags must be present—there are no optional end tags.   Unlike in HTML, where some end tags (such as </p> to end a paragraph) are optional, all end tags are mandatory in XHTML. Note in Figure 2.2 (relative to Figure 1.1) that a </p> end tag has been inserted near the end of the document. This tag properly ends the paragraph and is required for this to be correct XHTML.

Given these rules, note in Figure 2.4 how XHTML markup looks remarkably like HTML. Indeed, the goal of the XHTML 1.0 specification was to define an XML language as similar to HTML 4.0 as possible, so that XHTML documents could span the HTML and XML worlds, working well in both. This means that when authoring and managing documents, a Web site administrator (or the site management software) can take advantage of the stricter syntax rules of XHTML to help reduce the number of errors in the documents. Or, at the extreme, a site can use powerful XML-based document management systems to manage the XHTML documents (and any other XML data) on the site.

Then, when delivering data to Web browsers, the site can deliver XHTML documents as if they are standard HTML. This is important because many Web browsers are not XML aware, while those that are XML aware are generally limited in their ability to display and process XML data (we will revisit this issue in Section 2.4). Thus, a best-practice model for managing data on a Web site and distributing pages to Web browsers is as follows:

- Author and manage the pages (or design the Web interface pages) as well-formed XHTML.

- Deliver the pages to a browser as HTML data [i.e., using the Multipurpose Internet Mail Extensions (MIME) type *text/html*].

The former gives you the management and data processing advantages (at the Web server) of XML, while the latter lets you take advantage of the existing rendering capabilities HTML browsers.

In general, it is easy to write XHTML documents, although you need to be a bit more careful than when authoring HTML, since the XML syntax rules are stricter. Also, if documents are destined for use on HTML browsers, there are some advanced XML features you have to leave out. It is also generally straightforward to convert or upgrade existing HTML documents into HTML, so that you can migrate an existing Web site, over time, to an XML-based model. My book, *The XHTML 1.0 Language and Design Sourcebook*, describes these XHTML authoring and HTML-to-XHTML conversion issues in some detail. You may also find the *HTML Tidy* utility program (www.w3.org/People/Raggett/tidy/) useful in helping to automate the conversion process.

2.2.2 XML Namespaces

A particularly important feature of XML is the ability to declare the namespace for an element, or for a group of elements, using an XML *namespace declaration*. Such declarations are given by the attribute string **xmlns**, an example of which is used in the **html** start tag in Figure 2.4

```
<html xmlns="http://www.w3.org/1999/xhtml">
```

to declare the namespace for this XHTML document. The namespace mechanism is defined in an auxiliary XML specification (see the references section at the end of the chapter), and is used to group together element or attribute names that collectively have well-defined meanings. In the case of Figure 2.4, the namespace declaration xmlns="http://www.w3.org/1999/xhtml" means that the **html** element, and *all* the elements and attributes inside this element, are collectively associated with the "name" http://www.w3.org/1999/xhtml1. To put it another way, we can say that all the elements and attributes inside (and including) the **html** element are defined as belonging to the XHTML namespace.

When every new XML language is created, it can (and should) be assigned its own unique namespace. Indeed, all the languages described at the beginning of Section 2.2 have their own namespace Uniform Resource Locator (URL) names, defined as part of the language specification. Documents written in these languages can formally declare the namespace in their start tags, as in `<smil xmlns="http://www.w3.org/TR/smil1">` at the start of a SMIL document. Then, if software is configured to know about this particular name, it can use the namespace value to determine how this particular collection of tags should be processed. This description may seem a bit cryptic at this point, but it will be made clearer in Section 2.2.3.

The actual rules for using namespace declarations are somewhat more complicated than described here: This discussion has tried to outline the main features without going into too many details. The best place to find out more is the World Wide Web Consortium specification for XML namespaces. This is available at the URL listed in the references section at the end of this chapter.

2.2.3 Mixing XML Languages Together

The syntactic rules of XML, plus the namespace mechanism introduced in the previous section, make it possible to mix different dialects of XML together in the same XML document without losing a sense of where the different sets of tags come from. For example, Figure 2.5 shows a simple XHTML document that includes snippets of **mathml** and **smil** markup.

```
<?xml version="1.0" encoding="iso-8859-1"?>
<html xmlns="http://www.w3.org/TR/xhtml1" >
<head>
   <title> Title of XHTML Document </title>
</head><body>
<div class="myDiv">
    <h1> Heading of Page </h1>
      <mathml xmlns="http://www.w3.org/TR/mathml">
          ... MathML markup ...
      </mathml>
      <p> more html stuff goes here </p>
      <smil xmlns="http://www.w3.org/TR/smil1">
          ... SMIL markup ...
      </smil>
      <p> This is <em>fun</em>, isn't it.
</div>
</body></html>
```

Figure 2.5 An example XHTML document containing blocks of **mathml** and **smil** data (shown in boldface). The parse tree for this document is shown in Figure 2.6.

Figure 2.6 shows the parse tree produced after parsing the document in Figure 2.5. This can be parsed because all the components of the document, including the **mathml** and **smil** blocks, are well-formed XML and are thus always parsable. Indeed, a parser can always parse a document constructed in this way. At the same time, the namespace declarations distinguish the different dialects of XML. How this works in practice is described next.

If software is to process and display this document, it must be able to understand the difference between the different XML dialects. This is the role of the namespace declarations. Note the **xmlns** namespace declarations on the **html, mathml,** and **smil** start tags. The declaration on the **html** tag means, as stated previously, that all the elements and attributes inside (and including) this element belong to the "space" of XHTML. However, the namespace declaration on the **mathml** element overrides this statement, and says instead that the elements and attribute inside (and including) the **mathml** element belong to the space of MathML. Thus, the document is a valid XML document, but the namespaces help to distinguish the different meanings of the different parts of the document. Software can use this infor-

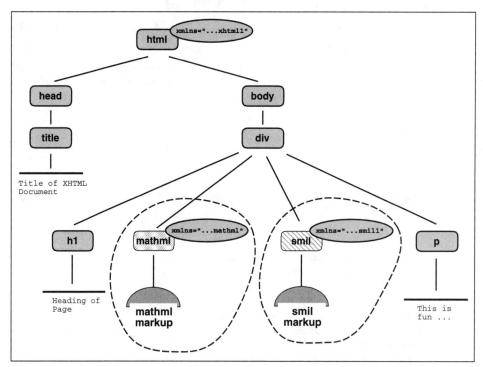

Figure 2.6 The parse tree arising from the document listed in Figure 2.5. Because the syntax rules of XML are followed, this document can be accurately parsed, even if the parser has no idea what the tags mean or what to do with them after parsing is completed. Note how the namespace declarations are available as "properties" of the nodes.

mation to process the different parts differently. In general, software will attach namespace-specific program modules to each element (or subtree of elements) associated with the given namespace, as illustrated in Figure 2.7. This approach, and the current problems associated with it, are discussed in a bit more detail in Section 2.3.

2.2.4 Distributing XML over the Web

XML itself is a distinct generic data type that must be distributed over the Web using a MIME type relevant to the type of data. For generic XML data, the most common MIME type is *text/xml.* This type corresponds to XML containing text data most likely to be displayed as text. An alternative is the application MIME type *application/xml.* This type is generally used for XML data being sent to an application for processing (such as to a purchase processing engine or a database integration tool), rather than to a Web browser for display.

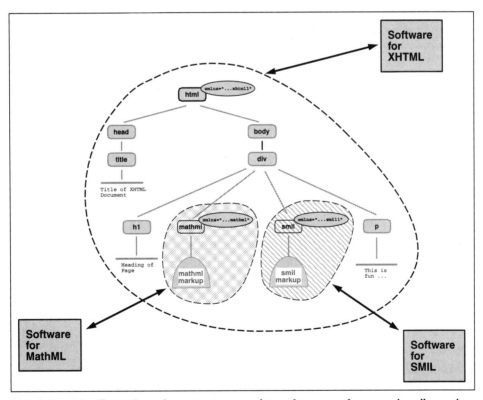

Figure 2.7 An illustration of namespaces used to reference software to handle markup coming from different namespaces. The namespace mechanism lets the parser attach namespace-specific program code to the different areas of the parse tree.

Specific dialects of XML may have their own MIME types. For example, it is expected that graphic files written using the SVG language will be delivered over the Web in the same way as GIF, JPEG, or PNG-format images. Thus, the SVG specification defines an *image/svg* MIME type for SVG-format graphics data. Other XML dialects may choose to define their own special types, depending on how the data is used.

In some senses, MIME type and namespace declarations fulfill similar roles, defining the type of a particular piece of data. However, MIME types are designed to work with all sorts of data, not just XML, and are moreover designed for specifying generic properties of "chunks" of data packaged for delivery by some transport mechanism. Thus, MIME content type statements can provide additional information relevant to the transport or encoding/decoding of data, such as the character encoding used within it or the type of character "escaping" mechanisms used to make the data safe for transport. Namespace declarations, on the other hand, are only used inside XML data, and allow specification of information about intermingled types of data within the space of XML data.

2.3 Nonbrowser Uses for XML

At present, XML is most commonly used for managing data "behind" a Web server, or for managing and processing data within software. For example, text data used in a Web site can be maintained as a collection of XML documents, which are managed by software that keeps the XML data consistent, reliable, and validly constructed, thereby avoiding human error in the authoring and editing process. Then, when Web pages are assembled—either dynamically for each Web server request, or statically, when pages are rebuilt on a regular basis—software can collect the required XML components, process them to extract and reformat the content, and write out a properly constructed HTML document.

This processing model is illustrated schematically in Figure 2.8.

There are many ways in which this processing can take place. In principle, you can create your own tools, because there is a lot of free (and commercial) XML software that you can use, as well as several standard programming interfaces for writing software that uses these XML toolkits. The references at the end of the next chapter list some useful software resource sites providing toolkits in various languages or site development environments.

A second approach is to choose an existing document management system that already includes these (and other) features. There are, in fact, many freeware and commercial tools available. Chapter 12 looks at some such tools and explains how to go about choosing a package appropriate to your needs.

XML is also important as a tool for automating business-to-business com-

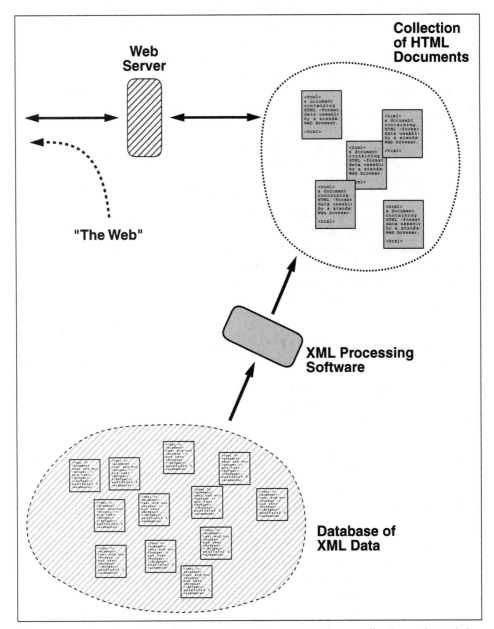

Figure 2.8 An illustration of the use of XML to manage large collections of text information used to generate HTML documents at a Web site.

mercial transactions. In this case, XML is used to encode the information needed for commercial transactions. These XML messages are then exchanged over the Internet to automate such transactions. As an example, a company could encode purchase order information in an XML document and then send this document to a computer operated by a supplier who handles such purchases. The supplier's computer can then process the XML message (since it understands XML in general, and the "purchase order" message format in particular), and can return an appropriate XML message outlining the status of the order—for example, that the requested items are available and will be delivered by the requested date.

Figure 2.9 schematically illustrates this process. Of course, for this to work, the companies have to agree on an XML language appropriate for the types of transactions they want to make. Indeed, one of the main efforts of companies such as Microsoft (with BizTalk), Commerce One [with Common Business Language (CBL)], and others has been to develop XML languages appropriate for business-to-business communication. This is a very large topic on its own, and is largely outside the scope of this book. The references at the end of this chapter provide links to Web sites that furnish additional information on this topic.

2.4 Browsers and XML Rendering

We will now suppose that an XML document (such as the one in Figure 2.4) is passed to a magical XML processing engine that reads the data and does something with it—in particular, renders it for display. In processing the data, the engine first sees the XHTML namespace declaration. The engine then knows that all the tags in that namespace should be processed for rendering according to the rules for XHTML. Most likely it has a special XHTML processing module and can pass the tags to that module for appropriate handling.

However, when the XML processing engine sees the MathML or SMIL start tags, it notes the additional namespace declarations. These declarations tell the processing engine that these tags (and the tags inside them) are not XHTML, but are instead different tags with meanings defined by the indicated name. Then, if the processing engine has software installed that is designed to process data with this name, the engine will pass the associated portion of the parse tree to this software and will use this software to process this part of the tree.

Ideally, this is how XML processing by a browser should work. However, at present there are no magical XML processing engines that actually process XML in this way (although the Mozilla/Navigator 6 browser, at www.mozilla.org, comes close). The reasons why this is not yet possible largely have to do with the absence of accepted standards for attaching pro-

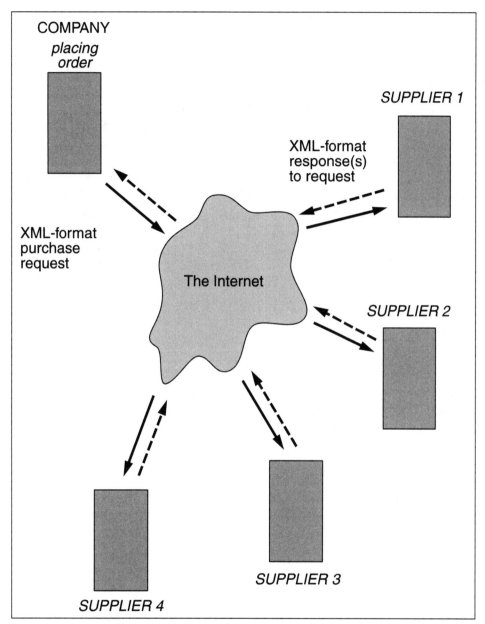

Figure 2.9 An illustration of XML as a dialect of machine-to-machine business communication. Here the XML messages encode all the information needed to automatically process a purchase order.

grammed functionality to parts of the XML parse tree. We will look into this in more detail in the next chapter.

2.4.1 Current Browsers and XML

Many common browsers, such as Navigator 4 (and earlier), Internet Explorer 4 (and earlier), Lynx 2.8.2 (and earlier), Opera 3.6 (and earlier), and others, do not understand XML data—they are only equipped with an HTML processor, and can only understand HTML data.

Newer browsers, however, such as Internet Explorer 5 (and greater), Mozilla Navigator 6 (and greater), and Opera 4 (and greater), are equipped with two processing engines: one for HTML and one for XML. When these browsers receive HTML-format data (indicated by the MIME type *text/html*), they process this data using the HTML processor, which has all the built-in knowledge of HTML elements and attributes. When the browsers receive XML-format data (indicated by the MIME type *text/xml*), this data is sent to the XML processing engine, which uses an XML parser to parse the data into a parse tree.

NOTE INTERNET EXPLORER MISHANDLING OF MIME TYPES **Internet Explorer 5 (and earlier) often ignores the MIME type for data received from HTTP servers, and instead reads the first few lines of the file to try to determine the type. Thus, if you store an HTML or XML document under the name *file.txt,* and serve it out as MIME type *text/plain,* Internet Explorer will not display it as plain text. Instead, Internet Explorer 5 looks for an XML declaration, and if it sees one it will process the data as XML. On the other hand, if the first text it sees is the string** `<html...>`**, and not an XML declaration, then it will process and display the data as HTML.**

This problem does not happen when accessing files from the local disk. In this case, all files with names like *file.txt* are displayed as plain text, regardless of the markup inside them!

However, once XML is converted into a parse tree, the browser has no idea of how to display it. Unlike the case with HTML, there are no default formatting rules for the XML elements.

For example, suppose that one of these more advanced browsers loads the document listed in Figure 2.10. This is a simple XML document [written in Ian's Markup Language (IML)]. Figure 2.11 shows how the two current browsers that support XML render this document. Internet Explorer 5 (top) shows a collapsible tree representing the hierarchical structure and content of the document, while Mozilla/Navigator 6 (bottom) treats all the elements as

```
<?xml version="1.0" encoding="iso-8859-1"?>
<iml xmlns="http://www.java.utoronto.ca/~igraham/iml1" >
<hd>
   <title> Title of text XHTML Document </title>
</hd>
<bdy>
<h1> A Heading: An XML (IML) Document </h1>
<p> here is a paragraph of text. I will include
    inside this paragraph a big whack of text. Isn't
    this exciting. Well, not really -- but then,
    what did you expect....</p>
<h3> Here is Another Heading </h3>
<p> here is another paragraph of text. But, unlike
    the previous paragraph, this one comes complete
    with a shiny, new exclamation point! </p>
</bdy></iml>
```

Figure 2.10   A simple example XML document. Browser renderings are shown in Figure 2.11.

being inline text and displays the content as a single, line-wrapped line of text.

Both of these presentations are perfectly valid, since each browser, although it has successfully parsed the document, has no better way of displaying the document's content.

A recent XML specification (www.w3.org/TR/xml-stylesheet/) defines how to specify, from within an XML document, a style sheet to use when rendering the document. An example illustrating this mechanism, using a CSS-language style sheet, is shown in Figure 2.12. The special line

```
<?xml-stylesheet href="style.css" type="text/css" ?>
```

references the style sheet *style.css.* Figure 2.13 shows browser renderings by Internet Explorer 5 and Mozilla/Navigator 6. Note how the styles are applied as specified, making the page readable as a regular text document.

This approach to rendering XML has significant limitations, however. This is because CSS can specify rendering properties for the markup content, but it cannot specify functionality associated with the content or markup, so that things like inline images or hypertext links cannot be properly handled. This is because there is as yet no standard way to attach such functionality. Thus, although Mozilla/Navigator 6 (and Internet Explorer 5 to some degree) provide some mechanisms for adding functions to XML markup components, the mechanisms that work on one browser will not work on the other.

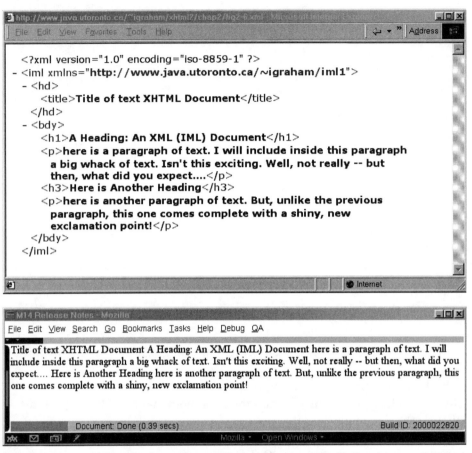

Figure 2.11   Rendering, by the Internet Explorer 5 (top) and Mozilla/Navigator 6 (bottom) browsers, of the XML document listed in Figure 2.10.

XSL and XML Rendering in Internet Explorer 5

Internet Explorer 5 provides a way around this problem by letting you attach an XSL transformational style sheet to an XML document. As mentioned at the beginning of Section 2.2, XSL is a second style sheet language with two important components: a formatting language (a bit like CSS), and a transformation language—known as XSLT—that can transform one XML document into another one. Although the formatting component of XSL is still being developed (and is largely unsupported), XSLT is fully specified and is supported by Internet Explorer 5. (Note: Internet Explorer 5 actually supports an early draft of the XSLT specification, which is somewhat different from the final version. Newer versions of Internet Explorer support the finalized standard.)

```
<?xml version="1.0" encoding="iso-8859-1"?>
<?xml-stylesheet href="style.css" type="text/css" ?>
<iml xmlns="http://www.java.utoronto.ca/~igraham/iml1" >
<hd>
   <title> Title of text XHTML Document </title>
</hd>
<bdy>
<h1> A Heading: An XML (IML) Document </h1>
 ... content as per Figure 2.10 ....
</bdy></iml>
```

Content of style.css

```
iml, bdy, p, h1, h2 { display: block;}
hd    { display: none; }
bdy   { font-size: 14pt;
          font-family: garamond, 'times new roman',serif;
          margin-left: 1em;      background-color: #ccffff;
          margin-right: 1em;     margin-top: 0.5em; }

p     { margin-top: 0.5em;     margin-bottom: 0.5em; }

h1    { font-family: arial,helvetica,sans-serif;
          margin-top: 1em;        font-weight: bold;
          margin-bottom: 0.7em; font-size: 1.5em; }

h2    { font-family: arial, helvetica, sans-serif;
          margin-top: 0.7em;      font-weight: bold;
          margin-bottom: 0.5em; font-size: 1.3em; }
```

Figure 2.12 The document listed in Figure 2.10, but with a reference (in boldface) to an external style sheet. The style sheet is listed at the end of the figure. Browser renderings are shown in Figure 2.13.

With Internet Explorer 5 (and greater), an XML document can reference an XSLT style sheet that transforms the XML data into a XHTML document, which is then passed to the HTML processor. The HTML processor then renders the HTML markup to the display. Recall that the HTML processor is hardwired to understand the functional nature of elements like **a**, **input**, **embed**, **textarea** and so on, so that this approach lets you regain the functionality lost by switching to XML—you simply transform XML markup into HTML elements that intrinsically have the desired functions.

This approach works quite well in most cases—some useful examples are found in Chapter 12 of *Applied XML: A Toolkit for Programmers,* listed in the references at the end of the chapter. On the other hand, this only works in Internet Explorer 5 (the new Navigator browser does not support XSLT),

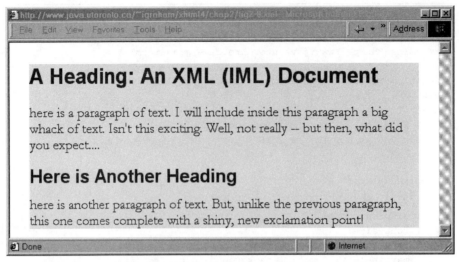

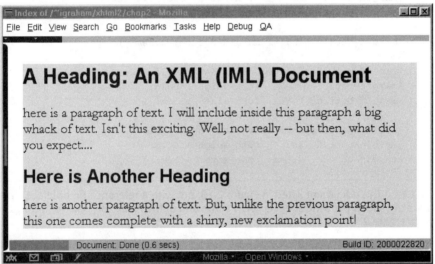

Figure 2.13 Rendering, by the Internet Explorer 5 (top) and Mozilla/Navigator 6 (bottom) browsers, of the XML document listed in Figure 2.12.

which means that this approach is not useful when developing pages for other browsers.

Internet Explorer 5: XML Embedded in HTML

Internet Explorer 5 and up let you embed XML data within an HTML document using what are known as *XML data islands*. This proprietary mechanism uses a special XML element to surround blocks of XML data to be passed to the XML parser. The Internet Explorer 5 programming interface then provides a mechanism for accessing the content of this island using script programs.

We won't go into the details of this mechanism here. A simple example is provided in the next chapter, where we look at XML programming tools in more detail.

2.4.2 XML in Mozilla/Navigator 6

The new open source version of the Netscape browser (code-named SeaMonkey, and available for download from www.mozilla.org) extensively uses XML in the design of the browser software and in specifying the layout and functionality of the browser user interface. Indeed, the Mozilla team developed a special XML dialect, called the XML User interface Language (XUL), for specifying the layout and functionality of the entire browser interface. The overall design also makes heavy use of namespaces to bind specific program functionality to specific sets of elements and attributes.

The implementation, however, required some extensions to the CSS language (to specify layout features required of the user interface components) as well as the definition of special programming interfaces so that functions could be connected to the various XUL components. These extensions are discussed at the Mozilla Web site's documentation area, which is listed in the references section.

2.5 References

GENERAL XML INFORMATION

wdvl.com/Authoring/Languages/XML/Intro/	Introductory XML article
www.w3.org/XML/	Draft standards and formal specifications
www.ucc.ie/xml/	XML FAQ
www-4.ibm.com/software/developer/education/xmlintro/xmlintro.html	Introductory tutorial
www.xml101.com	Tutorials
www.xml101.com/dtd/	Tutorial on DTDs
www.xml.org/xmlorg_registry/index.shtml	Common XML DTDs or schemas
www.xs4all.be/~stevenn/xml/xmlintro/toc.html	Tutorial

www.refsnesdata.no/xml/default.asp	Articles and tutorials
www.xml.com	Articles and tutorials
www.xmlhack.com	Articles and tutorials
www.xmlzone.com	Articles and tutorials
www.xmlinfo.com	Notes and resources lists
xml.org	Industry news
www.devdex.com/xml/	Resource lists
www.oasis-open.org/cover/xml.html	Resource lists

CORE XML SPECIFICATIONS

www.w3.org/TR/REC-xml	XML 1.0 specification
www.xml.com/axml/testaxml.htm	Annotated XML specification
www.w3.org/TR/REC-xml-names/	Namespaces in XML
www.w3.org/TR/xml-stylesheet/	Associating style sheets with XML documents
www.w3.org/TR/xpath	XML path language
www.w3.org/XML/	Drafts of new specifications
www.ietf.org/rfc/rfc2376.txt	XML-related MIME types

COMMON XML LANGUAGES

www.w3.org/Math/	Mathematical Markup Language (MathML)
www.w3.org/AudioVideo/ #SMIL	Synchronized Multimedia Integration Language (SMIL)
www.w3.org/RDF/	Resource Description Framework (RDF)
www.w3.org/Graphics/SVG/	Scalable Vector Graphics (SVG)
www.w3.org/TR/xhtml1/	XHTML
www.w3.org/Style/XSL/	eXtensible Stylesheet Language (XSL)
www.w3.org/TR/xslt/	XSL Transformations language (XSLT)
www.alphaWorks.ibm.com/ formula/bml	Bean Markup Language (BML)
www.mozilla.org/	XML User interface Language (XUL)
www.voicexml.org	Voice markup language (VoiceXML)
www.develop.com/soap/ soapfaq.htm	Simple Object Access Protocol (SOAP)
www.mozilla.org/docs/	XUL

www.uiml.org	User Interface Markup Language (UIML)
www.wapforum.org/what/ technical.htm	Wireless Markup Language (WML)

XML AND ELECTRONIC COMMERCE

xml.com/pub/Ecommerce	Overview of sites
www.commerceone.com/xml/	CommerceOne tools
www.microsoft.com/biztalk/	Microsoft BizTalk

XML BOOKS

The XML Specification Guide, by Ian Graham and Liam Quin, John Wiley & Sons (1999)—A good introduction to XML, and a good technical review of the XML specifications. This will be of interest to both technical and nontechnical readers.

Applied XML: A Toolkit for Programmers, by Alex Ceponkus and Faraz Hoodbhoy, John Wiley & Sons (1999)—A useful, technical book explaining how XML can be processed, with a bent toward the software tools available in the Internet Explorer 5 browser.

The XML Bible, by Elliotte Rusty Harold, IDG Books (1999)—Lots of XML information, as the title would suggest. The Web site, at metalab.unc.edu/xml/books/bible/, has useful updated chapters on topics such as XSLT, XLinks, and XPointers.

The XML Pocket Reference, by Robert Eckstein, O'Reilly and Associates (1999)—The title says it all: a useful pocket reference covering the essence of XML.

XML: A Manager's Guide, by Kevin Dick, Addison-Wesley (1999)—A semi-technical book that focuses on the ramifications of XML for those managing document management and software development projects.

Project Cool Guide to XML for Web Designers, by Theresa A. Martin, John Wiley & Sons (1999)—A semi-technical book that will be of interest to Web site designers and managers, as opposed to software developers.

CHAPTER 3

Software Processing of XML and HTML

Topics/Concepts Covered: XML parsing; SAX and DOM interfaces; using XSLT; browser processing of HTML; XML data islands

The previous two chapters described the purpose and structure of markup languages, and discussed the situations in which such languages are useful. This chapter continues from that point, and discusses how software is created that processes such data and makes it useful. Thus, this chapter introduces you to the tools and methods by which the data distributed by Web software applications can be processed and used. This chapter looks at this issue from the two main perspectives of interest to developers: processing eXtensible Markup Language (XML) and HyperText Markup Language (HTML) on a server (or offline from the Web) and processing XML and HTML on a Web browser.

Note that the goal of this chapter is not to make you an expert in all these areas. Indeed, the subjects of just about every section in this book (and possibly some subsections as well) deserve one or more books on their own. Instead, the goal of this chapter is to provide an overview of each of the tools you can use, to outline how they are used, and to give you an understanding of the situations in which the different tools are appropriate. From there you can investigate each mechanism further. The references section at the end of the chapter provides some useful and relevant online and print resources.

Section 3.1 discusses using an XML parser for integrating XML data into a general-purpose XML application. This section also discusses the common programming interfaces by which you attach functionality to the parser, thereby creating an application that processes the XML data and does something useful. This section also looks at how modern browsers handle XML data and provides examples illustrating browser-specific mechanisms.

Section 3.2 discusses eXtensible Stylesheet Language Transformations (XSLT), an XML language designed for transforming one piece of XML data into another (or into some other sort of data). Whereas a parser and parser programming interfaces let you build generic XML applications, XSLT is designed as a tool for easily doing this one specific XML processing task. It turns out that XML transformations are one of the most commonly performed tasks when working with XML, so that XSLT is often a very useful component of an XML application design.

Section 3.3 describes generic mechanisms for offline HTML processing. This is a short section—there are not a lot of tools of this type. Nevertheless, this section helps explain why there are so few such tools. We will also revisit this topic in Chapter 12 when we look at Web application development environments.

Section 3.4 discusses HTML processing by Web browsers. This begins with a brief history of browser scripting, but then quickly moves into a discussion of the Document Object Model (DOM) and its use on a Web browser for writing scripts that interact with a document's parse tree and the rendered version of a document. This section also discusses how XML fits into this model, and reviews the XML data island extension supported by Internet Explorer 5.

Finally, the chapter concludes with a detailed reference list of Web sites, books, and other resources related to processing XML and HTML data.

3.1 Parsing XML Data

The key to processing any XML data is the *XML parser*—the software that reads in XML data and makes the data usable by software. On its own, a parser does nothing useful—just reading and parsing the data in doesn't actually do anything. However, a parser also provides a programming interface whereby a programmer can attach code that interacts with the data or the treelike data structure produced upon parsing the XML document. It is by adding these custom components that you can actually process the XML or get the XML to cause something to happen. Sections 3.1.1 and 3.1.2 will discuss common programming interfaces for attaching custom functions to a parser.

There are two basic types of XML parsers: *validating* and *nonvalidating*. A validating parser reads both the XML document and an associated Document Type Declaration (DTD). While reading and processing the XML data, the parser tests the markup structure against the grammar rules defined in the DTD. If the document is inconsistent with the DTD (for example, the elements are improperly nested, or elements are used that are not defined in the DTD), the parser notes this as a fatal error and will refuse to continue processing the data.

In principle, a validating parser gives XML developers extra protection from error, since validation guarantees (more or less) that the XML document obeys a predefined grammar and is thus structured as expected. This reduces processing errors and can make a system using XML data more robust and less likely to fail. On the other hand, the validation phase does slow the software somewhat (since it does more work), which can be a problem in some circumstances. Also, it turns out there are many cases where the program processing the XML data does not have a DTD, in which case validation is not possible.

Validating parsers are particularly important within XML editors, since an editor needs to know the rules if it is to constrain the author to create a document consistent with those rules.

If you come from a programming background, you can think of validation as being a bit like type checking, since the validation phase really checks to see if a block of XML data is consistent with a specific set of grammar (read: type) rules. However, it turns out that DTDs are not actually very good for this role, since a DTD cannot define constraints on some important components of a document. For example, a DTD cannot constrain the text content of an element to be an integer or a date string having the syntax specified in RFC 1123.

To make up for the limitations of the DTD, the XML community is currently developing an XML language for specifying XML *schemas*—that is, a language for specifying the grammatical and syntax rules for XML data, but at a level deeper than is possible with a DTD. When this happens, XML parsers will be able to load in an appropriate XML schema definition document and use that document to validate XML data. This will give rise to a generation of schema-validating parsers that will use schemas instead of DTDs to validate documents.

A *nonvalidating* parser does not use a DTD and does not validate an XML document: Instead, it only checks to make sure that the document is *well formed* (no missing end tags, properly written empty-element tags, etc.). If a nonvalidating parser detects a syntax error, then the XML data is not well formed, and the parser stops processing the data and signals an error. This is a strict requirement of XML processing software, and ensures that badly formed XML data is always discarded.

It may seem silly to go to all the trouble of defining a DTD and then ignore it when processing the XML data.

NOTE In truth, a nonvalidating parser does not ignore the content of a DTD. Instead, a nonvalidating parser typically processes as much of the DTD as it can, ignoring parts that it cannot process. In particular, a nonvalidating parser *must* process declarations in a DTD that define entities representing blocks of XML. Such entities can be used inside the XML document to include text and/or XML markup into it. For example, the following entity declaration:

```
<!ENTITY myCo "Ian Graham Consulting Services Inc." >
```

defines an entity named "myCo". As a result, an entity reference &myCo; inside the XML document will be replaced by the defined string. Entity declarations can reference external files containing blocks of well-formed XML, as in:

```
<!ENTITY  section2
          SYSTEM "http://www.myserver.com/parts/sect2.xml" >
```

This statement means that the entity reference &section2; will be replaced by the content of the referenced file.

Additional details on how parsers process the DTD and on how they handle entity declarations are found in Chapter 2 (Section 2.3) and Chapter 4 of *The XML Specification Guide.*

However, not all data actually comes with a DTD—or is even consistent with a DTD. Indeed, one of the goals of XML—that it be easy to mix different XML languages together in a single document—means that in many cases it is impossible to define a DTD for XML data.

For example, consider two XML-based HTML (XHTML) and Mathematical Markup Language (MathML) documents, each of which is valid with respect to the DTDs of the respective languages. As described in the previous chapter, an author can write a perfectly well-formed XML document consisting of an XHTML document with embedded MathML data, as shown in Figure 2.4. However, doing so creates a very useful document for which there simply is no DTD. Thus, to process this sort of data, an application must use a nonvalidating parser.

For this reason, Web browsers that can process XML are typically equipped with nonvalidating parsers, or else are equipped with parsers that can work in either validating or nonvalidating modes.

Given an XML parser [Uniform Resource Locators (URLs) for some parsers are listed in the references at the end of the chapter], the next thing needed is a way of integrating the parser into the *XML application* you are designing—after all, it is the application that does all the interesting work. In principle, every parser could do this differently, having its own custom programming interface.

Fortunately, this is not what happened. Instead, the software development world has largely settled on two programming interfaces for writing programs that make use of an XML parser, each designed for a particular class of problems. These two are called Simple Application programming interface for XML (SAX) and the Document Object Model (DOM). These approaches are briefly discussed in the next two sections.

Both SAX and the DOM are general-purpose programming interfaces with—as we shall see—relative strengths and weaknesses. They are intended as generic tools for processing XML—whatever the application is supposed to do, programmers will have to implement every piece of functionality themselves.

There is, however, one set of XML processing tasks that reappears again and again in XML application design. This set falls under the generic name of *tree transformations*—that is, the transformation of one XML document into another, where the transformation depends on the content of the source document plus a set of transformational rules.

Because of this common need, the XML standards organizations have defined a special XML transformation language, called XSLT, that can define how one XML document should be transformed into another XML document. Using an XSLT engine, document transformations can be accomplished using two simple components: an XML document and an XSLT document defining the transformation rules. This is described in Section 3.2.

3.1.1 SAX: A Simple API for XML

The Simple Application Programming Interface (API) for XML (better known as *SAX*; see www.megginson.com/SAX/index.html) was the first general-purpose API developed for linking an XML parser to an XML application. The full name captures the intent of the API quite correctly: SAX was designed to be a simple, lowest-common-denominator tool for processing XML. Despite (and perhaps because of) its simplicity, SAX has proven to be exceedingly useful for a wide variety of XML application design problems, and is widely supported by commercial and noncommercial XML software.

SAX is an event-based API for processing XML. With an event-based API, the parser reports *events* (such as the start and end points of elements, or the value of an attribute) directly to the application through callback functions registered with the parser using the SAX API. The callback functions act as *event handlers* that deal with the different events (a "body" start tag, a "para" start tag, a "para" end tag, etc.) much in the same way a graphical user interface has handlers that respond to user events (a mouse click, a key press, etc.).

For example, Figure 3.1 shows a simple XML document and the sequence of events reported by a SAX-based application (the program is shown in Figure 3.2). Note how each part of the document (including each line of text data) is reported as an event. Note also that an empty element, such as `<boobie />`, is reported as two subsequent events: a start element followed by an end

(A) A Simple XML Document

```
<?xml version="1.0" encoding="iso-8859-1" ?>
<main>
  <part>Here is a Part</part>
  <boobie />
</main>
```

(B) Events Reported by SAX Application Listed in Figure 3.2

```
Event: Start of document
Event: start element: <main>
Event: text string [\0a]
Event: text string [ ]
Event: start element: <part>
Event: text string [Here is a Part]
Event: end element: <part>
Event: text string [\0a]
Event: text string [ ]
Event: start element: <boobie>
Event: end element: <boobie>
Event: text string [\0a]
Event: end element: <main>
Event: End of document
```

Figure 3.1 A simple XML document. Part (B) shows the sequence of events reported by the SAX-based XML application listed in Figure 3.2.

element. Indeed, as far as any XML parser is concerned, there is no difference between the markup `<boobie/>` and `<boobie></boobie>`—provided there is no text between the tags, of course!

Figure 3.2 shows a sample perl language SAX-based application that produces the output listed in Figure 3.1. In this case, the event handlers (contained in the file *MySAXHandler.pm*) simply print out a line explaining the nature of the event and some information about it (such as the name of the element, or the text content if the event was a string of characters). This example only defines handlers for some of the possible events, and ignores some of the data passed to the handlers. For example, the `start_element` and `end_element` event handlers can also access the attribute names and attribute values for the element. All in all, however, the SAX programming interface is small and simple to use—if you understand the example given here, then it will be straightforward to read the SAX documentation and add your own custom handlers. SAX documentation is available at www.megginson.com/SAX/index.html, but is also typically included with language-specific libraries (perl, Java, etc.) that implement the SAX interface.

```perl
#! /usr/bin/perl

use strict;
use XML::Parser::PerlSAX;
use MySAXHandler;

# XML::Parser::PerlSAX is the Perl XML parser object combined with
# the SAX interface.
#
# MySAXHandler is a class that defines the handlers to attach, using
# the SAX interface, to the SAX-ified parser.
#
# Now, create a new 'handler' object. Then, create a new parser
# object, and attach the 'handler' object to this parser using the
# SAX interface.

my &my_handler = MySAXHandler->new;
my &parser = XML::Parser::PerlSAX->new( Handler => &my_handler );

# now, invoke the parser on a filename passed from the command
# line -- let the thing look over all filenames passed to it.
# The syntax of the parse() method call is defined by the SAX
# specification.

foreach my &document (@ARGV) {
  &parser->parse(Source => { SystemId => &document });
```

MySAXHandler.pm

```perl
package MySAXHandler;

# This package contains the event handlers that will be attached,
# using the SAX interface, to the XML parser. The SAX interface
# specification defines:
#  + the names of the functions (methods)
#  + the arguments passed to the functions (methods), and their order
#  + the return values returned by the functions.

# 1) Create new MySAXHandler object
#
sub new {
  my (&type) = @_;
  return bless {}, &type;
}
```

continues

Figure 3.2 A simple perl program *test-sax.pl* that uses the SAX parser API. The handler functions are contained in the MySAXHandler object, defined in the file (a perl package) *MySAXHandler.pm.* Comments are shown in italics.

```perl
# 2) Handle Start of Document
#
sub start_document {
  my (&self) = @_;
  print "Event: Start of document\n";
}


# 3) Handle End of Document
#
sub end_document {
  my (&self) = @_;
  print "Event: End of document\n";
}


# 3) Handle Start of Element
#
sub start_element {
  my (&self, &element) = @_;
  print "Event: start element: <$element->{Name}>\n";
}


# 4) Handle End of Element
#
sub end_element {
  my (&self, &element) = @_;
  print "Event: end element: <&element->{Name}>\n";
}


# 5) Handle string of characters
#
sub characters {
  my (&self, &string ) = @_;
  my &data = &string->{Data};
  &data =~ s/\r/\\0d/g;
  &data =~ s/\t/\\09/g;
  &data =~ s/\n/\\0a/g;
  print "Event: text string [&data]\n";
}
1;
```

Figure 3.2 *(Continued).*

Figure 3.3 shows a Java program that is functionally equivalent to the perl program in Figure 3.2. The differences in the design are actually quite small. Indeed, the Java version is probably easier to understand, as the language is more grammatically straightforward (albeit less flexible!) than perl.

(1) DemoSaxApp.java

```java
// Load the SAX parser intefaces and helper classes
// Need to do this explicitly in Java. Note that this
// Example uses the Microstar XML parser (with SAX driver) --
// We could change parsers simply by modifying the parserClass
// String (if we had another one, of course ;-)
import org.xml.sax.Parser;
import org.xml.sax.DocumentHandler;
import org.xml.sax.helpers.ParserFactory;

public class DemoSaxApp {
  static final String parserClass = "com.microstar.xml.SAXDriver";
  public static void main (String args[]) throws Exception
  {
      Parser parser = ParserFactory.makeParser(parserClass);
      DocumentHandler handler = new MySAXHandler();
      parser.setDocumentHandler(handler);
      for (int i = 0; i < args.length; i++) {
        parser.parse(args[i]);
      }
  }
}
```

(B) MySAXHandler.java

```java
// Again, we need to explicitly load the SAX handler classes,
// as our own handlers will extend there.
// We then create methods for our handler, which overload
// those defined in the HandlerBase base class.

import org.xml.sax.HandlerBase;
import org.xml.sax.AttributeList;

public class MySAXHandler extends HandlerBase {

  public void startDocument (String name)
  { System.out.println("Event: Start of document"); }

  public void endDocument (String name)
  { System.out.println("Event: End of document"); }

  public void startElement (String name, AttributeList atts)
  { System.out.println("Event: start element: " + name); }

  public void endElement (String name)
  { System.out.println ("Event: end element: " + name); }
```

continues

Figure 3.3 A Java implementation of the SAX example described in Figure 3.2. Comments are shown in italics.

```
    public void characters (char chars[], int start, int length){
      myString = new String(chars[], start, length);
      System.out.println("Event: text string[" + myString + "]");
    }
  }
```

Figure 3.3   *(Continued).*

There are several things to note about SAX. First, SAX handles a document's parse tree as a *linear* sequence of events that occur as the document is read in and the parse tree is traversed. Consequently, the parser does not load the entire document into memory as a data tree (although event handler functions could create such a tree, if designed to do so). This is a disadvantage if you want the tree entirely in memory, but an advantage if that is not the goal. In particular, a SAX-based parser can be very useful when you need to parse particularly large documents that would be too large to fit into memory. In these cases, you can use the SAX event handlers to extract the desired data from a large XML document and then create the desired data structures containing just the data you need.

Also, a SAX-based approach can be useful if your application needs to read in one (or more) XML documents and create a custom data tree using data extracted from these other XML documents. It is often more efficient to use the SAX approach (and event handlers) to read the incoming data and write data into the custom data tree than it is to build multiple trees from the read XML data and then process these trees to extract and move data elsewhere.

3.1.2 Document Object Model (DOM) for XML

An event-based API is useful for single-pass processing of XML data, but is not as useful if the goal is to load in XML data and repeatedly manipulate the in-memory data. In this case, you probably want to store the entire document as an in-memory parse tree and then have an API that lets you "walk" the tree and process the data in the tree as desired. Such an API is called (amazingly enough) a tree-based API.

The Document Object Model (www.w3.org/DOM/) defines an industry standard tree-based API for processing XML. Indeed, the DOM was originally intended as an industry standard API for processing and manipulating HTML documents on a Web browser; we discuss the DOM in this context in Section 3.4.1. However, the need for a generic API for processing any treelike data (such as HTML and XML) was obvious, and the standard was quickly expanded to support XML data in addition to HTML.

When an XML application using a DOM-based parser reads an XML document, the XML data is converted into an in-memory tree representing the entire document. The DOM provides an object model for this tree (described as a hierarchy of nodes) and defines both properties for the different types of nodes and methods that can be used to explore the tree or modify the tree's structure or content.

An illustration of the DOM is found in the markup and code in Figures 3.4 and 3.5. Figure 3.4 lists a simple XML document with a root document element named **xmltest**. This document contains a hierarchy of element and text content. The program listed in Figure 3.5 uses the DOM to explore this hierarchy and report (as a generated HTML document) a list of all the elements and all the text content nodes found in that process.

The example document in Figure 3.4 uses the XML namespace mechanism to tell the browser how to load in the script. Thus, in the **xmltest** start tag, the markup

```
<xmltest xmlns:html="http://www.w3.org/TR/REC-html40">
```

tells the XML processor that any element names having the prefix html: (html followed by a colon) belong to the *HTML namespace* and should be handled as is appropriate for elements coming from that namespace. As a result, upon encountering the element:

```
<html:script src="tree-traverse.js" />
```

```
<?xml version="1.0" ?>
<xmltest xmlns:html="http://www.w3.org/TR/REC-html40">
  <fooBarNode />
  <bigHairyNode>
    <subNode>
      <subsubNode />
    </subNode>
  </bigHairyNode>
  <elem class="foo">
      This is some text content
      <blooble src="blookx" />
      Here is more text content
  </elem>
<html:script src="tree-traverse.js" />
</xmltest>
```

Figure 3.4 Example XML document *test-xml.xml* that references a script program. This program uses the DOM to traverse the document tree, producing an HTML list of the elements and text content of the tree, which is then written to a new browser window. The script program is listed in Figure 3.5. The XML namespace mechanism (markup in boldface), discussed in the previous chapter, is used to tell the browser that the script element is an HTML element and should thus be processed as such.

```javascript
// This is a recursive function, which traverses the
// entire document and prints out a list of all the
// element node names into string variable myString.
// We then erase the page and display this document.
// Now find document root node, then traverse the
// document tree (starting from the root node), and
// find out information about the tree.

root = document.documentElement; // Start here
contentString = traverseTree(root); // function returns a string

function traverseTree(node) {
    if(node.nodeType == Node.ELEMENT_NODE) {
        // Do this if the node is a markup element
        var name = node.nodeName;
        myString = '<li> <b> Element:</b> '+name;
        if( node.hasChildNodes() ) {
            myString = myString + '\n<ul> \n';
            var len = node.childNodes.length;
            var i;
            // If this node has child nodes, then re-call
            // this function for each of those nodes.
            for( i=0; i<node.childNodes.length; i++) {
                myString = myString +
                            traverseTree(node.childNodes.item(i));
            }
            myString = myString + '</li> \n';
        }
        myString = myString + '</li> \n';
    }
    else if (node.nodeType == Node.TEXT_NODE ) {
        // Do this if the node is a text node. Replace 'invisible'
        // characters by symbols (\n, etc. Replace space characters
        // by red 'times' symbols.
        var value = node.nodeValue ;
        value = value.replace(/\r/g,"\\r");
        value = value.replace(/\n/g,"\\n");
        value = value.replace(/\f/g,"\\f");
        value = value.replace(/\t/g,"\\t");
        value = value.replace(/\v/g,"\\v");
        value =
          value.replace(/\s/g,"<font color='red'><b>&times;</b></font>");
        myString =
          "<li><b>Text data: </b>[<tt>" + value + "</tt>]</li>\n";
```

Figure 3.5 Example JavaScript program file *tree-traverse.js* that uses the DOM to create a listing of all element and text nodes in an XML document. DOM-specific property and method names are shown in boldface. Comments are in italics.

```
    }
    return myString;
}


// Now, actually do stuff. First, put the start of an HTML
// document into text string.

startString =
        '<html><head>\n' +
        '<title>List of Elements and nodes</title>\n' +
        '</head>\n<body>\n' +
        '<h1>List of Elements and Text nodes </h1>\n<ul>';

// Add markup that ends the HTML document
endString      = '\n</ul>\n<hr></body></html>';
// Now, open a new browser window, open a new HTML document
// into it, and then write the document text we created
// into this new window.

myWin = window.open();
myWin.document.open('text/html')
myWin.document.write(startString + contentString + endString );
myWin.document.close()
```

Figure 3.5   *(Continued).*

the browser notes this as an HTML **script** element, and processes the markup accordingly by retrieving and running the indicated script program.

Indeed, this is the mechanism supported by the Mozilla/Navigator 6 browser; the following discussion describes how this browser processes the document. Internet Explorer 5 works somewhat differently. We discuss this browser's operation in the next section.

When Mozilla/Navigator 6 loads the document, the parser converts the document into an in-memory data tree representing the entire content of the document, including the elements, attributes, and text. Each different piece of information is turned into a node of that tree, with the type of the node indicating what type of data it is. For example, nodes that correspond to markup elements are called *element nodes,* while nodes that correspond to blocks of nonmarkup text are *text nodes,* and so on.

Since Mozilla understands XML namespaces, it understands how to specially process the **html:script** element, loads in the script program *tree-traverse.js,* and starts running the program. This program uses the DOM to explore part of the document tree. Figure 3.5 shows the program code, with the parts specifically related to the DOM shown in boldface.

How does this work? First off, the parser reads in the document and creates an in-memory data structure containing all the elements, attributes, and text content of the document (among other things). The namespace mechanism also causes the browser to load in the referenced script program. The first two lines of this program:

```
root = document.documentElement;
contentString = traverseTree(root);
```

locate the *document element* (the root node of the document) using a special DOM-defined document property (documentElement) and pass this node object to the function traverseTree(). This function recursively traverses the elements and text content nodes contained within the document node, and returns a text string containing HTML markup text that lists information about the element and text content nodes it has just visited.

This function works as follows. The first conditional statement:

```
if(node.nodeType == Node.ELEMENT_NODE) {
```

checks to see if the node is an element—the special nodeType and Node .ELEMENT_NODE properties are defined by the DOM specification. If it is not an element, then the program checks several lines down:

```
else if (node.nodeType == Node.TEXT_NODE ) {
```

to see if it is a text node (one containing text, but no markup). If the node is neither a text nor an element node, then the function ignores it, finishes, and returns an empty string.

If the node is a text node, then the program obtains the text content of the node:

```
var value = node.nodeValue;
```

and processes this string so that the "invisible" carriage return, tab, space, and other characters are displayed as text strings (\n for new lines, a multiplication character for spaces, etc.). It then constructs a new string of the form:

```
myString = "<li><b>Text data: </b>[<tt>" + value + "</tt>]</li>\n";
```

which is an HTML list item describing the node. This value is then returned by traverseTree() as the function's value.

Things are more complicated if the node is an element node. In this case, the function stores the name of the element in the string variable myString:

```
myString = '<li> <b> Element:</b> '+name;
```

(as the start of an HTML list item) and then checks to see if this node has
child nodes:

```
if( node.hasChildNodes() ) {
```

If it does, then the function adds a **ul** element start tag to the myString string:

```
myString = myString + '\n<ul> \n';
```

to start a **ul** sublist of subelements. The function then loops over the child
nodes:

```
for( i=0; i<node.childNodes.length; i++) {
```

calling the function traverseTree() for each node to recursively process this
node. When the call to traverseTree() returns, the string value returned by
the function is added to the end of the myString variable, adding to it HTML
markup that describes the child node. When all the nodes have processed,
the function adds a **ul** end tag:

```
myString = myString + '</ul> \n';
```

to properly end the sublist produced by the call to traverseTree(), and then
adds an **li** end tag:

```
myString = myString + '</li> \n';.
```

to mark the end of the list item that contained the element that started this
traverseTree() function.

As a result of this process, the function call traverseTree (root) returns
HTML markup that describes the document's tree structure. How are the
results displayed? The following five program lines accomplish this task:

```
contentString = traverseTree(root);
.... function definition for traverseTree() ...
myWin = window.open();
myWin.document.open('text/html')
myWin.document.write(startString + contentString + endString );
myWin.document.close()
```

The first line originally appears just before the traverseTree() function declaration, and means that the HTML markup describing the tree is stored in
the contentString variable. The next lines open a new window, open a new
HTML-format document into that window, and write the contentString
HTML markup into the window, preceded (and followed) by appropriate

HTML header (startString) and footer (endString) data. The HTML markup is then rendered into a new browser window, as shown in Figure 3.6.

Internet Explorer 5

Internet Explorer 5 does not support the XML namespace mechanisms just described (at least not the way we've used it), and cannot easily execute script functions from within an XML document. However, the browser does support several mechanisms for referencing XML data from—or for embedding XML data within—an HTML document. Thus, using Internet Explorer 5, you can first load an HTML document referencing the script, from this script reference and load in an external XML document, and then proceed as just described.

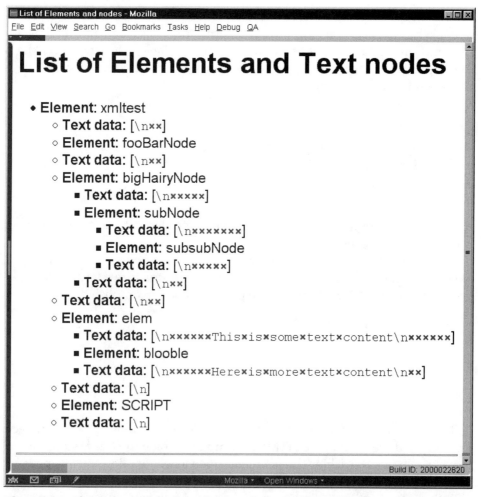

Figure 3.6   The document produced by the markup and script listed in Figures 3.4 and 3.5, as rendered by Navigator 6.

```
<html>
  <head>
   <title> Test of XML and DOM Processing in IE5 </title>
   <script src="tree-traverse-ie5.js"> </script>
  </head>
  <body>
  <h1>Test of XML and DOM Processing in IE5</h1>
  </body></html>
```

Figure 3.7 HTML document used to test DOM parsing of XML on Internet Explorer 5.

This approach is illustrated in Figures 3.7 and 3.8. Figure 3.7 shows the simple HTML document *test-ie5.html,* which simply serves as a placeholder for the script *tree-traverse-ie5.js.* This is a reworked version of the script listed in Figure 3.5, modified so that it directly references and loads in the desired XML document. To illustrate the changes made, the differences from the script in Figure 3.5 are shown in boldface. The main differences are due to the fact that the IE5 script must explicitly reference and load an XML parser, and then pass to the parser the URL of the document to be processed. The remaining differences are due to some limitations in the IE5 DOM implementation (in particular, the properties Node.ELEMENT_TYPE, etc., are not defined).

```
// This is a recursive function, which traverses the
.... other initial comments omitted to save space ....
// find out information about the tree.

ELEMENT_NODE = 1;    // MS parser doesn't define Node.ELEMENT_NODE
TEXT_NODE = 3;     // MS parser doesn't define Node.TEXT_NODE

// Create XML DOM parser object.
var xml = new ActiveXObject("microsoft.xmldom");

xml.async = false;        // Don't load data asynchronously
xml.preserveWhiteSpace = 1; // Treat whitespace as text data

// Load an XML document into the parser from a URL
xml.load("./test-xml.xml");

                                                 continues
```

Figure 3.8 Script program *tree-traverse-ie5.js.* The differences from the program listed in Figure 3.5 are shown in boldface. Italics denote lines omitted to save space.

```
// Check for parser errors.
if(xml.parseError.reason != "") {
   alert("XML Parser Error: " +xml.parseError.reason);
   exit;
}
root = xml.documentElement; // Start here
contentString = traverseTree(root); // function returns a string

function traverseTree(node) {
   if(node.nodeType == ELEMENT_NODE) {
       // Do this if the node is a markup element
       var name = node.nodeName;
       myString = '<li> <b> Element:</b> '+name;
       if( node.hasChildNodes() ) {
           myString = myString + '\n<ul> \n';
           var len = node.childNodes.length;
           var i;
           // If this node has child nodes, then re-call
           // this function for each of those nodes.
           for( i=0; i<node.childNodes.length; i++) {
              myString = myString +
                           traverseTree(node.childNodes.item(i));
           }
           myString = myString + '</ul> \n';
       }
       myString = myString + '</li> \n';
   }
   else if (node.nodeType == TEXT_NODE ) {
       // Do this if the node is a text node. Replace 'invisible'
       // characters by symbols (\n, etc. Replace space characters
       // by red 'times' symbols.
       var value = node.nodeValue ;
       value = value.replace(/\r/g,"\\r");
       value = value.replace(/\n/g,"\\n");
       value = value.replace(/\f/g,"\\f");
       value = value.replace(/\t/g,"\\t");
       value = value.replace(/\v/g,"\\v");
       value =
         value.replace(/\s/g,"<font color='red'><b>&times;</b></font>");
       myString =
         "<li><b>Text data: </b>[<tt>" + value + "</tt>]</li>\n";
   }
   return myString;
}

// Now, actually do stuff. First, put the start of an HTML
.... text omitted -- the rest is exactly as in Figure 3.5....
```

Figure 3.8 *(Continued).*

The result of running this script is shown in Figure 3.9; comparing this with Figures 3.6 and 3.9 shows that both parsers produce identical results. However, the two results are the same only because of the line

```
xml.preserveWhiteSpace = 1
```

in Figure 3.8. Setting this XML parser property to 1 (equivalent to "true") tells the parser to *preserve* white space characters. If this is not set, then the Microsoft XML parser will ignore situations where the text between two tags consists only of white space (carriage return, tab, or line feed characters) and no standard text characters. As an exercise, you can copy the example program code (or download it from this book's supporting Web site), edit the script file to remove this line, and then run the program, noting the differences in the output.

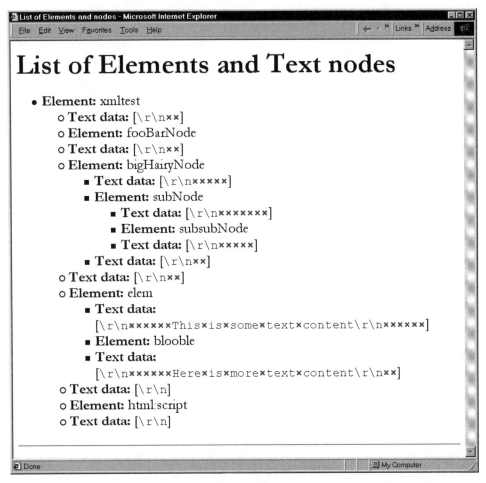

Figure 3.9 The document produced by Internet Explorer 5 after loading the document listed in Figure 3.7.

XML actually defines a special **xml:space** attribute so that a document can itself declare where white space is or is not relevant. This attribute and other details of the XML language are explained in the XML specification (www .w3.org/TR/REC-xml, Section 2.10) or in many of the books on XML, including Section 10.1 of *The XML Specification Guide.*

The preceding examples have provided a simple illustration of only a very few aspects of the DOM parser interface. The interface is actually much richer than this, and includes methods for modifying the content of a node, deleting a node, copying and moving a node to another location, attaching user interface (or other) event handlers to a node, creating and manipulating style nodes defining rendering properties, and so on.

Indeed, the goal of the DOM is to provide a generic interface for supporting rendering control as well as all sorts of complex tree manipulations—both event-driven and not—so that the DOM can be used to write complex, user-interface-driven applications. At present, this usage is most common with HTML, as discussed in Section 3.4.1.

DOM versus SAX

The DOM is obviously more powerful than SAX. However, being more powerful is not the same thing as being more appropriate. In particular, a DOM-based application needs more memory than a SAX-based one, since it must load the entire document into memory (as a tree), which can be a serious problem if the document being processed is large. Second, if doing simple SAX-like event-based processing of XML, DOM-based applications tend to be slower than SAX-based ones (assuming the code is of similar complexity) because the tree manipulation operations used by the DOM are more complex and slower than the simpler ones used by SAX.

Consequently, if you don't need an in-memory data structure for an entire document, don't need to handle external events, and are doing relatively simple processing of the XML that can be easily handled as a stream of event- or attribute-based "events," then SAX is the better choice. Conversely, if you need complex tree manipulation and reconstruction operations and need to keep the entire document in memory for this processing, then the DOM is the best game in town.

3.2 XSLT for Transforming XML

Both SAX and the DOM provide generic interfaces for writing programs that access the elements, attributes, text data content, and other properties of an XML document. Indeed, the goal of these APIs is to provide sets of tools for writing general-purpose programs, each tool set optimized for different classes of applications.

However, there is another set of more specific tools often needed in XML software applications—namely a set of simple tools for transforming one XML document into another. This is often needed for communication between different applications (so that XML messages can be translated into a format understood by another application), and also for communication within an application (so that various XML data sources can be transformed into a common format required by a particular software component).

Recently, the World Wide Web Consortium released a specification for a language—XSLT—that can specify such transformations. XSLT (short for *XSL Transformations*) is an XML language for specifying how XML documents should be transformed into other XML documents (or into non-XML formats such as plain text, PostScript, or other languages). XSLT is in fact one component of the as-yet-incomplete Extensible Stylesheet Language (XSL) specification, which is designed to be a general-purpose XML language for specifying how XML document should be formatted for display. However, XSLT is useful independently of rendering purposes, and is finding a growing role in doing simple XML-to-XML transformations independently of any interest in formatting or displaying the resultant data. Indeed, there are many implementations of XSLT available, some of which are listed in the references section at the end of this chapter.

XSLT is a complex language, and it is not the intention here to explain the details. The following simple example will help explain the basic mechanisms of XSL and give a sense of how XSLT can be integrated into XML-based applications.

3.2.1 A Simple XSLT Example

The goal of this example is to transform a simple XML document into an XHTML document. In practice, the purpose here could be to take XML data in a back-end database of information and transform it into a format (XHTML) that can be sent to a Web browser for display. Thus, although we are converting the document to XHTML, the data can be sent to a browser as text/html data, and will be processed by the browser's HTML-processing software.

An example of the type of documents we wish to transform is shown in Figure 3.10, while Figure 3.11 shows the XSLT style sheet that will transform this document into XHTML. Figure 3.12 shows the result of applying this style sheet to the XML document in Figure 3.10.

An XSLT style sheet works by taking the source markup and recursively searching for patterns in it, applying XSLT formatting templates to the portion of the document that matches the pattern. This process is recursive in that the XSLT templates are again applied to the markup extracted from the source document and copied (according to the templates) into the "output" document (often called the *target*): This process repeats until the entire document has been processed. For example, the template:

```
<?xml version="1.0" ?>
<doc>
   <title>A Happy Document is an XML Document</title>
   <chapter>
     <title>Chapter One: XML is Fun!</title>
     <section>
       <title>Section Title: Why XML?</title>
        <para>This is a test paragraph.</para>
        <note>This is a note, which is different
              from a paragraph.</note>
     </section>
     <section>
       <title>XML and Personal Happiness </title>
       <para> Here is another fancy paragraph.</para>
       <para> Here is an <important> important </important>
          paragraph that follows the previous paragraph.
       </para>
     </section>
   </chapter>
   <chapter>
     <title>Chapter Two: Don't Throw a Bird!</title>
     <section>
       <title>Section 2.2— Why a Bird! </title>
        <para>This is a test paragraph. My but don't
              these examples get more and more
              interesting ...</para>
     </section>
   </chapter>
</doc>
```

Figure 3.10   An example XML document to be transformed to XHTML using the XSLT style sheet listed in Figure 3.11.

```
<xsl:template match="doc">
   <html>
     <head>
        <title> <xsl:value-of select="title"/> </title>
     </head>
     <body>
     <xsl:apply-templates/>
     </body>
   </html>
</xsl:template>
```

is the only template that "matches" the **doc** element, which is the outermost element in the source document. This template produces as output the indicated XHTML template markup. However, it also "selects" the value of the **title** element inside the **doc** and inserts this inside the XHTML **title** element.

```
<!-- The first line says this is an XSL stylesheet: but note
     that it also says that XSL-related element names must
     have the xs1: prefix. If they don't have this prefix,
     then they are assumed to be XHTML elements! -->
<xsl:stylesheet version="1.0"
     xmlns:xsl="http://www.w3.org/1999/XSL/Transform"
     xmlns="http://www.w3.org/TR/xhtml1/strict">

<!-- Look for a 'doc' element -- then pull the content of
     the title element inside it, and paste it inside
     the template's 'title' element. Then recursively apply
     all templates from _inside_ the main template's XHTML
     'body' element. -->
<xsl:template match="doc">
   <html>
     <head>
        <title> <xsl:value-of select="title"/> </title>
     </head>
     <body>
     <xsl:apply-templates/>
     </body>
   </html>
   </xsl:template>

<!-- This template matches the 'title' element inside a 'doc'.
     When it finds one, it produces an 'h1' element
     that contains the content of the element it matched (i.e.,
     contains the content of the title element). It will then
     recursively apply templates to the text and markup 'included'
     inside that h1 element. -->
  <xsl:template match="doc/title">
     <h1> <xsl:apply-templates/> </h1>
   </xsl:template>

<!-- The next two templates do exactly the same thing, except
     in these cases for 'title' element inside a 'chapter' or
     inside a 'section' element. -->
   <xsl:template match="chapter/title">
     <h2> <xsl:apply-templates/> </h2>
   </xsl:template>
   <xsl:template match="section/title">
     <h3> <xsl:apply-templates/> </h3>
   </xsl:template>
```

continues

Figure 3.11 An XSLT style sheet that transforms the document in Figure 3.10 into an XHTML document. The template components of the document are shown in boldface italics.

```
<!-- This template simply makes sure that each 'chapter'
     element is converted into an XHTML 'div' element with
     an appropriate class attribute value -->
<xsl:template match="chapter">
    <div class="chapter"> <xsl:apply-templates/> </div>
  </xsl:template>

<!-- The next template matches 'para' elements wherever they
     are, and takes the para content and pastes it inside
     an XHTML 'p' element. It then recursively applies
     templates again. -->
<xsl:template match="para">
    <p> <xsl:apply-templates/> </p>
  </xsl:template>

<!-- And the following simply discards any 'note' elements and
     their content -->
<xsl:template match="note"></xsl:template>

<!-- The last template matches 'important' elements wherever they
     are, takes their content and pastes it inside
     an XHTML 'strong' element. It then recursively applies
     templates again. -->
  <xsl:template match="important">
    <strong> <xsl:apply-templates/> </strong>
  </xsl:template>
```

Figure 3.11   *(Continued).*

It also takes the content of the **doc** element and recursively applies all the XSLT templates to this content, inserting the results inside the XHTML **body** element.

As a result, the next template rule

```
<xsl:template match="doc/title">
   <h1> <xsl:apply-templates/> </h1>
</xsl:template>
```

again matches the **title** element inside the **doc,** and writes out an **h1** heading into the XHTML document. The content of the **h1** will be the result of processing the content of the **title** element using whatever other template rules are relevant inside that element—in this case, none. At the same level, the rule

```
<xsl:template match="chapter">
    <div class="chapter"> <xsl:apply-templates/> </div>
  </xsl:template>
```

matches the **chapter** element, writes out an XHTML **div** element with the specified **class** attribute, and then recursively processes the content of the **chapter** element, inserting the results inside the XHTML **div** element.

The rest of the templates are well explained by the notes in Figure 3.11. One thing of interest is the template

```
<xsl:template match="note"></xsl:template>
```

which matches **note** elements, but transforms them into nothing. This is one way in which nodes and their content can be eliminated from the output (or "pruned") during the transformation process.

Figure 3.12 shows typical output upon applying the XSLT style sheet in Figure 3.11 to the document listed in Figure 3.10. In this case, the transformation was made using an early version of the perl XSLT processor. This processor did not support all the XSLT features, so that Figure 3.12 was handcorrected to adjust for some errors of this software. The perl code used to invoke the XSLT processor is quite simple:

```
#! /usr/bin/perl
use strict;
use XML::XSLT;

my &xmlfile = "xsl-test-source.xml";
my &xslfile = "test-style.xsl";
&XSLT::Parser->open_project (&xmlfile, &xslfile);
&XSLT::Parser->process_project; # Apply the style sheet
&XSLT::Parser->print_result; # print the result
```

This simply applies the style sheet to the document and prints the result to standard output.

3.2.2 XSLT Strengths and Weaknesses

As described previously (albeit only briefly), XSLT is a very rich and flexible language for specifying how XML data should be transformed into other XML-format data or other data types. Indeed, for general-purpose transformations of this type, XSLT is much easier to use than handwritten code (using an XML parser and either the SAX or DOM interfaces) designed to do the same things.

However, this facility comes with some costs. For now, at least, XSLT-based transformation tools can be much slower than hard-coded transformation engines written using the SAX interface. This is partly due to the newness of the language and the newness (and nonoptimized nature) of existing XSLT software. However, it is obvious that any general-purpose transformation system such as XSLT will always be slower than a hard-coded transformation tool designed for a limited, special-purpose task.

```
<html>
    <head>
      <title> A Happy Document is an XML Document </title>
    </head>
    <body>
      <h1> A Happy Document is an XML Document </h1>
      <div class="chapter">
      <h2>Chapter One: XML is Fun!</h2>

      <h3> Section Title: Why XML? </h3>

      <p> This is a test paragraph. </p>

       <h3> XML and Personal Happiness </h3>

      <p> Here is another fancy paragraph. </p>

      <p> Here is an
      <strong> important </strong>
          paragraph that follows the previous paragraph.
        </p>
    </div>
    <div class="chapter">
     <h2> Chapter Two: Don't Throw a Bird!</h2>

      <h3>Section 2.2— Why a Bird!</h3>

      <p> This is a test paragraph. My but don't
          these examples get more and more
          interesting... </p>

    </div>
    </body>
</html>
```

Figure 3.12   The XHTML document produced by applying the XSLT style sheet in Figure 3.11 to the XML document listed in Figure 3.10.

Consequently, if speed is an important issue in your application design, you may end up developing a prototype using XSLT and then hard-coding the slowest transformations using a SAX- or DOM-based parser.

3.3 Processing HTML Data

In principle, the same sort of software described in Section 3.1 can be used to process HTML outside the browser. For example, a system could have a database of HTML documents (or of document fragments, where a fragment might be a heading, a **table**, or a **div** element and its content), and could use software to assemble these components into Web pages or break apart a page into reusable components. Indeed, some commercial site management tools—most based originally on SGML-based document management systems—work in this manner.

However, such tools did not become terribly popular for processing "run-of-the-mill" HTML. The main reason was that the input data—that is, the raw HTML authored by the writers and editors—tends to be badly formed, with missing tags, missing quotes (around attribute values), and other similar problems. This is not the fault of authors—it is simply the result of a system (i.e., Web browsers) that was designed to be tolerant of small mistakes. Unfortunately, the mistakes are less bearable when badly formed HTML components are input into a system (such as an SGML document management system) that needs correctness to work properly, or when such components are combined together (as in Web pages made up of different HTML snippets). Indeed, although such systems generally worked well for small collections of data (where mistakes could be corrected by hand), this approach was found to be not workable when the input consisted of large collections of hand-edited, error-filled HTML.

This is not to say that there are not a lot of commercial, open source, and shareware HTML processing tools available. Indeed, essentially all commercial site management systems use HTML processing tools to assemble and manage pages on a Web site, while most "dynamic" site production systems (such as Cold Fusion, PHP, and others) provide HTML processing libraries. We will look at some of these tools in Chapter 12, and compare some of their features.

However, in general these tools do not reuse large chunks of HTML markup, but instead use a simple *template* model. In this model, page designers build template HTML pages and then place instructions inside the templates that, when processed by a template processor, extract simple text strings from a database (or text source of some sort) and dynamically generate HTML tags and content. For example, such a template might look like

```
<table>
<tr> <td> heading 1 </td> <td> heading 2 </td> </tr>
<!-- loop over generated table rows -->
<? for i=0; I<20; i++ {
  println(' <tr> <td> %item(i)</td> <td>%item(i)-sub1 </td> </tr>)
} ?>
</table>
```

which effectively embeds a program inside the template document. The template processor then replaces this block of code with the 20 dynamically generated HTML table rows.

The similarity of such a statement to an XSLT-based approach is obvious. However, the advantage of XSLT is that the markup in the XSLT document can be directly tested for well-formedness even before the output is generated. This is because an XSLT document, since it is XML, must itself be well formed—and this includes the XHTML markup used inside the XSLT templates. As a result, the output of an XSLT processor will always be well-formed XML (such as XHTML).

Of course, this means that the source data also needs to be well formed, so that the entire system must use XML as the main technology and entirely avoid ill-formed HTML. This is the model behind many next-generation Web authoring and Web document management systems, including the XML-Apache project (xml.apache.org) and the Zope server XML document project (www.zope.org).

3.4 Processing HTML on Browsers

Browser processing (other than simple display) of HTML began early in the history of the Web with the Navigator 2 browser. With this browser, Netscape introduced the concept of *scripted* Web pages, with script programs written in the *JavaScript* language included in a document inside **script** elements. This language initially consisted of basic language features (syntax and grammar, plus some basic tools), plus a collection of predefined objects and functions that let JavaScript programs interact with the components on a browser (windows, status bars, document URLs, etc.). Such scripts could also interact, in a limited way, with the document itself, for example by printing text and markup tags into the document about to be displayed, or by changing the content of fill-in forms.

Microsoft quickly followed Netscape's lead by implementing JavaScript support in its Internet Explorer 3 browser. However, Microsoft did not have access to the details of Netscape's JavaScript implementation, so that Internet Explorer 3 was not entirely compatible with the version supported by Netscape (although Microsoft did try to make its version as compatible as possible). Indeed, Microsoft formally named its language *Jscript* partly to denote this difference.

> **NOTE** Microsoft also implemented a second scripting language, known as Visual Basic Script (VBScript). In terms of functionality, VBScript is similar to JavaScript, although the language is closer in look and feel to Visual Basic, from which it is derived.

However, the things that could be done with such scripts were quite limited. A script could open new windows and send HTML data to a window or frame, and could interact with the content of editable form fields (such as **input** or **textarea** elements), but could not interact with the already-displayed HTML markup. In this original model, once the content was rendered, the rendered page was static and could only be changed by erasing the page and redrawing it entirely. This made it difficult to design sophisticated, interactive Web interfaces using HTML and JavaScript.

With the release of Navigator 4 and Internet Explorer 4, Netscape and Microsoft extended scripting to support "dynamic" manipulation of the displayed page and interaction between the user and this displayed content. However, unlike the case with the previous browsers, where Microsoft attempted to duplicate the functionality of the Netscape scripting model, the two companies implemented entirely different tools for creating and manipulating dynamic content. Consequently, scripts written for one browser could not work on the other. To make the situation even more confusing, both companies referred to their dynamic scripting tools as *dynamic HTML*—Netscape with a capital D and Microsoft with a lowercase d. Today these two phrases, along with the abbreviation DHTML, are widely used to describe this functionality.

Of course, dynamic HTML, Dynamic HTML, and DHTML have little to do with HTML. Rather, these terms refer to programming interfaces that can let a program dynamically interact with the displayed Web page. In general, these interfaces allow for the following types of interactions between the software, the underlying HTML document, and the rendered appearance of that document:

- Support for multiple rendered "layers," stacked on top of the standard displayed page and capable of being positioned on the page under script control.

- Interaction with the actual content and attributes of elements. This extends the earlier ability to modify the values of form input elements, and makes it possible, for example, to dynamically change the value of any element attribute or change text content inside a paragraph and have the rendered view of the page dynamically "reflow" to reflect the changes.

- Control of display properties of elements, so that rendering characteristics, such as visibility, color, font family, and so on, can be controlled by a script program.

- Ability to detect events from any markup element (for example, a mouse passing over the content of an **em** element) and create script functions to handle such events.

Fortunately, Netscape, Microsoft, and various other industry members realized that it was not useful to have such incompatible software implementations for what was supposed to be a "universal" browser. Thus, in early 1997 the World Wide Web Consortium organized a working group, the goal of which was to define an industry standard way of implementing the features just mentioned. The result of this process was the HTML Document Object Model (DOM), a generic open standard programming interface for writing programs that interact with parsed HTML data.

However, if you are looking for books on programming dynamic Web pages, then you need to look for words such as *DHTML* or *Dynamic HTML* in their titles or descriptions. Very few books explicitly mention the DOM—although that will likely soon change.

3.4.1 Dynamic HTML and the DOM

Section 3.1.2 introduced the DOM as a generic programming interface for accessing and manipulating the content of an XML document. However, the DOM specifications (see the references at the end of the chapter) actually deal with several other issues related to the modeling of HTML or XML data and the processing/display of these structures. Indeed, the current specification defines the following seven things:

- A model for the parse tree representing the HTML document markup and content and for that representing the different special-purpose HTML elements (e.g., **img**, **form**, form input elements, **object**) and attributes (e.g., **id**, **class**, **href**, and **src**).

- A model for the parse tree representing XML document markup and content. Note that, unlike the case with HTML, the XML model does not make any allowances for special functional roles of any XML element.

- A model for the formatting properties associated with each markup element (HTML or XML).

- A model for user interface (and other) events, including how such events are detected and propagated (that is, passed up from an element to its parent element) through a document's parse tree (HTML or XML).

- A programming API for manipulating the HTML or XML trees.

- A programming API for manipulating the style information associated with a given element (HTML or XML).

- A programming API for attaching event handler functions to specific elements (HTML or XML) and for controlling how events propagate.

The first three items are simply the underlying model for the things the HTML or XML parser creates, and for the properties a program will wish to interact with. The last four define the mechanisms by which programs can be written to interact with the different parts of the model.

It is important to recall that there are two DOM models, one for HTML and one for XML. This was necessary for two reasons:

- For compatibility with the existing implementations on the Navigator and Internet Explorer browsers, which had special HTML-related names for some of the needed properties and functions. It was also felt that this approach would make it easier for page programmers, since the names helped simplify program design.

- Because there was no obvious way to define, in a generic way, special functionality and logic associated with certain HTML elements (for example, **img**, **applet**, **object**, **form**, or **input**) or the special meanings of special attributes (e.g., **id** for ID-based references, **class** for style sheet–based class formatting).

Thus, the HTML DOM is in fact much richer than the one for XML, as it defines special "objects" relevant to specific types of elements (e.g., `HTMLLinkElement`, `HTMLSelectElement`, and so on) and special methods for referencing elements (e.g., `getElementByID (idvalue)`) or for interacting with them.

Figure 3.13 schematically illustrates the relationships between these various parts. The retrieved HTML document is parsed by the HTML parser, producing a document object representing the HTML data. Any retrieved style sheet information "decorates" this tree, adding to each node in the tree data providing rendering instructions for the element. The dynamic renderer then processes this tree and renders it to the display. This renderer responds to a number of events, such as window resizing, and redraws the display when necessary.

The DOM interface lets the user create scripts that detect user interface events and that can interact with the data in the tree. Thus, the script can detect when the user interacts with the displayed document and can then act as programmed. Although in Figure 3.13 the script is shown as being separate from the HTML document, this script could be inside a **script** element inside the document.

Scripted DOM Example

Figure 3.14 is a simple document that illustrates how these programming interfaces can be used to dynamically control the rendering of HTML pages. The script element defines two functions. The function `setfonts()` sets the default font for the document. The first line in this function:

```
var myBody = document.getElementsByTagName ('body').item(0);
```

uses the DOM to get a list of all the **body** elements in the document, and sets the variable `myBody` to be the first (and only) element in this list. The next line:

```
myBody.style.fontFamily = "Garamond, 'Times New Roman'";
```

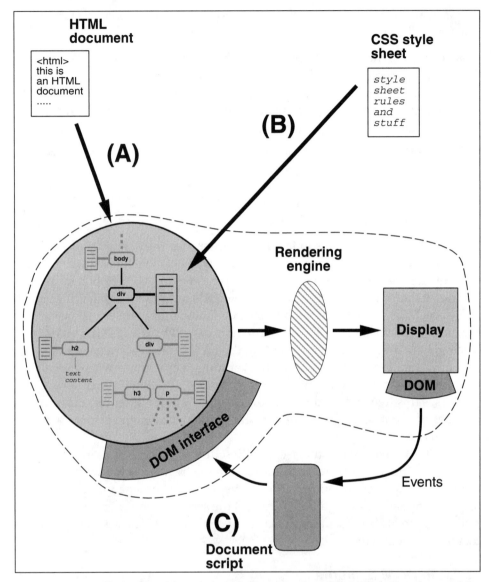

Figure 3.13   An illustration of the relationship between the DOM software interface and the software that renders and processes an HTML document. (A) The incoming HTML document is read in and parsed to produce the parse tree. (B) Any Cascading Style Sheet (CSS) rules are used to add formatting information to the parse tree. (C) A document script uses the DOM interface to detect events produced at the user interface and to interact with the HTML data.

sets the CSS font family property for this element to the indicated set of fonts. This, of course, will be inherited by all the elements inside the body. The font string is also stored in the variable font for future use. This function is run when the document loads (using the **onload** event handler attribute on the **body** element).

```
<html><head>
<title>Simple DOM Tests </title>
<script type="text/javascript"><!--

/* Set the default font for the body element */

function setfonts() {
  var myBody = document.getElementsByTagName('body').item(0);
  myBody.style.fontFamily = "Garamond, 'Times New Roman'";
  font = myBody.style.fontFamily;
}
/* Toggle toggles the ul list in and out, and changes the
   heading color */

function toggle () {
    var myList = document.getElementsByTagName('ul').item(0);
    var myHead = document.getElementById('varg');
    if (myList.style.display=="none") {
        myList.style.display="block" ;
        myHead.style.color="red";
        myHead.style.fontStyle="italic";
        myHead.style.fontFamily=font;
    }
    else {
        myList.style.display="none" ;
        myHead.style.color="green";
        myHead.style.fontStyle="normal";
        myHead.style.fontFamily="Arial";
    }
}
//--></script>
</head>
<body onload="setfonts()">
<h1 id="varg" onclick="toggle()"> This is the Heading </h1>
<p>This is a paragraph of text. Ipsum lorem dadak ilsum it
   plrimpkis dirlber di ilbert. dadak ilsum it plrimpkis
   dirlber di ilbert. fpllogn ilpsum slipsum lorendoar
   plrimpkis dirlber di ilbert. dadak ilsum it plrimpkis
   afleeble bloo. </p>
<ul>
  <li>Item one </li>
  <li>Item two </li>
  <li>Item three </li>
</ul>
<p>This is a paragraph of text. Ipsum lorem dadak ilsum it
```

continues

Figure 3.14 A simple HTML document containing a script that uses the DOM to manipulate the displayed content. Rendered results are shown in Figure 3.15. Please see the text for a detailed explanation.

```
    plrimpkis dirlber di ilbert. dadak ilsum it plrimpkis
    dirlber di ilbert. fpllogn ilpsum slipsum lorendoar
    plrimpkis dirlber di ilbert. dadak ilsum it plrimpkis
    afleeble bloo. </p>
</body>
</html>
```

Figure 3.14   *(Continued).*

The **h1** element uses the **onclick** event handler attribute to run the `toggle()` function when the user clicks on the heading. This function creates variables referencing two elements: the **ul** list (retrieved as discussed for the **body** element) and the **h1** element. The latter is found using the `getElementById()` function, which locates the element by its **id** attribute value.

The function then simply checks to see if the CSS display property value for this list is set to "none" (which causes the element to be removed from the rendering process). If it is, then the value is set to "block" (which makes the element appear as a block element) and the heading is transformed such that it uses the font, but with red, italicized text. If the value is not set to "none," then the second part of the statement sets it to "none," removing it from the rendering process. Also, the heading text is changed to use a green, nonitalicized Arial font.

Figure 3.15 shows the effect of toggling this heading. Of course, the dynamic nature of this transition is not apparent from this figure, so you are encouraged to visit the Web site and try it out for yourself.

This script uses standard DOM interfaces and works correctly on Internet Explorer 5 (and greater) and Mozilla/Navigator 6 (and greater). It does not, however, work on earlier browsers.

3.4.2 XML Mixed with HTML

As mentioned in the previous chapter, Navigator 4 and earlier, Internet Explorer 4 and earlier, and most other browsers have essentially no ability to process XML data. However, both Navigator 6 and Internet Explorer 5 understand the XML data type and can read in XML data, converting it into an in-memory data tree that can be accessed and processed using the DOM interface, as described in Section 3.1.2.

It would be nice if these browsers also supported mechanisms by which the browser could read in and process an HTML document, and from there read in and process XML data. In these cases the XML data would act as a data source for the HTML application. That is, the page could contain script components that use the DOM to access and manipulate both the HTML doc-

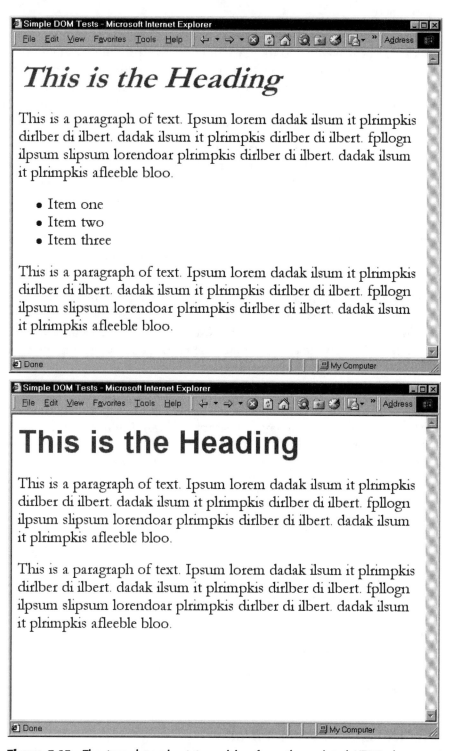

Figure 3.15 The two dynamic states arising from the scripted HTML document listed in Figure 3.14, here demonstrated by the Internet Explorer 5.5 browser.

ument being displayed and the XML data sources providing data to that page. For example, the page could consist of a formatted page providing information about a specific product, while the XML data source could contain, in XML format, detailed descriptions of many different products. The browser would then implement the application as follows:

- The browser would first render the default HTML document. This document would include some sort of HTML form (or other) mechanism that let the user select the product to be displayed. A script would then use the DOM interface to access this HTML document and detect selections by the user.

- The same script would use the DOM interface to load in the XML data source (as a separate DOM object), so that data could be extracted from that source per a user request.

- When the user made a selection in the HTML form, this event would be detected by the script, which would retrieve the data from the form and use this to extract data from the XML data source. This data would then be used to rewrite the portion of the HTML tree describing the product. This change would immediately cause the display to update and reflect the new content.

In practice, there are several ways to implement this model. Perhaps the most straightforward is to have the script program itself reference and load XML data referenced using a URL. Unfortunately, the DOM does not specify a standard for referencing external XML (or HTML) resources. Internet Explorer 5, however, supports some simple programming extensions that let the browser load in a remote XML data object, parse it, and make it available via the DOM. This mechanism is illustrated in Section 3.1.2 and Figures 3.7 and 3.8. Internet Explorer also supports a special "data islands" mechanism that lets an HTML document contain blocks of XML data. We discuss this mechanism in the next section.

Unfortunately, the Mozilla/Navigator 6 browser does not (yet) support a similar mechanism, although there is some hope that such a mechanism will exist with the released browser. If so, then this information will be provided on this book's supporting Web site. However, the current Mozilla browser does support user-defined HTML elements, so that it is possible (with a bit of work) to mimic the data islands mechanism in Mozilla/Navigator 6. We discuss this mechanism later in this section.

Internet Explorer 5: Data Islands

Internet Explorer 5 and up let you embed XML data within an HTML document using what are known as *XML data islands*. A simple example is shown in Figure 3.16. In Internet Explorer 5, data islands are indicated by a special **XML** element that either encloses the XML-format data (as in the first example in Figure 3.16) or references the XML-format data using a URL. The **id** attribute then labels each different block of data, so that each block can be individually referenced.

Internet Explorer 5 automatically hides the content of the XML islands from display. The islands can then be referenced and parsed exactly as in Figures 3.7 and 3.8, except that the reference is now to an internal data island, as opposed to an external URL. The browser will load the referenced XML document and convert it into a DOM-accessible object. The document script can then access these objects via some Internet Explorer extensions to the DOM. For example, the following function:

```
<html>
<head> <title> Example Document </title>
</head>
<body>
<XML id="data-1">
     <menu date="12nov1998">
       <rname>Liam's Chowder House and Grill</rname>
       <item type="appetizer" >
         <desc>Warmed leek salad, coated with a balsamic
             vinegar and goat cheese dressing</desc>
         <price units="usd">6.95</price>
         <graphic gtype="gif"
               src="http://www.goodfood.com/menu/leek-salad.gif" />
       </item>
       <item type="appetizer" >
         <desc>Prosciutto ham with melon</desc>
         <price units="usd">7.95</price>
         <graphic gtype="jpeg"
               src="http://www.goodfood.com/menu/ham-melon.jpeg" />
       </item>
     </menu>
</XML>
<!-- Here is an "external" data island -->
<XML id="data-2"
     src="http://www.remoteisland.com/file.data.xml"></XML>
<h1> Example Document </h1>
.... rest of document...
</body></html>
```

Figure 3.16 An example HTML document containing two data islands, one inside the document and one referenced via a URL.

```
function returnXMLDocument(IDvalue) {
return document.all(IDvalue).XMLDocument;
}
```

returns the XML document corresponding to the XML element having the given **id** attribute value. As a result, the statement

```
myXML = returnXMLDocument("data-1").documentElement;
```

means that the variable myXML refers to the root node (the document element) of the data island having **id**="data-1". This data island can then be processed using the DOM, just like any XML document.

Mozilla/Navigator 6: XML Namespaces

The Mozilla/Navigator 6 browser does not support data islands, so that the mechanism just described is simply not usable in this browser. However, the Mozilla HTML parser does support custom markup elements, provided they are written with both start and end tags. Thus, if you are careful with your document design, you can mimic the island mechanism by creating within the document a custom HTML tree containing the desired data. However, you must avoid using XML empty-element tags in the markup, as such tags are not understood by the HTML parser.

As an example, Figure 3.17 shows the document from Figure 3.16 modified so that it can work with the Mozilla/Navigator 6 browser. Note how the original XML markup is modified so that all the **graphic** empty-element tags are written using explicit start and end tags. This guarantees that the HTML parser will accurately parse the document—and still leave the document as valid XML.

Note that this will still function correctly with Internet Explorer 5, since the parse tree is unaffected by converting an empty-element tag into a start/end tag sequence.

However, with Mozilla you cannot use this mechanism to reference external data islands, as in:

```
<XML id="data-2"
src="http://www.remoteisland.com/file.data.xml"></XML>
```

This is because the current version of Mozilla does not provide a mechanism for loading and parsing XML data from within a script. The Mozilla developers hope to implement such a feature by the time the browser is released as Navigator 6.

```
<html>
<head> <title> Example Document </title>
<style><!--
XML {display: none } /* To hide the XML element and content */
--></style>
</head>
<body>
<!-- here is an XML data island -->
<XML id="data-1">
    <menu date="12nov1998">
      <rname>Liam's Chowder House and Grill</rname>
      <item type="appetizer" >
        <desc>Warmed leek salad, coated with a balsamic
           vinegar and goat cheese dressing</desc>
        <price units="usd">6.95</price>
        <graphic gtype="gif"
            src="http://www.goodfood.com/menu/leek-salad.gif" >
        </graphic>
     </item>
    <item type="appetizer" >
      <desc>Prosciutto ham with melon</desc>
      <price units="usd">7.95</price>
       <graphic gtype="jpeg"
            src="http://www.goodfood.com/menu/ham-melon.jpeg" >
       </graphic>
     </item>
    </menu>
</XML>
<!-- Here is an "external" data island -->
<h1> Example Document </h1>
.... rest of document...
</body></html>
```

Figure 3.17 The example HTML document from Figure 3.16, modified so that it contains virtual islands parsable by the Mozilla/Navigator 6 HTML parser.

3.5 References

XML PROGRAMMING INTERFACE SPECIFICATIONS

www.megginson.com/SAX/index.html   SAX specification

www.w3.org/TR/REC-DOM-Level-1/   DOM level 1

www.w3.org/TR/DOM-Level-2/   DOM level 2

www.w3.org/DOM/   DOM working drafts

XML PARSERS

www.alphaworks.ibm.com/tech/xml4j	Java (validating)
xml.apache.org	Java (validating; Apache Xerces Project)
www.cogsci.ed.ac.uk/~richard/rxp.html	C (validating)
msdn.microsoft.com/downloads/ webtechnology/xml/msxml.asp	COM (validating; COM object)
www.zveno.com/zm.cgi/in-tclxml/	Tcl (nonvalidating)
www.jclark.com/xml/xp/index.html	Java (nonvalidating)
www.textuality.com/Lark/	Java (nonvalidating)
www.jclark.com/xml/expat.html	C (nonvalidating; also available as perl and Tcl modules)
www.cogsci.ed.ac.uk/~richard/rxp.html	C (validating)

XML PROCESSING TOOLS/SOFTWARE

www.w3.org/XML/#software	Software list
www.cpan.org/modules/index.html	perl modules (many XML-related)
www.cpan.org/modules/ by-module/XML/	perl modules
www.python.org/topics/xml/	Python tools
www.alphaworks.ibm.com/tech/xml4j	Java tools
www.zveno.com/zm.cgi/in-tclxml/	Tcl language tools
www.jclark.com/xml/xt.html	XT: an XSLT processor
xml.apache.org/xalan/index.html	XALAN XSLT processor
www.jclark.com/sp/	SP: an XML/SGML toolkit
dir.altavista.com/Computers/ Data_Formats/41058/XML/Tools.shtml	Software tools list
freshmeat.net/	General list [search for "XML"]
www.xmlsoftware.com/	List of software

XML, SAX, DOM, AND XSLT TUTORIALS/INFO SITES

www.developerlife.com/	Java language
java.sun.com/xml/docs/tutorial/	Java language
wwwx.netheaven.com/~coopercc/ Xtech99/tutorial/index.html	perl and XML

www.python.org/doc/howto/xml/	Python XML HOWTO
www.perlxml.com/	perl articles
http://freespace.virgin.net/b.pawson/	XSLT FAQ
msdn.microsoft.com/xml/default.asp	Microsoft XML Information

LISTS OF XML-RELATED URLS

www.cetus-links.org:80/oo_xml.html	General XML and software

SOME XML EDITORS

www.stilo.com	WebWriter
www.arbortext.com	Adept*Editor
www.softquad.com	XmetaL
www.xmlspy.com	XML Spy
www.xmlwriter.net	XMLWriter
www.morphon.com	Morphon
www.webreference.com/xml/column8	Article on XML editors

LIST OF COMMON XML DTDS

www.xml.org/xmlorg_registry/index.shtml schemas	Common XML DTDs or

HTML TO XML/XHTML CONVERSION UTILITIES

www.w3.org/People/Raggett/tidy/	HTML Tidy
db.cis.upenn.edu/W4F/	Generic HTML-to-XML conversion tool

HTML, DYNAMIC HTML, AND DOM REFERENCES

cgi.din.or.jp/~hagi3/JavaScript/Mozilla/ SampleList.cgi?fmt=html	DOM examples
www.mozilla.org/docs/dom/samples/	More DOM examples
sites.netscape.net/ekrock/ standards.html	Guide to browser-compatible scripts
developer.netscape.com/docs/technote/ dynhtml/xbdhtml/xbdhtml.html	Cross-browser scripting guide
msdn.microsoft.com/workshop/author/	Microsoft DHTML references
developer.netscape.com/tech/dynhtml/ index.html	Netscape Navigator 4 dynamic HTML

BOOKS

XML IE5 Programmer's Reference, by Alex Homer, Wrox Press (1999)—A programmer's guide to using XML within the IE5 browser.

IE5 Dynamic HTML Programmer's Reference, by Brian Francis, Alex Homer, and Chris Ullman, Wrox Press (1999)—A programmer's guide to dynamic HTML (DHTML, whatever) as implemented on Internet Explorer 5.

Dynamic HTML: The Definitive Guide, by Danny Goodman, O'Reilly and Associates (1998)—A bit out of date, but an excellent guide to dynamic HTML on Internet Explorer 4 and Navigator 4. A related and also useful book is *Javascript: The Definitive Guide,* by David Flannagan, O'Reilly and Associates (1998).

Applied XML: A Toolkit for Programmers, by Alex Ceponkus and Faraz Hoodbhoy, John Wiley and Sons (1999)—A useful, technical book explaining how XML can be processed, with a bent toward the software tools available in the Internet Explorer 5 browser.

The Open Source XML Database Toolkit, by Liam Quin, John Wiley & Sons (2000)—A useful discussion of tools and tricks for designing XML-based database-driven applications using open source software tools. There are many working code examples.

The XML Specification Guide, by Ian S. Graham and Liam Quin, John Wiley & Sons (1999)—A useful review of XML markup and of the processing behavior required of XML parsers.

Technical Web Page Design

Topics/Concepts Covered: Setting requirements, project management, speed optimizations, cross-browser design, accessible design, printable design, component-based designs

This chapter discusses the high-level technical task of using technical skills when designing Web documents. Technical page design of course requires a detailed knowledge of and skill with HyperText Markup Language (HTML)/ eXtensible HTML (XHTML), Cascading Style Sheets (CSS), and JavaScript or Visual Basic Script (VBScript) if the pages use scripted components. Such knowledge, combined with graphical design skills (often provided by other members of a Web design group) and an understanding of overall Web site or application design issues (discussed in the next chapter) is essential to any successful Web project.

Indeed, many Web design projects start out with experts in these areas and then magically assume that everything will work out nicely. Unfortunately, this is rarely the case. This is because the preceding model misses some important components. In particular, it misses the fact that Web design projects do not exist in isolation—rather, they are strongly dependent on outside issues that constrain the design or design process in some way. For a project to succeed, these requirements must be well understood right from the start. If they are not, then you can pretty well guarantee that the project will have significant problems or may fail altogether.

What are typical requirements? Some are pretty obvious and quite general, such as the intended purpose of the site or the time, resources, and money available to build it. Others are more specifically technical and often less clear, such as the desired speed of the site or the types of browsers the site must support. Typically there are many technical requirements, and it is critical that the design team understand what these are before work begins. Otherwise, the team can easily waste time and resources developing pages that are unacceptable—often in ways so severe that the entire design has to be thrown out.

Therefore it is critical that requirements be discussed and agreed upon in the initial phase of a project. Establishing these requirements is typically the job of the project manager, but in practice it is the technical team that will best understand the ramifications of the proposed technical constraints. It is thus important that technical staff be involved in defining these requirements, typically by negotiating them with the customer or client and by helping to explain the ramifications and costs of possible choices.

Consequently, every technical designer needs to understand technical requirements in two ways:

- In a way understandable to nontechnical people, such as graphics designers, site architectural planners, or the customer contracting the work

- As technical issues with understood technical solutions

The first is needed because a designer typically negotiates requirements with people who do not understand or care about technical details, but who do care that the site works properly and who understand what makes a design work (or not work) from the customer's perspective. The designer must thus be able to discuss the requirements in a clear, nontechnical way.

The second is needed because a designer must turn requirements negotiated with a client into explicit technical requirements that can be used by the design team. Also, technical designers must have strategies for handling these requirements, so that they know how the requirements can be dealt with and so that they can estimate the costs associated with fulfilling the requirements. For example, knowing that a site must work with a certain set of browsers, designers should already know of approaches they can use to ensure this requirement is met, and should also have a reasonable estimate of how much additional development time this will require. Furthermore, they should also know how to test that the designs under development are consistent with the requirement.

The purpose of this chapter is to examine technical requirements from both these perspectives. Section 4.1 reviews design requirements from the perspective of a nontechnical person—that is, in a way understandable to nontechnical staff such as senior managers, marketing staff, or outside clients. This section presents a summary of the types of nontechnical issues that should be raised (and agreed upon) in the initial stages of any design project. This section also introduces some nontechnical issues that should also be discussed in the early stages—such as establishing the goals for the project—and other thematic requirements. Ways to deal with these requirements are discussed in Chapter 5.

The second part of this chapter looks at technical approaches to dealing with the issues raised in Section 4.1. For example, how can you increase the speed with which pages are rendered or make the design more accessible to users with visual impairments? In essence, then, the first part of the chapter tells you how to determine which issues are important, while the second part explains how the different technical tools can be used to resolve these issues and satisfy the established project requirements.

This chapter and the next one do not discuss graphic design, other than in a very abstract way. There are two reasons for this. First, there is no need to rewrite someone else's book—there are many excellent books covering the graphic and typographic problems of Web page layout and design. If these topics are of interest to you, then I encourage you to look at the references at the end of this chapter, where I have listed several good books and Web sites on these topics.

4.1 Page Design and Project Management

In every project, a Web developer is constrained by a set of technical requirements that strongly influence the final design. For example, if the pages must function under Internet Explorer 3, then the design simply must work correctly on this browser. Obviously this will lead to a quite different design than if Internet Explorer 3 did not need to be supported. And, of course, browser version support is only one of many possible requirements, any of which can strongly affect the ways in which pages can be acceptably designed.

It is thus important to establish the technical requirements at the beginning of each design (or redesign) project. If this is done, then all team members know right from the start the constraints they are under, and can use their skills and knowledge to develop designs consistent with those constraints. This saves both time and money, since the members can avoid approaches that are ruled out from the start, and can also test designs as they go, to verify that the evolving models and prototypes remain consistent with the technical goals.

At the same time, project planners and managers can use the constraints to properly estimate the costs (in both time and money) of a proposed project. After all, project planners or managers can only plan projects if they can predict the type and amount of work that will be required of them.

I cannot stress enough the importance of this process, particularly in an environment where you need to get buy-in on these requirements from many involved parties. After a new site is launched, a design group inevitably gets feedback from site users, from the client (if designing for an outside company), or from internal staff (if an internal project) commenting on perceived problems such as "the page looks crummy on browser X," or "I used my old PC and a slow modem connection and it took a minute for the page to load." You can only defend yourself (and your staff) from such complaints if you can demonstrate that the design does indeed match agreed-upon requirements. These requirements may change (they usually do), but at least they can change in a conscious, rational way.

Informally, requirements arise from a discussion of page design issues and of the ways in which these issues will be handled. From the perspective of a user (or a client), what are these issues? From this nontechnical perspective, they are:

How quickly must the pages appear on a browser?   Everyone wants the pages to download and render quickly. However, in practice you need explicit requirements for this, so that you can properly satisfy the users of the site and/or the client who has contracted the design work. To set this requirement, however, you need to ask two questions:

- What is the minimum-bandwidth network connection that must be supported?

- What is the acceptable worst-case time to load and render a page on a machine of specified speed using the minimum network bandwidth?

In most cases these speed requirements will vary depending on the type of page, with top-level pages needing to be faster than low-level ones.

Which browsers must be supported, and to what degree?   In most cases, the page designs will need to work on various browsers. However, to create appropriate designs, you must explicitly know which browsers need to be supported and to what degree. The degree of support has essentially two levels:

- *Functional* support—the critical features of the page work properly, but noncritical enhancements (e.g., pop-up navigation windows, rollover images, dynamic HTML pull-down menus) may not. The pages may also not look as attractive, as the browser may not support some of the advanced layout and formatting features used in the design. As a related issue, you need to know whether the pages must function if scripting (e.g., JavaScript) or HTTP cookies are disabled on the browser, since some users disable these features.

- *Full* support—all features of the page work properly, and the rendered page layout is exactly as specified by the designers.

At the extreme, your pages may also need to work on nonstandard browsers, such as TV-based browsers (WebTV, etc.) or palmtop browsers running on machines such as Palm Pilots. This again places further restrictions on the design.

Do some or all of the pages need to be accessible?   In some cases, it is important that some or all of the pages be accessible to visually impaired visitors, who may be using screen readers or limited-capacity browsers to read the pages.

Must the pages be printable?   The customer will probably want the user to be able to print pages containing content such as news articles, product information, and so on. However, many page design features (background colors, odd text colors, animated GIF images, and special style sheet rules) can make printed output ugly or unreadable. It is thus important to know which pages need to be printable and by which browsers. Conversely, you do not want to waste time designing printability into pages that don't need to be printed, so it is equally important to know where this requirement is not relevant.

Will the pages be integrated with databases or third-party content?   Your designs may involve an overall design template that contains data loaded in from a database. The design must then allow for appropriate variation in the way the database content is loaded in, without degrading the way the pages actually look.

Must the page content be re-usable?   If your pages contain a lot of content, it is often important that the content be reusable in new pages should you redesign or reorganize the site.

The issues that are relevant for each site will, of course, vary. For example, when designing for a single browser, you can ignore browser compatibility issues. Similarly, if you can guarantee that all users will access the site using a high-speed network, then you can largely ignore networking speed issues.

Not all design issues are directly technical: Many are related to the manageability of the pages. In this context, the most common issues are:

Maintainability of designs and content.   If you are planning to update the page content and/or design on a regular basis, then you want designs and content that are easy to modify.

Reusability of design and markup.   If the site will be expanding, with additional pages, then it is important that the page designs can be easily reused or updated to allow for new content or to allow for new navigational paths through the site.

Reusability of content.   Often a site will have content that originally appears in one page, but that will be reused in another. Good page designs can make it easy to reuse such content.

Although these are not technical issues, they are obviously important factors in establishing an appropriate technical design. This chapter discusses reusability and maintainability, but only in the context of individual pages. We will revisit this issue in the next chapter when we discuss overall site design and management.

Finally, every design must take into account semantic issues that reflect the purpose and usability of the design. Some of the most important issues here are:

Appropriateness of page design.   The design and layout must be appropriate to the function of the pages. For example, you would likely not use a modern "techno" look when designing a site targeted at retired people!

Uniformity of the design.   When many related pages are being designed, design components must carry through the different page designs, so that the pages can be recognized as coming from the same site, and so that users can become familiar with the organization of the site and the way the pages work.

Usability of the design.   The design must be usable by the intended audience, not by the designers of the Web site.

Effectiveness of the design.   Ideally, the design should make effective use of the display area available to the browser. This implies a scalable design that can adjust to the available rendering area.

This chapter looks a bit at effective design, but does not look at the other issues in any detail. These site design issues are examined in the next chapter.

4.1.1 The Testing Environment

Of course a design is only successful if it actually works—and the only way you can know it works is by testing it on the browsers you need to support. Thus it is essential that you create an environment and process with which you can test the designs to verify that they look and function as desired.

A testing environment consists of a set of machines matching the specified requirements, equipped with the required set of browsers, and connected to a test server using the specified types of network connections. For example, if the worst-case requirement is that the design must load and render in five seconds for a Pentium 200 Windows 95 PC connected to the server using a 56-Kbps modem, then one of the test platforms would have exactly this configuration.

Having a testing *process* is simply another way of saying that you have a *quality assurance* program for the designs. At the simplest, this would consist of a set of well-defined testing requirements that a tester could read and use to evaluate a test design. For example, a page-testing sheet might ask such questions as:

- Which design is being tested?
- What browser is this testing result for? (So you'll know which browser failed.)
- What is the loading time for the page?
- Are there any odd-looking colors or color errors? If so, where are the problems and what do they appear to be?
- Are there any other rendering problems/errors? If so, where are the problems and what do they appear to be?
- Does the page redraw properly when the window is resized?
- Do all the rollover images or other scripted functions work correctly? If not, where and how do they fail?
- Do all images have **alt** text? If not, which ones don't?
- Is the page functional if images are not being loaded into the page? If not, where are the problems?
- Does the page print properly?

Ideally, each page in the design should be tested after each iteration of the design. The designers can then use the feedback from the tests to fix the observed problems.

Of course, the preceding discusses only page design issues, and not problems related to the collective of pages that makes up a site or application. This aspect of Web design involves a whole other set of testing and quality assurance problems. These issues are discussed in the next chapter.

4.2 Managing Rendering Speed

Page rendering speed is determined by several factors. The most important is the network connection speed—something that the designer does not control. Indeed, a typical rendering speed requirement will be stated something like:

> "All main navigation pages must render in less than four seconds under Navigator 3/4.x and Internet Explorer 4.x running on a Pentium II at 150 MHz, connected to the network using a 56-Kbps modem."

This gives the designers a mechanism for measuring the acceptability of the design.

Given a fixed bandwidth and a desired rendering speed, designers are left with three things they can control: the size of the document (in bytes), the elegance and accuracy of the markup, and the types and amount of auxiliary content (plugins, images, scripts, applets) loaded into the page. If the pages need to be fast, then you will likely need to adjust all of these components to get the desired quality. The next few sections look at these issues from various perspectives and outline strategies for optimizing performance.

4.2.1 Optimized Markup and Layout

The first step for high-speed rendering is simply to use accurate markup. These issues are discussed in detail in *XHTML 1.0 Language and Design Guide,* the companion book to this one. Here I will summarize the main points:

Use accurate markup, and always include "optional" end tags.   This may seem pedantic, but on many browsers the rendering software is sensitive to markup errors and needs to do extra work if the document has missing optional end tags or improperly nested elements. There are particular problems with long tables that have missing `</td>` or `</tr>` tags to end table cells or rows. To avoid these problems, it is a good idea to pass all documents through a syntax verifier and/or markup validator before placing them online. A syntax verifier can point out (and often correct) obvious errors and omissions. The program *HTML Tidy,* provided for free by the World Wide Web Consortium, serves this purpose well. This utility, along with several validation tools, is listed in the references at the end of this chapter.

Give explicit sizes for all replaced elements.   The **img, embed, iframe, applet,** and **object** elements are graphically replaced by the thing they reference. As a result, the explicit size of the thing may be unknown until the referenced data is retrieved. Unless the browser knows the size ahead of time, it cannot render the page accurately, if at all: Older browsers such as Navigator 3 simply do not render the page until they have downloaded (and know) the sizes of any inline images. However, if you use **height** and **width** attributes (or CSS `height` and `width` properties, for sufficiently new browsers) to explicitly give the size in the markup, then the browser can happily render the page, leaving a blank box for the yet-to-arrive image, applet, or other resource.

Use small, simple tables, as opposed to big, complex ones.   Small and simple means tables containing few rows and columns, or tables that are not deeply nested inside other tables. Rendering of complex tables can be slow, particularly on older browsers. Moreover, most browsers use a multipass algorithm to render tables, adjusting column heights and widths as they process the tables to ensure optimal layout. This means that the browser needs the entire table in memory before the table can be rendered, which in turn means that nothing in the table can be rendered until all the markup has arrived. With newer browsers (Navigator 5, Internet Explorer 5), the CSS property `table-layout: fixed` can avoid this problem, as described later in this section.

Where possible, give explicit table and table cell widths.   To ensure accurate and reproducible table layout, you should explicitly provide table cell widths for each cell in the table. If using **td** or **th** element **width** attributes, you can give these either as percentages of the full table width or as sizes in pixels. CSS provides additional mechanisms for specifying these properties, and can be used to override attribute-specified values.

Where possible, use `table-layout: fixed`.   With fifth-generation browsers (Navigator 5 and greater, Internet Explorer 5 and greater), the CSS property `table-layout: fixed` (applied to **table** elements) causes a table to be laid out using explicit widths defined by the content of the first table row. This disables the automatic layout approach wherein table cell widths are adjusted with each row to optimize the display of the cells. Eliminating this row-by-row adjustment means that the table can be laid out more quickly (since the software does not have to reevaluate the layout with each row) and also progressively, since each row can be drawn as soon as it arrives.

Use Cascading Style Sheets properties to specify page formatting.   CSS lets you redefine the default formatting for elements, or add nonstandard formatting to them, without bloating the X/HTML markup. For example, if you want text inside **h3** headings to be of a specific color, font family, and text alignment, and to have an underline the full width of the heading region, then an appropriate CSS property could be:

```
h3 {font-family: garamond, "times new roman", times, serif;
    color: red;
    text-align: right;
    border-bottom: 2px solid black }
```

Then all **h3** headings of the form

```
<h3> Level Three Heading </h3>
```

will be formatted in this way. If, instead, you were to use markup to set the desired formatting, then each **h3** heading would look like

```
<h3 align="right"><font color="red"
    face="garamond,times new roman,times,serif">Level Three Heading
</h3>
```

repeated for every **h3** heading. Moreover, the CSS instructions can be removed from the document and stored in a separate, shared file, again reducing download times, as discussed in Section 4.2.3.

4.2.2 Use Optimized, Reusable Images

Image files are often, in total, larger than the X/HTML files into which they are placed—and most graphically intense pages contain lots of images. To make pages download quickly, it is critical to keep the sizes of these image files as small as possible.

Chapter 10 of *XHTML Language and Design Sourcebook* discusses image processing with an emphasis on these issues. From a pure design perspective, the first step is to choose a primary color palette for the site. If the graphical design must work well with Windows 3.1/9x/NT/2000 computers with 256 (8-bit) color displays (a common constraint), choose this palette from the 216 color values defined in the Windows default color palette (see, for example, www.lynda.com/hexv.html). This ensures that the colors will not be dithered on these computers.

Given a color palette, the next step is to create the images and icons you need for the site. The tool you use does not really matter—PhotoShop, Corel Draw, Paint Shop Pro, Illustrator, and others are perfectly appropriate—the choice largely depends on the tool you are comfortable with and the types of images you are working on. For example, PhotoShop and Paint Shop Pro are good for photographic image processing, while Illustrator and Corel Draw are good for line drawings or icon graphics.

In the case of icon graphics, you want to make sure that your tool is configured to use the desired color palette and that, if you are designing for compatibility with 8-bit Windows systems, you only use colors from the Windows palette.

Regardless of the tool you use, keep original, high-resolution copies of all graphics files and icons in whatever format is most convenient. Then, if you need to make additional graphics, you have the original images in high-resolution form.

Once the images are created, they need to be saved using Web-appropriate graphics formats. There are only three universally supported formats, which are summarized in Table 4.1.

Table 4.1   Graphics Formats Supported on the Web, the Browsers that Support Them, and the Type of Graphics Appropriate to Each Format

TYPE OF GRAPHIC	APPROPRIATE FILE FORMAT	BROWSER SUPPORT
Icons / solid color graphics	GIF	All browsers
Icons / solid color graphics	PNG	Navigator 4.2 and greater, Internet Explorer 4 and greater
Animated images	GIF	All browsers
Photographs or heavily textured icons	JPEG	All browsers

The GIF format is the most widely supported format for iconlike, solid-color graphics. GIF also supports animated images, discussed a bit later. PNG, short for Portable Network Graphics, is a newer format designed to supplant GIF for nonanimated images. PNG has several advantages over GIF (PNG supports more colors, supports alpha-channel transparency, and can produce smaller image files), but, as seen in Table 4.1, is not supported by all common browsers.

When saving graphics in GIF or PNG, make sure that they are saved with the desired color palette. Some graphics programs make unwarranted optimizations when saving an image to disk, and substitute a palette that is optimized for the image, but not for use on the Web. In particular, if the design must work well on 8-bit color displays, be sure that the GIF or PNG images are stored using the Windows color palette.

It is possible to reduce the size of the PNG or GIF image files without affecting the quality of the image. In particular, if an image uses only a small number of colors, you can reduce the stored color depth (number of bits stored per pixel) to reduce the file size. Some graphics programs do this automatically, but many do not: The references section at the end of this chapter lists several GIF optimization tools that help perform these (and other) optimizations.

Photographic images, or images that are heavily textured (and don't have large solid-color regions) should be saved in the JPEG format. JPEG is a lossy compressed image format—the higher the compression, the lower the quality of the image. In this case you can reduce the size of the stored file by applying as much compression as possible while making a conscious trade-off between size and quality. Note that you do not want to reduce the color depth, as is done for GIF images, because this actually reduces the effectiveness of the JPEG compression mechanism. Some JPEG optimization tools are listed in the references section at the end of this chapter.

Of course, for each type of image you process, you should document the compression/color processing steps used to create it. You can then reproduce these steps to create additional images and icons that match the existing ones.

Animated GIF Images

The GIF format supports a feature that allows for *GIF animation.* In this case, the GIF file actually contains a sequence of individual still images, along with instructions defining the delay between displaying each still image. Once the file is loaded, the browser "steps through" each of the images, waiting a specified delay time between one image and the next.

Obviously an animated GIF file will be larger than an unanimated one, since it contains more than one image. Indeed, as a worst case you can imagine a 10-frame animated GIF image as being 10 times bigger than the non-animated equivalent.

Fortunately there are optimizations that make the situation better than this. In particular, the format lets subsequent images contain only the image portion that is "different" from the preceding image. For example, if the first image shows a house, and the second image in the animation shows the same house, but with a newly open window, then the second frame can contain only the portion of the image encompassing the window frame. The rest of the frame is marked as transparent, so that it "shows through" the preceding frame. This approach can substantially reduce the size of subsequent frames and thus the size of animated GIF files.

Most animated GIF construction tools provide utilities that let you use these optimizations, although you often need to explicitly turn them on. The references at the end of this chapter list some sites providing more information on animated GIFs and animated GIF optimization, and also list some of the tools useful for creating such files. Most Web portal sites (such as Yahoo!, Lycos, and Alta Vista) have categories that list GIF resources, including software for creating GIF animations.

Perception of Download Times

Note that the *perceived* speed with which a page downloads is not the same as the *actual* speed with which the images arrive. For example, if a page contains a single large image, the reader may feel that the page downloads more slowly than an equivalent page containing several smaller images, even if the download times are the same. This is because viewers tend to focus on the first "active" item on the page and end up staring at the single downloading image, waiting for it to finish. This occurs even when the user can easily navigate off the page while the image is loading. At its extreme, this is somewhat similar to watching a small animal frozen by a bright flashlight shone in its face on a dark night.

To avoid this situation, you can try the following strategies:

Break large images up into smaller pieces, each piece stored in an independent file.   These images can be tiled together inside a **table**, as described in Section 14.3.3 of *XHTML 1.0 Language and Design Sourcebook*. For example, the bottom image in Figure 4.1 consists of four images tiled together using the table markup shown in Figure 4.2. The top of Figure 4.1 shows the four graphics components.

Redesign the page so that the slow-to-load image (or collection of images) is not the visual focal point of the page.   If you can do this, the reader will be much more likely to start using the page while the image arrives.

The latter strategy obviously takes the most work. However, if you are aware at the start that a single, slow-to-load, dominant image can make the page appear slow, you can avoid this problem right from the start.

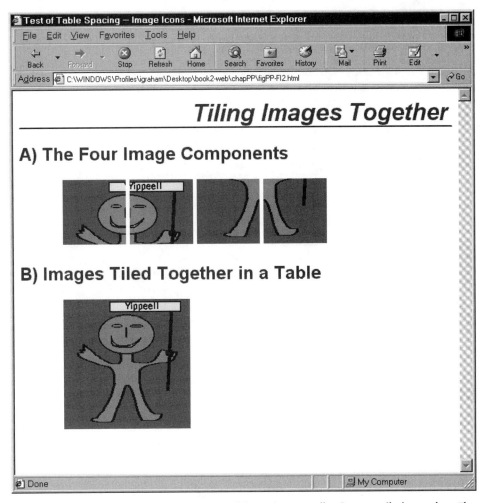

Figure 4.1 An example image composed from four smaller images tiled together. The corresponding XHTML table and **img** element markup is shown in Figure 4.2.

Reusing Image Files

Last, it is important, as much as possible, to reuse image files across the different pages of a Web site. By doing so, you take advantage of a browser's local cache, which retains copies of downloaded data, including images. As a result, images are only downloaded once, and are accessed rapidly from the local cache when referenced again. For example, if the first document downloaded from a site contains 10 images, the browser will download all the images, which will obviously slow the rendering of the page. However, if the next page contains 10 images, but 9 of those were used in the previous page, then the browser downloads only 1 image file, so that the download—and the page rendering—happens quickly.

```
<table cellpadding="0" cellspacing="0" border="0">
  <tr>
    <td><img src="top-left.gif" height="100" width="100"
            alt="Description of whole image" /></td>
    <td><img src="top-right.gif" height="100" width="100"
            alt="Description of whole image" /></td>
  </tr><tr>
    <td><img src="bottom-left.gif" height="100" width="100"
            alt="Description of whole image" /></td>
    <td><img src="bottom-right.gif" height="100" width="100"
            alt="Description of whole image" /></td>
  </tr>
</table>
```

Figure 4.2 Example XHTML table and **img** element markup used to produced a tiled image. This image is composed from four image files.

If you are feeling particularly sneaky, you can also use a piece of JavaScript to "preload" images into the browser cache. An example of this is discussed at the end of Section 4.2.3.

4.2.3 Break Documents into Components

As just mentioned, reusing images across multiple pages can significantly increase the page rendering speed for many pages, since the reused images only need to be downloaded once. You can extend this reuse to actual document text by moving program scripts and style sheets into external files. As with images, these external style sheets and scripts will be stored in the browser cache, and can be reused by other pages that reference them.

Markup illustrating this approach is shown in Figure 4.3. In this example, all the style sheet content and JavaScript program code is stored outside the XHTML document, and is included by reference using **link** and **script** elements.

Furthermore, script content that is not needed for the page rendering phase can be marked as "deferred" (see next section), such that the rendering process begins before these script components have been loaded. For example, script programs that operate rollover images can be run after the page is displayed: The rollovers simply won't work until the required rollover images are downloaded.

We will first examine the style sheet components. This document references three style sheets, namely:

```
<link rel="stylesheet" href="/styles/style-generic.css" />
<link rel="stylesheet" href="/styles/style-navigation.css" />
<link rel="stylesheet" href="./special.css" />
```

```
<html xmlns=" http://www.w3.org/1999/xhtml">
<head>
   <title> Smurfs and Beenies: the Next Generation </title>
   <link rel="stylesheet" href="/styles/style-generic.css" />
   <link rel="stylesheet" href="/styles/style-navigation.css" />
   <link rel="stylesheet" href="./special.css" />
   <script type="text/javascript"
          src="/scripts/defaults.js"> </script>
   <script type="text/javascript"
          defer="defer" src="/scripts/rollovers-1.js"> </script>
</head>
<body>
....... content goes here .....
</body>
</html>
```

Figure 4.3 An outline of an XHTML document in which most script and style sheet components have been moved to external files. The advantages of this architecture are described in the text.

In this example, the first style sheet, *style-generic.css*, defines global CSS rules that apply to all pages on the Web site. Consequently, every page on the site would reference—and thus reuse—this style sheet document. This style sheet might, for example, set properties such as the default text font and color, the default background color (and/or image) for the page, page margins and borders, and so on. It may also specify other generic formatting characteristics, such as default margins for paragraphs, indents for lists, and so on. The intention here, however, is to only define global properties that apply everywhere on the page—region-specific styles are defined in subsequent style sheets.

Note also that this must be the first style sheet included in the Web page. That way, subsequent style sheets can override formatting instructions set by this initial document.

The second style sheet, *style-navigation.css*, contains formatting rules specific to the part of the page containing navigational tools—for example, a sidebar with links to main page sections, or a collection of dynamic HTML pull-down menus. Again, many pages will contain such navigation tools, so that this style sheet can be referenced by many different XHTML documents.

Finally, the third style sheet, *special.css*, contains CSS rules relevant only for this page. These are essentially CSS "tweaking" rules designed solely for this (or perhaps a few) documents. If the content of *special.css* were used only in this page, then this style sheet might instead be inside a **style** element.

We now consider the script components. With Navigator 3 and greater and Internet Explorer 4 and greater, script programs can be stored external to the Web page, and can be referenced using the **src** attribute of a **script** element. Thus the markup in Figure 4.3:

```
<script type="text/javascript"
        src="/scripts/defaults.js"> </script>
<script type="text/javascript"
        defer="defer" src="/scripts/rollovers-1.js"> </script>
```

references two script files, which will be loaded inline in place of the **script** elements and then run by the browser.

Once again the goal is to use reusability to increase page loading speed: If the same script components are used by more than one page, subsequent references will retrieve the locally cached copy. Thus, the first element:

```
<script type="text/javascript"
        src="/scripts/defaults.js"> </script>
```

loads in default script components that are used on all (or most) documents on the Web site. When the user first retrieves a page from the site, it also retrieves this script. Subsequent accesses to different pages that reference this script will use the locally cached copy.

Consequently, it is often best to break scripts up into different files, each file containing a collection of script code designed to work together on a given task. For example, the file *defaults.js* might contain generic script components required by all pages, while the next script element:

```
<script type="text/javascript"
        defer="defer" src="/scripts/rollovers-1.js"> </script>
```

which includes the file *rollovers-1.js*, would contain code implementing a specific type of image rollover mechanism. Obviously, pages that don't use rollovers would not have this script element, while those that do can reference (and share) this script library.

Deferring Script Execution

The preceding procedure speeds up page rendering by reducing the need to download scripts or style sheet documents multiple times—once downloaded, they are stored in the local cache and can be reused in other pages.

However, the browser must still run the script programs. A browser processes a document sequentially, starting from the beginning. When it comes to a **script** element, it must load and finish execution of any script statements inside that element before proceeding. Consequently, if the content of a **script** takes a long time to run, there can be a long delay before the page is rendered: The browser is essentially blocked, waiting for the script to finish.

If a script is not needed for the initial rendering of the page, then there is no need for the browser to wait for it to finish. A good example would be a script that loads several dozen images to be used as rollover images. Obviously the page can be safely rendered before these rollover images arrive, so it is nice to mark such a script so that it can be skipped, or *deferred,* so that rendering can continue.

In principle, execution of script element content can be deferred by adding a **defer**="defer" attribute to the element: This was done with the second script element in Figure 4.3. A browser should then defer execution of the script in favor of rendering the page. A browser can do this either by running the script while simultaneously rendering the page or by simply holding up script execution until after the page is loaded.

Unfortunately, **defer** is not widely supported (it is supported by Internet Explorer 5 and greater, but not by Navigator or Opera). However, there are two alternate approaches that accomplish the same thing and that work on all browsers.

The first and simplest approach is to move to the end of the document any long-running scripts not needed when rendering the page. For example, if the rollover code is not needed until after the page is rendered, then the markup in Figure 4.3 could be rewritten as (the change is in boldface):

```
<html xmlns=" http://www.w3.org/1999/xhtml">
<head>
    <title> Smurfs and Beenies: the Next Generation </title>
    <link rel="stylesheet" href="/styles/style-generic.css" />
    <link rel="stylesheet" href="/styles/style-navigation.css" />
    <link rel="stylesheet" href="./special.css" />
    <script type="text/javascript"
            src="/scripts/defaults.js"> </script>
</head>
<body>
....... content goes here .....
    <script type="text/javascript"
            src="/scripts/rollovers-1.js"> </script>
</body>
</html>
```

The script code is now loaded and run at the end of the document, after all the content has been rendered.

This can be a problem, however, if the *rollover-1.js* block contains function definitions used in the document. For example, if the user clicks on an image that references a rollover function *before* the file *rollovers-1.js* has loaded, then the browser will report a JavaScript error, because the page has tried to execute an as-yet-undefined function. This solution is thus best used when the script inside the block is entirely independent of references from the preceding document or scripts.

The second approach avoids this problem. In this approach, the script is left at the beginning of the document, but the part that is slow is placed inside a function. This function is then executed via the **body** element's

onload event handler. This event occurs *after* the page is loaded—which effectively defers this slow JavaScript component until after the page is displayed.

For example, suppose the slow portion of the script *rollovers-1.js* (e.g., the portion that downloads all the images needed to make the rollovers work) is placed inside a function named `startRollovers ()`. This portion might, for example, load in all the images needed for rollovers to work. We can then rewrite the script portion of the XHTML document as follows (of course, the document *rollovers-1.js* has also been rewritten to wrap this functionality inside the function):

```
    <script type="text/javascript"
            src="/scripts/defaults.js"> </script>
    <script type="text/javascript"
            src="/scripts/rollovers-1.js"> </script>
</head>
<body onload="startRollovers ()">
....... content goes here .....
</body>
</html>
```

The script now loads quickly: The part that downloads the images is executed only when the *onload* event takes place. Since *onload* occurs *after* the page has loaded, this has almost exactly the same effect as the **defer**="defer" attribute, and in many ways is a more elegant solution to the problem.

Precaching Image Files

Another way to speed up page download is to preload images into the browser cache. This can be done using a JavaScript function that, after a page has loaded, retrieves a defined list of images and loads them into the browser. These images would not be ones that are used by other pages on the Web site and that thus are likely to be accessed by the user.

An example of how this might be done is shown in Figure 4.4. In this script, the function `loadImages ()`, which is run after the page is loaded, uses `addImage ()` functions to add new images into the browser cache. This function simply creates a list of images (in an array) and takes the function argument as the Uniform Resource Locator (URL) referencing the image. Images retrieved in this way are stored in the local cache and can be reused in subsequent pages. This function would be customized by site developers simply by adding appropriate `addImage ()` lines inside the `loadImage ()` function.

This function is not ideal for at least two reasons. First, if the list of `addImage ()` items is long, then this will repeatedly and heavily access the remote Web server, possibly leading to response problems for other users. This can be mitigated somewhat by rewriting the script to add a delay between each image request.

```
<script language="javascript1.1">
function loadImages () {
   imgArr = new Array;
   addImage("/images/image1.gif");
   addImage("/images/image2.gif");
   addImage("/images/image3.gif");
   addImage("/images/image4.gif");
   addImage("/images/image5.gif");
}
function addImage (name) {
   imgArr [name] = new Image();
   imgArr [name].src = name;
}
</script>
...
<body onload="loadImages ()">
```

Figure 4.4 A simple script that preloads a collection of images into the browser cache.

The second problem is that this script runs each time the page is loaded, resulting in unnecessary requests to the server. This could be avoided if the script checked to see whether it had already retrieved these files—which can be done by using an auxiliary function that stores in a cookie the date at which the cache function was last executed. Subsequent pages can then check for this cookie variable, and can skip execution of the addImage () functions when appropriate. A mockup of how such a script would look goes something like (changes in boldface):

```
function loadImages () {
   if ( !alreadyLoaded() ) { // Check if function already executed
      imgArr = new Array;
      addImage("/images/image1.gif");
      wait(1);        // Delay between requests
      addImage("/images/image2.gif");
      //... more addImage () functions ....
   }
}
```

4.2.4 Page Size Reduction and Compression

Last, you can preprocess the documents to reduce their download sizes. With X/HTML there are essentially two ways to do this:

■ Process the markup to remove unneeded characters, such as X/HTML comments or multiple space, tab, carriage return, and line feed characters between words or inside markup tags.

■ Compress the document using a compression mechanism (such as gzip or Unix compress), and then stream the file to the browser in compressed format.

The former approach simply eliminates unneeded characters, and can typically reduce the page size by between 5 and 25 percent, depending on the page. Of course, this also removes useful information, and so should only be done for the served-out documents, and not for the working copies retained on your site. Indeed, if you are going to use this mechanism you should be careful to retain unshrunken copies for future editing and reuse.

Furthermore, this form of optimization also means that the person receiving the document will have trouble reading the raw markup, since it will now appear as a single, unstructured, uncommented single line. On the other hand, if you are trying to make your markup difficult to understand, this may be quite useful!

The second approach is possible for browsers that support *content encoding* of data they receive. When a server sends data to a browser, the server indicates the type of the data using a Multipurpose Internet Mail Extensions (MIME) `content-type` field in the HyperText Transfer Protocol (HTTP) response header that precedes the data (see Chapter 9). But the server can also send the file using a special *encoding* as indicated by a MIME `content-encoding` field (see Chapter 9 for a description of these and other HTTP headers). This encoding mechanism allows for streamed data compression and lets you deliver compressed versions of HTML data that is uncompressed on the fly and displayed by the browser. Such files can be as much as 90 percent smaller than the original, which means they are much faster to download. Of course, the browser must uncompress the file before rendering it, but in many cases it takes far less time to uncompress a file than it does to download the uncompressed version.

To illustrate this I created a large (200-K) test file named *size-test.html.* By using the GNU ZIP (gzip) compression engine or the Unix standard compress compression engine, the example file can be compressed to a file 80 percent smaller than the original. The actual sizes for the original and compressed versions are shown in Table 4.2.

Table 4.2 Original Size of a Large HTML Document Compared with the Same Document Stored in gzip-Compressed *(size-test.gz.html)* and Unix-Compressed *(size-test.Z.html)* Forms. The Compressed Files Are up to 80 Percent Smaller

UNCOMPRESSED: SIZE-TEST.HTML	GZIP-COMPRESSED: SIZE-TEST.GZ.HTML	UNIX-COMPRESSED: SIZE-TEST.Z.HTML
content-type: text/html	content-type: text/html	content-type: text/html
	content-encoding: gzip	content-encoding: compress
content-length: 212425	content-length: 44008	content-length: 73433

Of course, it does no good to deliver content-encoded data to a browser that does not support content encoding. The browsers that do—and the types of encodings they support—are listed in Table 4.3. Fortunately, most Web servers support a mechanism known as *content negotiation,* which lets the server deliver the most appropriate version of a resource to a browser. This mechanism uses the fact that each browser indicates, when it requests a resource, the types of content encoding that it supports. With content negotiation, the requested URL references a *collection* of possible resources—for example, the same file in raw or compressed formats—and the browser returns the one best suited to the browser. In this way, compressed files are returned to browsers that support content encoding, while uncompressed files are returned to those that do not.

Content negotiation is a complex issue, and understanding how it works involves understanding how HTTP works and how Web servers can be configured to deliver appropriate data to a browser. These issues are discussed in Section 9.17.

Extreme Compression Strategies

Extreme compression strategies are those that work most of the time, but that can lead to problems in some cases. Such compression strategies include:

- Removing double quotes from around attribute values (except for **href** values and for any attribute values that have embedded white space characters).

- Removing unneeded closing tags (e.g., eliminating `</li>` tags).

- Removing alt attributes from spacer GIF images (requires that the software understand the difference between spacer and nonspacer GIFs).

- Shortening color names as much as possible (for example, #6699CC becomes #69C).

Table 4.3 Browsers that Support Content Encoding of Downloaded Data. Content Encoding Is Not Supported by Opera 3.6x, but Will Be Supported by Opera 4

BROWSER	SUPPORTED CONTENT ENCODING TYPES
Navigator 4.x	`gzip,`* `compress`† (also supports values `x-gzip` and `x-compress`; these values are not supported by other browsers)
Internet Explorer 4.x	`gzip, compress`
Internet Explorer 5.x	`gzip, compress`
Lynx 2.8.2	`gzip, compress`

* gzip: GNU zip compression format (Lempel-Ziv compression)
† compress: UNIX standard compression format (Adaptive Lempel-Ziv, or LZW)

Although these will work with most HTML browsers, the speed gains will be modest and do not, in my opinion, outweigh the problems they may introduce. In particular, the first two items produce code that is invalid XHTML (end tags and quotes around attribute values are mandatory for XHTML), which means that the pages will not be usable in an XML environment. The third trick will work, but will also produce pages that are unusable by those with text-only browsers or those using screen readers. The fourth strategy will work all the time, but is really not going to save you much—it's a lot of work for not much return.

4.2.5 Script Optimization

Finally, your pages may appear to display slowly simply because the script programs run slowly. In general, the only way to solve this is to redesign and rewrite the scripts, optimizing them for improved performance. This book does not discuss script optimization, as this is a complex task that depends on a careful determination of the script "choke points" that are actually causing the problems, and sometimes on an understanding of browser-specific script processing problems.

However, there is one simple optimization trick that, due to the manner in which scripts are processed, applies quite generally. The trick is simple: Shorten the names of all JavaScript variables and functions as much as possible, while keeping the names distinct. It turns out that many JavaScript processors must parse each JavaScript statement every time the statement is executed, and this parsing time is directly proportional to the lengths of the variable and function names. Thus, if the original script code is:

```
for(loopValue=0; loopValue<maxLoopValueIndx; loopValue++) {
    counterDecrement--;
    partIndexCounter[loopValue] = loopValue *
                        netArray[loopValue - counterDecrement];
}
```

it could be rewritten as:

```
for(i=0; i<mv; i++) {
    cd--;
    pC[i] = i * nA[i - cd];
}
```

which will run substantially faster on some browsers.

4.3 Browser Version Support

In many cases you will need to design pages that work effectively on different browsers. For example, you may need to have pages that work well on

Internet Explorer 4, 5, and 5.5, in addition to Navigator 3, 4, and 5, and perhaps Opera 3.6 or Lynx 2.8.2.

Obviously, the more browsers you must support, the more difficult the task. Technically, there are three components you need to consider:

- Level of support for HTML markup
- Level of support for CSS
- Level of support for JavaScript

Clearly HTML support is the most critical, as this is the foundation upon which every page is built. Because HTML and XHTML have evolved significantly over the past few years, more recent browsers support markup elements and attributes that are not understood by earlier browsers. This book's companion Web site provides a useful table listing browser support for all HTML elements and attributes defined in the official HTML 4.0 and XHTML 1.0 standards, in addition to proprietary elements supported by common commercial browsers. Given the browsers your design must support, you can use this table to determine which elements and attributes you can safely use.

The process for arriving at an acceptable XHTML and CSS design (we will exclude scripting issues for now) is essentially iterative, but the place to start is with HTML and the lowest-common-denominator browser. For example, if your design must both work and look great on Navigator 3, then you must initially restrict yourself to markup supported by this browser and ignore CSS at this first pass, since CSS is not supported by this browser.

Once you have arrived at a successful markup design, you can return to it and use CSS to fine-tune the design so that it looks better on browsers that support CSS. This may mean going back to the HTML markup and adding **class** attributes to elements that will take CSS-based styling, or it may involve grouping blocks of markup inside **div** elements (with specific **class** attribute values), so that you can use CSS to format a block as a group. Such changes to the markup will not affect the rendering by Navigator 3 (or other CSS-unaware browsers), but will let you add additional formatting instructions for newer browsers.

Of course, in the preceding case the formatting additions you can add using CSS will be small, since the physical layout and positioning will largely have been set using HTML **table** (or other) elements. Thus, in this case you will largely be restricted to using CSS to modify text font family or color or to control hypertext link colors, text decorations, or dynamic behaviors.

And, as outlined in Section 4.1.1, the process is iterative—you must test each new version of the design to make sure you haven't broken rendering on one of the supported browsers. It is important to test as you go. Even though the testing may seem to slow the process, it helps you find and fix problems early on in the design, before they become too big to solve easily.

4.3.1 Browsers and CSS

CSS is only supported by the most recent browsers—namely Internet Explorer 3 and up and Navigator 4 and up. However, the Internet Explorer 3 support is quite poor, mainly because the browser was released before the CSS Level 1 specification was finalized, so that many features were implemented in a manner inconsistent with the final specification. CSS support in Navigator 4 is better but still not very good: Some language elements are not supported at all, while others are very buggy and cannot be used reliably.

Eric Mayer, hypermedia systems manager for Case Western Reserve University, has summarized these various bugs, unimplemented features, and odd behaviors in a series of CSS compatibility charts, found online at webreview.com/pub/guides/style/style.html/. These charts explicitly describe the state of the different browsers' support for CSS, and make it easier for you to design using CSS. This chart is absolutely essential for anyone trying to build style sheets that work reliably across different browsers.

However, there is a lot in these charts, and it is often hard to translate the charts into a set of useful guidelines. The following short sections describe the most important features to consider if you need to design style sheets that support specific browsers.

Internet Explorer 3

Although Internet Explorer 3 supports some aspects of CSS, it is probably best to avoid CSS if designing for this browser. This is because it is almost impossible to design a style sheet that will work well with Internet Explorer 3 and also with any other CSS-aware browser. If you must use a style sheet, the best approach is to create a style sheet for Internet Explorer 3 independent of the style sheets used for other browsers. One possible approach for doing this is shown at the end of this section.

Navigator 4.x

Navigator 4 supports CSS Level 1, but in a manner best described as "shabbily." In particular, some features are not supported at all, while others are supported in buggy and inconsistent ways. The guidelines in this section will help you avoid the most glaring CSS problems, while at the same time letting you write CSS formatting properties that will work properly on other browsers, such as Internet Explorer 4 and greater or Opera 3.6 and greater. Please be aware that complex CSS designs will force you to do lots of extra design testing, since CSS can act very differently on different browsers—it is easy for a seemingly innocuous CSS change to cause odd and undesirable rendering on one of the browsers you must support!

The following, in point form, are some useful rules for using CSS with Navigator 4:

- Do not count on setting CSS properties for the **body** element, as they are not properly inherited by the content of the **body**. For example, if you want to set the default font family for the entire document, then you should use a rule such as:

```
body,div,p,blockquote,ol,ul,dl,li,dt,dd,td,th
        {font-family: arial,helvetica,sans-serif}
```

- Do not use `margin-`,`padding-`, or `border-` properties on *inline* elements, such as **em**, **strong**, or **big** (this causes significant rendering errors).

- Note that some block elements, such as **p**, **h1–h6**, and **blockquote** have default top and bottom margins that are not set to zero using `margin-bottom:0`, etc. If you want to be able to control top and bottom margins for a block element, you need to use **div** elements (which, by default, have zero-size top and bottom margins).

- Do not use `@import` rules to import one style sheet into another (it doesn't work, and crashes some early versions of Navigator 4). Instead, use **link** elements to import style sheets into X/HTML documents.

- Place external style sheet documents in the *same directory* as the documents they are used by, and place all images referenced by a style sheet in the same directory as the style sheet. Otherwise, Navigator improperly evaluates the locations of image files.

- Do not use `!important` declarations to raise the priority of a declaration (this declaration is not supported by Navigator 4).

- Apply rules explicitly to elements (for example, using **class** or **id** attributes) and do not assume that properties are inherited from parent elements or are cascaded down from other CSS rules—neither mechanism works reliably under Navigator 4. For example, Navigator 4 does not always pass properties down to other elements (e.g., setting a font family for a **div** element may not set this font for paragraphs inside the **div**). For example, to set formatting for a **div** element inside a **table**, write the element as

```
<div class="inside-table"> .. </div>
```

and create a CSS rule of the form

```
div.inside-table { ... css declarations ... }.
```

- Do not attach CSS rules to **table** or **tr** elements. Formatting for these elements must be set using markup attributes. Similarly, if you want to set CSS properties for the content of table cells, you must explicitly set these properties for **td** or **th** elements.

- Do not use `margin-`,`padding-`, or `border-` properties on **table**, **tr**, **td**, or **th** elements—these properties do not work properly here. If you need to set special margins, borders, or padding *inside* a table cell, then use the markup

```
<td><div class="table-cell"> ... content ... </div></td>
```

and apply the CSS rules to the **div** inside the cell.

■ Do not use `margin-`, `padding-`, or `border-` properties on list content elements (**li**, **dt**, or **dd**), as these properties do not work properly here. There may also be problems with such properties applied to entire lists (i.e., applied to **ol**, **ul**, or **dl** elements). The safest way to control margins, padding space, or borders around an entire list is to wrap the list element in a **div** element and then apply margins, padding, and borders to the **div**.

■ Be very careful about using `margin-`, `padding-`, or `border-` properties with floated elements—this can often introduce odd formatting bugs. In particular, you often cannot reliably set the position of a floated element using margin properties.

■ Note that `margin-top` and `margin-bottom` (and also `padding-top` and `padding-bottom`) only work properly for **div** elements—other elements, such as headings, paragraphs, or blockquotes, retain large top and bottom margins even when the CSS properties try to set them to zero. This is not a problem for **div** elements because the top and bottom margins are, by default, of zero width.

■ The `background-color` property, applied to a block such as a paragraph, colors only the region behind the words, and not the entire box. A workaround is to add a thin `border` to the block, but with the same color as the background (so that the border disappears). For example, to get a solid background color behind a paragraph, you could write:

```
p {background-color: green; border: 1px solid white }
```

■ When setting different borders on the four sides of an element, first use the `border` property to set identical borders on all sides, and then use side-specific properties to reset individual border widths.

■ The following CSS Level 1 properties or selectors do not work on Navigator 4, and should be avoided: `background-attachment`, `background-position`, `border-top`, `border-left`, `border-bottom`, `border-right` (use other `border-*` properties instead), `display` (except `display:none`), `font-variant`, `letter-spacing`, `list-style-image`, `list-style-position`, `vertical-align`, `word-spacing`, `white-space:nowrap`, the `!important` declaration, the `@import` statement, `:first-line` and `:first-letter` pseudoelements.

■ The following CSS Level 1 properties work, but are buggy or inconsistent (please see Eric Mayer's compatibility charts for details): `background-color`, `clear`, `float`, `line-height`, all `margin-` properties, all `padding-` properties, all `border-` properties.

- Note that, for left and right margins and paddings, and also for `width`, Navigator 4 always calculates percentage values relative to the width of the browser window and not relative to the width of the element they are inside. At present, only Navigator 6 and Opera 3.6 get this right.

Internet Explorer 4

Internet Explorer 4 supports CSS Level 1 fairly well, albeit with a few major problems. It certainly gets the main functionality of the language correct (inheritance, cascading mechanism, and so on), so that the problems do not lie in incorrect handling of style sheets. The main problems are due to CSS properties that are incorrectly implemented or not supported at all. In general, however, it is much easier to get things to work well on Internet Explorer 4 than Navigator 4.

In point form, here are the things that you most need to watch out for:

- Do not use `margin-`, `padding-`, or `border-` properties on *inline* elements (for example, **em**, **strong**, or **big** elements). They don't work, and can cause problems.

- The `background-repeat` property does not work properly under Windows (it works fine on Macintoshes, however). In particular, the browser only repeats the image down and to the right of the initial image position, but does not repeat the image upward and to the left.

- Do not use `margin-`, `padding-`, or `border-` properties on **table**, **tr**, **td**, or **th** elements—these properties do not work properly here. If you need to set special margins, borders, or padding inside a table cell, then use the markup:

  ```
  <td><div class="table-cell"> ... content ... </div></td>
  ```

  and apply the CSS rules to the **div** inside the cell.

- Do not use "named" `font-size` values such as such as `small`, `x-large`, etc. These values work but produce font sizes that are quite different from those produced on Navigator or Opera.

- Note that, for left and right margins and paddings, and also for `width`, Internet Explorer 4 always calculates percentage values relative to the width of the browser window, and not relative to the width of the element they are inside. In fact, only Navigator 6 and Opera 3.6 get this right.

- The following CSS Level 1 properties and selectors are not supported: `display` (except for `display:none`), `vertical-align` (the values `baseline`, `sub`, and `super` are supported), `white-space`, `width` (works for images and tables, but not for regular blocks like `p` or **div**), word-spacing, `:first-line` and `:first-letter` pseudoelements. Note also that margin, padding, and border properties are not supported on *inline* elements.

■ The following CSS Level 1 properties work, but are buggy or inconsistent (please see the compatibility charts for details): `clear`, `float`, and all `margin-` properties (in particular, `margin-left: auto` and `margin-right: auto` don't work, so you can't use `margin` properties to align blocks inside blocks).

Internet Explorer 5.x

Internet Explorer 5.x supports CSS Level 1 in essentially the same manner as Internet Explorer 4. Indeed, the only differences are that:

■ `Background-repeat` works properly under Internet Explorer 5.x.

■ Internet Explorer 5.x supports `display:block` and `display: inline`, but not `display:list-item`.

Otherwise, the support problems are exactly as described for Internet Explorer 4.

Internet Explorer 5 also supports some features defined in CSS Level 2. We won't go into the details here—this information is summarized in *XHTML 1.0 Language and Design Sourcebook*, and is also found at msdn.microsoft.com/workshop/author/css/reference/attributes.asp.

Opera 3.6

Opera 3.6 does a pretty good job with most of CSS Level 1, with the following exceptions:

■ Avoid using the `vertical-align` property, as support is buggy or nonexistent.

■ Avoid the shorthand `padding` property (it is buggy), and instead use `padding-left`, `padding-bottom`, and so on.

■ Note that `clear: left` does not work (but all other `clear` values work correctly).

■ The following properties are not supported: `background-attachment`, `white-space`.

Opera 4 and Mozilla/Navigator 6

Opera 4 essentially supports all of CSS Level 1 correctly, as does the newly released Mozilla/Navigator 6 browser. Mozilla, however, also supports most of CSS Level 2. For details on Navigator 6 support, please see *XHTML 1.0 Language and Design Sourcebook.*

Style Sheets for Multiple Browsers

Given these inconsistencies, it can be messy (if not impossible) to design a single style sheet that works properly on all the different browsers. One option is to use different style sheet documents for the different browsers you are supporting. In this way you can specify CSS formatting customized to the strengths (and weaknesses) of each different browser, without compromising for the average of the browsers.

There are essentially two ways to do this. The first is to use content negotiation to send the browser a browser-specific style sheet. This is analogous to the approach described in Section 4.2.4, except that here you use the browser's identity to determine which style sheet to return. With HTTP, a request for any resource (including a style sheet) will look something like (omitting several other pieces of information):

```
GET  /path/stylesheet.css  HTTP/1.0
User-Agent: Mozilla/4.61 [en] (Win98; I)
```

The `User-Agent` string uniquely identifies the browser (here Navigator 4.6). Most Web servers can be configured to return different style sheet documents depending on this value using a mechanism analogous to content negotiation (see Section 9.17).

The second way is to use JavaScript to test, on the browser, for the browser version and model number, and to then write **link** elements referencing appropriate style sheets directly into the document. Both Navigator and Internet Explorer will then process the script-generated **link** elements and will load the referenced style sheet. Of course, this will only work if JavaScript is enabled, but in many cases that may be an acceptable requirement.

An example of this is shown in Figure 4.5. This figure lists part of the content of a document **head**, showing the markup related to style sheets. The first **link** element is independent of the browser, and loads generic style sheet rules that apply in all cases. This, for example, could set generic font properties using CSS rules that are valid with all browsers.

The **script** elements set up a special JavaScript object, named *is*, that identifies the browser type and version. The code that does this is included from the external file *browser-detect.js,* so that this function can be shared across many different XHTML documents. However, some older browsers (e.g., Navigator 2, Internet Explorer 2) cannot include external scripts, in which case the *is* object is not created, so that subsequent code will fail. The two small script blocks before and after the browser detect script fix this problem. The first piece:

```
<!-- Load generic default style sheet ic -->

<link rel="stylesheet" href="style-main.css" />

<!-- The 'is' object contains browser version information.
     It is created by the downloaded browser-detect.js script.
     But older browsers don't load external scripts -- so
     just create 'is' now, and let the script replace it if
     the script runs -->

<script><!-- is = null; // --></script>

<!-- Now load browser-detection script. Original script from:
     developer.netscape.com/docs/examples/javascript/browser_type.html
-->
<script src="/browser-detect.js"> </script>

<!-- If browser couldn't load script set variable 'is' to be a
     new 'empty' object, so the rest of the script will work.
-->
<script><!--
if( is == null) { is = new Object (); }
// --></script>
<!-- Now load appropriate style sheets depending on the
     browser
-->
<script><!--
// Insert browser-specific style sheets. These can overload
// The rules from the 'main' style sheets, to correct for
// idiosyncracies in particular browsers.
if (is.nav5up) {
  document.write('<'+'link rel="stylesheet" href="style-moz5.css" />');
}
else if (is.nav4) {
  document.write('<'+'link rel="stylesheet" href="style-nav4.css" />');
}
else if (is.ie5up) {
  document.write('<'+'link rel="stylesheet" href="style-ie5.css" />');
}
else if (is.ie4) {
  document.write('<'+'link rel="stylesheet" href="style-ie4.css" />');
}
else if (is.ie3) {
  document.write('<'+'link rel="stylesheet" href="style-ie3.css" />');
}
```

continues

Figure 4.5   A document that uses a script to insert browser-specific style sheets.

```
else if (is.opera) {
  document.write('<'+'link rel="stylesheet" href="style-op.css" />');
}
// -->
</script>
```

Figure 4.5   *(Continued).*

```
<script><!-- is = null; // --></script>
```

sets `is=null`, ensuring that the variable exists and is assigned a null value.
Then, if the next line:

```
<script src="./browser-detect.js"> </script>
```

successfully loads the script, the variable *is* is reset to be the *object* containing
the browser data. However, if the script is not loaded, then the value remains
`null`. The next **script**

```
<script><!--
if( is == null) { is = new Object(); } //
// --></script>
```

tests for this case: If the value is still `null`, then it assigns a new, empty object
to the variable.

The remaining script uses the `is` object to test for the browser version. The
function *browser-detect.js* (available from the URL listed in the references at
the end of this chapter) adds properties to this object according to the type of
browser. For example, if the browser is Navigator 6 or greater, then the property `nav5up` is created and is assigned the value `true` (for quirky historical reasons the keywords `nav5` and `nav5up` correspond to Navigator 6). In this case,
the statement `if (is.nav5up)` is true, so that the following block of code

```
if (is.nav5up) {
  document.write ('<'+'link rel="stylesheet" href="style-moz5.css" />');
}
```

will write into the document a **link** statement referencing a Mazilla/Naviga-
tor 6–specific style sheet. Mazilla/Navigator 6 then loads this style sheet into
the browser and caches a copy in the local browser cache.

There are many browser detection scripts available on the Web. The one
used in this example is available from the Netscape Web site, at developer
.netscape.com/docs/examples/javascript/browser_type.html. Unfortunately, this mechanism does not work with the Opera 3.6x browser—Opera

executes this script code, but does not process the inserted **link** element, and thus does not load the Opera-specific style sheet instructions.

4.3.2 Browser Scripting Support

Different browsers support different versions of the JavaScript language—and these differences can be extremely big problems when designing complex JavaScript applications. The differences occur at two levels:

- The basic language rules and syntax.
- The browser-specific objects, properties, and methods.

and due to two reasons:

- Additional basic language features added in newer versions of the language.
- Basic incompatibilities between the browser-specific objects, properties, and methods defined by Microsoft (for Internet Explorer) and Netscape (for Navigator).

Basic language rules and syntax refers to issues such as what the browser returns when a number is divided by zero, or the types of (and behavior of) functions and properties defined for the core language, such as the value returned by a Date() function, or the functions and properties of the Math object. Navigator and Internet Explorer have somewhat different understandings of these core issues. However, such differences should disappear with the recent standardization of core JavaScript by the European Computer Manufacturers Association (ECMA) standards organization. The standardized core language is now referred to as ECMAScript, and is defined by the ECMA-262 standards document (this document is available via the Web at www.ecma.ch).

Browser-specific objects refers to the object model supported by a browser—namely the functions, methods, and properties related to the browser and the document, such as window.open(), document.write(), and so on. Beyond some core functionality, Navigator 4 and Internet Explorer 4 implement these quite differently. However, the recent Document Object Model (DOM) standards promise a new common denominator of browser functionality, as discussed in Chapter 3 (Section 3.4.1). These standards are being widely adopted by newer (Internet Explorer 5.5, Opera 4, Navigator 6) browsers.

However, the practical problem for Web application designers remains that different browsers support different versions of the evolving language, making it difficult to write programs that work well on multiple browsers. Thus, a designer is left with two choices: Write a script that uses limited features and that works on as many browsers as possible, or write a script that uses advanced features and that works only on a limited number of browsers.

For basic scripting issues, such as rollover images, simple manipulation of form data, and simple management of browser windows and frames, a programmer can often create a single generic JavaScript program that works successfully on most browsers. However, this is not possible if the script calls for complex functionality, such as dynamic manipulation of document content (so-called dynamic HTML). In this case, the programming approaches are so different that the designer essentially needs to write multiple programs, each one designed to work with a different browser.

There are essentially four ways to control which piece of code is executed by a browser:

Using server-side content negotiation.   Store the scripts on the server as external script files (always a good idea), and use content negotiation to determine which script to send to the browser. This is analogous to the use of content negotiation to return appropriate style sheets, described in the previous section.

Using browser detection to write appropriate script elements into the document.   Use a generic browser detection script on the browser to detect the browser type and write into the document **link** elements referencing browser-appropriate external script programs. This is analogous to the mechanism described previously for style sheets.

Using conditional execution of the script code, depending on browser type.   Store all script code in a single location (either in an external referenced file or inside the HTML document), and use a browser detection script to define which sections of the program should be run, given the indicated browser type. That is, the program contains browser-specific blocks of code that are run (or skipped) depending on which browser the script is loaded into.

Use script element language attribute to identify the script language and to control which script is loaded.   Many browsers (such as Internet Explorer) support languages other than JavaScript, so it is important to be able to identify the language of the script so that the browser can ignore scripts it does not understand. Moreover, the language attribute can indicate the version of the language the script is consistent with, letting the browser ignore scripts too advanced for it. This mechanism is discussed in the next section.

Most scripts found in online script libraries use the third approach. The fourth approach is actually better suited to making sure that scripts do not run on incompatible browsers, as discussed in the next section.

The Script Element Language Attribute

The **script** element can take a **language** attribute to define which version of JavaScript the script conforms to. Netscape originally set attribute values for the Navigator browser, with values as follows:

LANGUAGE ATTRIBUTE VALUE SUPPORTED BY

JavaScript   Navigator 2.0

JavaScript1.1   Navigator 3.0

JavaScript1.2   Navigator 4.x

JavaScript1.3   Navigator 4.5 and up (similar to 1.2, but core language conforms to ECMA-262 standard)

JavaScript1.4   Navigator 5 (ECMA-262, DOM Level 1 and DOM Level 2 compliant)

JavaScript1.5   Navigator 5 (with extra core language features defined in ECMA-262, revision 3)

In general, a Navigator browser understands all previous versions of JavaScript, so that Navigator 3 understands the special names "Javascript1.1" and "Javascript", the first corresponding to JavaScript as implemented in Navigator 3 and the second to generic JavaScript. Navigator 4 supports the additional values "JavaScript1.2" and, for browsers with versions greater than 4.5, "JavaScript1.3".

Navigator browsers will ignore **script** content when the browser does not support the JavaScript language version. Also, Navigator browsers will ignore **script** content if the **language** value refers to an unsupported language, such as "vbscript", "python", or "jaavascript" (note the spelling mistake in the latter example). So, if a script does not run, but otherwise looks fine, make sure that the **language** value is spelled correctly!

Internet Explorer understands the values "javascript", "jscript", and "vbscript", but will interpret "javascript1.1", "javascript1.2", or (for Internet Explorer 5) "javascript1.3" as indicating a generic JavaScript program. A summary of the names understood by different popular browsers is given in Table 4.4. Note that Opera recognizes any **language** value beginning with the string "javascript" as indicating a javascript program, regardless of subsequent text.

Browsers should ignore scripting languages or language versions that they do not understand. Thus, Navigator (all versions) ignores scripts with **language**="jscript" or "vbscript", while Netscape Navigator 3 ignores script sections labeled by **language**="javascript1.2" or higher, and Internet Explorer ignores scripts with language="javascript1.4" or higher. Unfortunately, in these cases these browsers do not display the **noscript** content.

You should also identify the language type using a **type** attribute, with allowed values text/javascript (for JavaScript) or text/vbscript (for VBScript). Thus, a complete script element would look like:

```
<script language="javascript1.2" type="text/javascript"
      src="/scripts/stuff.js" > </script>
```

Table 4.4 Language Attribute Values Understood by Common Web Browsers. A Y Means That the Browser Will Load and Run a Script with the Indicated Language Name. Here NN Corresponds to Netscape Navigator, IE to Internet Explorer, and OP to Opera

LANGUAGE NAME	NN2	NN3.X	NN4.X	NN6	OP3.6*	IE3	IE4	IE5
JavaScript	Y	Y	Y	Y	Y	Y	Y	Y
JavaScript1.1	--	Y	Y	Y	Y	Y	Y	Y
JavaScript1.2	--	--	Y	Y	Y	--	Y	Y
JavaScript1.3	--	--	Y (NN 4.5+)	Y	Y	--	--	Y
JavaScript1.4	--	--	--	Y	Y	--	--	--
JavaScript1.5	--	--	--	Y	Y	--	--	--
JScript	--	--	--	--	--	Y	Y	Y

* Opera will run any **script** element whose **language** attribute value begins with the string "javascript"—for example, **language**="javascriptzzzz".

4.3.3 Supporting Nonstandard Browsers

In some cases you will need to design pages that work on nonstandard browsers, such as WebTV, cell phone, or Palm Pilot–based browsers. Unfortunately there is often no easy way to design pages that work well on these devices and also on regular computers. This is because the devices are profoundly different, with display user input technologies that can be quite different from those of a standard computer.

Indeed, special languages and protocols are being designed for wireless (and other) devices—and these often replace JavaScript or XHTML with new languages (or dialects) targeted specifically at the limitations and features of the specific device. For example, the Wireless Application Protocol consortium (www.wapforum.org) has defined a special markup language called the *Wireless Markup Language* (WML) for use with wireless devices such as pagers or cell phones. Although WML is similar in many ways to HTML, the model is quite different—WML treats a page as a collection of stacked views (designed to appear one after the other), and has special formlike elements that attach functions to the buttons on a telephone keypad.

In these cases, the best approach is often to deliver different Web page data to each device, and thereby provide data appropriate to the different devices. Doing so is not trivial, since you want to make it easy to add new interfaces or modify existing ones without having to make costly modifications to the entire Web application. The best way to do so is to create the entire Web application delivery system in two parts. One part contains the actual data (and perhaps program) components that are largely independent of the browser interface. The second part consists of the "interface manager" that controls the way Web interfaces (XHTML, WML, CSS files, etc.) are assembled and shipped out to the browser. This component may, in turn, load in special script code, CSS files, or document templates optimized for these different devices, as illustrated in Figure 4.6.

Media-Specific Style Sheets

CSS Level 2 provides an `@media` rule that lets a designer define different style sheets depending on the device capabilities of the display device. For example, the style sheet:

```
@media screen {
      body {font: 12pt Verdana }
}
@media handheld {
      body {font: 10pt Garamond }
}
@media screen,print {
      p {margin-left: 5%; line-height: 1.4; }
}
```

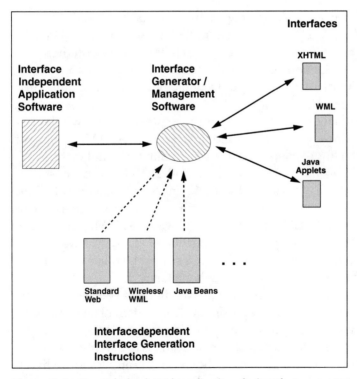

Figure 4.6 Example back-end application design that supports multiple browser devices.

contains three blocks of rules, the first and third applying to on-screen presentation and the second to handheld devices (such as a Palm Pilot).

CSS defines several media types, summarized in Table 4.5. `@media` types are supported by Internet Explorer 5 and by Navigator 5, although Internet Explorer does not give the user a way of switching between different equivalent style sheets (e.g., switching between a `screen` and `projection` format). Other browsers essentially ignore CSS rules inside an `@media`, so that this mechanism is not compatible with older browsers, such as Navigator 4, Opera 3.6, or Internet Explorer 4, or with browsers that run on current "alternate media" devices such as Palm Pilots or cellphones.

NOTE @MEDIA RULES ONLY SUPPORTED BY NAVIGATOR 5 AND INTERNET EXPLORER 5
`@media` **rules are only supported by the indicated browsers, and only for a limited number of media (typically** `all`, `print`, **and** `screen`**).**

At present the most common use of `@media` types (supported by Mozilla/Navigator 6 and Internet Explorer 5) is to provide alternate style sheets for printed content, as discussed in Section 4.5.

Table 4.5 The Different Media Types Defined in the CSS Level 2 Specification. Only the `all`, `screen`, and `print` Types Are Widely Supported

MEDIA TYPE NAME	DESCRIPTION
`all`	All media
`aural`	For aural presentation via speech synthesis
`braille`	For Braille tactile feedback devices
`embossed`	For printed Braille documents
`handheld`	For portable handheld devices (typically with small, low-resolution displays and limited color capabilities)
`print`	For printed material (or for a browser's print preview mode)
`projection`	For projection display (such as a PowerPoint presentation)
`screen`	For display on a standard computer display
`tty`	For display on devices such as teletypes, text terminals, or low-resolution displays such as cell phone text displays
`tv`	For display on a television (or similar device)

4.4 Page Accessibility

For many sites it is important that the site be functionally accessible to a user with visual (or other) impairments. There are several reasons why this may be the case. Most important is the need to serve the people reading the pages. In this sense, it is important to recognize that many site visitors have some form of vision impairment, ranging from the extreme of complete blindness to more common impairments such as color blindness, nearsightedness, or blurred vision due to cataracts. Even a minor impairment may lead to problems reading some Web pages—indeed, all of us have on occasion visited a page that annoyed or frustrated us by the small size and illegibility of the text.

Second, there may be a legal imperative for providing accessible content. Many government agencies, public service agencies, or government-regulated corporations are by law required to provide accessible services. Such obligations extend to online media produced by such organizations, so that they are legally obliged to create accessible Web pages.

In practice, accessible page design must take into account the degree of accessibility to be supported by the design: In general, the wider the audience you intend to reach, the more complex the issues you need to consider. When implementing the design, you will then need to deal with two main points: making sure the content can be read and making sure that the site can be navigated. These are, of course, the same issues page designers always deal with. However, in this case the designer will have to consider different needs of the readers (due to color blindness, complete blindness, deafness, etc.) and different modes of navigation (tab selection of links, audio browsers, etc.). Moreover, you will not be able to "see" when you get the design wrong—a person with normal vision simply can't appreciate when an image is inaccessible to someone who is colorblind!

Moreover, the designer may also be implicitly designing for unfamiliar technologies. Many browsers commonly used by (or specially designed for) users with disabilities do not support common Web browser technologies, such as frames, plugins, applets, scripting, or table-based layout. This can make it very hard to design sites accessible to these users, unless you are aware of what is supported and to what degree.

It is thus important to do extensive testing with prototype designs to ensure they are accessible. It is also often useful to bring in outside accessibility consultants during the design and testing phases.

This section does not give a complete review of strategies for improving page accessibility, but does cover some of the approaches that are the easiest and most straightforward to implement. For more details, you should visit the Web Accessibility Authoring (WAI) guidelines, at www.w3.org/TR/WAI-WEBCONTENT. Please also see the relevant references at the end of this chapter.

4.4.1 User-Adjustable Font Sizes

The most basic accessibility feature is also the simplest: Make sure that the user can increase the displayed sizes of the text, so that the display can be enlarged if the text is unreadable. Navigator 4 and greater, Internet Explorer 4, and Opera 3.6 and greater provide simple keyboard shortcuts or pull-down menus that let you adjust the default text size. This lets the reader increase the font size and make the document easier to read.

However, on many browsers (e.g., Navigator and Internet Explorer) this feature does not work if the CSS style sheet or **font** elements specify a *fixed* font size. This is the case, for example, if the style sheet uses any of the fixed length units (points, pixels, millimeters, inches, etc.) to set the size. To make the text size scalable, you must specify sizes using relative sizes defined using em or ex units or percentage values. Thus, to make the text size scalable, your default document style sheet must look something like:

```
body        {font-size: 1.0em
              font-family: Garamond, 'times new roman', serif; }
div.navbar  {font-size: 0.8em;
              font-family: arial, helvetica, sans-serif; }
```

which sets the default font size for the document to be that set by the reader, and which also sets the font size inside the navigation bar div element to be 80 percent of the default size.

Note that you must make sure that the default **body** font size is set using relative length units: If it is set using fixed units, then this fixes the size for all text inside the **body**, including any relative sizes in side it. For example, the style sheet

```
body        {font-size: 10pt
              font-family: Garamond, 'times new roman', serif; }
div.navbar  {font-size: 0.8em;
              font-family: arial, helvetica, sans-serif; }
```

fixes the default size at 10 points, and the size inside the navigation bar as 8 points. Adjusting the browser's default size will affect neither of these sizes, since they are both set as fixed values.

However, if you absolutely need to fix the font size somewhere inside the page, you can instead use a style sheet such as:

```
body        {font-size: 1.0em
              font-family: Garamond, 'times new roman', serif; }
div.navbar  {font-size: 8pt;
              font-family: arial, helvetica, sans-serif; }
```

This fixes the font size inside the navigation bar div element, but lets the sizes freely adjust elsewhere in the document.

4.4.2 Appropriate Use of Color and Contrast

In general, it is best to avoid using color to denote important meanings or functions on a Web site, since the colors will not be meaningful to users with color vision impairments. However, you obviously don't want to omit color entirely, or else the site will be ridiculously bland. The following are some simple guidelines that will let you incorporate color as accessibly as possible.

When you have colors that contrast, make sure to choose colors that will be distinguishable to color-blind users. For example, it would be a bad choice to use red and green to distinguish between different types of links, as a person with red-green color blindness would not be able to see the difference. Similarly, it is helpful to choose contrasting colors that have different overall intensities. That way, if the user is completely color-blind—or if the page is viewed on a grayscale display—the difference will still be visible.

It is also important to ensure that the foreground (usually text) and background colors have sufficient contrast, as otherwise the text may be obscured. Indeed, you should always check to see that, if the page is transformed to a grayscale, the text can still be read and page functionality is not otherwise reduced. You can do this by doing a screen capture of the displayed page and then using an image processing program to collapse the image to grayscale. If the content is still understandable after this is done, then the page should be easy to read.

Note that these color-related issues also apply to the content of inline graphics—an icon only has meaning if it can be read or interpreted!

4.4.3 Text Alternatives for Images

It goes without saying that inline graphics are useless to a blind user unless you include appropriate **alt** attribute values to describe the images. Note that this applies to *all* images in the page, including spacer or decorative graphics that serve no functional role. This is because a nongraphical browser has no way of distinguishing the nature of a graphic, and must treat all graphics as potentially being of importance. The author must then add appropriate markup (via **alt** attributes) to define each graphic's role.

Obviously, for important graphics, the **alt** text string should provide a good description of the content of the graphic, or the functional purpose of the graphic (should it, for example, be inside a hypertext link). For purely decorative graphics, use the assignment **alt**=" ". This assigns an "empty" string description to such graphics, which generally means that they will be ignored by text-based browsers.

When the meaning of an image is important but cannot be explained using **alt** text, you can also include a D-link. This is a standard accessibility trick, and involves adding, next to the image, a small hypertext link of the form:

```
<a href="target.html" alt="description of the image">D</a>.
```

By convention, users will know that the D stands for *description,* and will access the link to obtain information about the associated image.

4.4.4 Tabindex: For Keyboard Navigation

Many users find keyboard navigation an improvement over pointing and clicking. This is particularly true for users who do not have the fine motor control needed to easily navigate with a mouse or other pointing tool, and even more so for nonvisual users. You can make such navigation easier using **tabindex** attributes.

Tabindex attributes let you define the tabbing sequence in which anchor and form input elements are accessed. For example, you can choose **tabindex** values such that the tabbing sequence first steps through all the main navigational links on the page and then proceeds to the links within the body of the page. This can then bypass the natural tabbing sequence, which simply proceeds linearly through these components in the order in which they appear in the markup.

Whatever the sequence you choose, be sure to use the same approach in all your pages. This lets users become familiar with your navigational model. In essence, you are using **tabindex** to reproduce, using tab keys, the same sort of navigational model you otherwise create using graphical layout and positioning of navigational links and buttons.

The use of **tabindex** attributes is discussed in detail in Sections 5.5.1 and 16.3.6 of *XHTML 1.0 Language and Design Sourcebook.* Examples from these book sections are available online at www.utoronto.ca/ian/books/xhtml1/chap5/ and www.utoronto.ca/ian/books/chap16/.

4.4.5 Accessible Screen-Readable Layout

Many people who have visual impairments use screen readers to read Web pages. At the simplest level, a screen reader scans the text displayed on the page and uses a text-to-speech synthesizer to dictate the text to the user.

Most current screen readers, however, have limited ability to interpret complex HTML formatting—they directly read the rendered text from left to right across the screen, and cannot infer when text has been organized into columns using HTML **table** elements. For example, given the following simple text table:

The remaining accessibility-enhancement attributes apply to the table cell **td** and **th** elements. The **abbr** attribute specifies	an abbreviated text description for the cell—this would typically be used with a header cell (**th**), as opposed to a data cell.

a typical screen reader would dictate this as follows:

> The remaining accessibility-enhancement *an abbreviated text description for* attributes apply to the table cell **td** and **th** *the cell—this would typically be used* elements. The **abbr** attribute specifies130 *with a header cell (**th**), as opposed to a data cell.*

where the text in italics comes from the right column, and the text in normal font from the left. Obviously this reads as total gibberish, and will be incomprehensible to someone using a screen reader!

For optimum accessibility, designs should avoid column-based layouts. Needless to say, this is a major blow to elegant page design. Fortunately, next-generation screen reader (and other) technologies will be able to do a better job of reading the HTML markup structure, and should be able to handle structured text.

Advanced Screen Readers and Table Structure

X/HTML provides several attributes to help make tables more accessible to users with visual impairments. The most basic—and most important—is the **table** element **summary** attribute. **Summary** serves a role similar to the **img** element **alt** text, providing a text summary description of the table suitable for use by a speech synthesizer or screen reader. For example, if a table contained a collection of automotive parts with part numbers, descriptions, and pricing, then the **table** start tag might be:

```
<table summary="A list of carburetor component parts with
    descriptions, part numbers, graphics and prices" cellpadding="4" >
```

where the **summary** explains the purpose and general structure of the table. **Summary** is supported by some screen readers, and thus should always be included to provide basic accessibility to tabular data.

A second issue for accessible table design is proper use of **th** elements for column or row headers and **td** cells for table data. Some adaptive software can differentiate between these two components, can recognize which headers belong to a given table cell, and can thus provide header information alongside the data in a data cell. Indeed, the remaining accessibility enhancements provide ways of furnishing summary information for explicit **td** or **th** cells, and ways of relating data cells to appropriate headers.

XHTML 1.0 and HTML 4.0 also provide **abbr**, **headers**, **scope**, and **axis** attributes that can be used to add information to the table elements that can be used to simplify navigation and understanding of the table design by blind users. These attributes, and the ways in which they are used, are discussed in Section 15.3 of *XHTML 1.0 Language and Design Sourcebook.* Please note, however, that to date there are no browsers that take advantage of the additional information provided by these attributes.

4.4.6 Other Quick Tips

Some of the generic good habits of Web authoring are also important for creating accessible designs. For example, if you use HTML markup elements according to their meaning (**p** for paragraphs, **h1** for headings, etc.), then the content will work much better across many rendering technologies. Similarly, providing **title** attributes for anchor and **frame** elements will help make those components easier to navigate and use. Last, avoiding blinking or scrolling text is both good for design and good for accessibility.

Finally, you should validate your X/HTML documents using an HTML validator (some are listed at the end of this chapter), and also check the pages at the Bobby accessibility evaluation Web site (www.cast.org/bobby/). Bobby is an online utility, provided by the Center for Applied Special Technology, that checks a page for accessibility issues and reports common problems. This is very useful when checking a design for accessibility problems.

4.4.7 Aural Style Sheets

A final hopeful option would be to provide Aural Cascading Style Sheets (ACSS) documents with your delivered Web pages. ACSS works just like regular CSS, except that the ACSS rules define aural queues explaining how the text content should be spoken, typically by voice synthesis software. Thus, a well-designed XHTML document equipped with an ACSS style sheet can be rendered quite accessibly to a blind user—or to a sighted user who might be listening to the Web page on an audio "car-based" browser.

Unfortunately, there are no browsers that presently support ACSS.

4.5 Printable Page Designs

Web pages are generally designed solely for viewing on a screen, with no thought given to printing the pages on a printer. However, in some cases printing is important—for example, for a page containing a product description, for a news announcement, or for directions to an event or conference. In these cases the printability of the design is important and must be considered in the design of the markup and the style sheet.

The requirements of a printed page are quite different from those of a screen display. In particular, you must consider that many pages will be printed on black-and-white printers, so that colors on the page may cause problems—particularly if two "contrasting" colors both correspond to the same shade of gray. Thus, for pages destined for printing, it is best to minimize the use of color. Ideally, you should use a white page background color and black text—no one who has ever printed a Web page containing white text on a black background wants to do so again!

Of course, printability is not just about the look and feel of the existing page content. In many cases, a Web page contains content (for example, animated GIF images, long footers and headers, transient text from a discussion forum or chat tool), that is simply inappropriate for printed output. If you are writing only for Navigator 6 or Internet Explorer 5 and greater, you can use advanced print media CSS style sheets (see Section 4.5.1) and `display: none` to hide these items. However, this is not always possible, particularly if you need to support older CSS-aware browsers.

A common alternative is to provide a second, print format version of each page, which users can select using a simple hypertext link. Then, should users wish to print the page they are reading, they can select the print format version and print that instead.

Of course, if printing is a goal, then printing must be tested. Make sure to do so if this is a requirement of your design!

4.5.1 Print Media Style Sheets

Newer browsers such as Navigator 6 (and greater), Internet Explorer 5 (and greater), or Opera 4 (and greater), support special CSS style sheets targeted at printed output. Such style sheets are contained inside an `@media` rule that designates the media for which the style sheet is intended, or are imported as external style sheets using `@import` statements containing a parameter specifying the media with which the style sheet is associated. For example, the following two statements:

```
@import url('printformat.css') print;
@media print {
```

```
h1,h1,h3 {color: black;
            background: white; }
}
```

reference an external style sheet and an internal style sheet (inside an `@media` rule), both marked as being of use for printed output only. These rules are only used when the page is printed, thus letting you design a style sheet specific to the needs of printed output. Indeed, with Navigator 6 and Internet Explorer 5 you can prepare different style sheets for the different media, as in

```
@media screen {
    h1,h1,h3 {color: yellow;
            background: #333333 ;}
}
@media print {
    h1,h1,h3 {color: black;
            background: white; }
}
```

where the first block of rules would be used for screen display, and the second for printed output.

Unfortunately Navigator 4 and Internet Explorer 4 do not understand `@media` rules and ignore both blocks of instructions in the preceding example. However, as an alternative you can create a print media style sheet that overrides formatting instructions of a default (media-independent) style sheet. For example, if the entire style sheet for a document is:

```
h1,h1,h3 {color: yellow;
            background: #333333;}

@media print {
    h1,h1,h3 {color: black !important;
            background: white !important;}
}
```

then the first default style sheet applies for both print and screen media, but heading formatting rules of the second one override those set by the default style sheet.

Since Navigator 4 and Internet Explorer 4 do not support `@media` rules, this approach can be useful in providing default formatting for these browsers, along with special printing rules for more advanced browsers.

4.6 Component-Based Design

When designing pages, it is easy to get lost in the technical details of a single design problem and forget about the global issues the design must solve. By *global* I mean that a design typically does not stand on its own, but must instead be easily usable across many different documents and easily adaptable to changes in design, layout, and content. Thus, the design needs to be useful across both space (that is, across many different pages) and time (as the site grows), and must be flexible enough to support various types of content.

For ease of use and for long-term maintenance of designs and content, it is best to think of documents as being made up of reusable page *components.* In a sense, most Web designers do this already, thinking of page headers, footers, and so on, as they work through possible designs.

A component-based design, however, goes beyond conceptualization by asking that you *explicitly encode* this type of information in the design. Experience shows that the best way to do this is to use a component-based approach to the design process. That is, you consider the layout as consisting of page components, and design the layout model so that each component appears as a complete, self-contained collection of markup statements.

Page components have the following general characteristics:

- Each component is a unique block of markup, so that it can be processed independently of other components.

- Each component can be individually modified, updated, or restyled (using CSS) without affecting other components.

- Properties can be globally set (for fonts, text colors, and so on) for the entire document, but can be locally changed within each block.

For example, a typical page design might have the following components:

- A page header, identifying the site and the location within the site.

- Navigational components, providing links to other regions in a Web site.

- A footer, typically at the bottom of the page (so that the user knows the page has ended).

- The main page content.

Figure 4.7 shows a typical Web page and illustrates these various components.

This design model can now be turned into a markup model. Ignoring formatting for now, the **body** of the document design can be marked up as follows:

```
<body>
  <div class="page-header"> ... header content ... </div>
  <div class="navigation-bar"> ... side navigation bar ... </div>
  <div class="main-content"> ... main content region ... </div>
  <div class="page-footer"> ... page footer ... </div>
</body>
```

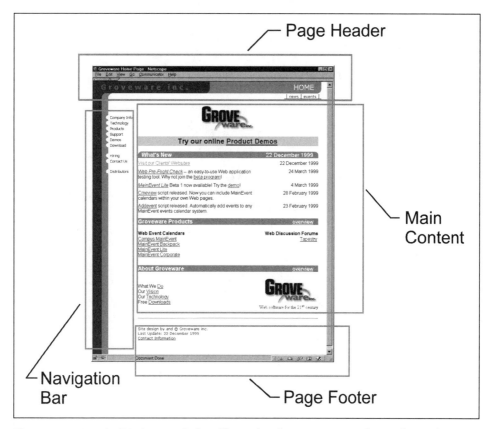

Figure 4.7 A typical Web page design, illustrating the components that make up the page.

Using CSS, these components could be rendered as shown in Figure 4.7 by floating the navigation bar to the left (and stretching it to the full height of the browser window) of the main content and page footer blocks.

However, one requirement of the design shown in Figure 4.7 was that the design needed to display well on Navigator 3. As a result, the design uses **table** elements to obtain the desired layout. The resulting markup is similar to that illustrated in Figure 4.8 (this figure excludes **body**, **table**, **tr**, **td**, and **th** attributes used to control page formatting).

The markup tricks actually used to ensure uniform layout across all browsers (i.e., appropriate use of **table** and **body** element attributes) are discussed in Chapter 14 of *XHTML 1.0 Language and Design Sourcebook*.

Note how this design still encloses the different blocks inside **div** elements, making it easy to assign specific formatting rules to the different regions. For example, global design characteristics (such as font families, link colors, and text rollover effects) can be set using generic rules that apply to the entire document, while area-specific rules can be set for the different blocks. A simple example style sheet looks like this:

```
<body>
<div class="page-header">
  <table width="100%"><tr>
      <td align="left"> Left side heading </td>
      <td align="right"> Right side heading </td>
  </tr></table>
</div>

<table width="100%">
  <tr>
   <td width="33"><img src="spacer.gif" height="1" width="33" /></td>
    <td width="105" align="left">
        <div class="navigation-bar">
        ... navigation bar content ...
        </div>
    </td>
    <td width="100%">
        <div class="main-content">
        ... main body content ...
        </div>
        <div class="page-footer">
        ... footer content ...
        </div>
    </td>
  </tr>
</table>
</body>
```

Figure 4.8   Body-level markup incorporating page components. The markup denoting the components is shown in boldface.

```
body, td, div, p {
        font-family: arial, helvetica, sans-serif;
        color: black;
        font-size: 1em; }
div.navigation-bar {
        font-size: 0.8em; /* smaller text in navbar */
        font-family: verdana, arial, helvetica, sans-serif; }
div.navigation-bar a:link {
        text-decoration: none; }
div.navigation-bar a:hover {
        text-decoration: none;
        background-color: yellow ;}
```

where the first CSS rule defines global text properties for the entire document, while the second provides font and anchor formatting rules specific to the navigation region (a different, smaller font is used, and hypertext links have their underlines removed. Also, the links will take on a yellow background when the mouse passes over them.).

Missing from Figure 4.8 is the **head** content. Obviously the document **head** will contain an appropriate **title** element, along with **link** elements referencing relevant style sheets, and any relevant script elements. You can think of the **head** as just another component of the design.

However, we have not discussed **meta** elements. **Meta** elements play an important role in communicating information used by Web indexing engines, and in some cases by browsers. Section 3.4.3 of *XHTML 1.0 Language and Design Sourcebook* discusses these uses in detail, and we will not reproduce this discussion here. However, we will mention three **meta** elements that should be used whenever you want pages to be indexed appropriately—or to be skipped and not indexed. The forms for these elements are:

```
<meta name="keywords"
      content="dogs, cats, wild animals, frogs, ponies" />
```

The preceding element lists keywords that a Web indexing engine can use to appropriately index the page. Note that if you use keywords that seem wildly unrelated to each other or to the content of the document, then most indexing engines will ignore this information.

```
<name="description"
      content="Long description for page (longer than the title)" />
```

The preceding element provides a long description for the page. Many search engines will store this string as a description of the page, and will use this when providing descriptions when information about the document is returned as the result of a search.

```
<meta name="robots"
      content="noindex,nofollow" />
```

The preceding element provides instructions to Web indexing robots—the tools that index pages for Web search engines. This instruction tells the robot that this page should not be indexed (`noindex`), and that links from this page should not be followed (`nofollow`). Possible keywords to use in the **content** value are `noindex`, `nofollow`, and `noimageindex` (the images are not indexed, but the page is indexed).

4.6.1 Design of Page Components

The overall page markup model, such as the one in Figure 4.8, defines the main content components and the relationship between them. However, it does not define the structure of these parts. Just as with the overall page, it is useful to think of these parts as being made up of components, and to establish good design models for these subcomponents. As with the global design, the design of each component should be such that it is easy to modify the design (for different content) and (where possible) easy to change the layout using a style sheet.

For example, in Figure 4.8 the markup for the navigation bar on the left consists of text labels for the section links (Company Info, Technology, etc.) preceded by small GIF images that produce the white cutouts to the left of the text (a page background image provides the two solid vertical stripes). These images also control the horizontal position of the anchor text—recall that one of the design constraints was that this design must work on Navigator 3.

One possible markup model is as follows (with the markup surrounding the components shown in boldface):

```
<div class="navigation-bar">
  <div class="nav"><img src="bul2.gif" alt="*" height="17"
        width="19" /><a href="/dir/file.html">Company Info</a></div>
  <div class="nav"><img src="bul2.gif" alt="*" height="17"
        width="19" /><a href="/sec/par2.html">Technology</a></div>
</div>
```

and so on, where each **div** element contains a single navigational component. Using **div** elements ensures that the blocks appear one after the other, while the use of **class** attributes (**class**="nav") means that we can use CSS to apply special formatting to these blocks.

Additional navigational components, such as for sublist items, can then be written as:

```
<div class="navigation-bar">
  <div class="nav"><img src="bul2.gif" alt="*" height="17"
        width="19" /><a href="/sec/par2.html">Products</a></div>
  <div class="first-sub-nav"><img ...
        width="19" /><a href="/sec/subpar2.html">Campus
        MainEvent</a></div>
  <div class="sub-nav"><img ...
        width="19" /><a href="/sec/subpar3.html">MainEvent
        Backpack</a></div>
  <div class="sub-nav"><img ...
        width="19" /><a href="/sec/subpar3.html">MainEvent
        Lite</a></div>
        ... more div blocks ...
  <div class="last-sub-nav"><img ...
        width="19" /><a href="/sec/subpar3.html">Web
        Pre-Flight Check</a></div>
  <div class="nav"><img src="bul2.gif" alt="*" height="17"
        width="19" /><a href="/sec/par2.html">Support</a></div>
</div>
```

Note how the items in this list have class attributes that define their role in this list, so that CSS can be used to assign different formatting for the first and last items in the sublist. An example of how this might be rendered is shown in the navigational link menu from Figure 4.10, shown on the right side of Figure 4.9, in comparison with the original link menu from Figure 4.7.

Of course, this design is significantly constrained by the requirement that it succeed on Navigator 3. If we relax this constraint, then we have much more freedom to simplify the markup design and place more of the formatting instructions in the style sheets. We can then use appropriate CSS rules to control the text font colors for the links, to control the indents and vertical margins around items in the lists, and even to change the display from a vertical layout model (as in Figure 4.9) to a horizontal one.

The other components of the page require their own structural models. For example, the main body content of a page, contained inside a **div** element of

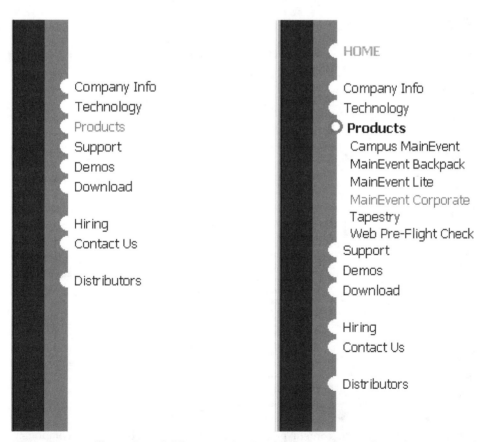

Figure 4.9 An illustration of different navigational link components from Figures 4.7 and 4.10. A possible markup design is discussed in the text.

class="main-content", might be constrained to have the following design model:

- Use **h1** for main page heading. To support CSS styling using Navigator 4, give these headings the attribute **class="main-head"**.

- Use **h2** for subheadings on the pages. To support CSS styling using Navigator 4, give these headings the attribute **class="main-subhead"**.

- Use `<p><b class="para-head"> ... <br /></b> ... </p>` for text leader headings at the beginning of paragraphs (see Figure 4.10).

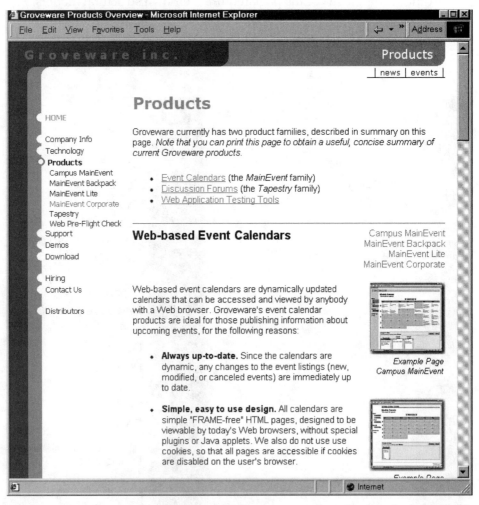

Figure 4.10 An example content page from the example Web site. The component model is the same as in Figure 4.7, although the content of the components is different due to the different role of the page.

The last rule is a compromise between HTML and CSS-based formatting mechanisms. Thus, the markup corresponding to the content region of a page, such as the example shown in Figure 4.10, will look like:

```
<div class="main-content">
  <h1 class="main-head">Technology</h1>
  <p> This page contains a brief overview of our approach to
     application development. For additional information, please
     see the
     <a href="white-papers.html">white papers</a> that outline our
     ... omitted content ....
  </p>
   <p><b class="para-head">Document-Centric
      Applications<br /> </b>
      Groveware designs and sells <EM>document-centric</EM>
      Web applications. By document-centric we mean that the
      basic components of the application, such as stored
      ... omitted content ...
      a requested transaction (e.g., retrieve all documents of
      a given type, subject to search criteria), and for
      converting XML messages into other formats, such as
      Web pages or Java applets.
   </p>
   ... more content ...
</div>
```

where again the parts in boldface come from the design rules and mark out the main design components. The text in italics refers to text omitted to save space in this illustration.

4.6.2 Integrating and Reusing Content

Many large-scale Web sites go one step beyond component-based design and actually *manage* the documents as components, keeping the different document parts in separate files (or a database) and then assembling the documents for use on the Web when needed. For example, the content page shown in Figure 4.10 might be constructed from three parts: a main component document, providing the overall markup model for the page plus the page header and the navigation portion, combined with the main content of the page and the footer. A person might then author and/or edit just the content portion of the page. When new content is ready, the software can combine the parts, automatically adding the correct "Last Update" date in the page footer, and write out the newly updated page, as illustrated in Figure 4.11.

There are many advantages to this approach, such as:

■ Each component can be maintained separately, reducing the risk of accidentally "breaking" a page while editing it.

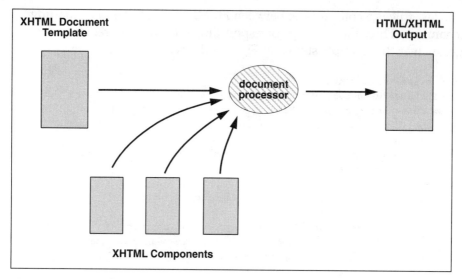

Figure 4.11 An illustration of dynamic page generation from page components.

- Software can check for inconsistencies when the full page is assembled, reducing the risk of creating pages with errors in markup or in hypertext links.

- When appropriate, the components can be reused in other documents.

- Some components can be dynamically generated by databases, making it easy to use and reuse database-driven content.

Obviously you can build your own tools to facilitate this sort of management, but there are also many existing commercial and freeware software tools that can do many of these things. Some XML approaches for implementing such tools were discussed in Chapter 3. Chapter 12 will also look at commercial systems that implement such features.

4.7 References

X/HTML SYNTAX CHECKERS/VERIFIERS

www.w3.org/People/Raggett/tidy/	HTML Tidy syntax checker
www.chami.com	HTML-Kit editor (incorporates HTML Tidy)
htmlworks.com/	Web-based HTML validation
validator.w3.org	W3C HTML and XHTML Validation service
arealvalidator.com/	Shareware validation tool

SITE OPTIMIZATION TUTORIALS

Please note that some of the optimizations recommended at the listed sites, such as removing quotes around attribute values, will lead to nonvalid markup, and can cause problems on some browsers.

hotwired.lycos.com/webmonkey/design/tutorials/tutorial2.html

www.glostart.com/webtrimmer/fluff.html

www.webreference.com/authoring/languages/html/optimize/

IMAGE FILE OPTIMIZATION TOOLS

www.lynda.com/hexv.html	Nondithering Windows color palette
www.webreference.com/ dev/graphics/	Review of optimization concepts
www.gifwizard.com	Online GIF optimizer
www.jpg.com	JPEG Wizard optimization tool
www.webreference.com/services/ graphics/jw/	Online JPEG Wizard demo
www.boxtopsoft.com	GIF, JPEG optimization tools
www.spinwave.com	GIF, JPEG optimization tools
www.equilibrium.com/index.html	deBabelizer GIF utility
www.gimp.org	Linux/Unix graphics tool

BOOKS ON WEB GRAPHICS

Designing Web Graphics, 3d ed., Lynda Weinman, New Riders (1999).

Designing Web Site Images: A Practical Guide, Gene Berryhill, Delmar Publishing (2000).

Creating Great Web Graphics, 2d ed., Laurie McCanna, IDG Books (1997).

Animation on the Web, Sean Wagstaff, Corbin Collins (ed.), Peachpit Press (1998).

Effective Web Animation: Advanced Techniques for the Web, J. Scott Hamlin, Addison-Wesley (1999).

ANIMATED GIF OPTIMIZATION

http://member.aol.com/royalef/gifanim.htm	Tutorial on GIF animation
www.webreference.com/dev/gifanim/	Review and products list

CSS COMPATIBILITY INFORMATION

webreview.com/pub/guides/style/style.html	CSS compatibility charts
css.nu/pointers/bugs.html	Browser CSS bugs list
developer.netscape.com/support/bugs/ known/css.html	Navigator 4.x bugs
www.css.nu/	CSS information

JAVASCRIPT BUGS AND COMPATIBILITY INFORMATION

developer.netscape.com/docs/examples/ javascript/browser_type.html	Browser detection script
www.it97.de/JavaScript/JS_tutorial/ bstat/navobj.html	User-agent strings for various browsers
www.it97.de/JavaScript/JS_tutorial/ bstat/Browseraol.html	User-agent strings for various browsers
sites.netscape.net/ekrock/standards.html	Guide to browser-compatible scripts
developer.netscape.com/docs/technote/ dynhtml/xbdhtml/xbdhtml.html	Cross-browser scripting guide
www.webdevelopersjournal.com/jsweenie/	Browser compatibility
www.webreference.com/js/column6/	Browser compatibility
javascriptweenie.com/articles/ javascript_limitations.html	Browser compatibility
builder.cnet.com/Programming/ ErrorFree/ss02.html	Browser compatibility
www.netscapeworld.com/netscapeworld/ nw-03-1997/nw-03-coin.html	Nav3/IE3 compatibility
developer.irt.org/script/bugs.htm	JavaScript bugs
developer.netscape.com/support/bugs/ index.html?content=known/javascript.html	JavaScript bugs

JAVASCRIPT STANDARDS AND RELATED SPECIFICATIONS

www.ecma.ch	ECMA (Java/ECMA-Script standards body)
msdn.microsoft.com/workshop/author/	Microsoft dynamic HTML (DHTML) references
developer.netscape.com/tech/ dynhtml/index.html	Netscape Navigator 4 dynamic HTML
developer.irt.org/script/vfaq.htm	JavaScript FAQ

www.ecma.ch/stand/ECMA-262.htm	ECMAScript Standard
www.ecma.ch/stand/ECMA-290.htm	ECMAScript components specification
www.w3.org/TR/REC-DOM-Level-1/	DOM Level 1 standard
www.w3.org/TR/DOM-Level-2/	DOM Level 2 standard

NONTRADITIONAL WEB BROWSERS

www.wapforum.org	Wireless devices
www1.wapforum.org/member/ developers/overview.htm	Wireless Application Protocol (WAP) technical specifications
developer.webtv.net/	WebTV technical info
www.palmpilot.com/devzone/ webclipping/	Palm Pilot

ACCESSIBLE DESIGN GUIDELINES

www.w3.org/TR/WAI-WEBCONTENT/ guidelines	Web authoring accessibility
www.w3.org/WAI/	Overview of accessibility issues
aware.hwg.org	Accessible Web authoring resources
www.webable.com	Web accessibility resources
hotwired.lycos.com/webmonkey/ geektalk/97/11/index4a.html?tw=design	Accessible design article
www.cast.org/bobby/	Online accessibility evaluation tool

CHAPTER

5

Web Site Architecture and Design

Topics/Concepts Covered: Linear and hierarchical Webs; multimedia and hypermedia; themes in site design and implementation; site design tips; site indexes and searching; dynamic content and user tracking

The previous chapter provided a review of the main issues to consider when designing individual Web pages, focusing on usability of the design, reusability of the markup, and accessibility of the content.

This chapter takes a higher-level view and looks at the design of *collections* of Web documents and associated resources. In the printed world, there are differences between designing a single page and designing a complete magazine, book, or library. Such collections require organizational and design elements that are neither necessary nor apparent from the perspective of a single page. The same is true of hypertext collections, although here opportunities of the design—and the required design elements—are quite different from those needed in the purely printed world.

Why such differences? The reasons lie in the nature of the presentation media: Books are spatial, physical, static collections, with a fixed *linear* structure, whereas hypertext is nonspatial, nonphysical, possibly dynamic, often *nonlinear*, and often *interactive.* Good hypertext design must embrace these differences while preserving the easy navigability and ease of use of printed books. This chapter looks at some ways of accomplishing these goals and provides references for additional reading on this subject.

We begin with a short introduction to general models of multimedia, which explains some basic ideas and helps position the Web among the various other multimedia and hypermedia technologies in common use. Section 5.2 then examines detailed models for Web design, focusing on two important aspects: the architecture of how sites and content can be designed and the themes that are currently seen as important for making popular, attractive sites. This section is an odd mix of design and social sciences—as, in many ways, is the Web itself!

Section 5.3 looks at some basic technical issues related to the implementation of the design points discussed in Section 5.2. This is not at all detailed, but is rather designed to give you a rough understanding of some of the technical aspects important in site design. References are provided to sections later in the book, where these points are described in more detail. Finally, Section 5.4 presents my own idiosyncratic list of references related to multimedia and hypermedia design, Web design in particular and design in general. The references should help you quickly expand your knowledge.

5.1 Models for Web Multimedia

The easiest way to introduce architectural models for multimedia is to start with a simpler, familiar media example—namely, a printed book. This lets us introduce, using a familiar model, the ideas behind structured collections of information. The issues that arise in *hypertext* design can then be introduced and analyzed with respect to this more familiar case.

In simplest terms, a book is a collection of related, printed pages. Of course, there is much more to a book than that! After all, a large collection of unbound and unnumbered pages would be, to say the least, a cumbersome format (rather like the floor, desk, and hallways of this author's home as he writes this chapter). Given a pile of printed pages, a reader cannot distinguish between pages arising from different books or documents (should there be pages present from more than one collection) and cannot, even within a set of associated pages, determine the proper reading sequence without explicitly checking for page-to-page continuity. The problems are essentially navigational: There is no easy way for the reader to figure out how to read the pages as a coherent whole.

Book or magazine designers solve such problems by giving pages a uniform design (top and bottom page banners, typeface, and so on) so that they have a distinctive look, by numbering the pages to give *linear order* to them, and by binding the pages together to enforce the correct order. If there are many pages, or if there are explicit organizational requirements, there is often a table of contents listing the page numbers of important starting pages, and perhaps an index providing references to other significant locations in the book. By convention, such content-listing or indexing tools are placed at the beginning or end of the volume (the exact location varies according to linguistic and national conventions) to make them easy to find. Additional cross-referencing is possible through internal page references, footnotes, bibliographies, and so on, and additional indexing components are present within specialty books such as dictionaries or encyclopedias. Indeed, the organizational technology of printed material is very sophisticated, covering everything from the production of simple pamphlets to multivolume encyclopedias. This is not surprising given that this technology has been refined over 500 years of practical experience.

5.1.1 Linear Documents

Books and other printed media are essentially *linear.* By linear, I mean that they have an obvious beginning and end and a fixed sequence of pages in between. While indexes, tables of contents, or cross-references are often added and are often critically important, they do not change the underlying linear structure. In fact, they count on the underlying linear nature, page numbers, and so on, to provide fixed reference points.

The reasons for the popularity of this linear model are both physical and psychological. Physically, the only easy way to organize printed pages is as a bound, linear entity. Psychologically, a well-defined linear structure is comfortable, familiar, and convenient, since it is easy to read, easy to reference, and easy to communicate to others. Indeed—and it is important to remember this above all else—the goal of all publishing is *communication,* and books are tried and true in this role, as they can be reliably communicated to others (through duplicate copies) and reliably referenced and compared (through page number references).

It is also important to note that the physical aspect of a book provides a psychological comfort zone to readers by letting them know both the exact size of the book and where they are *within* the book. This makes it easy to browse a book, for example by jumping from the table of contents to a selected location or by simply selecting pages at random, all the while retaining a sense of location with respect to the beginning, end, table of contents, or index.

Figure 5.1 illustrates both the structure of a book and how the table of contents and index merely provide referencing on top of the underlying linear structure.

Other traditional media, such as music, video, and film, are also linear in this sense, being predetermined presentations of sounds or images created by a musician or director. This, in part, reflects the temporal nature of these media—music and film move forward in time in a fixed, linear way. This also reflects the technical limitations of the media, as it is almost impossible to make nonlinear presentations with traditional film, video, or audio technology, just as is the case with printed text.

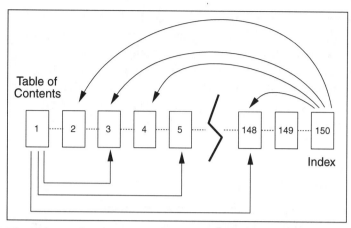

Figure 5.1 The structure of a linear document collection, in this case a book. The ordering is implicit in the page numbering. Tables of contents and indexes simply provide referencing on top of this underlying structure.

5.1.2 Nonlinear Media

The appearance in recent years of inexpensive yet powerful computers and graphic displays has made it possible to step beyond these linear approaches and has opened up enormous—and still largely unexplored—possibilities in the organization and presentation of information. This is because a computer has no preferred organization for stored data and can easily store, index, relate, and access data in a number of different ways, subject to the design of the database holding the data and the capabilities of the software. In addition, a computer can create a representation of the underlying data quickly, efficiently, and *inexpensively* by following instructions provided by the software and/or the reader. In a sense, you can think of the stored data as a collection of book pages or page components (paragraphs, images, etc.) that can be shuffled and rearranged almost instantaneously by the computer at practically no cost. This is in stark contrast to the difficulty and high cost of modifying the order of printed material, or material on tape or film.

NOTE This flexibility and speed also applies to audio and video, which in large part explains why text, audio, and video editing are now commonly performed on computers.

At the same time, modern computer interfaces can directly and at low cost present this data to a user—a Web browser is just one example. This also is a new phenomenon, since high-resolution computer display systems capable of rapidly displaying finely formatted text and graphics have become affordable only in the last 10 years. Thus, not only can a computer rapidly organize data, it can also nearly instantly present the data to a user in almost any format (text, graphics, audio, video, for example). To make an analogy to traditional media, a computer can be thought of as a customizable, personalized printing press, capable of organizing and presenting information in decidedly nonlinear ways, limited only by the capabilities of the underlying software and the interests of a user.

Computer Games

These technological possibilities have led, over the past 15 or so years, to the birth of several new media. The first and likely still most popular is video games. Games are inherently nonlinear in the sense previously described, since they evolve in an unpredictable way according to the input (that is, the "play") of the user. Video games preserve this model through environments that incorporate both the game scenario and rules—the user plays in this environment and can explore nearly endless game variants, or number of possible variations, depending on the sophistication of the game. The first games were very simple, with primitive graphics and limited scenarios, but today's games, such as *Myst, Quake* (my favorites), and others, provide enormously rich environments and allow for enormous flexibility in the way a player can explore the game's virtual world. Indeed, anyone interested in understanding current and future directions of digital media should spend time playing modern computer games—even though it may be hard to convince your friends that this really is work!

Hypertext and Multimedia

At the same time, it was apparent from the earliest days of computers that this technology could realize the long-dreamed notions of hypertext and multimedia.

Inexpensive computers and easy-to-use programs like HyperCard and Macromedia Director opened up exciting new ways of presenting combinations of otherwise weakly connected media. Very quickly, hypertext and

HYPERTEXT

A collection of text and graphics that can be explored by the reader in a nonlinear way. *Multimedia* is the mixture of text, graphics, sound, and video in a single presentation. Note that many multimedia presentations are often *linear.* The combination of multimedia in a nonlinear hypertext format is often called *hypermedia.* In this book, the term *hypertext* can be taken as synonymous with hypermedia.

multimedia became the basis of new media design, with products ranging from multimedia wine guides and hypertext encyclopedias to multimedia/hypertext training packages. Indeed, today many corporations commission multimedia promotional presentations instead of the more traditional videos or films.

Designing linear multimedia is relatively straightforward, whereas the design of *hyper*text or *hyper*media introduces enormous design complexities. This is because each hypertext presentation must incorporate—*within* the presentation's structure—the tools that let a user successfully and comfortably explore the collected material. Since the components can now be related in decidedly nonlinear ways, there are no simple organizational schemes, such as page numbering, that can serve as universal and commonly understood tools for navigation and location. And, unlike those in a game, the navigation rules in multimedia systems should be nonintrusive and easy to follow, since the goal is to communicate *content*, without the reader having to worry about navigation. Designers and researchers are still exploring ways of designing easy-to-use hypertext and hypermedia structures, and it is not surprising that good design is something of an art as well as a science.

5.1.3 The Web as Hypertext/Multimedia

Most of the preceding design problems are relevant to large collections, or webs, of HTML documents. Indeed, Web collections are a form of hypermedia, limited by the current technologies of the Web and the Internet (a Web collection is clearly not as dynamic or multimedia-oriented as a Macromedia Director presentation, although the differences are getting smaller as the Web technologies advance), but at the same time enriched by the ability to interconnect with resources around the world. Most important, the Web is inherently nonlinear, since there can be a nearly (often frustratingly) endless number of ways of getting from one page to another. Figure 5.2 shows a simple figure of a possible Web document collection—as in Figure 5.1, the solid lines indicate the links (in this case, hypertext links) between the pages, with the arrows indicating the directions of the links.

Do you see the problem inherent in Figure 5.2? Suppose you are reading document A and want to go to a topic discussed in document B. How do you get there? The answer is that you have absolutely no idea. If a collection were to have no structure other than the links indicated in Figure 5.2, the reader would be forced to move randomly through the collection until he or she wandered, largely by chance, to the desired page. In the absence of additional navigational cues, the reader does not know where to find the table of contents (or even if there is one), the index, or even the beginning of a section.

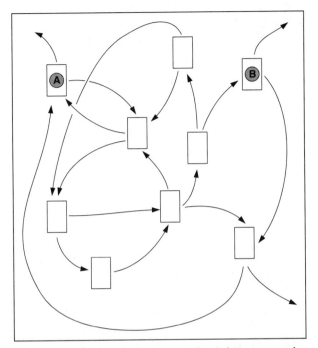

Figure 5.2   An illustration of a web of documents—the arrows show the links between documents. The collection is *nonlinear*, in that there are a number of different routes by which the collection can be explored. It is very easy to get lost in such a web.

Even if the links are sequential (the documents connected one after the other as in a book), a reader could not find these places since, with the Web, there is no way to step back, see the entire book, and just turn to the front for the table of contents. Indeed, a reader has absolutely no idea of the size of the collection: There could be one page or a thousand.

Conversely, a book gives you both a local and global feel for its size and for your location in it. Page numbers tell you where you are and where the next and previous pages are, and the feel of the book tells you more or less where you are in the entire book (for example, halfway through) and where to find the table of contents (at the front) or index (at the back). The reader's ability to see the whole picture, plus conventions for the location of contents' pages and indexes, are part of the technology of books that makes them so easy to use. And it is the absence of these features that can make hypermedia design so difficult. It is your goal, when designing a Web, to include navigational tools that will allow visitors to easily explore and find what they are looking for without becoming lost or frustrated.

5.2 Models for Web Design

Given this quick introduction, it is time to look at some practical models for Web design and at the design features a Web designer must account for in designing such collections.

We first look at a linear model for a Web—just because the Web is nonlinear doesn't mean you always have to give up linearity! A linear approach is often ideal when converting a printed document to hypertext, for online documentation, or when you have a particular sequence that you want followed by your readers, such as a sequence of slides.

5.2.1 Linear Collections

Figure 5.3 shows a schematic layout for a linear document collection—the solid lines with directional arrows show the critical navigational links. Figures 5.4 and 5.5 illustrate some designs for pages in a linear collection. The structure in Figure 5.3 very much follows the book layout shown in Figure 5.1, except that there are now explicit links to places such as the index and table of contents. Recall that, in a book, the reader could easily find these components because of their physical place in the book. This is not possible with hypertext, so Web documents must provide explicit links to these navigational aids.

Some examples of Web designs using the linear model are shown in Figures 5.4 and 5.5. Figure 5.4 is one page from a large, online HTML documentation site. The first thing to notice is the large title banner text at the top of the page. This quickly identifies the page as part of a particular collection (the "Introduction to HTML" collection) so that users immediately know, from page to page, where they are. Every collection should carry an identifying marker (text or graphics) such as this at some prominent location reproduced from page to page.

Navigational Links

The linear navigation tools are provided by the collection of text buttons just under the page heading. These lines are connected to related documents and replace the navigational cues available in a printed book. Using the *Prev* and *Next* buttons, the document can be read sequentially; or it can be accessed nonsequentially, using *ToC* (for Table of Contents) or *Index*. The *Up* button is linked to the top page of the local section—for example, because this is a page from Section 2, the *Up* button might link to the first page of Section 2. Part (B) of Figure 5.3 shows how such pages could be organized. A top-of-section page might contain a brief section introduction and perhaps a content

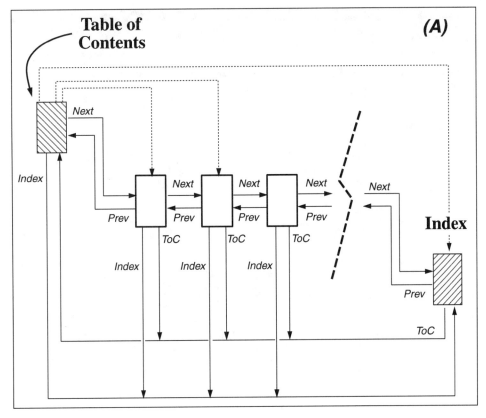

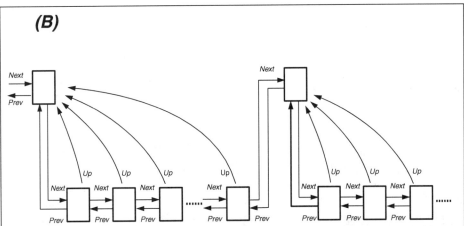

Figure 5.3 A linear collection of hypertext documents. Lines show the main navigational links; the thin lines illustrate secondary links superimposed on the linear structure. Part (A) illustrates the basic linear structure—note the links to the *Next, Previous, Index,* and *ToC* (Table of Contents) pages. To make the figure easy to follow, links from the *Index* to the individual pages are omitted. Part (B) shows a possible linking structure for section headings. *Up* links connect each page to the top page of the section—for clarity, the links to the *ToC* and *Index* are omitted.

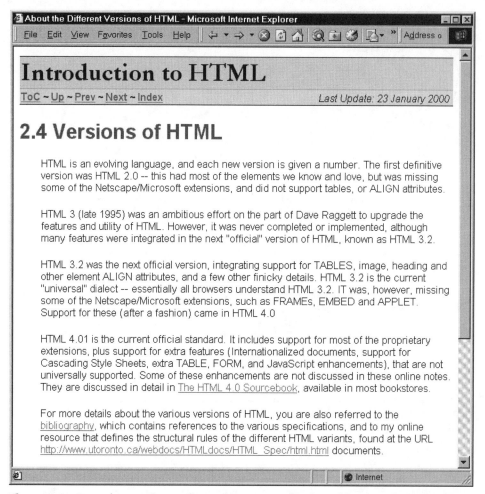

Figure 5.4   Example page from a linear document collection. This example is taken from an online HTML tutorial found at www.utoronto.ca/webdocs/HTMLdocs/NewHTML/.

listing for the section. This lets the user move *Up* for a section overview without having to return all the way to the full table of contents.

The design in Figure 5.4 does not explicitly state how many pages there are in the "linear" collection. Indeed, most online linear navigation mechanisms do not mention page numbers or page counts, as these are often not meaningful to a reader, who is quite likely to jump back and forth (using the *ToC* or *Index*) through the collection looking for information of interest. In principle, such information could be provided, but in practice this is usually done only when the collection of pages is small.

An example of this case is shown in Figure 5.5(A), which shows two (out of seven) pages from a short article on using nonstandard characters in

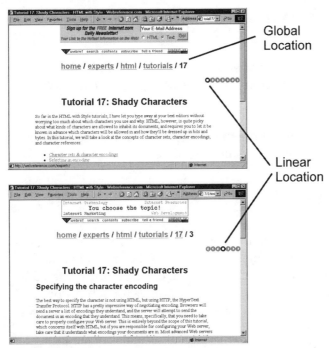

Figure 5.5(A) Two example pages from a seven-page article on character sets in HTML documents, found at webreference.com/html/tutorial17/. The "page" being displayed is indicated by the small image icons, as noted. The hierarchical location of the page within this site is shown at the top of the page.

HTML documents. In this case, the page being viewed is indicated by the small circular icons to the right and just above the article title—this figure shows the first and fourth pages from this article. Thus, this site explicitly marks each page in the sequence by its own icon: The number of icons tells the user how many pages there are, and the selected icon (the darker icon) indicates the page being viewed. This makes it easy to see the extent of the article and the reader's position in it. Of course, this approach does not scale well if there are many pages in the collection—this design would be very cumbersome if the collection had many dozens of pages and hence dozens of small icons.

Also, note that this design does not provide *Table of Contents, Up,* or *Index* links. Such large-scale navigational components aren't needed with small collections like this and would be more of a hindrance than a help.

Figure 5.5(A) uses graphical icons to mark the page location and navigational choices. An alternative would be to use page numbers (or other text) for the links. Indeed, text links provide some additional functional features, since the links can show (by changed link color, for example) when a particular page has already been viewed.

Last, note how the tops of the pages show global location links that mark the position of this linear collection within the structure of the entire Web site—article 17 in the "tutorial" section in the "HTML" section, inside the "experts" section. This information is kept separate from the local navigational mechanisms so that local (within the article) navigation does not get mixed up with global navigation across the site.

Clean Design, Dated Content, and Generic Information

From a design perspective, clean page design is important, as is the use of a similar design for all pages in the collection, to enable the reader to find the navigational components on the page. Thus, if you decide to use centered **h2** headings for main sections and left-justified **h3** headings for subsections, you should do this for all pages. This reinforces the familiar pattern implied by the graphic and banner design and makes it easy for a reader to navigate within each page, as well as across the collection.

Note also in Figure 5.4 that the page is dated so that the reader knows when the content of the page was last changed. The document shown in Figure 5.5(A) is also dated, but in this case at the bottom of the page (see Figure 5.5(B)). Although not needed on every page, creation and/or modification dates are useful for pages that are regularly modified, because this lets regular visitors know if the page has been updated since their last visit.

As shown in Figure 5.5(B), the page footers in both examples provide important generic information about the page. Commonly included (or referenced) information includes legal notices, the page URL (so that the user can return to this page if they have only a printed version of it), links to generic information about the site, links to a user feedback tool, and so on. Date information should be presented in a *universal* date format. In particular, the common form 8/9/1998 is a bad choice, since some countries use the order day/month/year, whereas others use month/day/year.

If you don't want feedback, you can omit a feedback tool—but my experience is that feedback is very helpful when building and maintaining large Web sites.

5.2.2 Hierarchical Collections

The next hypertext model is a hierarchical document collection—the treelike structure is illustrated in Figure 5.6. There are many real-world examples of such structures, including the Open Directory (dmoz.org) and Yahoo!

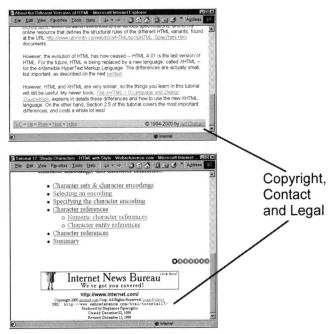

Copyright,
Contact
and Legal

Figure 5.5(B) The bottom portions of the documents shown in Figure 5.4 (top) and 5.5(A) (bottom). Note how the page footers reproduce the linear navigation tool and also provide links to copyright, user feedback, or licensing information relevant to the page or the Web sites.

The bottom figure is © 2000 internet.com, Corporation. All rights reserved. Reprinted with permission from www.webreference.com.

(www.yahoo.com) Web sites, among others. These sites consist of a list of Web-accessible resources, organized hierarchically so that visitors can easily look through the collection for things they are interested in. In a sense, you can think of this as a hierarchical "library," with the categories in the hierarchy chosen to make it easy for people to browse through the shelves of information, or "drill down" quickly to a specific topic.

For example, the Yahoo! page covering "Asthma," shown in Figure 5.7 lies under the category "Diseases and Conditions," which in turn is under the category "Health." This natural progression of categories ("Health" to "Diseases and Conditions" to "Asthma") makes it straightforward for people to navigate down to this category. Indeed, if you have information that naturally organizes itself in a hierarchical manner, this is the obvious approach for presenting the information on a Web site. Of course, the hierarchy is useful even for small collections—your site does not have to be as large as Yahoo!

The navigation tools needed in a hierarchy are different from those needed in a linear collection. For example, *Next* and *Previous* are no longer meaning-

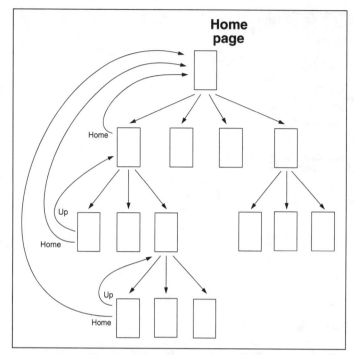

Figure 5.6 An illustration of a *hierarchical* document web. The documents are organized in a treelike structure, descending from a single home document.

ful, and links to *Up* are usually equivalent to the browser's "back" button and are often not necessary. Indeed, instead of *Up*, you want to provide links "up" to a number of locations. Typical locations are the root or home page of the tree (the link to "Yahoo!" in Figure 5.7—the image is clickable), the sequence of pages to which an *Up* button would take (since you can go "up" more than once), and a *Search* or *Index* tool (essentially a searchable index). These links are all found in Figure 5.7 at the following places:

- The Search box provides a Search tool.
- The link to "Home" or clicking on the word "Yahoo!" takes you back to the top-level page.
- The "Diseases and Conditions" and "Health" links take the user one or two levels up in the hierarchy.

The top of the page also has links to general-purpose service links, including a *Help* link (for general information about the Yahoo! site and services), and two links (*Check Email* and *Personalize*) connected to special Yahoo! services. Not shown in Figure 5.7 are the *Suggest a Site, FAQ,* and *Company Information* links found at the bottom of the page. Obviously, each collection will

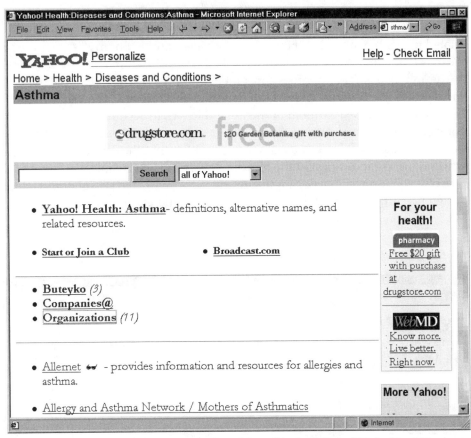

Figure 5.7 Example page from the Yahoo! hierarchical catalog of Web sites. This shows the page in the "Asthma" section, which is below the "Diseases and Conditions" section, which in turn is in the "Health" section. Note how links to other category pages are in boldface. The "@" after link indicates that the target lies in a different "branch" of the hierarchy. For example, selecting the link "Companies@" produces the page shown in Figure 5.8.

have its own special-purpose utilities and links, depending on the site's function and purpose.

In general, the structural design of a page also provides important information, and this is certainly true at Yahoo! For example, in all Yahoo! index pages (e.g., Figure 5.7), links to *category* pages use boldface hypertext anchors, and the bracketed numbers after the anchors give the number of items in that subcategory. Also, a trailing "at" (@) character after the category name means that the referenced category is actually a subcategory below another parent. When such a link is accessed, the top of the page lists the primary route through the hierarchy to the page. For example, clicking on the link to "Companies@" in Figure 5.7 (the result is shown in Figure 5.8) links to a subcategory in a different (company-related) tree containing information related to asthma, namely: "Home" → "Business and Economy" → "Companies" → "Health" → "Diseases and Conditions" → "Asthma."

The Yahoo! design undergoes constant evolution as the collection of references grows and as dead references are removed. Moreover, the Yahoo! tree keeps growing new document branches and leaves to account for new categories under which resources are cataloged. Overall, the design has evolved very well (at least as far as a user is concerned!) within the original structure, which is a good indication of the robust nature of the hierarchical approach. One of the goals in every design (including your own) is to ensure the original design has sufficient flexibility that such growth and evolution are possible.

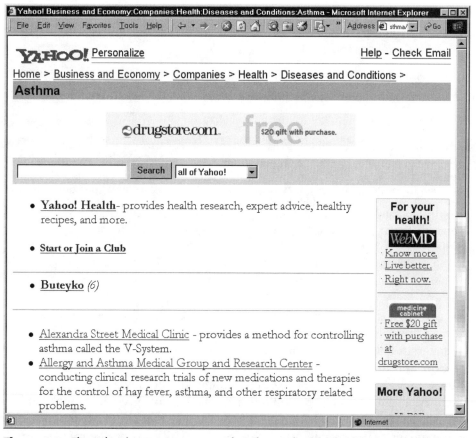

Figure 5.8 The Yahoo! category page produced on selecting the "Companies@" link in Figure 5.7. Note how this page is in a different branch of the hierarchy, as discussed in the text.

Not all hierarchies are as obvious as this one. Revisiting Figure 5.5 you will note how the "Global" site navigation tool is presented as a hierarchical list representing the section of the site the user is viewing and the various sections up from there. Indeed, almost all Web sites use a hierarchy to provide access to the main content of the site. The main issue, then, is making the hierarchy effective for the users.

Designing an Effective Hierarchy

The hierarchical approach is by far the most common and useful site design theme. However, you need to consider two things when designing the hierarchy:

- The physical navigability of the hierarchy
- The logical navigability of the hierarchy

The former refers to the structure of the links and the organization of the pages, whereas the latter refers to the categories you choose and their meaningfulness to the site visitors. We will talk about the first of these issues here and mention the second one only briefly (we'll discuss the second issue in detail in the next chapter).

Whatever hierarchy strategy you choose should be easy to navigate. Structurally, you want to avoid two extremes: a hierarchy that is too deep (has too many levels) or one that is too shallow (has too few levels). If the hierarchy is too shallow, then there will be too many items at each level and it will be difficult for visitors to find what they are looking for. The same problem occurs if there are too many levels in the hierarchy: After four or five selections down into the hierarchy, users will lose confidence (or patience!) that they are on the right track. You should thus strive to keep the depth as shallow as possible without making each level too unwieldy. A depth of three to five is ideal, and anything greater than six is likely to cause problems.

Most important, your design—the number of levels and the names and labels of your categories—must reflect the material you wish to present and the way you wish to present it. There is no one universally appropriate hierarchical structure. Thus the Yahoo! layout, which works well for Yahoo!, is not where you should start. You should start by looking at *your* data and determining how you want it to be organized and accessed.

Logically, however, the design must reflect the *navigation model desired by the site visitors*. This is an important point, since site visitors typically have very different expectations of a site than the site designers or senior corporate executives. One of the keys to implementing a design is making sure that this design, including the site organization, reflects the users' needs. Approaches for making sure this actually happens are discussed in the next chapter.

Hierarchies and Linear Components Together

Obviously, it is easy to include linear collections within a hierarchical model: A single page within the hierarchy simply becomes the starting point for the linear collection. The hierarchy then gives an overall and easily navigable structure to the collection, rather like shelf labels in a library.

Indeed, the HTML article shown in Figure 5.5 is an example of this model—a short linear article placed in an overall hierarchical structure. Similarly, if the documents illustrated in Figure 5.4 were stored inside a hierarchically organized site, the location to this region could be shown in the pages as well, in the same manner as Figure 5.5.

5.2.3 Sites as Collections of Collections

A Web site usually follows the hierarchical approach, but with a few twists. Figure 5.9 illustrates a possible organization of a large site's Web collection. In general, a Web has a single top node, or *home page,* which is the publicly advertised location for the document collection. The home page then has links to other pages that lead down to the remaining resources. In this example, the home page has links to small introductory documents that explain the origins of the site and that outline copyright rules associated with the site content. There are also links to the top-level nodes of the various hierarchical collections beneath the home page. Figures 5.9 through 5.11(C) show three example home pages illustrating these features. Despite their superficial dissimilarity, all these pages follow precisely this model.

Distinguishing Branches in a Large Web

Often, a Web site will have many different main sections, or branches, rooted at the home page. The site manager may want to use similar document layouts and design models in the different branches, since this makes it easier for users to navigate through the collection. At the same time, the designer will probably want to give each section a distinctive look so that the readers have a sense of location and know where they are.

One way to do this is to modify the page banner design to reflect the identity of the site and the specific features of the specific branch—this is just what we prescribed for linear collections earlier in this chapter. An example of this is shown in Figure 5.11(B), which shows a subsection page within the CNET site—the home page is shown in Figure 5.11(A). Note how the CNET logo is smaller in the subsection pages and the design of the header has been

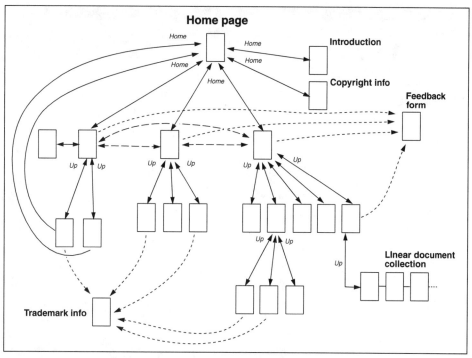

Figure 5.9 Schematic layout of a large Web collection, showing the hypertext links between the home page, the top-level organizational nodes, and other documents. Solid lines indicate main links between items within the hierarchical (or linear) structures; long-dashed lines indicate links between "siblings" at the same level in a hierarchy. The arrows indicate the possible directions of the links, as coded into the HTML anchor elements. The short-dashed lines indicate links to general-purpose pages—note that these links are unidirectional, since it is unreasonable to code in all the possible return paths. Typical home pages from large collections are shown in Figures 5.10 and 5.11(A).

modified—there is an advertising graphic between the top page banner and the hierarchical location banner giving the location of the current page. This is a simple structural change, yet it quickly gets across the message that we are in a CNET site subsection and, moreover, quickly identifies the specific subsection.

There are of course many variations to the CNET approach. A popular alternative is to use a tab bar at the top of the page, with each tab denoting a different area of the site. Amazon.com and Snap.com, among others, use this approach. The advantage here is that the location can be indicated both by text label (in the selected tab) and also graphically (by the position and possibly color of the tab). An example of this is shown in Figure 5.12—note how strongly the tab mechanism marks the area of the site being viewed.

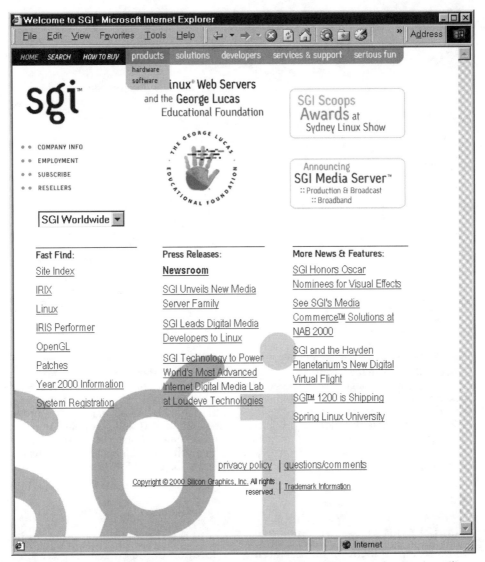

Figure 5.10 The home page (www.sgi.com) of SGI, corporate Web site for Silicon Graphics, Inc. For discussion see the text and also the caption for Figure 5.11(A).

5.2.4 Themes in Site Design

The preceding sections have roughly outlined the main ideas behind site design and layout. However, they did not explain when the different styles of design should be used or when they are or are not relevant. These sections also did not go into the finer details of design, such as what colors palette to use or how to best design a page.

Figure 5.11(A) The home page (www.nando.net) for the *Nando Times,* an electronic newspaper. Both this design and that shown in Figure 5.10 are graphically oriented, with links to the main site areas. Note that the home page for *Nando Times* has a link to a "no frames" alternative: Both sites were carefully designed to support a wide range of users.

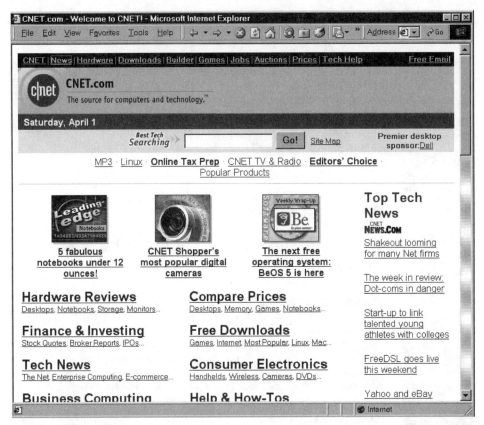

Figure 5.11(B) The home page (www.cnet.com) for CNET, a computer and technology news and information source. Note how the top bar provides quick shortcut links to the most popular sections of the site.

Reprinted with permission from CNET, Inc. © 1995–1999. www.cnet.com.

There are no simple or short answers to these questions. In fact, the tools or tricks you need to use will vary depending on the type of site and the intended audience and, moreover, will vary with time, as the technologies get better and as users' expectations change. Indeed, instead of starting with a list of design tools and tricks, it is better to start with questions about the purpose of and the intended audience for the site. Understanding—and answering—these questions will put you in a far better position to understand the design parameters for the site, the requirements you must satisfy with the design, and the appropriate approaches to take.

Note that Chapter 4 of this book covered many technical issues related to effective page design, and the companion book, *XHTML 1.0 Language and Design Sourcebook*, covers these technical issues in great detail.

Sites serve many different purposes, ranging from providing information and/or services to selling products. However, within these very general func-

Figure 5.11(C)   A subsection page from CNET, a computer and technology news and information source.

Reprinted with permission from CNET, Inc. © 1995–1999. www.cnet.com.

tions, three common themes commonly are used to make the site more interesting and "sticky" to visitors and to provide additional marketing information useful to the site owners. These three themes are *personalization, community building,* and *user tracking.* These issues—which are strongly related to each other—are briefly described in the next section.

Personalization

The personalization theme lets site visitors create personalized views of the site content. This is typically accomplished by having visitors create an account at the site through which they can set preferences for the types of information they wish to see or the services they wish to use. When the user visits the site, he or she can log in at the site and can obtain a custom, "personalized" view of the site information.

Figure 5.12   Examples from Snap.com illustrating tab-bar navigation for indicating the main sections of the site. Note how the pop-up menus highlight the section of the site.

Personalization approaches are most relevant for portal (or vertical portal, or *vortal*) sites which attract regular, repeat visitors.

NOTE A portal is simply a Web site that serves as an access point to a spectrum of information generally originating from many different sources. A *vortal* (short for vertical portal) is a portal that focuses on information in a specific vertical market. For example, www.netscape.com or www.altavista.com are general-purpose portals, while mp3.com is a vortal, because it focuses on the music industry market.

As examples, a college or university might create a portal site providing university-centric news, where students and staff could create personalized views of the site. In the commercial realm, such personalization services are offered by almost all commerce sites, some good examples being mp3.com (with the my.mp3.com personalized portal), Netscape (www.netscape.com), with the my.netscape.com portal, and Yahoo! (www.yahoo.com), with the personalized portal at my.yahoo.com.

Personalization can be a powerful tool for attracting repeat visitors, provided, of course, the site is easy to use and offers compelling, regularly updated content. Personalization is less critical if the site does not have lots of changing content, since users are then unlikely to return often—and when they do return are unlikely to remember their account names or passwords!

On the other hand, once a user has registered, the site may then have useful contact information for that user, so the site itself can "push" important updates to registered users (typically by e-mail) based on the user's declared interests. For example, a personalized "Internet Security" site might be configured to e-mail notification of important security updates to registered users—for many, this would be a compelling service and a good reason to register for personalized services.

Community Building

The community theme attempts to build site loyalty by creating a shared community of interest that is attractive to site visitors. This is possible for a site that deals with a topic of particular interest to users and thus attracts a community of people with shared interests. However, a community can develop only if the members of the community can communicate with each other and build community identity. Thus, many Web sites provide community services that let registered users exchange messages, resources, or other information—or even contribute to the content of the community Web site.

For example, the mp3.com site offers many community-related tools, such as message boards, chat rooms, custom "Web radio" stations set up by users, and e-zines (electronic fan magazines authored by members of the community). Such services lead to enormous brand loyalty (also called visitor "stickiness") and keep people coming back to the site again and again. Indeed, if you go to the mp3.com Web site (see Figure 5.13) you will notice that links to these community services are provided right from the site's home page. If you then visit these community areas, you will find a great deal of material there, all authored by members of this community.

A second example of this is the Slashdot.org Web site. Its home page is illustrated in Figure 5.14. This is a news and information site, but one where *all* the news and information is added to the site by the Slashdot.org community members. To a large extent the value and stickiness of this Web site is entirely due to the members of the site community.

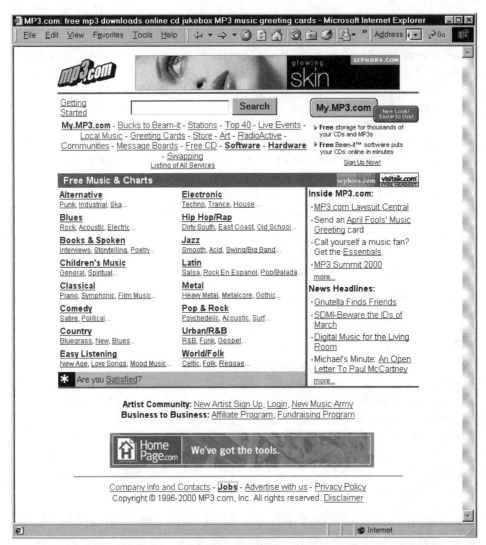

Figure 5.13 The home page for mp3.com. Note how the home page provides direct links to community-building services such as "Message Boards" and "Stations."

User Tracking

The user-tracking theme lets the site management track the activities and interests of the users visiting the site. This is a powerful tool for Web site developers and marketers, as it can provide enormous amounts of information about their customers or prospective customers. For example, by knowing the personalization preferences of a registered user, by monitoring the types of pages the user requests, or by analyzing the keywords used in site-

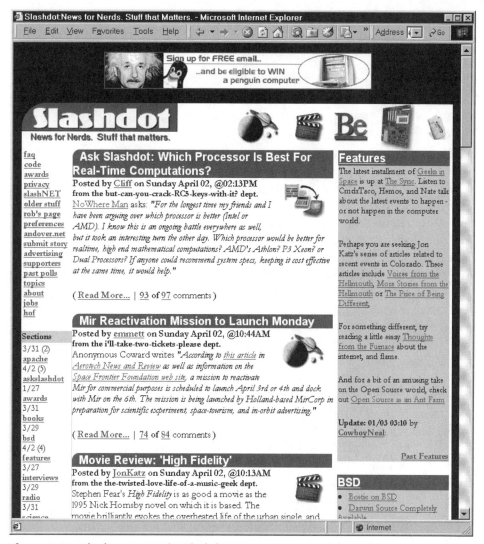

Figure 5.14 The home page for Slashdot.org. Every news article on this page is authored by one of the Slashdot community members (this does include some of the principal staff members at Slashdot.org).

specific search queries launched by the user, software can quickly develop a profile of the interests of registered users, and this information can be used to do the following:

- Develop a better personalized service by tuning the delivered content or services based on this additional information.
- Deliver targeted advertising placements, should the site use advertising.

- Develop user information databases, which can be used to extract averaged demographic data (for example, removing all personal data) about the site customers, for use in selling advertising, and so forth.

- Develop user information databases for sale to other organizations.

Almost any user who joins a personalization service at a Web site expects the site to use tracking information for the first three tasks. However, essentially *every* user will balk at the fourth possible use—and indeed will likely refuse to accept the service if they know you will use the information in this way.

Moreover, the integrity of such demographic information is questionable. Many users intentionally provide misleading information about themselves—particularly personal identity or address information, which means that detailed user data can be of very poor quality and not terribly useful. Thus, although user-tracking data can be very useful for understanding the average demographics of users and for adjusting the site design to better serve user interests, it is less reliable for understanding details about specific registered users.

Regardless of these issues or of the information you choose to collect, you *must* (for both legal and ethical reasons) provide your users with a clearly stated privacy policy telling them exactly how the information you gather will be used, both in the present and in the future. Note that in doing so you are effectively making a contractual obligation with your customers—so make sure you get it right the first time!

It is also possible to extract useful information about site usage without knowing any personal details of a specific user. For example, even if you don't know the identity of the users, you can still track their activities as they explore the site. By doing so you can learn how people actually use the site, which can help you improve the site design. Similarly, you can use user session–specific information, such as the words typed into search tools, to tailor advertising or other site information to the user, even if you don't know the identity of the user. Examples of these features are common throughout the Web. As an exercise, try visiting some commercial sites (e.g., amazon.com or www.altavista .com) to do some exploring and searching; note how the pages end up with auxiliary content (advertising, hot links) tightly related to the path you explored or the keyword you entered.

We will look at user tracking again in Section 5.3.3, when we review the technical features of the Web that make user tracking possible.

5.2.5 Page and Site Design Tips

The following are some simple page and site design tips that will help you to design better individual pages and better overall sites. This list, of course, should not be seen as complete, and you are urged to look to the references at the end of this chapter for additional ideas. Also, to add to this list yourself, based on your own experiences and observations.

Design with navigability in mind.   Site visitors will want to navigate within a site to do or find something. Your goal in the design should be to make that task as quick and easy as possible.

Design with the site visitor in mind.   You are designing the site for the people who use it, not for the designers and not for senior management. You must understand what the visitors want to do if you are to design successfully for them.

Embrace the dynamic nature of the Web.   Users expect sites to be dynamic entities, with updated and changing content and with interactive components they can use.

Emphasize important links.   For example, boldfaced links at the start of a sentence or paragraph are more likely to be accessed than links embedded in the middle of a paragraph or in other block of text. Thus, if you want to attract users to a particular location, make sure to emphasize links to it!

"Chunk" the information in a page.   Group related information together so that it is easy to find. For example, note in Figure 5.11(A) how the content in the bottom left is organized into chunks that form natural groups.

Use the full width of the browser window.   A good design uses "rubber" right margins and lets the page size expand or contract depending on the browser width selected by the user. This makes the design more flexible for different users and for monitors of different sizes and resolutions.

Don't overdesign the home page.   Keep the page designs as simple, straightforward, and consistent as possible so that it is as easy as possible for visitors to navigate the site and find what they are looking for on the page.

Don't overdesign the features of the site.   Just because you have a 600-MHz Pentium V with 256MB of RAM doesn't mean everyone else does. You want to restrict your designs to layouts, components (e.g., Java applets, Shockwave plugins), and scripts that work on your visitors' browsers.

Simplify, simplify, simplify.   Make the site navigation and operation as simple as possible. The content (and software) beneath the site may be terrifically complicated, but your users don't care—they want things to be simple, easy, and straightforward. Remember that you only have one minute (or less) to impress first-time visitors—they don't have the time (or inclination) to read a long page of instructions or to proceed through a complex sequence of Web pages to complete a simple transaction.

Keep the URLs simple. People actually use these things, either by mailing them to friends or jotting them down on pieces of paper. They can't do this if the URL is long or confusing.

Provide a search tool. Users will expect the site to have a search tool, particularly if the site is large. Indeed, search-based navigation is one of the most popular methods of finding content on a Web site.

Keep downloading time short. Once again, visitors do not have patience for slow-to-arrive pages. Make sure your pages all download and render quickly.

We will revisit some of these issues in the next chapter, when we discuss Web site planning, implementation, and management.

5.3 Technical Issues in Site Architecture

The preceding two sections provided a quick overview of the main issues in site layout and design. However, at this point it is useful to look at three technical issues related to Web site implementation, since they are important for understanding how certain aspects of a site are designed.

5.3.1 Searching a Site: The Site Index

Searching is one of the most common and powerful paradigms of Web navigation. Indeed, almost every user will expect a site to have a search utility—and will be tremendously disappointed, if not annoyed, if one is not available. Indeed, you can think of a search tool as being the equivalent of a book's index or a telephone system's 411 service—just as useful and just as essential.

Moreover, the search tool must be very simple and must be simply integrated into the page design. Indeed, the consensus for search tools is that they should have at most two components:

■ A text box for the text of the query (the text is typically just keywords or phrases)

■ A "Go" or "Submit" button to start the search (although pressing the Enter key will also start the search)

There may also be an adjacent link to an "advanced search" page that provides more complex search tools. However, almost all users (over 90 percent) will never explore beyond the simple two-component tool, since it is sufficient in almost all cases.

If you go back and visit the figures from this chapter, you will see that almost all have a search tool similar to the one described here. And, in the cases where you don't see such a tool, it was probably present in the page, but outside the view area. You can check this by visiting the different sites yourself.

Site Indexing Engines and Services

Commercial Web site indexing engines are available from a number of companies, including Infoseek (www.infoseek.com), Alta Vista (www.altavista.com), and Verity (www.verity.com). Typically, these are expensive products, with prices that increase as the number of pages in the database increases. There are some less expensive open source products, such as ht:/Dig (www.htdig.org), which are worth considering for small- to medium-sized sites.

For small sites you can often lease indexing services from an index service provider. Such sites will remotely index your site: You simply include, in your search page, an appropriately encoded link to the remote search engine. Companies offering this service include Atomz (www.atomz.com) and FreeFind (www.freefind.com), but there are many others. A good list of such tools is found at www.searchtools.com/search/search.html.

There are, of course, many other tools and service providers for you to choose from. Additional information on site indexing and search tools is found at dmoz.org/Computers/Software/Internet/Servers/Search/ and www.searchtools.com.

5.3.2 Dynamic Content and User Tracking

Many Web sites have very little static content; that is, very few of the Web pages are simple HTML documents stored on disk as files. Instead, these sites generate their documents on the fly, typically using page templates and server-side preprocessing tools (such as Cold Fusion, Active Server Pages, Java Server Pages, PHP, and so on) to process the templates, inserting content on the fly as the template is converted into the served-out HTML page.

Of course, tools like this allow for personalized Web services, dynamically assembling pages according to the interests of the user (and the marketing interests of the site owner!). We won't go into the details of such tools here—there are literally dozens of books and Web sites devoted to the different packages. We will describe some of these tools and the roles they serve in more detail in Chapter 12, but only after we've looked at the underlying technologies that make this possible in Chapters 7 through 11.

Personalized content is, of course, possible only if the Web site can track users as they explore the site. This means that each request coming from the browser must contain information identifying the user so that the server knows who the request is coming from. There are only two ways that a browser can actually send this sort of information to a Web server:

- As information encoded in a URL
- As a cookie sent as part of the HTTP message sent from the browser to the server ahead of the actual HTML document

The URL is just the string that tells the server which resource it should return to the browser. However, a URL can contain information that both references the resource and contains information explaining who is requesting the resource and what filters they would like to apply to that resource. For example, in the URL

```
http://www.msite.com/@userid/list/music/list.html?prefs=ctry:rk
```

the value `@userid` might be a string that identifies the user, while the appended string `?prefs=ctry:crk` might indicate some preferences selected by that user (for example, this user has selected to see listings of country and rock music). Of course, this URL would need to be written into the Web page the user was viewing, so that he or she could simply click a link (or press a button) to access this resource. Thus, the document containing this link would need to be custom-generated for each user. Obviously this is one common role of CGI programs or the more complex page-generation system mentioned previously.

Cookies and Session Information

As an alternative to placing session information in the URLs (and dynamically editing all the URLs in a document to reflect this information), a Web application can use HTTP *cookies.* Cookies are small pieces of data sent from the server to browser and then back from the browser to server, but as part of the HTTP message separate from the HTML document. For example, the first time a user identifies him- or herself to the server, the server can return a cookie that encodes the user's identity along with any special user preferences. Then, when the user makes another request for a resource from that server, the cookie will be sent along as part of the request, providing the same user identity and preference information, but by a different means.

Cookies are a useful way of tracking users and user sessions, and they have the advantage that they can also persist after the user shuts down the browser. That is, if the user shuts down the computer on Friday, turns it on again on Monday, and then reconnects to the same site, the cookie from the previous week will be sent along with the request, letting the server know that the same user has returned. This, of course, is not possible with the URL mechanism previously described, since in that case users must identify themselves *before* the URLs are created.

However, cookies have two important disadvantages:

■ Users can disable cookie support on their browser so that it will refuse to accept and transmit cookie data.

■ Proxy servers (intermediary servers between the Web browser and the server actually delivering the Web resources) can also be configured to refuse cookies.

Thus, although cookies can be very useful in identifying and tracking users, they can't be counted on 100 percent of the time. Typically, then, Web applications use both mechanisms at the same time. The cookie mechanism is discussed in detail in Chapter 9, Section 9.12.

Tracking URLs Sent by E-Mail

If your site uses e-mail to send recommended URL links to your users, you can encode information in the e-mailed URLs to uniquely identify the user to whom the link was sent. Then, when the recipient accesses the URLs, you can identify which users actually bothered to do so and develop better personalization profiles for those users.

For example, suppose that your site is recommending an exciting news article about Mars to a collection of your site subscribers. The links you send could then easily be of the following form:

```
http://mx.msite.com/mlinks?/path/mars.html/023112A01b21
```

where the program *mlinks* (running on your server) redirects the incoming request to the actual article. In this example, the document is indicated by the first part of the query string, */path/mars.html.* The second part of the URL (the string *023112A01b21*) would be different for each mail message sent out to the registered site users, and this encodes the *identity* of the user to whom this URL was sent. It could also encode the date on which the message was sent out if you wish—the information it encodes is entirely up to you. The program *mlinks* can then use this key to determine the likely name of the user making the request (of course, the user could forward this URL to someone else) and use this information to develop a better personalization profile of that user.

5.4 Thematic Issues in Site Architecture

Thematically there are several important issues that come up again and again when designing or redesigning a Web site: *continuity* (the site functions in the same way to outside users over time), *navigability* (the site is always easy to navigate), *containment* (you retain visitors who come to your site), and *community* (your visitors feel a "part of" your site). These themes should be ingrained in the minds of every Web site designer or architect. The next six sections describe some important design concepts related to these four themes.

5.4.1 Continuity: Never Move Existing Pages

Once you have built a popular site, some visitors will bookmark pages at your site or will write up Web pages containing links to your site so that they can return directly to these locations or can direct others to your site. Therefore, once you have put pages in place, you should *never, ever* move them! Doing so will break visitors' bookmarks, disconnect any pages with links to your site, and cause no end of grief. Indeed, by removing pages you are effectively throwing away all the link advertising you have probably fought long and hard to generate!

Sometimes, however, you do need to move pages, or at least change the URLs. This is often true after a management reorganization of an internal Web site, when the URLs end up containing a name that reflects a now nonexistent division or department. As well, a product may be dropped or renamed, in which case the original pages are obsolete. However, this is no reason to delete the page without providing any forwarding information! If you must delete and relocate pages, make sure to provide server redirection from the old locations to the new, or provide replacement pages in place of the old ones that reference other appropriate locations on the site.

NOTE All servers can be configured to redirect a request from a specific URL to a different location.

If you use the latter option, you should avoid using **meta** redirect headers (see Section 4.6 and *XHTML 1.0 Language and Design Sourcebook*), since they break accurate functioning of the browser's Back button. Instead, simply place a link in the page referencing the new location—and include a **meta** header that informs Web indexing robots that this page should not be indexed (see Section 4.6).

When expanding a collection, you should similarly avoid eliminating pages—only add new ones. This avoids the problem just mentioned, but reiterates the importance of thinking through the organization of your collection before you start building it. A well-organized collection has room for easy expansion, whereas an ill-thought-out jumble of pages will not grow easily and will lead to problems when reorganization is required.

5.4.2 Navigability: Never Return Dead-End Pages

A site should never serve out pages that don't contain links back to somewhere else on the Web site. There are two reasons for this. First, users may arrive at this page using a bookmarked link or a URL someone mailed them—and without such links they will have nowhere else to go! Second, someone who has diligently navigated down through your site to get to this page really doesn't want to press the browser's Back button to try and get somewhere else.

As a corollary to this rule, no Web site should ever return a blank "404 Not Found" page. Instead, you should configure your server, in case someone requests a page that does not exist, to return a well-designed document that explicitly states that the page does not exist and that provides links to useful starting points on the Web site. To test out the usefulness of this, try accessing various commercial sites using wildly incorrect URLs (e.g., www.groveware .com/adfafafasfas). Note how much easier a site is to use if you receive a navigational tool in response.

5.4.3 Navigability: Make Information Easy to Find

The goal is always to make it as easy as possible for visitors to find what they are looking for or to do what they want to do. The designs should reflect this and should be modified only to improve this feature. In particular, make sure that, when adding a new feature, you don't make other features harder to use or find!

Making information easy to find *also* means letting people know when resources are *not* available. For example, a visitor to an airline Web site will probably be looking for airline flight information and ticket prices. However, since ticket prices are notoriously variable (or subject to complex pricing schedules), it may be impossible to keep Web-based data relevant or up-to-date. If this is the case, the site should have a page that says exactly this and that provides an alternative (yes, even a 1-800 number) for further inquiries regarding fares.

5.4.4 Containment: Retain Site Visitors

No doubt you want people to stick around at your site once they arrive, and if you have followed all the rules of elegant design presented in this chapter, they are bound to do so! However, one easy way to unwittingly send visitors away is to explicitly give them, just after they have arrived, links to locations outside your local Web. Thus, it is generally a bad idea to include external links on your home (or other high-level) pages, because your visitors will be tempted to head right there—and never come back.

Instead, place any links to external sites further down in your collection so that users have to step through and see some of your own content before arriving at these external references.

5.4.5 Community: Solicit User Feedback

Your pages should allow for user feedback so that users can make inquiries, point out problems (broken links, nonfunctional search tools, etc.), or provide commentary on the site in general. This can be done using simple mailto links (and e-mail responses) or **form**-based fill-in feedback forms. Of course, if you use such a tool, you must also be ready to cope with the mail. You must make sure to respond to the mail you receive—after all, if a visitor goes to the trouble of sending you commentary, it would be very impolite not to respond.

5.4.6 Community: Design for Users, not Managers

When you design the site you should design it for those who use it and not for the managers who have commissioned the design. A site will be successful not because managers like it, but because users use it.

Similarly, you want to use technology that is appropriate for your users—there's no point in building fancy Java applets if your users are unable to run them. Your primary goal should be to design a site that works, even if this means omitting some elegant and attractive content. Once you know the site works properly, you can add these features, thus providing added value to those who can use them without breaking the site for everyone else.

Figuring out what a site needs to do is one of the most difficult aspects of implementing a Web site, often because the actual reasons for the site are not well known or well articulated. The next chapter describes ways in which the site purpose can be better defined and understood, and it outlines approaches for implementing a site that reflects the real goals.

5.5 Annotated References and Bibliography

This bibliography is not comprehensive, and mentions only sites and books I have personally found useful. Many other books and sites can be found by searching bookstore sites, such as amazon.com or chapters.com, or by searching the various Web index sites, such as yahoo.com, altavista.com, and so on.

WEB-SPECIFIC BOOKS AND SITES

info.med.yale.edu/caim/manual/—This site contains an excellent online discussion of hypertext design issues and their relevance to the Web. This resource has a large and very useful annotated bibliography. The authors of the collection are Patrick J. Lynch, director of the Center for Advanced Instructional Media at the Yale University School of Medicine, and Sarah Horton, a multimedia applications specialist for Academic Information Resources at Dartmouth College.

www.useit.com—This is Jakob Nielsen's personal site, which contains many useful articles on Web site design and usability.

usableweb.com—Another site devoted to Web design and Web usability. Contains a good collection of articles, plus many links to other resources.

dmoz.org/Computers/Internet/WWW/Web_Usability/—A list of links to sites covering Web usability topics.

Designing Web Usability: The Practice of Simplicity, by Jakob Nielsen, New Riders Publishing (2000)—An opinionated book by someone whose opinion on Web design is well worth reading. This is a must-have book for all Web designers.

Web Navigation: Designing the User Experience, by Jennifer Fleming, O'Reilly and Associates (1998)—One of the first books to summarize the issues and problems associated with designing Web architectures that work from the users' and designers' perspectives. There are many useful examples and case studies, plus a nice chapter on the process of developing a Web site.

Information Architecture for the World Wide Web, by Louis Rosenfeld and Peter Morville, O'Reilly and Associates (1998)—A good review of technical architectural issues related to Web design.

GENERAL ISSUES IN DESIGN AND HYPERMEDIA

The Non-Designer's Design Book, by Robin Williams, Peachpit Press (1994)—This small, outstanding book covers all the basic elements of good typography, page layout, and book design. Although written for the printed page, this is a must-read book for anyone who wants to design Web pages and who does not have a background in design and/or typography.

Designing Visual Interfaces: Communication-Oriented Techniques, by Kevin Mullet and Darrell Sano, Prentice-Hall (1995)—An excellent book on visual interface design concepts for computer graphical user interfaces. A bit out of date and not focused on Web design (which has constraints from generic computer interface design), but still a useful book to read.

Designing and Writing Online Documentation, 2d ed., by W. K. Horton, John Wiley & Sons (1994)—An excellent book that covers in detail all aspects of electronic document design. There are also many useful references.

Visual Design of the User Interface, by E. R. Tufte, IBM Corporation (1989)—An excellent review of the issues associated with designing usable interfaces of all types for users.

Envisioning Information, by E. R. Tufte, Graphics Press (1990)—Simply a lovely book that illustrates the many ways in which information can be graphically communicated, with some reflections on computer interface issues. This is a must-have book for any serious interface designer, and it makes a wonderful addition to any coffee table.

The Visual Display of Quantitative Information, by E. R. Tufte, Graphics Press (1983)—This is considered by many to be the best book ever written on the graphical presentation of data. It is an outstanding book, which nicely complements Tufte's later work, *Envisioning Information*.

Hypertext, by George P. Landow, Johns Hopkins University Press (1992)—This is a discussion not of the technical aspects of hypertext, but of the literary meaning of hypertext and of its impact on our understanding of text and literature. If the term *critical theory* and the name Michel Foucault mean anything to you, then this is the book to read.

The Gutenberg Elegies, by Sven Birkerts, Fawcett Columbine (1994)—Some thoughts on the usefulness of hypertext and hypermedia and on the advantages of print. This is much easier to read than *Hypertext*. Birkerts's newer book, *Readings*, published in 1999 by Graywolf Press, apparently brings some of these arguments up-to-date. Unfortunately, I haven't read it.

Web Site/Application Design and Management

Topics/Concepts Covered: Process and management of Web projects; project research, brainstorming, and design; establishing testing procedures; deployment and ongoing maintenance

Planning, implementing, and managing of a Web site or Web-based application are in fact complicated tasks that require brilliant technical skill, the wisdom of Solomon, and nerves of steel. Or, at least it often seems that way. This can be the case because Web projects typically straddle many layers of an organization—both vertically from senior management (who often launch the endeavor) on down, and horizontally across many departments or divisions. Consequently, the person (or people) managing a Web project must be able to:

- Explain the functionality of a proposed (or existing) site in ways that all can understand.

- Negotiate the design so that it works well for all parties.

- Work with all groups to "capture" the real requirements so that the site designers do the right things.

- Plan the development and testing of the design.

And, of course, it all has to be done in a ridiculously short time frame, with insufficient funds and staff. The goal of a Web applications design manager is to be able to do all these things while keeping all the participants happy— and themselves sane and healthy!

The key to doing so successfully is having both a good understanding of the process and a methodology for managing that process. There are many different methodologies, many adopted from the software development world. In general, the purpose is to let you define, monitor, and manage an ongoing project while keeping all the external players informed and involved so that they can see how it is going and feel that they're a part of the process. At the same time, the approach must do all of this without overloading the project with too much extra work—you don't want to spend all your time managing as opposed to developing.

This chapter describes the process stages of a Web development project, and it outlines the issues that you need to manage throughout these stages. It is notably not a prescription for *how* these things are actually managed, but rather a set of suggestions for how the process can be organized to work effectively. In practice, the management practices that you put in place will depend on the tools you have, the existing business or communication process you have to work with, and the size of the project. For example, if you are designing a 40-page "public affairs" Web site that will have simple page updating and little programmed functionality, then you won't want a complex, detailed process. On the other hand, if you are implementing an Intranet application that will replace large portions of the company's IT infra-structure, then you'll want a careful, well-defined process, because you have a lot to deal with and can't afford to make any mistakes.

In general, every project can be thought of as having six stages:

1. *Project definition/understanding the project.* Before you begin a project, you need to know the real purpose—not as a Web project, but as a strategic business (or other) decision, with critical business objectives and priorities.

2. *Researching the project.* Once you know the real purpose or goal, you need to do some research to establish quite generally the types of things you want to do with the site. This is often called the *requirements capturing* phase during which you work with the senior management staff, and Web implementation experts determine what the site is supposed to accomplish, given the real business goals and priorities for the sites. You should also research comparable services offered on the Web, and start determining what types of resources you have in-house or will need to purchase/outsource to attain the desired goals.

3. *Roughing out or brainstorming the design.* The design team and other important parties can work through possible system designs, evaluat-ing their effectiveness or appropriateness. In particular, you can test the appropriateness of a design against the requirements set during the research phase. This activity can also provide suggestions for other approaches that should be researched further.

4. *Prototyping the designs.* Given some possible designs, you can now implement prototypes of portions of the design. The goals should be twofold: (1) to test the appropriateness of the Web page designs and site architectures, and (2) to test complex, high-risk software components.

5. *Design, implementation, and testing.* After you have prototyped the design and determined which way to go, it is time to actually design and implement the site. Critical to this stage is ongoing testing, or quality assurance, so that you can catch small problems quickly and fix them before they become big ones.

6. *Deployment and maintenance.* Once the site is ready to go, you need to deploy it and keep it operating successfully. This would include updating content, in addition to ongoing testing to ensure that links (or software) have not been inadvertently broken. You also need to evaluate the site so that you can decide what corrections and updates are needed and how to proceed with the next version (or revision) of the site.

Of course, the stages are never as distinct as this—research often overlaps brainstorming, which often overlaps prototyping, and so on. Moreover, in the long run, the process is actually a cycle—a project is never really done, and by the time you are deploying and maintaining a site, you are probably already reanalyzing the site and its purpose (step 1) and researching ways to update/upgrade it (step 2).

Note that the process is the same if you are an employee of an organization, working on internal Web projects, or if you are a consultant/developer brought in from outside to implement a project. The advantage of the former position is that you probably better understand the organizational players and how they work together, and can better ferret out the real business case for the project. The disadvantage is that you probably don't want to lose your job, so you may be reluctant to tell the unvarnished truth about a proposed design! Of course, if you are a small design company, you may be nervous about telling your client that there is a major problem they haven't dealt with, for fear of losing the contract. On the other hand, doomed projects such as these are generally bad for staff morale and—because they will fail—will invariably tarnish your relationship with the client.

6.1 Understanding/Defining the Project

Many Web projects fail not for technical reasons, but because no one really understood the true reason for the project. By *true reason*, I mean the purpose of or goal for the project independent of its being a Web project of some sort. It is important to remember that a Web site or application is simply a tool— and a tool can succeed if it is designed to accomplish some well-defined function. However, a business project can only succeed if the tools successfully achieve some specific business goals.

For example, suppose that the stated goal for a project is "to make it easier to access online documentation." This may in fact be true, but it is probably not the real *business* reason for this goal. The real reason might be "to reduce customer support costs." This might be accomplished by letting customers answer product-related questions themselves, or by improving efficiency for the customer service agents who answer support calls. Obviously, the system you design could be very different in either of these cases.

You also need to understand the players, or participants, who will be affected by the project. In the preceding example, the players might consist of those who maintain documentation and/or convert it into online form, the customers who might be looking for information, or the customer service staff who deal with customer calls. Obviously, these people must be able to effectively use the system you build, so you'll want them involved in the process of designing that system right from the start.

There will also be political players—people who have management responsibilities over the areas your project will impact, and who can help or hinder your project, depending on how they feel the project will affect their own position in the company or the operation they manage. You need to find out who these people are and what their level of involvement with the project is. If some of these people seem ambivalent or even hostile to the project, then you should delicately try to find out why. It may simply be a personal sentiment about the project—or the person may have serious and valid concerns that you should know about.

In particular, you need to know what organizations or services you will need to work with in implementing the project. For example, if the online documentation is stored in a database that is managed by a computer services group, then you will need to work closely with this group. Similarly, if the Web application must interact with accounting systems or other software applications, you must build a working relationship with the relevant stakeholder groups.

6.1.1 Preliminary Goals and Timelines

At this stage, you also need to establish a preliminary project plan that outlines the different tasks to be done (research, brainstorming, prototyping, implementation, and deployment), the resources (people, equipment, money) you have to draw upon, milestones for completion of these tasks, and an overall time frame for completing the project and delivering the product. The details of these will no doubt change somewhat as you research (Section 6.2), brainstorm (Section 6.3), and prototype (Section 6.4) the project. However, this preliminary schedule is important for keeping your feet firmly planted on the ground, and ensuring that the project does not get lost and drift far away from any meaningful deadlines or staffing and fiscal constraints.

6.2 Researching the Project

The next step is to do a bunch of project-related research. In essence, the research phase complements the first one by defining in more concrete terms the purpose and function of the project, and by establishing the working relationships with important stakeholders (customers, clients, users, or partners). The former is necessary so that you know what you're actually trying to do, and to determine how you can measure success and failure. The latter is necessary so that you can get important individuals or groups involved in the project, and can get them to "buy into" it. This is essential, as these groups will either be users of the Web project you are building, or they will be providing services or support critical to making the project a success.

6.2.1 Competitive Survey

It is important to know what is possible, and the best way to know that is to survey various Web sites and note the types of services they offer. An obvious place to start is with sites of business competitors. This will not only help you understand the competitive landscape, it will also help you to appreciate how well your competitors are providing service over the Web. In particular, this will give you a sense of the types of functions and services that your competitors are offering, and this will also give you the opportunity to see what does—and does not—work well. In a sense, you can learn from the mistakes and successes of your competitors. You will, of course, make your own mistakes—but this type of research will help you avoid the most obvious ones.

But you don't want to limit yourself to competitors' Web sites. Feature and design ideas will come from all over the Web, so it is important to not restrict yourself to one type of site. Also, there are a large number of Internet trade magazines [*Internet World, PC Week* (recently renamed *eWeek*), and *Information Week,* for example) and Web sites (www.zdnet.com and www.cnet.com, for example] that provide useful (if not always critical) descriptions of new Internet services and products. Every Web project manager should regularly browse these magazines to identify new products, ideas, and trends.

If you are planning a public site or Web application, this is also a good time to start defining how your site or application can be differentiated from competitors' sites, or to provide functions and services that better serve or target a specific market. At this stage, you can simply think in terms of features, designs, or functions that might serve this role and that are consistent with business goals defined during the project definition phase. Of course, there can be significant overlap between these two activities, with interesting ideas from the research activities actually changing the business model for the project.

6.2.2 Define Site Requirements

While you are researching ideas for the Web site, you also want to start defining more explicitly what users should be able to do at the site—keeping in mind, of course, the business reasons for the site.

To do this you need to determine first who the audience will be—only by understanding your site's visitors can you design for their interests, needs, and preferences. This was illustrated in Section 6.1, which described how a Web site designed for internal call center support staff (that you can train if the site is complicated) would be implemented quite differently from one designed for the general public (for whom training is not an option)! Of course, in most cases the user demographic is not so well defined as for an internal call center. However, you can still use an understanding of a site's audience demographics (either the existing audience, or an audience being targeted by a new site) to create a design in keeping with that demographic. For example, a site designed for 18-year-old male trance music fans is going to look quite different from a site designed for 50-year-old female business executives.

On a related note, understanding your users helps you determine the technologies you can use for delivering content and services. Thus, if you are delivering services only over a high-speed Intranet, and all your customers use the same Web browser, then you can significantly simplify your technical page design requirements. However, if you must deliver content over the Web to users with different browsers and different network connection speeds, then your design must allow for this fact.

Also, if you need to market your site to generate customers, understanding your user demographics will help you determine where to market your site. You can then target your various advertising or other marketing strategies at sites or media that target similar demographics, and get a better return on your marketing investments.

Functions and Service Requirements

Given an understanding of the user demographics and the purpose of the site, you then need to think about the services and features that the site should provide. For example, if this is a customer support site, what types of support should be provided: Should you provide online searchable manuals or other support tools? If it is a site that will provide specific functions (such as an online store), what should those functions be? Similarly, if the site is going to depend on customers or site visitors, what functions and services can the site provide that will make it attractive (and "sticky") to those visitors?

At this point, you don't want to define *how* you will offer this function or service on the Web site—there are many ways a function or service can be provided on a Web site, and you can't easily know at this point which way is best. Indeed, the best way will likely vary depending on the other services that are offered. The next section will explore a useful way of capturing the requirements of particular features without specifying how they are implemented on the Web site.

You also need to understand what requirements each proposed feature has in terms of existing or new back-end technology. For example, will a particular service require connection to an existing database, or will it need a new one? Making note of these requirements helps you when you begin to prototype design possibilities and lets you weight the cost of each design element. Similarly, at this stage you can note what special front-end functionality will be needed—for example, that users will need to log in, and the system will need to be able to track users to maintain a user session. This is useful when you start to mock up possible page designs.

An understanding of the people who will be using the system and the ways in which they will be accessing it will let you start writing down technical design requirements for the actual page designs. This process was discussed in detail in Section 4.1 of Chapter 4 and is not repeated here. However, it is at this stage that you can start defining answers to important questions such as:

- What browsers do you need to support?
- What should be the worst-case time for pages to load onto a browser (given slowest supported network connection, slowest computers, and slowest browser)?
- What other page design limitations need to be imposed on the design?

Beyond page-specific details, you can also establish overall performance requirements for the system, to ensure that you can provide appropriate service to users. This means that you need some estimates of the number of users the system will have and of how often (and at what times of the day) those users will access the system. For example, if you are developing an internal intranet system that operates at only one location, you can quickly determine how many users the system will have and the times during the day they will be using it. Later on, when you start to model the design, you can estimate how often users access the system, so you can estimate a *hit rate* per user. Some statistical analysis will then let you estimate the *number of hits per second* that the system will need to handle on the average, and at peak demand times.

The issues are somewhat different if your site is counting on a rapidly growing public audience, because the number of hits per second will likely increase rapidly as the number of users increases.

NOTE This hit rate can often increase faster than linearly with an increasing number of users, particularly for community-oriented sites. This is because each user is likely to stay longer when there are more things to do, and there are more things to do when there are more users at the site!

In this case, you need to estimate a doubling time for the number of users, and make sure that the implemented site has sufficient hardware and bandwidth growth capacity to service this growing number of people. This will be crucial information for the people planning the technical implementation.

You also should try to estimate how noisy the hit rate will be—that is, how likely it is that the number of hits will increase enormously for a short period of time—and how important it is for your site to perform well when the hit rate grows suddenly and dramatically. This type of issue is seen, for example, with day trading sites such as Etrade.com, where sudden stock market trading crises can lead to a 20-fold (or more) increase in requested trades.

You may also need to understand how the site content will be managed and updated so that you can build a system that works well with a specific management model. With large or growing sites, you may wish to consider Web site management systems (see also Section 12.2, Chapter 12), which can automate portions of the management process and reduce the risk of errors by human editors or authors. In either case, you want to analyze carefully how the content will need to be managed once the site is up and running.

Use-Case Analysis

For complex applications, it is often best to capture the essential functional requirements using a technique known as *use-case analysis*. This approach was developed as an object-oriented software-engineering tool for capturing the high-level requirements of a software system. It is a flexible and semi-informal tool designed to be used by nontechnical people, to let them define *what* a system needs to do, not *how* it should do it. The software (or Web site) developers can then take the use cases as a set of requirements for the design, using the documents produced by the use-case analysis to define what the system needs to do.

Basically, a use case is a simple statement describing how an actor in the system accomplishes a specific task, or goal (where an *actor* is someone, or something, that interacts with the Web site or software). Each step in accomplishing that task is often called a *scenario* (object-oriented design experts seem to love defining special-purpose vocabularies), so that a use case consists of a sequence of scenarios that lead to the desired goal.

For example, suppose that we are developing a customer-response Web site. One of the possible use cases will be a customer (the actor) sending in a product query about a specific product. The use case for this could be written as shown in Figure 6.1. Note how the different steps (scenarios) in the use case outline in a very simple way the things that need to be done to successfully complete the use case. At the same time, the *Alternative* section allows for other possible ways that the scenario could evolve. The *Preconditions* section outlines possible things that might need to happen before this use case can start. For example, if this use case could only be used by a customer who has already logged in and identified him- or herself, then this activity (e.g., the "customer logs in" use case) could be a precondition of the "Submit a product query" use case.

A real system will have many use cases and several different actors. In the case of our product customer response system, other actors might include *agents* (the people who handle customer response requests), *managers* (a person who tracks the agents, and makes sure responses are handled in a timely way), and *monitors* (the super manager who is flagged when something goes wrong). Actors are not always people, however: an external piece of software—such as the system that handles incoming or outgoing mail—can itself be an actor because it interacts with the system you are trying to build.

The example use case in Figure 6.1 is pretty simple—use cases don't have to be terribly complicated to get the idea across. If the use case is complicated, or if it interacts strongly with other use cases, you might want to provide more detail than is shown in Figure 6.1. However, it's best to keep things simple at the start, so that you can quickly get a sense of how things work and how different use cases are related. The software experts (who will know all the details of use-case analysis) can help the team simplify and organize the use cases.

Of course, there is more to use-case analysis than this—although this should give you enough to see how it works and get you on the right track. The references at the end of the chapter provide additional information on this topic.

Setting Priorities and Risk Assessment

As you are establishing the functions and services the site might provide, you also need to start estimating the relative importance—and risks—of each component, and document this information in the design specification. The first is needed because you inevitably won't be able to do everything on the list given the allotted time and resources, so that some functions will need to be dropped from the product. However, in the "heat of the battle," it is easy to lose track of the relative importance of specific functions or features—par-

Submit a Product Query

1. Customer chooses to submit a product query.
2. Customer provides e-mail, telephone, and any other needed contact information.
3. Customer identifies the product about which information is wanted.
4. Customer provides a description of the problem.
5. System sends e-mail confirmation to user of their problem submission.
6. System takes customer query and queues it up for a customer support agent.
7. System confirms receipt of support request, provides a tracking number to the user, and tells the customer how long before they can expect a response.

Preconditions: None.
Alternative: User already registered.

Preconditions: User is logged in. The user is logged in so that the system already knows the user's identity when he or she goes to the submission page. The user can thus skip step 2.
Alternative: Product already identified.

Preconditions: Product identity is known. The system knows the identity of the product for which information is being requested (for example, because the user was previously looking at specific product-related information). Thus, at step 3, the system assumes a default product identity. The user can accept or change this product selection.
Alternative: E-mail failure at step 5.

   The system attempts to send mail to the customer at step 5, but discovers that the e-mail address is invalid.

6a. The system informs the user of the error.
6b. The user corrects the e-mail address and resubmits the query.

We then return to the primary scenario at step 5.

Alternative: E-mail failure after step 7.

   Error cannot be reported to user. See "User submits product query with invalid e-mail" scenario.

Figure 6.1 An example use case for the customer support system. Here, the main actor is the customer. The main use case consists of seven scenarios. The *Alternative* use cases show possible variations. The *Preconditions* blocks indicate things that must take place before this use case can occur. For example, an alternative design might require that users be logged in before they can access the "Submit a Product Query" scenario. "Logging in" would then be a precondition.

ticularly if you have invested a lot of time in a feature that someone wants to drop. It is thus best to assign priorities early on, so that you can concentrate work on the most important components—and know which components should be dropped, when push comes to shove.

Moreover, in many large projects, the people doing the development are not necessarily the same people who did the original research and design modeling, so they won't know what items are more important than others, unless this information is formally written down for them.

Risk assessment is a tool for estimating the riskiness of a particular part of the design, the purpose being to identify possible problem areas so that they can be tackled and solved early on. In general, the likelihood of a project's failing is critically related to the number of high-risk design components—so it is essential to identify the highest-risk issues and to work to minimize that risk.

Risk assessment actually comes in three parts: (1) political, (2) financial, and (3) technical. By *political risk*, I mean possible problems associated with the popularity or usability of a proposed feature or service. An example might be a component that records detailed information about users. In this case, the risk is that users will balk at revealing such information, unless the design of the tool—and the privacy policies of the site—guarantee sufficient confidentiality. Alternatively, within a company's intranet, a political risk might be that the designed tool is not used, either because the design does not match the workflow needs of the users, or because the people who will use the tool have no vested interest in its success.

A *financial risk* corresponds to an item that you know how to do, but for which the costs are unknown. For example, you might want to include special database content (such as an interactive map) on your Web site, but not know the cost. You need to properly cost such items so that they can be properly budgeted for.

Technical risk corresponds to possible services or features you don't know how to do and that run a high risk of costing too much in time or money. For example, you may know that you need to integrate the Web application with an internal user database, but you're not sure how to do it, or whether the performance will be satisfactory. Alternatively, you may know how to set up a shopping cart site that can handle a single purchase a second, but you are not sure if the same software will work at the expected rate of 10 purchases a second.

High-risk items will be the first things you test in the prototyping phase, so you can reduce the risk of the item by finding a technical or architectural solution, or by finding there is no easy solution and dropping that feature from the design.

6.2.3 Locating Required Content

Most sites will require external content of some sort—the time is long past that a Web site consists solely of home-grown information or services. Part of the research phase may then be to identify the types of content that are needed and to find places to obtain them. Some such content may come from sources within a company (for example, a product database). However, Web sites will often require other sources of information [e.g., news feeds with articles related to the Web site's function, or Geographical Information System (GIS) databases] that are not owned outright and that will need to be obtained elsewhere. In some cases, a company will know of likely databases or data sources directly related to their business. However, this is not always true for the Web site, particularly if the site reflects a real change from the existing business model. Thus, the Web design team will likely themselves have to search for such information sources.

Such data sources will also come in many shapes and forms—from databases stored on magnetic tape using proprietary data formats to millions of compressed PDF documents to dynamic Internet feeds marked up in XML. In addition, these resources will come with different costs and different currency (i.e., Internet feeds are likely to come in hourly, if not more often, whereas new tape archives of a database are probably made available every three months or so). The research team must analyze the type, quality, costs, and digital formats of the available data sources so that the value of each different type can be properly assessed. These options will need to be presented to the project management team (and possibly to senior management, because these data sources will represent an ongoing cost to the site's operation) who can decide which way to go.

6.3 Roughing Out/Brainstorming the Design

Given a good idea of the purpose of the site and the type of functions you'd like to provide, and the priority and risks associated with different features, the next step is to start trying out some possible site layouts, features, and technologies. The purpose of doing so is threefold:

- To validate some of the initial assumptions about features and functions.
- To get a rough idea of how the site or application should work, so that you can verify this design with possible users.
- To test risky technical problems and research technical solutions for these problems.

Of course, *storyboarding* is best done with some preexisting models for site or Web application architectures. Such models were the topic of Chapter 5.

The best way to validate the overall concept is by storyboarding the design or application. For example, the design team can take a large piece of paper, draw boxes for the various pages on the site, and use lines and arrows to show how the pages are connected—a simple example is shown in Figure 6.2. You also want to annotate the different pages, explaining what each page is generally supposed to do, as well as any special requirements of, or services offered on, that page. If you have special page functions that you want to provide on each page, you can note that also. You can also test functional page sequences (such as "buy this product") by sketching a sequence of pages reflecting the different stages of the purchase.

Storyboarding should be a very experimental, brainstorming-style process, and not one steeped in process—the idea is to obtain interesting and novel ideas about how things might be done without fixing on any particular approach. There are always many ways in which a particular design require-ment can be implemented, and thus potentially millions of ways that all the requirements could be combined to provide the desired services—so, obvi-ously, you're not going to get it right the first time. Storyboarding and brain-storming let you quickly skim over the millions of possible designs that can satisfy the site requirements, and they help you avoid getting stuck with one particular point of view.

Indeed, the storyboarding phase can produce ideas that were not thought of in the research phase. If you have sufficient time, you can take these ideas and research them in detail, producing associated requirements and a risk assessment. If you don't have sufficient time, then you can simply put this idea on the back burner and look into it in more detail at the next site

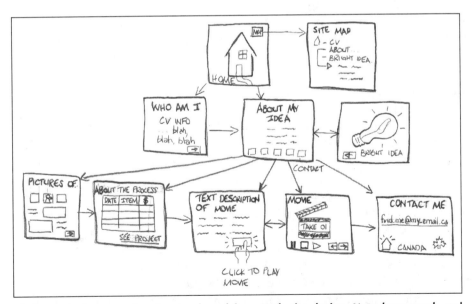

Figure 6.2 An example of a storyboard for a Web site design. Note how rough and ready this is—at this stage you are only concerned with the global way things hook up together, not with the page layout details or how they are connected.

redesign. A team should be encouraged to ask questions of the initial design requirements and should be willing to recommend implementation changes based on the ideas they come up with.

Given some rough storyboards, you can test the designs by pretending to be a site user and by attempting—using the navigational or other tools noted in the storyboard—to perform the types of activities a user is likely to do. Of course, if you've done things right, you already have a good list of these activities from the requirements capturing phase of the project.

For example, if you are designing a site for a bank and you know that visitors are very likely to want to log in and check their bank balance, try exploring this scenario within the storyboard, and see how easy it is to do. If this operation seems to take a lot of clicks, then you can redesign the storyboard to make this operation easier.

Sometimes, it is easier to storyboard using Post-it® Notes or index cards to represent the pages. These can then be posted on a whiteboard, and you can use marker pens to draw and annotate the links between pages. You can even use different colored pens to denote different types of relationships. This approach also makes it easier to rework the design, as you can simply move the Post-it Notes and erase and redraw the lines. However, if the storyboarding phase lasts more than a few days or involves people who do not make it to all the design meetings, you might want to photograph some of the intermediate designs and write down the functions that did or did not work well. This lets you avoid wasting time rehashing issues at later design meetings, and it also helps you avoid repeating already discarded designs.

In some cases, you can even use flowcharting software [such as Visio (www.visio.com), SmartDraw (www.smartdraw.com), or Micrografx Flow-Charter (www.micrografx.com)] to document the designs. This can be useful to provide working drawings for the team implementing the site—indeed, many of these applications can produce HTML output that you can put online as a set of design documents. However, these tools are generally not appropriate during the brainstorming sessions, as they tend to get in the way of the brainstorming process.

This is also the time when the software developers should take some of the technical high-risk issues and try to find technical solutions. For example, if you need software to connect to back-end databases, or need a totally new database, this is the opportunity for the technical staff to look for products that will satisfy the anticipated needs. Similarly, if the site is going to need some sort of content management system, you should be looking into the different sorts of systems that are available and finding out which ones best meet your requirements. The references at the end of this chapter provide links to some well-known content management tools, ranging from HTML editors with site management components (e.g., Microsoft FrontPage, Macromedia Dreamweaver) to complex high-end management systems (e.g., Vignette's StoryServer). These tools are also discussed in Chapter 12.

Note also that, although you may drop support for a feature at this stage or later on, it is useful to know what that feature was going to be. That way, the design (both in the Web interfaces and in the software) can leave room for that feature, so that it can be easily added later on.

6.4 Prototyping the Design

Prototyping is an essential stage in a Web or software design project, and it lets you evaluate—using real pages and real software—whether things will work the way you want. It is a mix of experimentation with different designs and testing of those designs, the goal being to arrive at one or more design options that best match the requirements of the site. The goals in the proto-typing phase are fourfold:

- To test various page layout and design alternatives and see what works best
- To verify the navigational model and make sure the site layout works well
- To test critical functional components of the site and make sure they work properly
- To refine and extend the technical requirements so that the people designing the site will know exactly what to do

6.4.1 Test Page Layout and Design

You now need to work out some real page layouts and designs (for various parts of the Web site) and test how well these work for the user. Graphically, you need to make sure that the content of the page is clear and easy to follow, so that the user can easily find critical information on the page and navigate from the page to elsewhere. Of course, you also want the pages to look good, but usability should always be the primary goal.

One way to test natural usability, due to Thomas S. Tullis (see www.useit.com/alertbox/980517.html), is to create so-called mumbled pages. With mumbled pages, the page text is replaced by nonsense words (our friends "ipsum lorem . . .") so that the functions on the page are defined only by the page layout and not by the words. Using mumble text, you can quickly create different possible mock-ups for a page and test which one works best by asking test users to identify the main navigational components of the page. Because you don't need real Web pages to do this, the design can be quickly laid out with standard graphics or page layout programs, making this a very easy process.

Of course, you also need to create HTML versions of promising page designs and make sure that they can satisfy the speed, accessibility, and other page design–specific requirements. Indeed, the last phase of prototyping may involve iterative changes to the HTML designs as you try to balance functionality with design quality. At the same time, you can prototype and test any page scripting components that might be needed across the site.

Near-to-final versions of the page designs can be converted into page templates, as described in Chapter 4. The implementation team can then work with these templates to finalize the design and create working templates for the staff who create the content (or who use the templates in script-generated pages).

With application-based Web designs, there will be many cases (e.g., form layout, URL string construction, user identification text, etc.) where the page design is defined in large part by the software that creates or interacts with the page. In these cases, the Web page designers will have to work closely with the software designers to ensure that the two designs mesh smoothly.

6.4.2 Verifying Usability and Navigational Model

Good site navigation depends both on the clarity of the page design and on appropriate navigational links between parts of the site. You can verify the overall navigational design by creating mock-ups of the proposed site architecture, and then by asking users to navigate through the design to perform specific tasks. These tasks will be the ones you previously determined to be the critical functions at the site. You can monitor the users (e.g., watch them as they work) to see how quickly they can perform the tasks and can ask qualitative questions about their perceptions of the process. Mock-ups should be simple—you don't need all the functionality or fine graphic design—but you want to include enough graphical layout to accurately reflect how the pages will look to real users.

Ideally, you would like to compare several different designs and find out which one is best. Practically, however, there are too many things to vary at one time (e.g., graphic layout, organizational structure, etc.) for this to be practical. It is thus best to stick with a few basic designs and tweak only the site architecture, looking at each step for improvements (or the opposite) in navigability.

If there are critical Web application services as part of the site, you want to test the usability of the pages that implement these services. For example, if you are offering personalized Web page services, then the pages by which a user provides personal data will be crucial to the success of this application.

You thus want to prototype and test these pages and make sure that you've made this part of the site particularly easy to use.

In this latter case, you can test the design using nonfunctional mock-ups and, thus, don't need to write a lot of software. However, the software designers will need to be involved in this process, because they will need to write the software that actually implements the designs you choose.

This verification phase is absolutely essential when designing Web application services for an intranet, because it is critical that the tools, users, and business process work well together. You therefore must test your prototype designs with real users, making sure that each user can successfully (and easily) perform their tasks.

6.4.3 Testing Critical Software

At the same time as you are testing page and site design approaches, you also want to test critical (i.e., high-risk) software components of the site and make sure that they work. During the prototyping phase, the software team should be busily developing prototype back-end software needed to drive the various features of the Web application. This testing phase will indicate which components are likely to work properly, given the time and other constraints on the project—and which will not. This helps reduce the risk that things will blow up during the design-and-implementation phase—indeed, if you're lucky, things will blow up here. You can then choose to drop features (if they are not critical to the application) or to allocate extra people and resources to the problem (if it is absolutely critical to the project's success).

This is also the time when you should be selecting and testing the programming languages, databases, and other tools with which you will build the Web side of your application. In general, scripting languages such as perl or python, or page scripting languages such as ColdFusion, ASP, JSP, or PHP (see Chapter 12 for a description of these different packages), lead to faster development of prototype Web interfaces and are often quite sufficient for building the final application. The choices are often quite pragmatic, based on the skill set of the developers and on how well these tools integrate with the other components (databases, server software, and server operating systems) that you will be using.

Obviously, these different activities are all tightly coupled: Changing the page design may lead to architectural changes in the site, whereas dropping features may lead to changes in the page design and site organization. However, dropping a feature does not mean that it is gone forever—you may revive it later on, when you have time to update the site and incorporate new components. If you're careful, you can leave a place in the design for an unimplemented feature, making it easier to add the feature back in at a later date.

This is also a good time to test-develop any special multimedia content (e.g., streamed audio or video, or Macromedia Flash animations) that the site may use in quantity. It is generally inexpensive to implement only one such component, but the total cost (and the financial risk) can increase dramatically if your needs many dozens of them. Developing prototypes up front can help you realistically estimate the total cost for all the desired content.

6.4.4 Refining and Extending Requirements

Once the prototyping phase is drawing to a close, the team is ready to start designing and implementing the site. Before doing so, however, the team needs to prepare a set of formal requirements and design documents for the design team to use while the site is being built. This set of requirements should include:

- A list of required features (the use cases).
- A list of page design, rendering speed, and other requirements (as described in Chapter 4).
- An outline of the desired site architecture, with example page layout templates for main page in the design.
- An initial graphical design specification, with a color palette and some example pages.
- An overview of the software design model and of how the design will interact with the Web pages.
- An idealized specification for the Web pages attached to back-end software, with templates.

The first two items reflect hard design requirements that the site (however it is built) must satisfy. The third and fourth items provide pretty firm guidelines for the design and layout, based on the design prototypes. Of course, here, there is somewhat more flexibility, because the design can be changed somewhat without damaging the usability of the site.

The final two items provide software guidelines for the developers who will be writing the server-side programs (and possibly page scripting programs as well) and some suggestions for how the interfaces can best be designed. However, in the rush to get things done, it may be easier to change Web designs than it is to write the software, so you want to give the designers more flexibility here, so that the project can be finished on schedule.

At the same time, the design and implementation team will be handed any raw data (or content) to be used in the Web site, information about data feeds (for dynamically fed data), and the various pieces of software to be used in building the back-end components.

6.5 Design, Implementation, and Testing

The design-and-implementation phase should now be easy, because all the possible problems were worked through in previous phases. Or, as is commonly said, "What possibly could go wrong *now*?" The answer, hopefully, is not much—if you've done the preceding tasks well, the likelihood of something bad jumping up and biting you in the foot is small. However, it can still happen, so you need to carefully monitor the implementation phase so you can quickly detect when something is amiss.

Moreover, by this point, the client is probably desperate that the project be up and running as quickly as possible—no matter how quickly you can implement a site, it is invariably slower than desired. It is thus important to use a controlled implementation process that reduces the risk of errors, maximizes efficiency, and lets you set a real and realistic launch date for the site.

6.5.1 Assigning Roles, Responsibilities, and Timelines

When you begin the implementation stage, the number of people involved in the project generally grows significantly, as graphics designers, writers, and programmers come on board to finalize the design and implement the site. To coordinate all these activities, you need to establish a formal production schedule that defines the tasks to be done, the people who will work on each task, and *milestones* for completion of those tasks (for example, "all graphics for part X of the site will be finished on day Y"). In doing so, you will also need to estimate the level of *connectedness* of the tasks, because some tasks cannot begin until others are successfully completed. You also need to assign staff to the different tasks and estimate how long each task will take to complete.

Doing this helps you stay aware of how well (or not!) things are going—with a large project it is impossible to keep track of the overall status without measures such as these. By comparing the actual progress on each task with scheduled milestones, you can tell when and why things are behind schedule. You can sit down with the relevant staff and work out how best to get things back on track. This may mean moving staff from an area that is ahead of schedule to one that is behind, or it may mean dropping features so that you can get the project released on schedule. You may also be able to delay the launch date, although this is often the hardest option of all!

With small projects, you can often manage the process using Web pages listing the tasks and people involved—the staff can edit the pages to update everyone on the status of the different components. It is also often useful to have a plasticized time management sheet posted in a public place, outlining the various tasks, the people assigned to the task, and the current status (e.g., percentage completed). This helps to keep people aware of how things are going overall.

With large projects, you may wish to use project management support tools, such as Microsoft Project (there are many others), Gantt charts (that show the task schedules and the relationships between tasks), or other approaches. Although these tools are complicated to use, large projects often have tightly coupled components, and it is hard to see how to adjust the development process without software to help analyze the ramifications of possible choices.

Project management is both an art and a skill. Art is hard to learn without practice (and some innate talent!), but skills can be learned by taking a project management course. Microsoft, IBM, and others offer courses on software project management, and the skills they teach are also largely applicable to Web-based projects. The "References" section also lists some books that go in more detail into both the technical and artistic sides of software project management.

6.5.2 Before You Implement

Before you start implementing, you need to organize the results from the previous activities so that you can structure the implementation process. You also need to finalize the graphics and page layout designs for the various classes of pages on the site. Last, you need to put in place a process so that you can properly farm out the development work, monitor the development process, and detect problems as they occur.

Finalize the Design

The first thing to do is to finalize the graphic and page layout designs for the different pages on the site. The place to start is with the page layout and design templates inherited from the prototyping phase, as they were almost what you want, barring some fine-tuning of the markup or graphics. Typically, you will go to the various classes of pages in the navigational hierarchy of the site and create template designs for those pages.

This is where a component-based markup design approach, discussed in Chapter 4, comes to great advantage. Component-based designs translate naturally into overall page templates, or into templates for specific content components (for example, as a specification for the markup that goes inside a navigation bar). Reusing these templates means that you reduce the risk of introducing errors in markup. Also, reusing these templates means that you can use sitewide CSS style sheets to control the global look and feel of the site.

Make sure to test these designs with the testing approaches discussed a bit later. You will also want to get senior management to sign off on the look and feel of the final design. You definitely don't want to surprise people with the final product—project sponsors, system users, and all other important stake-holders must be involved throughout the process so that the look or function-ality of the site surprises no one.

Implement Back-End Hardware

At the same time you are finalizing the layout and design, someone should be getting the Web servers up and running. Ideally, you should set up three different classes of servers:

> **Development servers** for development of completely new site designs and software (e.g., *dev.mycompany.com*)
>
> **Update servers** for doing regular fixes and updates to the running site (e.g., *update.mycompany.com*)
>
> **Production servers** that are seen by the outside world (e.g., *www.my-company.com*)

In principle, these different services could reside on the same machine, but under different domain names. However, in practice, it is best to keep them on separate machines if at all possible. This reduces the risk that someone working on the development or update servers will accidentally break the Web pages or software your customers are using. This is particularly true if your site uses a lot of software, because it is generally hard to upgrade soft-ware on a machine without affecting all applications running there.

At the same time, you want to make sure that the hardware and network connection speeds match the anticipated site load. Also, the technical people implementing the site will need to know the anticipated load so that they can design the hardware to support this load level.

Establish a Testing Process and Environment

You will need to establish a testing procedure to verify that the site looks and functions the way you want. Various page-specific requirements, and some of the page-specific details you may need to test, were described in Section 4.1 of Chapter 4. You also need ways to test how the functional components of the site work so that you can verify that these aspects of the site work cor-rectly. There may also be nonbrowser-accessible features (e.g., e-mail notifica-tion systems, tools that automatically place advertising graphics, or automated tools that analyze log files to produce site usage statistics). You need to test these features also.

If the project is large or complex, you may wish to obtain software that automates aspects of the testing process. For general Web site testing, these tools come in three common varieties:

Load or stress testing tools. These tools stress the Web site (or Web application) with repeated requests for pages. These tools test performance under heavy loads.

Functional testing tools. These tools test that the particular parts of the site work correctly, for example by testing links, testing for bad markup or missing images, or testing that XHTML forms connect to the back-end software correctly. A sophisticated functional testing tool can even test that Web pages connected to back-end functions (e.g., search engines, forms, etc.) work correctly, although many functional tools are not that clever.

Regression testing tools. These tools test that the Web site functionality does not change as the underlying software is modified, by comparing newly generated pages with those obtained on a previous occasion. Typically, a person first "walks" the regression testing system through a sequence of pages and makes sure that the response pages are correct. This response sequence is stored in the testing system, which can then automatically repeat the sequence, testing at each page to make sure that the application still returns the correct information.

The "References" section at the end of the chapter provides links to some common tools and to Web sites with additional information on testing tools and procedures. Software developers will be familiar with these testing approaches and will know of several other tools and approaches necessary when developing complex software. Consequently, before you set up such tools, you will want to talk with the software staff to find out what they are using and if it can also be used for Web site testing. In general, these tools will need to be installed and managed by the software staff, so you don't want to give them unneeded extra work.

You will also need a way of tracking the problems that show up, so that you can note what problems occur, and when they are fixed. If the site is small, you can probably get by with a mailing list to which all bug reports are sent and to which all developers are members. You could then use *Hypermail* (www.hypermail.org) or a similar tool to provide a Web-browsable listing of these mail messages, so that developers can see a complete list of all the reported problems and note whether problems have been dealt with and by whom.

If the project is large, or if you are running many different projects at the same time, then you will want to set up a proper software-managed bug tracking system. These tools let developers report problems, assign problems to particular staff, prioritize problems, and mark the status of problems as they are being worked on. Such tools are invaluable communication devices for large projects and make it much easier to manage problem tracking and resolution.

There are several commercial bug and problem tracking systems, many of which were designed for software development projects, although some also allow a more general help-desk style of support. The "References" section at the end of this chapter lists some common open-source tools. Some of these systems (*Bugzilla* from the Mozilla organization, and the GNU *GNATS* package, for example) are open-source packages with simple Web interfaces—these can be implemented easily without buying additional software.

Organize and Prepare Written Content

Someone, of course, has to write all the stuff that goes into the Web pages—and if it's not coming from some contracted external source, then you will need to do this yourself. Typically, the source material for your content will come from many different places, and you will need to integrate this content so that it all fits together smoothly. This is a job for a writer or editor who is familiar with Web design, so if you have a lot of content to convert over, you will need someone proficient in that task.

Typically, the content will flow into the page templates you have designed, although often a single, long file will need to be split into multiple Web pages. Often, this will mean converting the source documents from their original formats (e.g., Microsoft Word, WordPerfect, PageMaker, etc.) into HTML—or with newer systems, into XML as an intermediary format—and then processing the HTML (or XML) to create the desired pages. Most word processors can save files as HTML, but you will then need to process the result to remove unneeded markup and to integrate the content into your own page templates. The tools you use will then depend on the page editing and content management tools (if any) you are using.

The site also may require that some content be distributed in alternate formats, such as Adobe PDF files or as Word documents. These instances should be noted when the site requirements are being established.

The content developers should test their pages as they go, making sure that they have not created broken links or bad markup. It is important that all developers (Web page or software) understand that they are responsible for testing the components they create.

Configure Content Management System

If the site will use a content management system, now is the time to get it up and running. Ideally, you should use this tool as you are building the site, because this will help you debug the package and test how well it works. This knowledge will be particularly useful if you have to train those who will use the system once the site is up and running.

If you are implementing a new content management system, then it is likely that part of the project includes configuring this system, training users, and providing documentation for those users. These activities can, of course, begin now.

6.5.3 Phased Implementation

You are now ready to build the site. Basically, you just want to tell people to start and let them develop as quickly as possible! However, you also want to make sure the process proceeds in a controlled manner, so that you can monitor progress, watch for problems, and test things as you go.

The site being developed should be tested on a regularly scheduled basis, so that each developer knows when to polish up his or her part and get it ready for testing. At each testing phase you should test the pages and software according to the testing procedures defined previously in the development cycle, noting any problems in the problem-tracking system. This ensures that the problems are known and can be worked on.

Where possible, you also want to branch off regular *milestones* of the project—where a milestone is a snapshot of the site or application at a particular stage of development reflecting important new features. Then, while the developers continue work on the site and content, you can show the milestones to the senior management team (or client) and, where appropriate, test it with prospective users and stakeholders. This is very important—you and your people may think that things look and work great, but the people who really count (in particular, the users) may have decidedly different opinions. If you regularly test and verify the site components as you go, you will catch such problems early on before they have the chance to grow into big, difficult-to-solve crises.

Development is more or less finished when the pages and software are finished, and when most of the bugs have been fixed. Of course, you will never fix all the bugs, and at some point the management team will need to decide which bugs won't be fixed and which will be handled as enhancements or fixes for future versions. Indeed, as the development and testing process proceeds, people will invariably come up with new ideas that could be incorporated into the site. These should be noted as feature enhancements, for consideration in the next version of the site.

6.6 Deployment, Maintenance, and Management

When you are ready to deploy the site, you first need to test-deploy it to a test server, and then rerun all your tests on that server. This helps make sure that the process of installing the new version onto a new machine works as expected, and that no data or program code was inadvertently omitted.

If this test is successful, then you are ready to deploy the new system on the production server. Even now, however, you should be wary of possible problems. If you don't have an existing site, you can simply copy the system over to the new server and retest it, just to ensure that everything went okay. If it did, then the site is up and you are ready to start publicizing and marketing it.

After you've deployed the new site, you want to actually have two (or more) versions of the site up and running: (1) the *production* site seen by the outside world, and (2) one or more update servers used to develop site upgrades. The update sites will be used to make regular updates to the site content and to develop patches, fixes, and upgrades to the existing software. The development team can now go back to the drawing board—and the first phase of the development cycle—and start thinking about developing the next generation of the Web site.

If you already have an existing site, then the process of deploying an entirely new site will be much more complicated that the outline just provided. In particular, if the site already runs complex software that requires user tracking, you will need to take special care so as not to interfere with users who are already using the system. Indeed, you may need to schedule a downtime for the site, so that you can make changes without affecting any users. Make sure to schedule—and publicize—this downtime well in advance!

6.6.1 Ongoing Maintenance Policies

Once the site is up and running, the site managers need to do regular maintenance on the site. Maintenance involves many tasks: adding updated content; fixing spelling mistakes; adding new graphics; or upgrading software to newer, more stable versions. Regular maintenance could also involve fixing technical problems with the site that simply could not be fixed by the time the site was formally released.

All such work should be done on the update server, which will be a system exactly like the production server, but with the updated content or software and not publicly accessible. After changes are made, you can test the update server to make sure that the changes didn't break the site. Once the changes have passed the tests, you can publish the changes to the production server, bringing the updated Web site online.

Because sites are expected to be dynamic, updates should be regular events. Moreover, it is safer to do small, regular updates than irregular, large-scale ones. This is because the probability of something going wrong grows rapidly with the number of changes you make. Making smaller, incremental changes reduces the risk of introducing a major problem with any given update.

However, there is always the possibility that something will go wrong. To protect yourself from this possibility, your site management tools should let you undo an update and return to the previous incarnation of the site. Then, if a problem is found that can't easily be fixed, you can back off the change and return to the previous version. This process can be quite complicated for large Web sites and applications (and you were wondering why complex site management systems are so expensive?). However, for small sites, this task can be as simple as making a backup copy of the existing site before it is updated. Then, if something goes wrong, you can simply replace the existing collection of pages with the backed-up copy.

Monitoring and Performance Testing

Once a site is up, it needs to be continuously monitored to make sure that users can access the server(s), that response time is adequate, and that all the dynamic content is working properly. Some of this work can be done in-house, although such services can also be bought from Web service firms—some such companies are listed in the "References" section. We revisit this issue again in Section 12.1.4 of Chapter 12.

You also need to monitor log files and analyze user usage patterns. Analyzing server logs will tell you a lot about the parts of the site that are popular and can give you some estimates of how the users are exploring the site. More such information is available if you track users using HTTP cookies or some other form of session management, although actually mining this information to extract useful data can be a slow and costly process. There are some Web server log analysis tools that can help (see Chapter 12, Section 12.1.3), but most provide only simple forms of analysis. If you are really serious about analyzing this data, then the best option is to hire a statistical analyst who can design analytical data-mining tools to effectively analyze the data you are collecting.

Last, you want to be sure to do regular link checking and maintenance—there is nothing more unprofessional than a site containing broken links! There are many automated link-checking tools available, and every site should incorporate automated link testing as part of the ongoing site testing process. Some such tools are discussed in Chapter 12, Section 12.1.2.

6.6.2 Evaluation and Feedback

Of course, you also need to evaluate the site or application. If this is an internal Web application project, you can simply interview the users and other stakeholders of the system and explicitly ask them what works or doesn't. You can also monitor users while they use the system and determine, by observation, those features that work, those that do not, and those that work but are confusing. In addition, user feedback or feedback from training or support staff who are supporting the users can tell you a lot about how well things are working and what needs to be improved for the next version.

Note that you can also test your initial assumptions about how the system would be used against actual usage patterns. Often, a Web application represents a true paradigm shift in the way an organization operates. As a result, the organizational models upon which your Web application was designed may quickly become outdated as the organization changes as a consequence of the Web application. For example, the application may have been designed to work with a multilayer management model (e.g., managers, submanagers, etc.), but the new Web system may end up causing a flattening of the management hierarchy, making this model obsolete. This may mean that you need to redesign how the application works, to reflect the new approach.

If the site serves the general public, it can be harder to measure user satisfaction, or determine if users are actually using the site in the way you expected or wished. For example, I know of a Web site developer that originally thought their service, because of the enormous number of users, was very successful. Unfortunately, a more detailed analysis of usage patterns showed that most people were not using the system as intended (a product marketing site). Instead, they were using the system's bulletin board tool as a chat system and were bypassing the content entirely.

For sites open to the public, the best ways to determine how the site is being used are by careful analysis of the server log, cookie or other data-tracking usage across the system, and by observing actual user focus groups. Log analysis (using the tools described in Chapter 12) can also provide useful information about how the site is being used. Focus groups, on the other hand, let you address very specific questions about how the site is used or perceived and are an excellent way of finding out the truth about your site.

Everything you learn is grist for a redesign of the site. Indeed, a Web site's effective lifetime is well under two years, so that by the time a new (or redesigned) site is launched, you already need to be working on the next version. Therefore, based on the information that you gain at this stage, it is already time to go back to Section 6.1 (*Understanding/Defining the Project*)—and start the process again!

6.7 References

BOOKS ON WEB PROJECT MANAGEMENT

Secrets of Successful Web Sites: Project Management on the World Wide Web, by David Siegel, Hayden Books (1997)—A great collection of case studies, plus some useful observations on how the process works in real-world environments.

Collaborative Web Development: Strategies and Best Practices for Web Teams, by Jessica R. Burdman, Addison-Wesley (1999)—I am afraid I haven't read this book, but others have told me that it is an excellent choice for anyone thinking of a career in Web project management.

Death March: The Complete Software Developer's Guide to Surviving "Mission Impossible" Projects, by Edward Yourdon, Prentice-Hall (1997)—A thoughtful yet entertaining discussion of how software (read: Web) projects really work, with useful guidelines for managing such projects.

Web Navigation: Designing the User Experience, by Jennifer Fleming, O'Reilly and Associates (1998)—Chapter 3 has a nice discussion of the Web site development process. Examples of the site design process are found throughout the book.

Microsoft Solutions Framework (training program; see www.microsoft.com/MSF/courses/taking.htm). Microsoft teaches a series of courses on software project management, and many of the skills and processes are directly relevant to managing Web projects. Similar courses are offered by IBM (see www-5.ibm.com/services/learning/uk/courses/ms02u.html) and no doubt by others.

USER DEMOGRAPHICS AND OTHER WEB SURVEYS

www.gvu.gatech.edu/user_surveys/	10 years of Web user surveys
www.internetstats.com/	General demographics
www.nua.ie/surveys/	General demographics
http://freespeech.org/terrabay/	International usage statistics
http://glreach.com/globstats/	International usage statistics
www.emarketer.com	General demographics
http://cyberatlas.internet.com/	General demographics
www.statmarket.com	General demographics and marketing
www.upsdell.com/BrowserNews/stat.htm	Browser usage statistics
www.browserwatch.com	Browser usage statistics
www.webreference.com/internet/statistics.html	List of Web demographics/market research resources
www.internetnews.com/IAR/index.html	Advertising/marketing report
www.wilsonweb.com/webmarket/	Web marketing resources
www.jup.com/home.jsp	Jupiter Communications

www.neilsen.com	Nielsen online
www.iab.net/	Internet Advertising Bureau
http://home.netscape.com/ads/links.html	Web advertising references

USE-CASE ANALYSIS

UML Distilled: A Brief Guide to the Standard Object Modeling Language, by Martin Fowler with Kendall Scott (Second Edition), Addison-Wesley-Longman (2000)—Chapter 3 has a short, elegant introduction to use cases.

usecasehelp.com/	General information (a bit technical)
www.pols.co.uk/usecasezone/	Collected articles (less technical)
members.aol.com/acockburn/ papers/usecases.htm	Use-case analysis guidelines
members.aol.com/acockburn/ papers/uctempla.htm	Simple use-case templates
www.awl.com/cseng/titles/ 0-201-89542-0/articles/	Some nice articles

WEB SITE AND SOFTWARE TESTING

Client Server Software Testing on the Desk Top and the Web, by Daniel J. Mosley, Prentice-Hall (1999)—A good text on software testing of client-server and Web-based software. This is an advanced book, but it will be useful to anyone who has to manage a large-scale Web software development project. There are many other books that cover this topic; you can find them by searching most bookstore Web sites.

wwwlis.iei.pi.cnr.it/LIS/Overview/index.html	Software testing tutorial
www2.umassd.edu/cisw3/coursepages/ pages/CIS311/LectureMat/test/test1.html	Testing overview
www.data-dimensions.com/testersnet/ docs/web_testing.htm	Article on Web site testing
www.data-dimensions.com/testersnet/ docs/web_testing2.htm	Another article on Web site testing
www.data-dimensions.com/testersnet/ archive.htm	List of articles on testing

WEB SITE TESTING

www.webperfcenter.com/	Server load testing
www.radview.com/	Server load testing

www.oclc.org/webart/	WebArt: functional, regression, and load testing
www.segue.com/	SiklTest: functional and regression testing
www.soft.com/Products/Web/	Various tools
www.mercuryinteractive.com/products/	Various tools
www.softwareqatest.com/qatweb1.html	List of tools
www.aptest.com/index2.html?resources2.html	List of tools

BUG/PROBLEM TRACKING TOOLS
Web-Based Mailing List Archives

www.hypermail.org	Hypermail (open source)
www.oac.uci.edu/indiv/ehood/mhonarc.html	Mhonarc (open source)
www.ii.com/internet/robots/procmail/	Procmail (open source)

Bug Tracking Systems

www.alumni.caltech.edu/~dank/gnats.html	GNATS (open source)
www.mozilla.org/bugs/source.html	Bugzilla (Mozilla tool; open source)
www.iac.honeywell.com/Pub/Tech/CM/PMTools.html	General list of tools

WEB SITE PERFORMANCE MONITORING

www.wrqwam.com/prodserv/	Various tools
sitealert.computacenter.com/index.html	External uptime monitoring
www.mercuryinteractive.com/products/	Various tools
www.softwareqatest.com/qatweb1.html#MONITORING	List of tools

WEB SITE CONTENT MANAGEMENT TOOLS (SEE ALSO CHAPTER 12)
Large-Scale Management Systems

www.vignette.com	StoryServer
www.documentum.com	Documentum
www.ebt.com/dynabase/index.htm	Dynabase/Dynaweb
www.sitestation.com	SiteStation
www.infooffice.com	RedDot
www.symantec.com/vpage/	Visual Page

www.mks.com/products/wi/	Web Integrity
www.egrail.com	Egrail (open source)

Small-Scale Management Systems

www.macromedia.com/software/ dreamweaver/	Macromedia Dreamweaver
www.microsoft.com/frontpage/	Microsoft FrontPage
www.hotmetalpro.com	Softquad HoTMetal Pro

Content Management Information Sites

dmoz.org/Computers/Software/ Internet/Site_Management/ Content_Management/	General list of tools
www.xmlsoftware.com/dms/	XML-based tools

CHAPTER 7

Internet Networking

Topics/Concepts Covered: IP protocol, TCP and UDP, IP addresses, domain names, domain name system (DNS), security and firewalls, IP masquerading

Of course, the Web runs on top of the Internet—the worldwide computer network that connects all the machines together. Most of the time (at least to users) this network is invisible: Things magically work properly (well, most of the time), and users do not have to worry about why this is so.

However, Web designers—and particularly Web *application* designers—cannot afford such blissful ignorance. This is because Web designers must make use of core Internet issues—such as domain names, numeric IP addresses, port numbers, virtual host addresses, and so on—and must consequently understand what these things are and how they work. Furthermore, with most fledgling companies, a Web application designer is often a jack of all trades, called on not only to design the new Web site, but also to help determine how the Web server network should be designed and implemented. Thus, it is important to understand some of the issues associated with network design and security, if only to be able to understand when important issues need to be outsourced to networking or security experts!

These topics are the goals of this chapter. Section 7.1 explains the basics of the Internet protocols: how the Internet works, how machines are addressed, and how messages get passed from one machine to another. Section 7.2 then reviews standard Internet services: These are the services (such as HTTP, FTP, or DNS) that the Web applications you create actually use. Finally, Section 7.3

looks at physical network design issues and briefly covers topics such as network security and Web server management. If you do not expect to be involved in such issues, then you can easily skip this section.

Of course, this chapter can cover these topics only in a very superficial way—there are specialty books covering the many issues related to Internet networking. If you are interested in finding out more, check out the references at the end of the chapter, which point to some starting points for learning more on these topics.

7.1 IP: The Core Internet Protocol

The Internet consists of a family of software services designed for delivering data between computers connected on a network. Technically, these services act as an *abstraction layer* between the computers and the network. In less technical words, this simply means that the messages passed between computers are handled identically on all computers, independent of the type of computer or operating system and of the physical network (wire or fiber-optic, Ethernet, token ring, or ATM) carrying the data. Thus, Windows PCs, IBM mainframes, PCs running Windows or Linux, Sun or other Unix systems, cell phones, and more can all send, receive, and forward messages on the Internet, once equipped with the right software.

The core communication tool of all Internet software is called the *Internet Protocol* (IP). This provides the base-level functions required of all Internet software—namely, the ability to send data from one machine to another. With IP, data is sent as a collection of *packets,* more formally called *datagrams.* You can think of a packet as an envelope, with address information on the cover and data inside. When a computer wants to send data to another computer, it constructs IP packets, addresses them with both the address of the destination and the sender (just as on an envelope), and sends them on their way. Internet software running on the other computers on the Internet network can read the address labels of such packets and can decide what to do based on the address information. In essence, a computer can do one of three things with a packet:

- Accept it (if the packet is addressed to this machine)
- Ignore it (if the packet is not addressed to this machine)
- Forward it on to the destination (if the machine acts as a *gateway* between different networks and the address on the packet indicates that the packet needs to go outside)

Machines that connect one network to another are often called *gateways,* since they act as gateways between networks. Machines designed specifically

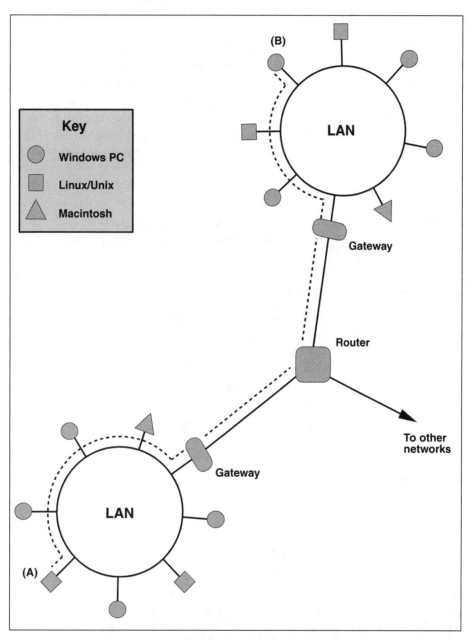

Figure 7.1 A schematic illustration of a portion of an Internet network. The machine labeled G is a gateway that connects the local area network (LAN) to the outside world.

to act as gateways between multiple networks are typically called *routers*, since they reroute packets to their intended destinations. An illustration of this is shown in Figure 7.1.

Of course, the Internet packets are actually carried on some kind of physical network (wires, fiber-optic cable, microwave, or satellite links), which uses some sort of physical layer transport mechanism [Ethernet, token ring, Asynchronous Transfer Mode (ATM), for example]. This lower-level hardware and software on which Internet software works is often called the *network access layer.* Figure 7.2 illustrates how IP is built on top of this layer—and how IP-derived tools are in turn built on top of IP, as discussed later in the chapter.

7.1.1 Numeric IP Addresses

Each IP packet has a data *header* (essentially the envelope part) that contains the return and destination addresses for the packet, plus some additional

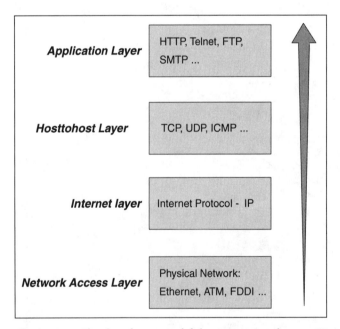

Figure 7.2   The four-layer model for Internet software. IP packets, defined in the *Internet layer,* travel over the physical mechanisms (e.g., wires and fibers) of the *network access layer,* which uses different transport software [Ethernet, ATM, Fiber Distributed Data Interface (FDDI), etc.] to move the data. You can think of the Internet layer as an abstraction layer that lets IP software work independently of the physical systems that transport the data. *Host-to-host layer* IP protocols define special types of IP packets, while higher-level *application layer* protocols define special syntax rules for the data carried inside the packets.

bookkeeping data to help the computer understand what to do with different types of packets. These addresses are more formally called *numeric IP addresses,* often shortened to *IP addresses.* Written in decimal form, they are written as four numbers separated by periods, such as:

```
132.206.9.1
```

Each number must be between 0 and 255 and corresponds to a single byte of a 32-bit address. This 32-bit word address space in principle supports 2^{32}, or 4,294,967,296, unique addresses. However, many of these numbers are reserved for special uses (to identify special types of networks, for testing purposes, etc.), so the number that can be used in practice is less than this.

Physically, the rightmost digits correspond to local address information and the leftmost to global information. Thus, given an office full of computers, they will probably have addresses such as 132.206.9.1, 132.206.9.2, 132.206.9.3, and so on. The numbers you can use depend on the type of network you have and the global numbers your network was assigned. For example, being assigned the network 142.321.21.* would mean you could assign some 254 unique numbers inside your own local network (the numbers 0 and 255 are reserved for special purposes and can't be used in an address).

It is important to realize, however, that every IP address must be *unique*— no two computers on the Internet can use the same IP address. Thus, when a computer is attached to a local network, the local network administrator must configure the machine to use an as-yet-unused address.

Of course, there is nothing to stop a single machine from having more than one address. Indeed, *gateway* machines or *routers* that connect one network to another generally have two or more addresses—one connected to the internal network, the others connected to different networks and to the world outside. On the computer, each of these different connections is typically called a *network interface.*

IP addresses do more than identify a machine—they also provide *routing* information explaining where on the Internet each machine lies. Thus, if machine A in Figure 7.1 wishes to send a message to machine B, the numeric address for machine B helps machines in between determine the most appropriate way to forward the message.

IP does not guarantee delivery of the packets. Packets can be lost in transit, or the data in them could be damaged in some way before they are delivered. Reliable delivery is provided by higher-level transport protocols, discussed in the next section. IP does, however, guarantee that packets do not wander the Internet forever, like an IP Flying Dutchman. To avoid this, every IP packet header starts out with a special positive integer value called the *time to live* (TTL), which is decreased by 1 very time the packet is forwarded from one router or gateway to another. Once this number reaches 0, the next gateway machine or router that sees the packet will remove the packet from the network and throw it away.

7.1.2 IP Transport Mechanisms: TCP and UDP

IP provides the fundamental services—packet addressing and transport—but is not in itself sufficient for most Internet-based applications. For example, most applications (such as Web services) want to deliver large messages, not small packets, to a specific destination. Such applications also need to be able to guarantee the delivery of data—or, failing that, they need to be informed that delivery failed so that they can try again.

The extra information is provided by the *Transmission Control Protocol* (*TCP*), which defines additional transmission control information that is placed *inside* an IP packet, just after the IP header (envelope) data. Indeed, if you were to look at an IP packet containing TCP data, you would see that it consists of an IP header followed by a TCP header followed by the actual data. Alternatively, you could think of this as an IP envelope that in turn contains a TCP envelope that in turn contains the data being sent.

The extra information in a TCP header allows for explicit *connections* between computers and the controlled, reliable, transmission of data from one computer to the other. To do this, TCP (often written as TCP/IP to reflect the fact that TCP is built on top of IP) provides the following services:

Message decomposition/reconstitution. TCP can take a long message and break it into fragments, each fragment placed in a single TCP/IP packet. These packets are then numbered so the receiver can reassemble them in the correct order to reconstruct the complete message.

Reliable transfer. Upon receipt of a packet, the recipient sends back to the sender an acknowledgment message, effectively saying something like "I received TCP packet number 231." If the sender does not receive such an acknowledgment, it assumes that the packet was not delivered safely and resends it. Only after acknowledgments have been sent back for all the sent packets will the sender conclude that the message was successfully delivered. Furthermore, TCP sends additional information (a checksum) in each packet, which the receiver uses to check whether the packet contents were damaged in transit.

Multiplexed communication. To allow a single computer to run many different TCP-based services at the same time, TCP supports the concept of host *ports*—essentially different subaddresses on a computer. Thus, with TCP, each packet contains the IP address and the *port number* from which the packet was sent, plus the IP address and port number to which the packet is being sent. This is illustrated in Figure 7.3.

Explicit connections between machines. To manage all the preceding issues (tracking all the sent/received packets, allocating port numbers,

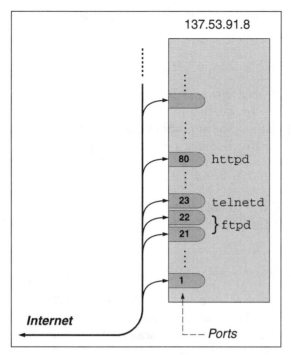

137.53.91.8

Internet

Ports

Figure 7.3   An illustration of a single computer listening for messages coming in on different ports.

etc.), TCP software keeps track of information while the data is being transferred. In Internet terminology, this is referred to as a *connection.* In other words to transfer data to or from a machine, TCP must first make a *connection* between a port on the local machine and a port on the remote one. TCP then breaks the connection when the transaction is complete.

Example: Browser Connections to Web Servers

Most of these issues are visually demonstrated by the information displayed in a browser's status bar when a user requests data from a URL. This is because the Web's HyperText Transfer Protocol (HTTP) uses TCP/IP to send and receive data between Web clients (such as browsers) and Web servers. When a Web browser connects to a remote Web server, it connects to a specific port on that server. Indeed, port numbers can be explicitly given in a URL, as described in Chapter 8. While this connection is being made, the browser typically displays a status message such as:

```
... connecting to host 132.121.1.1...
```

Once a TCP/IP connection is made, this status message changes to something like this

```
Connect: host 132.121.1.1 contacted, waiting for reply...
```

which means that the browser was able to send a TCP message to the remote machine and is waiting for a TCP response. If, on the other hand, the browser is unable to contact the remote machine, the attempt to make the connection will time out, and the browser typically displays a message such as

```
Description: Could not connect to the server "132.121.1.1".
```

which indicates that the computer was unable to make a TCP connection to the machine at the indicated IP address.

User Datagram Protocol: UDP

TCP is the best known of the IP transportation services. However, the *User Datagram Protocol* (*UDP*) is also important and worth mentioning here. UDP is much more limited that TCP/IP. Basically, a UDP packet contains only two pieces of packet information beyond those provided in the basic IP header:

- The *port numbers* corresponding to the sender and destination addresses
- A *data checksum* so that the computer receiving the packet can verify that the data content was not damaged in transit

Unlike TCP, there is no header data defining connections between sender and receiver. Thus, packets may be lost before they reach their targets, and there is no guarantee of delivery. For this reason, UDP is typically used only in a local network, where it is less likely that packets will go missing.

Why use UDP if information can be lost? The short answer is *speed*. Because TCP/IP packets contain lots of additional bookkeeping information, there is less data per byte in a TCP packet than in a UDP one. Also, TCP software works harder than UDP when processing the same-length message, since the TCP protocol has more overhead for managing the connection. Thus, UDP can be faster and more efficient—provided, of course, the packets don't get lost!

Network Management: ICMP, Ping, and Traceroute

Management, control, and diagnostics of IP communication are provided by additional message protocols packed inside IP packets. For example, the *Internet Control Message Protocol* (*ICMP*) defines special messages related to network operation or failures. Such packets can announce network problems, such as when a router is congested and should be avoided or when a particular network is entirely inaccessible. These messages are used by IP software to control how data packets are routed to the intended destination. ICMP also provides tools that can be used to diagnose problems. For example, the *ping* utility program uses a special echo ICMP message to see if a particular machine is alive by bouncing a packet from the machine and seeing if it can answer. Similarly, the *traceroute* program (called *tracert* on Windows 98/NT/2000 systems) uses ICMP packets with different TTL values to determine the route by which a message is being sent to a specified destination. In essence, *traceroute* bounces messages off all the machines between the client and the remote machine being contacted and lists the addresses of all the machines in between.

There are other special-purpose IP protocols, but they are beyond the scope of this book. If you are interested in learning more, please see the references at the end of this chapter.

7.2 Internet Services

The Internet services we know, love, and actually use are built on top of the TCP and UDP data communication protocols. For example, HyperText Transfer Protocol (HTTP), Network News Transfer Protocol (NNTP—for distributing Usenet news articles), Telnet (remote terminal connections via the Internet), and *Simple Mail Transfer Protocol* (SMTP) use TCP/IP to send data back and forth between machines. However, other tools, such as Network Time Protocol (NTP) for synchronizing system clocks on network-connected computers, and Domain Name System (DNS), discussed in Section 7.2.2, use UDP. And others, such as the Network File System (NFS), are designed to use either TCP or UDP, depending on the nature of the network connection.

In all these cases, the service defines its own unique *application protocol* to control the transfer of data (HTTP) or the synchronization of times (NTP). For example, HTTP defines a rich message syntax, described in Chapter 9, for HTTP clients exchanging messages with HTTP servers. However, the data or text of these messages is communicated between the computers using TCP.

All high-level Internet services, such as the ones just mentioned, operate using what is called the *client-server* model. In this model, illustrated in Figure 7.4 for the case of SMTP, a request for service (here, to send an e-mail message) comes from an Internet client, and a response to this request is returned from an Internet-accessible server. For example, to send an e-mail, an Internet mail client (such as a user's e-mail program) contacts an e-mail SMTP server (the machine that receives and possibly forwards e-mail messages) using TCP. The e-mail client then sends the SMTP server a request, consisting of SMTP control messages (perhaps identifying the sender should authentication be needed to send mail via this machine) and address information for the e-mail message. The SMTP server then sends a response, either approving or rejecting the request.

7.2.1 Services and Port Numbers

For convenience, all well-known Internet services are designated to receive (or *listen* for) messages addressed to specific ports on the server. Thus, if a client wants to contact an HTTP server on a specific machine, it will do so by sending a message to the server at the default HTTP port number (port 80). Table 7.1 lists some common Internet service protocols and the default ports at which such services are provided.

Table 7.1 is very much abbreviated: There are literally dozens of special services offered at well-defined port numbers. On Unix systems, the file */etc/services* lists most of the common services and the ports they use. Fortunately, most of these are not relevant to Web application designers.

You will note from Table 7.1 that most standard services operate from port number values smaller than 1024. Port numbers in the range 0 through

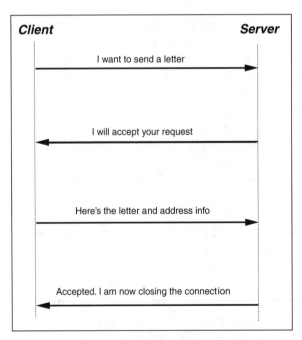

Figure 7.4 An example Simple Mail Transfer Protocol (SMTP) client-server session in which a mail client sends a letter via a mail server. The actual messages passed back and forth are transported using TCP/IP.

Table 7.1 Common Internet Services and Their Default Server Port Numbers

PROTOCOL/SERVICE	DEFAULT SERVER PORT(S)
Telnet	23
HTTP	80
FTP	21 (receive) and 20 (send)
NNTP	119
7P	123
DNS	53
SMTP	25
NFS	2049

1023 are called *well-known ports* and are reserved for standard services defined by the Internet Engineering Task Force (IETF) working groups that develop Internet standards. Furthermore, on most systems these ports are accessible only to programs run by the operating system or by specially privileged users. Thus, a regular user cannot start up a program that accesses these ports.

The ports in the range 1024 through 49151 are designated as registered ports, designated for services that will run consistently at a port, listening for connections. Thus, if regular users wants to run their own Web server, they need to configure the server to use a port number in this range. This is why you will see many "test" or personal Web servers running on ports 8000 or 8080.

Finally, ports in the range 49152 through 65535 are called *dynamic* or *private ports* and are intended for transient use. For example, a Web browser uses such ports when it opens a local port so that it can connect to a remote port on a remote Web server. Local ports are usually selected at random, so each time a browser connects to the outside world, it uses a different local port number to do so.

7.2.2 Basic Service: DNS

We won't discuss services such as NFS, NTP, or NNTP, because these are not terribly important to Web designers. However, the *domain name system* (DNS) is extremely important, because this service lets us use names for computers as opposed to numeric addresses.

The domain name system was designed to make the Internet usable to people—after all, no human can make sense out of hundreds of millions of numeric IP addresses and port numbers! The idea behind the domain name system was to define a naming scheme that uses human-understandable domains. In the domain name system, these names are organized hierarchically by organization. The names are chosen to express both logical information about the placement of a machine or a network of machines and the relationship of that machine or network to other machines in the same network or elsewhere on the Internet.

For example, the computer on my desk has the domain name:

smaug.infocommons.utoronto.ca

In a domain name, the different *domains* in the name are separated by periods, with the main domain farthest to the right and less significant ones to the left. The rightmost string is called the *top-level domain,* and the allowed top-level domain names were formerly defined by an organization called the Internet Assigned Naming Authority (IANA), recently replaced by an organization called the Internet Corporation for Assigned Names and Numbers (ICANN). These can either be two-letter country codes (such as *ca* for Canada) or special three-letter codes listed in Table 7.2 (more top-level names are being planned). The three-letter codes date from the early days of the Internet. The various country codes are listed and explained at www.utoronto.ca/ian/books/xhtml1/appc/iso3166.html. The official list of country codes is found at the IANA registry at www.iana.org/domain-names.html.

Moving to the left are subsequent *subdomains.* In the DNS model, each higher-level domain is assumed to be responsible for the names in the domain just below it. Thus, since the *utoronto* domain is one level below the *ca* domain, the managers of *ca* domain are responsible for knowing (and pub-

Table 7.2 Nonnational Top-Level Domain Names and Descriptions

TOP-LEVEL DOMAIN	DESCRIPTION
.com	Commercial organizations
.edu	Educational institutions
.gov	U.S. government
.int	International organization
.mil	U.S. military
.net	Internet network service organizations
.org	Nonprofit organization

lishing information) about the *utoronto* (and any other) domain lying just below it. This approach proceeds hierarchically through the names. Thus the domain infocommons.utoronto.ca is responsible for knowing (and publishing information) about the names directly below it, including information about my machine *smaug.infocommons.utoronto.ca.*

Names are assigned and maintained by a domain naming authority. For example, to create, or *register,* a new name under the *com* domain, you must contact the naming authority for this domain. Network Solutions Inc. (www.internic.net) currently manages this particular top-level domain, but other organizations can register names in this domain. On the other hand, to create a new name underneath *ducky.com,* you would need to contact the organization that registered—and owns—the *ducky.com* domain: This organization has sole rights to register names beneath it (such as *lucky.ducky.com*). Similarly, all domains below *utoronto.ca* are controlled by the University of Toronto, which has a Network Operations group that manages names inside this domain.

Of course, machines on the Internet are actually addressed by number so that, given a specific domain name, there must be a way to convert the name into an IP address. This is one of the functions of the *domain name system*—a distributed database that stores information about domain names (and other information) and the related IP addresses. For example, to contact the machine with domain name *smaug.infocommons.utoronto.ca,* you must first find the IP address that corresponds to that name. Consequently, if I want to create a domain and provide names for machines in that domain, I must somehow publish those names so that you can look them up and find out the IP addresses corresponding to the names.

Publishing Domain Name Information

Information about domains is stored on the Internet in a distributed database of name information, collectively known as the *domain name system.* The domain name system provides two main functions: a mechanism for *publishing* information about new domains or about machines or subdomains in a given domain and a mechanism for *interrogating* this database and obtaining information (such as IP addresses) about a domain or about a specific machine. Information about domain names is published via *domain name servers,* also called DNS servers or simply name servers. A name server is an Internet service that maintains a database of information about domain names and related IP addresses. Remote clients can query this database for information about specific names—if the name server does not have the desired information, it can query other name servers to obtain it. This section looks at the publishing process, whereby information is published on these servers. The next section looks at how computers obtain information from this database.

Adding a New Domain

To create a new domain, you must contact the authority for the parent domain to register the new domain. For example, to create the new domain *bigcompany.com,* you would need to contact the registration authority for the *.com* domain and give them the following information:

- Name, address, and organization name for the contact who will manage the new domain.
- The desired domain name (*bigcompany.com*).
- The names and IP addresses of one or more name servers that will serve as *authoritative* name servers for that domain. An authoritative name server is simply one that always has correct and up-to-date information about the new domain. If you are looking for the most accurate DNS information, then you need to contact an authoritative name server for the desired domain.

If the preceding request is accepted, then this information is added to the DNS database for the top-level *com* domain. Then, when a request is made for information about machines or subdomains inside *bigcompany.com,* authoritative name servers for the top-level *com* domain will direct the request to one of the name servers designated as an authoritative name server for the *bigcompany.com* domain.

Note that this delegates responsibility for managing the *bigcompany.com* domain to the people who manage the authoritative name servers for that domain. The organization that manages the *com* domain doesn't need to know anything about the machines or domains inside *bigcompany.com*—it only needs to know where to redirect requests about this domain.

Managing Names within a Domain

Once a domain name is created, the domain managers can add new names inside their own domain without needing to inform the *com* domain managers of this change—they need only update the DNS records in their own authoritative domain name servers regarding the new machines or networks. Thus, once the domain *bigcompany.com* is created, the owners of that domain can add any subdomains they like (*my.bigcompany.com, www.bigcompany.com, datacenter.db.bigcompany.com,* etc.) simply by updating the information to their authoritative domain name servers. Any computer trying to find the IP address corresponding to a domain name ending in *bigcompany.com* will end up contacting one of these authoritative domain name servers. For example, at the University of Toronto, several authoritative domain name servers maintain information about all the machines and networks in the *utoronto.ca* domain.

Resolving Domain Names to IP Addresses

When a computer such as a Web browser wants to contact a machine with a given domain name, it must first translate that name into the appropriate IP address—recall that machines on the Internet are really addressed by number, not by name. Machines do this by using the DNS protocol to contact a local name server, which does this lookup on the machine's behalf. Every machine connected to the Internet must be configured to know the IP addresses of one (or more) such local name servers. Then, when it has to look up a name, the machine contacts the local name server using the DNS protocol and asks the server to do this. The local server will return the resolved IP address—or a message stating that the lookup failed and why.

The contacted local name server must then obtain information about the specified name by contacting other name servers. In many cases it doesn't have to do so—most name servers maintain local caches of name information, and if the information is available in the cache, it will immediately return this data. However, if the information is not available, it must locate a name server that actually maintains a record of names and IP addresses in the target domain and contact that server.

In principle, the local name server does this lookup by first contacting a name server for the top-level domain and asking it for the location of a name server for the next domain in the hierarchy. It then proceeds through a sequence of name servers until it finds one with the information it is looking for. This process is called *name resolution,* as the server is attempting to resolve the name into the correct IP address.

For example, suppose that a Web browser wants to make a connection to the machine at domain name *smaug.java.utoronto.ca.* The first step is to contact the local name server and ask it to resolve the name into an IP address. If the local machine does not have this information already, it will do the following:

1. The local name server contacts an authoritative name server for the *ca* domain and asks for the location of a name server that retains authoritative information for the *utoronto.ca* domain. In general, all name servers are configured with a list of primary domain name servers (for *edu, com, ca,* etc.), so they always know where to start their search.

2. The *ca* name server returns an IP address of a name server hosting authoritative domain information for the *utoronto.ca* domain. The local name server then contacts this name server and asks for the address of a name server that manages authoritative information about the *java.utoronto.ca* domain.

3. The *utoronto.ca* name server returns the address of a name server that handles the *java.utoronto.ca* domain. The local name server then contacts

the authoritative name server for *java.utoronto.ca* domain and asks for the address of the machine *smaug.java.utoronto.ca.*

4. The authoritative name server for the *java.utoronto.ca* domain returns the DNS database record for the machine named *smaug.java.utoronto.ca.* This record includes the IP address for the machine.

5. The local name server returns the desired IP address to the client that asked for it. The local name server also will likely cache this record (and perhaps other information gathered in the preceding request) so that if someone else asks a similar question, it can get the answer from the local database without repeating the procedure.

The Web browser, now equipped with the needed IP address corresponding to the name *smaug.java.utoronto.ca,* can proceed with the request.

In practice, a local DNS server query will probably not proceed as just described—DNS servers are carefully optimized so that shortcuts in this procedure are possible. Thus, a local DNS server may obtain cached DNS data from a neighboring server instead of actually contacting the authoritative server for the targeted domain. Alternatively, the local name server may already know the address of the authoritative server for the target domain, in which case steps 1 through 3 can be skipped.

Lifetime of Cached DNS Records

As noted, name servers will likely cache a copy of any DNS records they retrieve so that they do not have to repeat the entire (and time-consuming) query. However, such cached information must not be kept forever, since DNS information changes over time as new machines are added or as IP addresses change.

To make sure that they expire after some time, each DNS record comes with a time to live (TTL) value, which tells a name server how long it can keep the record before discarding it. Of course, the server may discard the DNS record before the expiry date (name servers generally have room for only so much data and will discard older or less-used information if the cache becomes full). Thus, one can best think of the TTL value as defining the record's maximum lifetime. In general, this lifetime ranges from one to three days.

As a result of this design, it can take some time for the world to know about changes to your local domain. This is because when you change the information in your authoritative name servers, it can take several days to replace the outdated data cached elsewhere on the Internet. Until the outdated data is replaced, Internet users will continue to use old DNS data and may have trouble reaching machines on your network.

You can reduce the time it takes to flush obsolete DNS records by intentionally reducing the TTL value set for your authoritative DNS records several days before you change the DNS data. By doing so, you ensure that cached DNS information is being rapidly purged and refreshed by the time you actually make the DNS changes. Then, when you update the DNS data, it takes less time for this information to percolate across the Internet. After making the DNS change, you can increase the TTL value to a more reasonable value, letting the local DNS caches work more effectively as soon as they have retrieved the new, accurate records.

TIP   REDUCE DNS TIME TO LIVE PRIOR TO CHANGING DNS RECORDS   **If you know you will be changing the DNS records, reduce the TTL value for the authoritative name servers a few days before you make the change. This causes cached DNS entries to be more quickly updated with correct data when you actually change the name server data, as discussed in the text.**

Domain Names and Aliases

The domain name system lets you define different domain names for the same IP address. This is illustrated in Figure 7.5, which shows a single IP address that corresponds to six different domain names. In general, one of these names is called the *primary name* (this is largely up to whoever creates the DNS database describing this machine), and the rest are called *aliases.* Thus, the machine in Figure 7.5 has a single primary name and five aliases.

There are several reasons for defining and using aliases. For user convenience, you can use names that obviously correspond to the common services offered by your network (FTP, Web, Usenet, DNS, as illustrated in Figure 7.5) and then tell everyone to refer to these services using these names. This is useful because such names are easy to remember or guess (i.e., most people will try typing "www," "ftp," or "my" in front of a domain name if they can't remember the correct URL). Initially, you could offer all these services from the

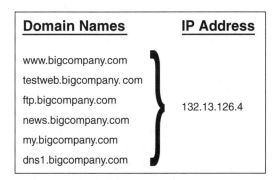

Figure 7.5 An illustration of domain name aliases. All six domain names correspond to the same IP address.

same machine, using aliases to have all the names correspond to the same IP address. Later on, should you decide to use a separate machine for a specific service, you can simply reconfigure the DNS data so that the name now refers to the IP address of the new machine. Since the rest of the world knows the machine by name and not number, they do not have to change their references—the DNS system takes care of this automatically. This makes it much easier to evolve your network, as you can make relatively large-scale changes without needing to change the public names by which machines are identified.

Also, aliases let a single machine provide different virtual services depending on the name by which the machine is addressed. For example, HTTP servers can be configured to return different data—essentially acting as a different server—depending on the domain name used to reference it. Using this mechanism, the requests

http://www.bigcompany.com

http://testweb.bigcompany.com

can return different data, since they reference the server by different names. With HTTP, this is possible because the HTTP request actually lists (with the host field, as discussed in Chapter 9) the domain name being used in the request. The server then uses this information to determine which resources to return.

Multiple IP Addresses per Domain Name

Just as DNS lets a single IP address correspond to many different domain names the system also lets a single domain name correspond to multiple IP addresses. There are physical reasons why this may be desirable: For example, the same machine may have multiple network interfaces and can thus be contacted at more than one IP address.

However, it also reasonable to set up the DNS records such that multiple machines with different IP addresses share the same domain name. This allows for a simple form of *load averaging,* wherein multiple different computers can share the requests coming to a given domain name. We discuss this approach in Section 7.3.4.

Other DNS Services

The domain name system provides a lot of services other than domain name resolution. For example, DNS lets you do *reverse lookups*—that is, convert an IP address into a list of possible domain names. It also lets you inquire and find out at what ports various Internet services are offered. Finally, the DNS database entries contain special data fields (called MX or Mail eXchange records) related to e-mail address resolution—the domain name portion of an

Internet e-mail address is handled somewhat differently than regular domain names.

Indeed, DNS is one of the more complex systems (and protocols) on the Internet, and this brief section has touched on only the main features. For additional information check out the references listed at the end of this chapter.

7.3 Network Issues

The actual design and physical layout of a network is a complicated job, requiring a detailed understanding of IP networking as well as in-depth knowledge of the physical networking technologies (Ethernet, ATM, etc.) being used to "connect the boxes." Indeed, there are long professional courses—and many books—devoted to these topics. Clearly, this short section is no substitute!

The goal of this section is simply to introduce the basic concepts and terminology of the Internet part of a network and to give you a feel for the basic issues that need to be considered when designing a network. This will help you better understand the implications of certain design decisions and appreciate the roles that quality of service (QoS) and network security requirements play when implementing an appropriate network design.

7.3.1 Routers, Hubs, and Gateways

In the early days of the Internet, there was little distinction between the roles that a computer played on a network: A machine could be a simple client or server or a network gateway, simply depending on how it was configured. However, as network designs evolved, special-purpose computers were developed for serving network management roles. Thus, today, the machines that manage network communication are still just computers, but they are specially designed ones, optimized for managing and delivering network traffic at the expense of other functions. This section describes some of these special-purpose machines and their roles.

A machine that connects different IP networks together is called a *router*. It is called this because the software on the machine is optimized for routing incoming IP packets to the appropriate networks according to their destination. In general, routers are equipped with special network management software so they can keep track of the best place to forward outgoing packets and so they do not forward packets that don't need to go outside a specific network. The details of this management software depend largely on the underlying hardware and software of the network (Ethernet, ATM, etc.) and won't be discussed here.

A *firewall* (discussed in more detail in Section 7.3.2) is essentially a special-purpose Internet router optimized for network security. A firewall contains special software for controlling packet flow so that access can be restricted to specified networks.

A simple *hub* is a box via which computers can be connected to the same network: Hubs are most commonly used to connect machines that reside on the same local area network, or LAN. With a simple hub, the computers are effectively connected to the same communications line, in which case the local network looks much like a party line. Thus, a packet sent by one computer is seen by all the other computers on the network. This, of course, limits the effective speed of the network, since if one machine is attempting to use the full network bandwidth, there is nothing left for the others.

An *intelligent hub* acts in a more intelligent manner. With an intelligent hub, data sent between two machines connected to the hub is not seen by the other machines on the network: Instead, the hub automatically switches the packets to their destination and avoids sending them to computers they are not destined for. This eliminates the party-line aspect of the simple network and means that each circuit can in principle operate at its maximum speed when connecting to another machine on the same hub. In general, an intelligent hub has many connection points for individual computers, plus a smaller number of connection points that can connect to other networks.

Note that an intelligent hub may not know anything about IP networking, as the intelligence may be applied entirely at the physical network layer (Ethernet, etc.).

Figure 7.6 shows a simple IP network that illustrates these various network components. Some of these, such as the firewall computer and others, are described further in later sections.

7.3.2 Network Security

When considering Internet network security, an organization is hopefully thinking of four things:

- Protecting the network from outside intruders.
- Protecting communication between computers so that the messages cannot be read and interpreted by a third party.
- Protecting the data stored on machines inside the network from being stolen or damaged.
- Ensuring that the network services are provided with a high quality of service, 24 hours a day, seven days a week.

At the same time, the security technologies you use will represent a compromise between accessibility and security. The most secure server is one that

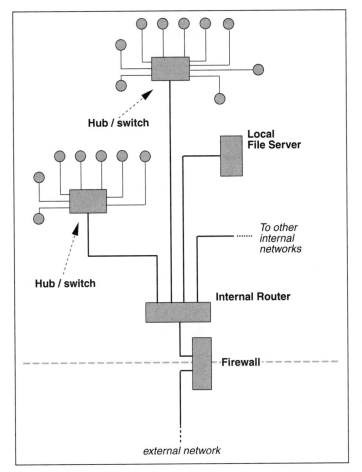

Figure 7.6 An illustration of a simple IP network showing the different hardware components.

is not connected to anything, but this is not a terribly useful network architecture! Furthermore, the compromises you make will vary depending on the part of your network being considered. For example, you will want far more protection for your internal corporate network than for the network hosting publicly accessible Web servers.

Some of these issues can be dealt with by creating an appropriate network design. For example, the network illustrated in Figure 7.7 has publicly accessible Web (and other) servers outside the company's firewall and hides the internal network's services (Web servers and file servers, for example) inside it. The firewall (discussed later in this section) protects the internal network from intruders while giving users inside the internal network safe access to external resources such as Web sites.

However, to understand these approaches, it helps to understand the basic ways in which people (or software) can break into a network or monitor network communication. These issues—and some of the technical solutions for them—are discussed in the next few sections.

IP Packet Sniffing

The information transported in an ordinary IP packet is easy to read and understand. It is easy to create software that can read the packets going over an IP network and display their contents. Indeed, network monitoring software does—and must do—exactly that! Thus, there is, in principle, no privacy on the

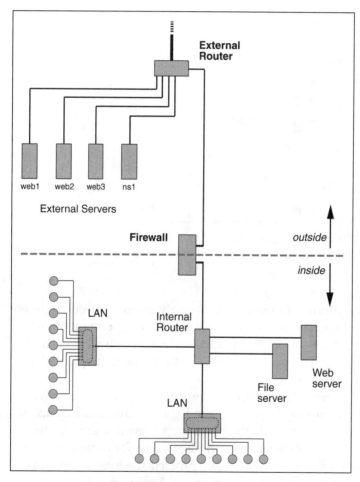

Figure 7.7   A simple corporate network with publicly accessible servers outside the corporate firewall.

Internet other than the fact that it takes a lot of work to extract all the packets and process them, so you need a good (or heinous!) reason for doing so.

Within a local network, network security must be managed by a combination of network design, usage policies, and monitoring software. Design policies include making sure that the network wiring is not easily accessible, thereby making it difficult for someone to surreptitiously connect a machine to the network. Management policies include careful screening of users and computers to make sure that only authorized people are using the machines and ensuring that "network sniffing" software is not being installed or used.

At the same time, software can be installed to ensure that only authorized computers are connected to the network. Such software can signal an alarm whenever an unauthorized machine is connected. Of course, this does not stop someone from running network sniffing software on one of the authorized machines, but it helps reduce the opportunities for doing so.

Such policies cannot apply outside the physical network you control. Thus, it is important to separate your internal network as much as possible from the outside world. At the lowest level, this can be done by using a router to connect the internal network to—and isolate the internal network from—the outside world. The router can be configured so that IP packets traveling between machines on the inner network never pass through the router to the outside world. This means that machines on the outer network cannot sniff information related to machines inside your network. Note in Figure 7.7 how all the internal networks are connected to the outside world via an internal router.

IP Spoofing

Just as IP packets are easy to read, so are they easy to produce. Indeed, a computer on a network can easily create an IP packet that pretends to be coming from a different computer, simply by creating a packet with a faked return address. *Spoofing* refers to the case where one computer uses this facility to pretend to be another by sending packets as if they were from another machine and then intercepting the returned data. Thus, if a network is protected from some IP addresses but not others, then a person can infiltrate the network by spoofing the address of a machine that is allowed access.

With standard TCP packets it is difficult to tell the difference between spoofed and nonspoofed data. However, there are approaches that can protect an IP connection, for example, by adding special signature data in the packets that changes with each packet in a manner that cannot be predicted by the spoofer but that is understood only by the actual client and server. In this case, the crackers may be able to intercept a packet and replace it by their own, fake, packet, but they will be unable to insert the signature data that verifies the packet as coming from the correct source. Thus the interlopers can read the packets, but they can't send their own for lack of the proper signature data.

IP Packet Encryption

At a deeper level, privacy and security can best be guaranteed by combining packet *data encryption* with the antispoofing mechanism just mentioned. With data encryption, data inside a packet is encrypted such that only the intended recipient has the digital key needed to decrypt it. Consequently, even if the packet is intercepted, the contents are unreadable. Using this approach, only the authorized client and server can exchange encrypted data and decrypt and read each other's messages, ensuring a private connection that cannot be monitored by anyone listening in on the packets. Combined with the antispoofing mechanisms described previously, this guarantees that an interloper cannot read the data passed between two parties and that the interloper cannot break into the transaction and spoof the role of either party.

On the Web, the *secure sockets layer* (SSL) technology is the most common technology that provides both antispoofing and IP-layer data encryption. This technology, developed by Netscape in cooperation with RSA Security Incorporated (www.rsasecurity.com), encrypts the IP packet contents more or less as just described. All commercial browsers are equipped with SSL software, as are most commercial Web servers. We talk a bit more about SSL in Chapter 9 when we review the HTTP protocol.

Internet Firewalls

To further protect a network, you can isolate the network from the outside world using a *firewall*. A firewall is essentially a region of your network consisting of specially equipped routers configured to prevent packets from the outside network from entering the internal network and vice versa. Figure 7.7 shows a typical use for such a firewall: Here the firewall is protecting the internal corporate network from the outside world. Note, however, that the public portion of this organization's network (the public Web and name servers) are outside the firewall since they are designed to be accessed by anyone.

Firewalls are typically highly configurable, letting the firewall administrator control the type of traffic that can pass from inside to outside and vice versa. For example, a firewall can be configured to let Web browsers inside the network send packets to servers outside the network and to let the response packets pass through the firewall back to the browsers. There are several ways of doing this, some of which are discussed in Section 7.3.3. In many cases these approaches involve running a proxy server on the firewall that can communicate with the outside world on behalf of computers inside the local network. The proxy server then hides the inner world from the outside one and is designed to let in only those packets that have been explicitly requested by machines on the inside.

Denial-of-Service Attacks

Protecting a network from unauthorized access is one thing—but this is not the only way in which a network can be attacked. Another approach is to simply make the network resources unusable: Your e-commerce Web servers may still be running, and the data may be safe, but this doesn't do much good if no one can access your servers to purchase your products or read your Web pages!

This approach is called a *denial-of-service* (DoS) attack, and there are literally dozens of ways in which such an attack can be launched. These attacks typically try to flood your network with too much data, for example, by sending you millions of e-mail messages or by flooding the network with invalid IP packets. Modern network software can protect a network from such attacks by detecting sudden surges in incoming traffic and then blocking incoming messages from the guilty network(s). However, such detection and protection software needs to be installed before it will do any good. Many organizations have found this out the hard way!

Most recently, these attacks have been implemented in a distributed fashion, as what is known as *distributed denial of service*, or DDoS. With DDoS, a machine or network is attacked simultaneously by dozens of machines from many different networks. Such attacks can in principle flood a corporate network with literally billions of bits of data every second, easily swamping the networking hardware (not to mention the servers) and rendering the network resources inoperable. Indeed, many companies, such as Yahoo!, Amazon.com, eBay, and others have had their Web sites disabled for hours at a time by such distributed, coherent attacks.

Once again, network security software can be installed to detect these problems and to block the incoming data before the network is flooded and rendered inoperable. And, once again, it's best to install such software before such an attack rather than after!

Network and Systems Security

Obviously, maintaining a secure network is an ongoing task. Most break-ins or attacks take advantage of flaws in network or server software—and such flaws are being uncovered every day. Thus it is imperative, if you want to maintain good network security, to be constantly on the lookout for security patches to your network or server software. All hardware and software manufacturers (including open source vendors) provide regular security advisories and system patches designed to fix major bugs. It is important to carefully monitor such messages and to apply the patches as soon as possible.

The Computer Emergency Response Team (CERT), at www.cert.org, is a well-known clearinghouse for general, Internet-related security problems.

This organization regularly releases announcements of new security problems and possible solutions for them. You can also subscribe to its mailing list and have these notifications sent to you automatically. Every organization that wants to maintain a secure network should have someone on staff who monitors this site and who can report on possible problems that could affect the network. Some resource sites are listed in the reference section at the end of the chapter.

7.3.3 Connecting through a Firewall: IP Masquerading

As mentioned earlier, a firewall is a special type of gateway that either blocks or tightly restricts the passage of IP packets across it. This can be used to keep intruders from getting into the internal network from outside, to keep internal staff from retrieving data from the outside world, or to keep internal users from copying data (such as confidential files) to the outside. With most firewalls, the degree of restriction can be quite finely controlled. You can thus create a very hard firewall, which allows virtually nothing to cross, or a very porous one, with very few restrictions. Obviously, the harder the firewall, the more secure the internal network. On the other hand, a hard firewall is often not practical should you want your own staff to have access to the Web.

Indeed, organizations often want people inside the network to have Web access to the outside world while simultaneously restricting the reverse situation (access from outside users to the internal network) and without revealing details (such as the IP addresses) of the machines inside. One way to do this is by using a mechanism called *IP masquerading*. With IP masquerading, all IP communication to the outside world is processed by the firewall machine, which takes each packet coming from inside and rewrites it so that it looks, to the outside world, as if it is coming from the firewall machine itself. Thus, as far as the outside world is concerned, all the connections are coming from the firewall machine, which *masquerades* as a machine inside the network.

This is schematically illustrated in Figure 7.8, which shows two internal browsers connecting to the outside world: Note how both machines, to the outside world, appear to be coming from the same IP address (that of the firewall), the only difference being the port number they are using. These external numbers change with each transaction, since the port is closed when the browser closes the connection and a new one is selected essentially at random the next time the browser opens a connection.

This has important implications for Web server application designers, who may be tempted to track individual users on the assumption that each user is coming in from a unique IP address. This is obviously not true for users coming in via a firewall, so IP addresses are unreliable for this purpose.

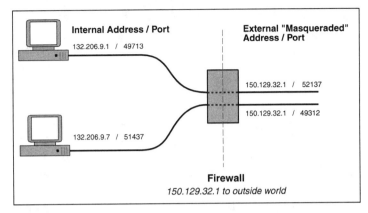

Figure 7.8   An illustration of IP masquerading across a firewall. As far as the outside world is concerned, the two machines inside the network have the same IP address (150.129.32.1) and are connecting to the outside world using the indicated port numbers.

IP Proxy Services Using SOCKS

As an alternative to IP masquerading, many secure networks use a SOCKS (for "SOCKet-S") proxy server. SOCKS is a special client-server protocol: The SOCKS server runs on the firewall machine, and each client inside the network must be equipped with SOCKS client software. The SOCKS server is a type of *proxy server* that connects to Internet-accessible application servers (such as Web servers) on behalf of the client and relays data between the client and the outside server. Thus, when a Web browser inside the network wants to contact a Web server outside, this request is sent to the SOCKS proxy, which contacts the outside server on behalf of the browser and then returns the response to it.

SOCKS sounds much like IP masquerading. However, SOCKS requires special software on the browsers (unlike IP masquerading) and also supports user authentication and data encryption, so it provides additional tools for applying and managing a network security policy. Please see the references section for links to more information about SOCKS.

Service-Specific Proxy Servers

Finally, for specific services such as HTTP, an organization can configure an application-specific proxy server that handles just that service. For example, an organization could configure a specific firewall machine to run an HTTP proxy server, then configure all browsers inside the network to use that proxy server when accessing Web sites outside the local network. Since the proxy server is on the firewall machine, it can access Web servers outside, and can thus proxy requests on behalf of browsers.

HTTP proxy servers are themselves quite complex, and they are obviously very important when designing Web applications. These issues are reviewed in Chapter 9.

7.3.4 Multiple Web Servers

As mentioned at the end of Section 7.2.1, a DNS record for a network can associate several different IP addresses with the same domain name. When a name server then asks an authoritative name server for the IP address corresponding to this domain name, the server will return just one of the possible addresses. Indeed, the authoritative name server will return a different IP address at each such request, essentially looping through the list of possible values and then starting again. This mechanism is informally called *DNS round-robin,* and it ensures that, in a sufficiently large network, machines on the Internet will have obtained one of these addresses essentially at random when attempting to resolve this name.

Using this mechanism, several Web server machines can serve out the resources for a single domain name. For example, a company can have five different machines with each machine delivering the same content. Since outside users will locate the machines using different DNS servers, these users will be using different IP addresses—thus spreading the load across the different machines. Formally, this is a form of *load averaging,* since the load is being spread, or averaged, across the different servers.

This approach is particularly useful if the load becomes too great for a Web server and the server is simply unable to process all the incoming requests. This mechanism then lets you share the load among several machines and ease the load on any individual one. This makes it simple to scale up service simply by adding new machines and new addresses in the DNS pool.

This approach is also useful for distributing a Web site across multiple different networks. For example, the different IP addresses for the different Web servers could be on distinctly different physical networks, so that if one network fails (or is slow), the service will still be operating properly on the other networks. Thus, even if one network goes down, only a portion of your clients are affected, as opposed to all of them. Similarly, if one network becomes saturated (i.e., there are too many requests for the network to handle), the servers can be distributed among many different high networks, providing additional bandwidth to the distributed servers.

Of course, for this to work you must also implement software to ensure that these different Web servers have the same static data (Web pages, image files, slowly changing database content) to serve out. The situation is more complicated for dynamic content; in this case you will need some sort of replication technology to ensure that data changed at one site is properly synchronized with the other servers. However, there are commercial packages that support these features (typically referred to as *Web caching* or *Web replication*). We will revisit this subject when we discuss site management and implementation software in Chapter 12.

7.4 References

IP NETWORKING AND IP SOFTWARE

freesoft.org/CIE/index.htm	Online IP notes and tutorials
www.armory.com:457/NetAdminG/ CO7E7S.html	General networking, including IP
www.ktek.com/ktek/Lans-Wans.html	Networking terms dictionary
www.private.org.il/tcpip_rl.html	Long list of TCP/IP resources
www.iana.org/domain-names.html	List of top-level domains

Internetworking with TCP/IP Vol. I: Principles, Protocols, and Architecture, 3rd ed., by Douglas E. Comer, Prentice-Hall (1995).

IP Fundamentals: What Everyone Needs to Know About Addressing & Routing, by Thomas A. Maufer, Prentice-Hall (1999).

DOMAIN NAME SYSTEM

www.hill.com/library/staffpubs/dns.html	Introduction to DNS
michael.iserver.com/dns/	Tutorial
www.lantimes.com/handson/97/ 706a107a.html	Simple article
hotwired.lycos.com/webmonkey/ webmonkey/geektalk/97/03/index4a.html	Somewhat longer article
www.dns.net/dnsrd/	DNS resources site

NETWORK ARCHITECTURES AND TECHNOLOGIES

www.cisco.com/univercd/cc/td/doc/ cisintwk/ito_doc/index.htm	Technology overview

INTERNET SECURITY

Firewalls and Internet Security: Repelling the Wily Hacker, 2nd ed., by W. R. Cheswick and S. M. Bellovin, Addison-Wesley (2000). Considered the bible of security issues: well written and detailed.

Maximum Security: A Hacker's Guide to Protecting Your Internet Site and Network, anonymous, Sams (1998). A more introductory book; discusses many different computer systems.

www.eeye.com/html/	Resources and book lists
www.informationweek.com/775/ security.htm	Security overview
www.geocities.com/Silicon Valley/ Bay/9952/	Introductory security articles
www.clark.net/pub/mjr/pubs/fwfaq/	FAQ on firewalls
www.socks.nec.com/aboutsocks.html	SOCKS overview
www.securityportal.com	Information site on Internet security
www.cert.org	Computer and network security advisories
www.sans.org	System Administration, Networking, and Security Institute

WEB SERVER LOAD AVERAGING AND DISTRIBUTED CACHING

www.web-caching.com/	Overview
ircache.nlanr.net/Cache/FAQ/ ircache-faq.html	Overview and company list
www.caching.com/	Overview and company list
dir.yahoo.com/Computers_and_Internet/ Internet/World_Wide_Web/Caching/	Yahoo! resource list

Uniform Resource Locators (URLs)

Topics/Concepts Covered: URL syntax, URL character encoding and escaping, query strings in URLs, common URL schemes, URIs and URNs

Uniform Resource Locators (*URLs*) specify the location of Internet-accessible resources using a single string of ordinary characters: A URL simply indicates where a resource is and how to access it. All URL schemes share a common syntax, which was designed to be simple, clear, and flexible. Indeed, there exist schemes for all the major Internet communications protocols, including FTP, Gopher, e-mail, HTTP, and many less familiar ones. And most of these schemes are easy for a human to read and understand!

Within X/HTML documents, URLs are used as values of **href.src.** or **class** attributes (among other places) to reference the target of a hypertext link, the source of an image, the location of applet or object program code, or the location of a linked style sheet. However, use of URLs is not restricted to the Web. Indeed, the URL syntax was designed so that it would be easy to communicate URLs in many ways—including in print (as in this book) or on scraps of paper.

This chapter describes the general syntax for URLs and the details of commonly implemented URL schemes. Section 8.1 begins with an overview of URL properties and the syntax for constructing valid URLs. This includes a description of character-encoding mechanisms used when writing URLs (or when including special characters in a URL) and a discussion of the syntax rules for partial URLs. Section 8.2 then looks in detail at the most commonly implemented URL schemes, such as **http**, **ftp**, **mailto**, and others. The different subsections also describe special encoding rules (or other special characteristics) relevant to the different schemes. Section 8.3 briefly reviews other proposed (but not widely implemented) schemes.

URLs are in fact only one of the methods designed for identifying resources on the Internet. Another approach is called a *Uniform Resource Name* (*URN*), and, collectively, all possible identification schemes (URLs, URNs, and any others) are called *Uniform Resource Identifiers* (*URIs*). Section 8.4 reviews these different identification mechanisms and the relationships between them. Finally, Section 8.5 concludes with references for standards documents and other resources that define the URL syntax, the various URL schemes, and other related Internet standards.

If you are reading this chapter to get a simple overview of URLs, you may want to skip Section 8.1.4 and most of 8.2, which is largely a reference section on the most common URL schemes (but you should read Sections 8.2.5, 8.2.7, and 8.2.14). Section 8.1.4 is particularly useful if you are writing software that must process URLs—such as CGI programs processing query data that is sent by a Web browser.

8.1 URL Overview and Syntax Rules

As mentioned in the introduction, a URL is simply a tool for referencing the location of an Internet resource. Most of the time, a URL contains the following four pieces of information (some of which are optional, depending on the scheme):

- The *protocol* to use when accessing the resource (HTTP, Gopher, WAIS, for example). This is always required and is indicated by the *scheme identifier* at the start of the URL. An example is the scheme identification string `http:`, which indicates the HTTP protocol. Such identifiers are case-insensitive, can only contain ASCII letters (*a–z, A–Z*), numbers (*0–9*), or the characters +, –, and ., and must begin with a letter.

- The Internet *domain name* or numeric IP address of the site on which the server is running information. If present, this information appears just after the protocol identifier and is identified by two leading slash characters. An example is `//www.utoronto.ca`. This portion is not required by some schemes (such as **mailto** URLs). Some schemes support username and password information in this portion of the URL: This information appears just in front of the domain name or IP address. The syntax for doing this is discussed in Section 8.1.1.

- If a URL specifies the domain name or IP address of a resource, then it can also specify a *port number* on the server being referenced (each Internet service offered by a machine is made available via one or more such ports, as discussed in Chapter 7, Section 7.2.1). This information is optional: If present, the port number is indicated by a colon after the domain name or IP address, then followed by the number. An example is :80. If the port number is not specified, then the software processing the URL assumes a default value corresponding to the indicated protocol. For example, the default port number for **http** URLs is 80.

■ The *location* of the resource on the server—often a file or directory specification. This is sometimes optional, depending on the protocol. If the URL contains a domain name, then the location portion appears after the domain name and port number, separated from it by a forward slash. An example is www.alphabeta.com:80/location. If the URL scheme does not give a domain name or IP address, then the location portion appears just after the protocol specifier.

URLs are written as a sequence of ASCII characters (see Appendix A on this book's companion Web site), although there is an encoding scheme (discussed in Section 8.1.4) that lets a URL contain characters not defined in the ASCII character set. Figure 8.1 shows three URLs that illustrate these basic parts of a URL. The first URL

```
http://www.address.edu:8096/path/dir/People.html
```

references the file *People.html* in the directory *path/dir/*, accessible via port *8096* from the server at domain name *www.address.edu*, using the HTTP protocol. The second URL,

```
telnet://gopher.guts.edu
```

references a Telnet connection to the machine at domain name *gopher.guts.edu* at the default Telnet port (port 32). Note that **telnet** URLs do not take any resource location information. Alternatively, a remote server can be referenced using the actual numeric IP address, as in:

```
telnet://132.206.23.1
```

Finally, the URL

```
mailto:john.cleese@fawlty-towers.org
```

references sending a mail message to *john.cleese@fawlty-towers.org* using an appropriate mail client. Note that this scheme does not include a domain name or IP address, so the double forward slash after the protocol specifier is absent.

Domain name or IP address information is not present in URL schemes that do not depend on a specific server, such as those for sending electronic mail (**mailto**) or accessing Usenet newsgroup (**news**) articles. In these cases, users have, and must somehow specify, their own default mail or news server. With Web browsers, domain names for these servers are usually set using a browser configuration menu.

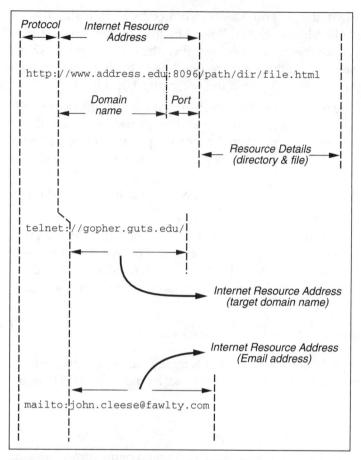

Figure 8.1   Three example URLs (here http, telnet, and mailto URLs), showing the main components. Not all URLs follow these models, as discussed in the text.

NOTE BOOK NOTATION FOR HTTP URLs   In this book, **http** URLs that reference Internet-accessible resources are given without the http:// portion of the string—for example:

```
www.w3.org/pub/WWW/People/W3Cpeople.html
```

This takes advantage of the fact that most current browsers interpret strings, typed into the "Location" text field at the top of the browser window, or into the "Open File..." or "Open Page..." pop-up text input windows, as **http** URLs, if no other protocol is specified.

This, however, is *not true* for **http** URLs used as attribute values in HTML, XHTML, or XML documents. In these cases, an author must not leave off the http:// portion when specifying a full HTTP address. The reasons for this are discussed in Section 8.1.5 (*Relative URLs*).

8.1.1 Usernames and Passwords in URLs

Some schemes allow for username and password information in the URL—this is supported by schemes corresponding to protocols that may require user authentication. In such cases, the username and password information can be placed ahead of the domain name or IP address, using the following syntax

```
username:password@domain.name.edu
```

where *username* is the username, *password* is the password, and the colon character separates the two. However, URLs that show the password are generally a bad idea, as this lets anyone who can read the URL know the user's password! The password can usually be omitted, though, in which case this portion of the URL can be written as:

```
username@domain.name.edu
```

If this is done, the program accessing the resource specified by the URL will typically prompt the user for a password. For example, the URL

```
ftp://joe_blow@machine.internet.com
```

requests an FTP access to the indicated machine, but as the user *joe_blow*. A browser accessing this URL will make the connection and will prompt the user for *joe_blow*'s password.

8.1.2 The Location Portion of a URL

The location portion of a URL specifies the location of a resource on the designated server. This is often given as the path to a resource, where the path corresponds to the directory, folder, or other hierarchical location of the resource on the server (relative to some starting position, of course). For example, the URL

```
http://www.utoronto.ca/webdocs/HTMLdocs/NewHTML/intro.html
```

references the file *intro.html* available in the subdirectory *webdocs/HTMLdocs/NewHTML/*, relative to the top-level directory of resources accessible to the Web server.

The forward slash character (/) has a special meaning in the location portion of the URL and references a change in directory (or some other hierarchical relationship) on the server. Note that this character is used in place of *all* system-dependent symbols defining such relationships, such as the backslash (e.g., *dir1\dir2\file.html*) on DOS, OS/2, or Windows computers, the colon (e.g., *folder:my folder:file.html*) on Macintoshes, and the dot notation (`[dir.sub-dir.subsubdir]`) on VAX/VMS systems.

Query Strings in URLs

Some URL schemes (such as **http** URLs) support *query strings*—this is a way of writing a URL that references a resource on a server and that also contains information (the query string) to send to that resource. A query string is included in a URL by appending the query string data to the resource location, separated from it by a question mark. An example (with the query string in boldface) would be the following

```
http://www.somewhere.edu/cgi-bin/srch-data?archie+database
```

which references the resource *cgi-bin/srch-data* and requests that the data *archie+database* be passed to that resource. This, of course, means that the resource *srch-data* must be able to process the data (i.e., that it is a program of some sort and not just a document).

Fragment Identifiers

URLs referencing resources can also contain *fragment identifiers* that reference specific locations within the resource. This is done by appending a hash character (#) at the end of the URL followed by a string that references the location. An example is (with the fragment component in boldface)

```
http://some.where.edu/Stuff/Path/plonk.html#location
```

where the string `location` references a specific location within the resource (here, inside the document *plonk.html*). Within targeted HTML documents, such named locations can be marked in one of two ways:

1. Using an anchor element and a **name** attribute, as in `<a name="loc23">text marker</a>`

2. Using an **id** attribute, as in `<p id="loc23">This paragraph ... </p>`

where the string `loc23` is the text string marking the location. Note, however, that only recent browsers (e.g., Internet Explorer 4 and greater, Navigator 6 and greater, Opera 4 and greater) support the latter syntax.

When a browser accesses a resource specified by a URL, it first strips off *all* characters following and including the hash (#) and uses the remaining string as the resource URL. Consequently, for the stripped URL to be valid, a fragment identifier must be the very last substring on a URL. The browser preserves the fragment identifier as local information and, after retrieving the indicated resource, looks for the indicated spot in it. The browser will then present the document to the user such that the location is prominently displayed, either by placing the location at the top of the screen or by highlighting it in some way.

This means that the fragment identifier must be the last thing on a URL, after both the location and any query data. Thus, if a URL has both a query string and a fragment identifier, then the latter portion of the URL must be written as:

```
...../path/to/resource?query-data#fragment-id
```

The use of fragment identifiers is discussed in detail in Section 5.2 of the *XHTML 1.0 Language and Design Sourcebook.*

8.1.3 Allowed Characters in URLs

All URLs are written using so-called *printable* ASCII characters (see Appendix A on this book's companion Web site). However, several ASCII characters are not allowed in URLs, mainly because these characters are often interpreted in special ways by software that might process text containing a URL. For example, XML or HTML documents use single or double quotation marks to delimit (i.e., enclose) a URL in a hypertext anchor, so that a quotation mark inside the URL could cause the browser to end the URL prematurely. Therefore, the single and double quotation marks are disallowed. Similarly, the space character is disallowed, because many programs will consider the space as a break between two separate strings and might add a line break at that point when formatting or otherwise processing the text.

> **NOTE** The actual discussion of disallowed, reserved, and other characters in URLs is complex: The material here tries to simplify the discussion, but should in no way be seen as definitive. The technical details are discussed in Section 2 of RFC 2396 and also at the Internationalized URI's overview at www.w3.org/International/O-URL-and-ident.html.

Table 8.1 summarizes the disallowed ASCII characters [including TAB (although TAB, formally, is a control character)], alongside their positions (in hexadecimal notation) in the ASCII, ISO-8859-1, and Unicode character sets (these characters appear at the same positions in all three sets). Also disallowed are the 33 control characters (hex codes 00 to 1F, and 7F).

Escaping of Disallowed ASCII Characters

Of course, the disallowed ASCII characters in Table 8.1 may be needed in a URL, particularly in the location or query string portion. For example, file or

Table 8.1 ASCII Characters That Are Disallowed in URLs and Their Hexadecimal Positions

CHARACTER	HEX	CHARACTER	HEX
TAB	09	SPACE	20
"	22	<	3C
>	3E	[	5B
\	5C	]	5D
^	5E	`	60
{	7B	|	7C
}	7D	~	7E

directory names may contain space characters, as in the filename *Network Info* (where there is a single space character between the words *Network* and *Info*).

To allow these characters to appear, the URL syntax supports a special *escaping* mechanism by which disallowed ASCII characters can be represented in a URL by the special ASCII character sequence

`%xx`

where *xx* is the hexadecimal code (see Table 8.1) corresponding to the character's position. Thus, the code corresponding to the space character is `%20`, and the filename *Network Info* would need to be represented in a URL as the encoded string `Network%20Info`.

You will sometimes see disallowed characters (for example, the tilde, ~) in a URL without any special escaping. Such URLs will work correctly most of the time, but to be safe, you should escape them.

Special ASCII Characters

Also, as noted earlier, several ASCII characters can have special meanings when they appear in a URL. In particular, the percent character (%) is special, because it starts a character escape sequence. Similarly, the forward slash character (/) is special and either divides portions of the URL (when it separates the domain name from the protocol specifier, or the domain name from the location information) or denotes a change in hierarchy, such as a directory change (when in the location portion of the URL).

These special characters must also be escaped if they are to be treated as ordinary characters and not be interpreted as special. Thus, to include the string:

```
ian%euler
```

in a URL (for example, as part of a directory name), it must be written as

```
ian%25euler
```

where `%25` is the escape code for the percent character. If this is not done, then the program parsing the URL string will try to interpret `%eu` as an escape sequence. Conversely, special characters *must not* be encoded if their special meaning is needed. For example, in the location portion of a URL, the string

```
dir/subdir
```

means that *subdir* is a subdirectory of *dir*, whereas

```
dir%2Fsubdir
```

simply represents the character string *dir/subdir* (`%2F` is the encoding for the slash).

The characters that are special actually depend on the particular scheme. The characters that are most often special in the location portion of a URL are as follows:

The percent sign (%). This is the escape character for character encodings and is special in all URLs.

The hash (#). This separates the URL of a resource from the *fragment identifier* for that resource. A fragment identifier references a particular location within a resource. This character is special in all URLs.

The slash (/). This indicates hierarchical structures, such as directories.

The question mark (?). This indicates a *query string;* everything after the question mark is query information to be passed to the server. This character is special only in Gopher, WAIS, and HTTP URLs.

Other characters that are special in certain schemes are the colon (:), semicolon (;), at (@), equals (=), and ampersand (&). These cases are noted in Section 8.2, where the different schemes are discussed in more detail.

Table A.1 in Appendix A on this book's companion Web site lists all ASCII characters alongside their hexadecimal positions in the ASCII, ISO 8859-1 (a.k.a. Latin-1), and UCS (Unicode) character sets.

TIP URL ASCII CHARACTER ENCODING RULE **Encode any ASCII character that might be special if you do not want to use its special meaning.**

Special ASCII Character Encodings in Query Strings

Characters in query strings, because they are part of a URL, are also escaped as just described. However, query string data is typically also *encoded* in some way, with the encoding mechanism typically varying depending on the mechanism by which the query string is generated. As an illustration, space characters in a query string corresponding to a Gopher server query are encoded as plus (+) signs, and not as the escape sequence %20. Indeed, query string encodings are specific to the protocol being used and to the mechanism used to gather data from the user (e.g., was the data gathered by **isindex**, **form**, or **ismap** active image markup). The different mechanisms are discussed in Sections 8.2.6 (**gopher** URLs) and 8.2.7 (**http** URLs).

8.1.4 Encoding Non-ASCII Characters in URLs

To this point, we have discussed URLs that contain only characters defined in the ASCII character set—a set that defines only 128 possible characters. In practice, the URL syntax allows for non-ASCII characters as well, using two different *encoding* mechanisms. The first mechanism, which was defined in the original URL syntax specification (RFC 1738), lets a URL contain only those characters defined in the ISO 8859-1 character set—this set consists of some 232 characters common to Latin alphabet–based Western European languages. The second mechanism, defined in the newer syntax specification (RFCs 2396 and 2718), lets a URL contain any of the millions of characters defined in the UCS/Unicode character set, which is obviously far more flexible. However, this second approach is not backward-compatible with the original one.

This section first describes the original encoding mechanism, which is widely supported by most current browsers. In particular, this is the only mechanism supported by older browsers such as Navigator 4 (and earlier), Internet Explorer 4 (and earlier), Lynx 2.8 (and earlier), and Opera 3.6 (and earlier). The next section then describes the newer (next-generation) approach.

Note that to understand the details of these two sections, you will need a good understanding of character sets and character set encoding. These issues are discussed in some detail in Appendix A on this book's companion Web site.

Original URL Character Encoding

In traditional URLs, as supported by Navigator 4.x and earlier, Internet Explorer 4 and earlier, Opera 3.6 and earlier, and Lynx 2.8 and earlier, URLs could only contain or encode characters defined in the ISO 8859-1 (also called

Latin-1) character set. This is a character set that defines some 256 characters—the first 128 of which are the characters defined in the ASCII character set. The additional 128 positions reference many accented and other characters common in Latin alphabet–based languages. For example, the character *é* (*e* with an acute accent) is at position 233 (hexadecimal e9), and the character *õ* (*o* with a tilde on top) is at position 245 (hexadecimal f1). Table A.1 in Appendix A on this book's companion Web site summarizes the different Latin-1 characters and their positions.

ISO 8859-1 was designed so that each character could be stored in a single byte—this is why the set only supports 256 characters. In ISO 8859-1, each character is stored as a byte that encodes the position of the character in the character set. Thus, the character *é* (at position 233 or hexadecimal e9) is stored as the byte 11101001 (eight bits corresponding, in binary notation, to the decimal integer 233).

In the original URL encoding scheme, any non-Latin-1 character can be encoded using the mechanism

%*xx*

where *xx* is the *hexadecimal* position of the character in the ISO 8859-1 character set. Thus, the string %e9 encodes the character *é*, while %f1 encodes the character *õ*. Note that this is the same as the escaping mechanism used for the disallowed and special ASCII characters. As a result, *decoding* a URL and recovering the original character is easy: Just look for a percent character and replace the sequence %*xx* with the character at (hexadecimal) position *xx* from the ISO 8859-1 character set.

The advantage of this approach is that both encoding/escaping and decoding are simple and straightforward. The obvious disadvantage is that such URLs cannot contain characters from other languages, such as Hebrew, Greek, or Chinese, as these characters are not defined in the Latin-1 character set.

The URL syntax rules were recently modified (RFC 2396 and 2718) to allow for a more complex URL encoding mechanism that allows for characters not defined in ISO 8859-1—these new rules and their implications are discussed next. Note, however, that this new approach is not yet widely supported. At present, only Internet Explorer 5 (and greater) and Navigator 6 (and greater) understand the newer scheme.

Next-Generation URL Character Encoding

To define the problem precisely, a URL is actually a *double encoding* because it encodes, as a sequence of printed ASCII characters, the binary data in which the original URL text is actually encoded. This fact can be glossed over in the case just described because the URL was by definition always encoded using the ISO 8859-1 character set, so that the relationship between bytes and characters is straightforward (one character corresponds to one byte value). However, this distinction is critical to understanding how non-Latin characters can be used in URLs, because here the relationship is not so simple.

This is because the next-generation URL syntax lets the text in a URL be digitally encoded using many different character sets and *character set encodings*. The ramifications of this statement are actually quite deep, and understanding these ramifications in detail requires a detailed understanding of character sets and encodings (discussed in detail in Appendix A on this book's companion Web site). However, the next two sections provide a brief review of the most important issues, with a particular focus on the recommended way of constructing internationalized URLs. But to summarize briefly the process of creating a URL would go as follows:

1. Write down the desired text for the various portions of the URL as the desired sequence of characters—this can include any characters you want, including Arabic, Greek, and so on, and will use any of the special URL encoding mechanisms used by HTML forms (e.g., `input1=Φ&input2=Öffnen`, etc.) and so forth. Some of these, of course, will be ASCII characters. Any ASCII characters that are special, in the context of the portion of the URL being created and that need to have this special meaning escaped, must be noted at this point. For example, if the filename `fich /Φr` (with a space character and a forward slash in the name) appeared in a URL, you would note that the space and forward slash characters are, respectively, disallowed and special and need to be escaped in some way.

2. Look for all the characters not allowed in a URL (i.e., non-ASCII characters, the disallowed ASCII characters, or special characters that need to be escaped), and convert these characters into the byte sequence produced by the UTF-8 encoding of the UCS character set.

3. Replace the original character now by the ASCII escape sequence corresponding to the sequence of bytes. For example, the character Φ corresponds to the bytes `00000011 10100110`, which would be escaped as the character sequence `%ce%a6`.

Of course, to undo this process the software must know which character set and encoding was used at step 3 to transform the original text into binary data. This is only possible if you know which character set and encoding were used at step 2. The current (and proposed) standards recommendation (that URLs always be encoded using UTF-8) helps to avoid these problems.

By now, this complex algorithm and barrage of terminology have probably hopelessly confused you. The next few sections (and Appendix A on the Web site) will help make these issues clearer and also help explain why these steps are necessary.

Character Sets

A *character set* simply defines a collection, or *set*, of characters and the *positions* of the characters in the set (i.e., the character *B* is at position 66; the character *õ* is at position 245; and so on). For example, the ASCII character set allows for 128 characters—it defines 95 printable characters at positions 32 (the space character) through 126 (the tilde, ~) and reserves positions 0 through 31 and position 128 for so-called control characters. The ISO 8859-1 character set allows for 256 characters, but the first 128 positions are occupied by the same characters as in ASCII, at the same positions for compatibility with that character set. Thus, the character at position 66 is the letter *B* in both sets. The upper 128 positions in ISO 8859-1 contain characters common in Western European languages: for example, the letter *Ö* (capital *O* with an umlaut) at position 214.

There are lots of other character sets that define 256 characters. For example, *ISO 8859-7* puts the ASCII characters in positions 0 through 127, but defines Greek characters in the remaining 128 places. Thus, in ISO 8859-7, the character at position 66 is the letter *B*, whereas the character at position 214 is now Φ (the Greek letter phi).

The *Universal Character Set*, or *UCS* (see Appendix A on this book's companion Web site), is a much larger character set that allows for several million characters. However, once again, the characters at positions 0 through 255 are identical with those characters defined in ISO 8859-1, whereas the characters at positions 0 through 127 are identical with those defined in ASCII. Thus, the character at position 66 is the letter *B* in all three of these character sets, whereas the character at position 214 is the letter *Ö* in both UCS and ISO 8859-1. Finally, in UCS the character Φ is at position 934—which is different from its position in ISO 8859-7, because you can't have two different characters at the same place in a character set.

Character Set Encodings

A *character set encoding* defines how the numerical *position* of a character in the character set is encoded as binary data. For example, when using the ASCII character set, the characters can only be encoded in a single way: As a bit sequence corresponding to the numeric position of the character in the character set. Thus, the letter *B*, at position 66, is encoded as the byte `01000010` (binary for 66). Note that, for ASCII characters, the leading bit is always zero, which is why ASCII is often also called a seven-bit character set.

NOTE Character set specifications generally define a set of characters and their positions in the set, along with one or more binary character set encodings that can be used with that character set.

Similarly, when using the ISO 8859-1 character set, characters can only be encoded in a single way: As a bit sequence corresponding to the position of the character in the character set. Thus, the letter *B*, again at position 66, is encoded as the byte `01000010` (binary for 66) and the character *Ö*, at position 214, is encoded as the byte `11010110` (binary for 214). Indeed, the ISO 8859-1 character set is often called an eight-bit character set, because the binary encoding makes use of all the bits in a byte to encode the positions of the characters.

There are lots of other eight-bit character sets that use this same encoding. For example, when using the ISO 8859-7 character set, the byte `11010110` corresponds to the Greek letter *Φ* and not to the letter *Ö*. Thus, given the encoded binary data, you need to know both the encoding and the character set to figure out the characters the bytes represent.

UCS allows for several different encodings of the character positions. To illustrate this, we will consider three characters defined in UCS: the characters *B* and *Ö* at positions 66 and 214, respectively (just like in ISO 8859-1), and the character *Φ* (Greek capital letter phi) at position 934 (note that this is different from the position in ISO 8859-7). We will now look at two ways in which these characters can be encoded.

One encoding, called *UTF-16*, stores each character in two consecutive bytes, where the bits in the two bytes correspond to the position of the character in the UCS character set (as a 16-bit integer). Thus, as shown in Table 8.2, the UTF-16 encoding for *B* is `00000000 01000010`, while the encoding for *Φ* is `00000011 10100110`. Note how each character is digitally encoded using two bytes.

UCS also supports a second encoding called *UTF-8* (UCS Transformation Format: eight-bit encoding). In UTF-8, characters are encoded in one, two, or more bytes depending on the position of the character in the character set. The UTF-8 encodings of the example characters we have been considering are shown in Table 8.2. Note how the number of bytes in the encoding

Table 8.2 Three characters defined in the UCS character set and their UTF-16 and UTF-8 binary encodings. The digits in boldface are specific code sequences added, in the UTF-8 encoding, to pad out the bit sequences to 8 bits—the nonboldface bits encode the character's actual position. The number of set (i.e., with a value of 1) leading bits in the first byte of the encoding sequence (here, 2) gives the number of bytes used to encode the character.

CHARACTER	UTF-16 ENCODING	UTF-8 ENCODING
B	00000000 01000010	01000010
Ö	00000000 11010110	**11000011** **10**010110
Φ	00000011 10100110	**11001110** **10**100110

sequence differs depending on the position of the character—indeed, the higher (larger) character positions are encoded using as many as six bytes!

The special aspect of UTF-8 is that all ASCII characters are encoded using the standard ASCII (or ISO 8859-1) encodings—note how the UTF-8 encoding of the letter *B* is simply the byte 01000010, which is exactly the encoding this character has when encoded using the ASCII character set.

UCS supports other possible encodings, and there are many other character sets that in turn support their own encoding mechanisms. However, these three examples are sufficient to illustrate the main issues.

Character Encodings and URLs

A URL, on the other hand, is a sequence of characters, and not a sequence of bytes. In fact, it is a sequence of characters that *encodes* a sequence of bytes that, in turn, corresponds to a *character set encoding* of the original characters. With the old encoding mechanism, this two-stage correspondence was straightforward. Only characters defined in ISO 8859-1 were allowed in the URL text, and after all the disallowed and unsafe ASCII characters were escaped (using the %*xx* encoding mechanism) in the original text, all characters were uniformly encoded into a single byte (for example, *B* became 01000010, and *Ö* became 11010110). Then, to URL-encode the *bytes*, any byte with a value greater than 7f was encoded as the sequence %*xx*, where *xx* is the hexadecimal value for the byte (so that 11010110 became %d6). Then, any byte with a value less than this was simply URL-encoded as the corresponding ASCII character encoded it (e.g., 01000010 was encoded as the letter B).

Indeed, because these steps are straightforward they can easily be collapsed into a single encoding phase, where characters are immediately turned into analogous ASCII character sequences—that is, disallowed ASCII, special ASCII, and extra Latin-1 characters are converted to %*xx* sequences—without having to think much about the character set being used.

If we don't use ISO 8859-1, then the situation is much more complicated, as the character set and encoding now play a major role. To simplify the situation, the current recommendation is that URLs always be binary-encoded, using the UTF-8 encoding. Given this constraint, the procedure for encoding a URL text is as follows:

1. Write out the URL text as the desired sequence of characters, leaving any non-ASCII, disallowed ASCII, or special ASCII character as is. However, note any special ASCII characters (such as the forward slash, /) that are present and not being used for their special meaning in the URL. Of course, the characters that are special vary depending on the URL scheme and, indeed, on the portion of the URL being considered (domain name, location, query string, query string from an HTML **form**, etc.).

2. Encode and escape the nonallowed characters (ASCII and non-ASCII), as well as the special ASCII characters that need to be escaped, as follows:

   a. Take each such character and use the UTF-8 encoding to encode it as a sequence of one or more bytes. For example, the character / would become the byte `00101111`, and the character Φ would become the two-byte sequence `11001110 10100110`.

   b. Character-encode these bytes using the URL escaping mechanism. That is, the byte `00101111` becomes the character sequence `%2f`, and the bytes `11001110 10100110` become the character sequence `%ce%a6`.

   c. Replace the original character in the URL text by the resulting character encoding sequence.

The URL has been properly constructed after the entire text has been processed. As an example, let us suppose that we want to convert the following text, produced as a query string from an HTML **form**, into a correctly encoded string that can be attached to a URL

```
String1=a=1/&String2=Φ
```

where the characters in boldface are treated as special in the URL. The composition rules for creating the URL string are now as follows (the numbering corresponds to the numbering sequence in the preceding list):

1. Take each character in the string and look for the disallowed characters and any special characters that are not using their special meaning. In the example, the character Φ is disallowed, whereas the characters = and / (as part of the value assigned to `String1`) are special but here are being handled as regular characters. These characters have the following UTF-8 encodings:

UCS character	=	/	Φ
UTF-8 byte encoding (hex)	3d	2f	ce a6

2. Now, take each byte in the encodings, and encode it using the URL escaping mechanism. Thus, the escape sequences for these characters are as follows:

UCS character	=	/	Φ
ASCII escape sequence	%3d	%2f	%ce%a6

3. Rewrite the string, replacing these characters by their escaped forms. Thus, the original string

   ```
   String1=a=1/&String2=Φ
   ```

   becomes the URL string:

   ```
   String1=a%3d1%2f&String2=%ce%a6
   ```

Browser Encoding of URLs

Of course, a browser automatically gathers **form** data and dynamically generates the URL-escaped query string based on the data entered or selected by the user. However, when doing so, the browser must know if you want the URL data to be encoded using the original URL escaping mechanism, which only supported ISO Latin-1 characters, or if you want to use the new UTF-8 mechanism—or, indeed, if you want to use some other character set and encoding mechanism. Although the aforementioned mechanism described how to encode the URL using UTF-8, the specifications actually let you use any character set and encoding you want!

At present, you can use a **meta** element in the X/HTML document **head** to indicate which encoding to use when the URL is constructed. In fact, the **meta** element indicates the character set encoding used in the document, as in the following two examples:

```
<meta http-equiv="content-type"
      content="text/html;charset=UTF-8" />
<meta http-equiv="content-type"
      content="text/html;charset=ISO-8859-1" />
```

The first of these indicates that the document itself was distributed as binary data using the UTF-8 character encoding: Browsers that support the UTF-8 encoding of URL data then use the UTF-8 encoding when they encode **form**-based data.

Of course, including the **meta** element

```
<meta http-equiv="content-type"
      content="text/html;charset=UTF-8" />
```

means that the document itself must be encoded using UTF-8. Thus, there is no way to write a document using one character encoding (e.g., EUC-JP) and then have an HTML **form** produce URLs that encode using the UTF-8 encoding.

Problems will also occur if the document contains characters not supported by the indicated document encoding. For example, if the document is encoded using the ISO 8859-1 encoding, but contains character or entity references in form fields that reference non-Latin characters, then the form has no way of including this character in the URL. In this case, Mozilla/Netscape 6 replaces such characters by an escaped question mark (`%3f`). Internet Explorer 5, on the other hand, uses some sort of Microsoft code pages switching notation to reference the character using nonstandard notation.

The best practice, then, is to encode documents using UTF-8 whenever necessary and to indicate this encoding using a **meta** element in the document **head**.

Problems Decoding a URL

Encoding a URL is in principle easy, because the encoding software knows the character set and character set encoding being used. However, the reverse is not so easy: Given the URL

```
http://www.wooble.org/path/my%20prog.pl?Val=21&B=%CE%A6
```

and no additional information, the software processing the URL does not know the character set and encoding used to create it; thus, it does not know if the sequence %CE%A6 corresponds to the character Φ (if UTF-8), the character sequence Î¦ (if ISO 8859-1), or some other character or characters (if another character set).

This means that the software decoding the URL needs to know how the URL was created—that is, which character set and character set encoding was used. There is no standard way of communicating this information, and this lack of a standard places extra demands on the Web application designer to make sure that this information is somehow communicated or otherwise understood in a Web application. In particular, the application design must ensure that all URL requests generated by a Web browser encode URL data in a manner that can be properly parsed by the server-side software processing the request.

8.1.5 Relative URLs

From within a document, an author does not always need to specify the full URL of a second resource. This is because being *in* a document implies knowledge of the URL location of that document, which lets you reference neighboring resources relative to that location, using a *relative* URL. More formally, the URL string is called a *partial* URL, because it contains only part of the full URL—that is, the part *different* from the URL used to access the current document.

For example, suppose a user accesses the document *file.html* using the full URL

```
http://www.stuff.edu/main/docs/file.html
```

and that, within this document, there is a hypertext reference containing the *relative* URL:

```
<a href="stuff.html">anchor text</a>
```

Where is this file? Any information not present in a URL reference is considered to be the *same* as that used to access the current document. Thus, the partial URL stuff.html is transformed into a full URL by appropriating the missing URL components from the URL that was used to access *file.html*. The completed URL is then:

```
http://www.stuff.edu/main/docs/stuff.html
```

which indicates, as expected, that *stuff.html* is on the same server and in the same directory as *file.html.* Other, equivalent, relative URLs would then be:

```
/main/docs/stuff.html
//www.stuff.edu/main/docs/stuff.html
```

The former appropriates `http://www.stuff.edu` from the current URL to complete the reference, and the latter appropriates only the `http:` part from the *base* URL of the current document.

You can also use partial URLs to reference resources at other locations on the same server. For example, from within the file *file.html,* the partial URL

```
../../main.html
```

references the file *main.html* in the root HTTP directory, namely:

```
http://www.stuff.edu/main.html
```

Note how, with partial URLs, the special symbol . . (two periods) indicates a location one up in the directory hierarchy, just as it does in DOS or UNIX. Furthermore, the symbol . (single period) denotes the current directory.

Practical examples illustrating the use of partial URLs are also found in *XHTML 1.0 Language and Design Sourcebook,* Section 5.3.

Relative URLs and the Base Element

Relative URLs are very useful when constructing large collections of documents that will be kept together. However, relative URLs become invalid for a single document that is moved to a new directory or a new Internet site. Using a **base** element in a moved X/HTML document can mitigate this problem. **Base** records the *base,* or original, location of the document. Relative URLs are evaluated *relative to* this recorded base URL. Thus, when the document is moved, all relative URLs are determined relative to the URL recorded by **base**, and the linked resources are correctly accessed from the original server. For example, suppose a document contains the **head**-level element

```
<base href="http://www.flopsy.com/dir1/path/file2.html" />
```

and also the **body**-level hypertext reference:

```
<a href="../stuff.html">link to some stuff</a>
```

Then, this hypertext link references the URL

```
http://www.flopsy.com/dir1/stuff.html
```

regardless of the actual location of the document containing the reference, because the **base** always directs relative URLs to an address relative to the base location.

8.2 URL Specifications

This section reviews in detail the most common URL schemes. These schemes are summarized in Table 8.3, which provides a brief description of the protocol plus a list of the browsers, browser plug-ins, or other software that support the scheme. Italicized entries indicate schemes that are not widely supported by current browsers. The section labeled "Special Schemes" lists those that are currently only supported by **object** elements in the indicated Web browsers. The section labeled "Pseudo Schemes" lists URL schemes that, formally, are not resource locators, but that are commonly encountered in Web browsers and Web applications.

Table 8.3 Description of URL protocol specifier strings. The "Supported by" column indicates level of browser support.* "Special" schemes are currently supported only by **object** element **classid** values. "Pseudo" schemes do not reference well-defined Internet Resources.

PROTOCOL SPECIFIER	PROTOCOL OR FUNCTION	SUPPORTED BY
castanet:	*Apparent synonym for HTTP urls (Netscape Navigator 4 only)*	*NS 4*
cid: (see also mid:)	Content-id resource reference; for mail and USENET messages	NS 4 (Mail/News Client), other mail clients
data:	Inclusion of inline data	IE 4, NS 4
file:	Local file access (various protocols)	All
ftp:	FTP protocol	All
gopher:	Gopher protocol	All
http: (https:)	HTTP protocol	All
https:	Secure HTTP	All
imap:	IMAP post office access protocol	NS 4
lav: (lavs:)	Liquid Audio streaming audio protocol	Liquid Audio player
ldap: (ldaps:)	Lightweight Directory Access Protocol	NS 4 (addressbook client only), IE 4
mailto:	Internet mail address	All

(continues)

Table 8.3 (Continued)

PROTOCOL SPECIFIER	PROTOCOL OR FUNCTION	SUPPORTED BY
mid: (see also cid:)	Message-id resource reference; for mail and USENET messages	NS 4 (Mail/News Client), other mail clients
mms:	Microsoft media server protocol	Microsoft Media Player
news: (snews:)	NNTP USENET *protocol*	All
nntp:	*NNTP USENET protocol*	*IE 4*
pop3:	POP3 post office access protocol	NS 4
prospero:	*Prospero directory services protocol*	*None*
rtsp: (rtspu:)	Real Time Streaming Protocol	Real Audio Media Player (and server), Apple QuickTime 4 player (and server)
telnet: (*rlogin:,* tn3270:)	Telnet protocol	All (provided browser is configured to know of a telnet client)
wais:	*WAIS protocol*	*Some (via a proxy server)*
SPECIAL SCHEMES		
clsid:	Microsoft COM class identifier	IE 3
java:	Java classes	NS 4, IE 4
javabean:	A Javabean class	NS 4
PSEUDO SCHEMES		
about:	References information about the browser	IE 4 (partially), NS
addbook:	Add vCard entries to Address Book	NS 4
javascript:	References inline JavaScript code	IE 3/4, NS
mocha: and *livescript:*	References inline JavaScript code (obsolete—do not use!)	NS 2 through 4 only
mailbox:	References Access to local mail client	NS 4
pnm:	Progressive Networks Metafile data	Real Audio players
res:	References a resource accessible from a loadable (DLL) module	IE 4
view-source:	References a source listing of a resource	NS 3, IE 4
wysiwyg:	References JavaScript-derived HTML output	NS 2 through 4 only

* NS: Netscape Navigator (Versions > 1); NS 4: Netscape Navigator 4 (and greater); IE: Microsoft Internet Explorer (Versions > 2); IE 4: Microsoft Internet Explorer 4 (and greater).

8.2.1 Castanet URLs (Navigator 4 Only)

Castanet URLs were apparently designed as a reference to Marimba *Castanet* resources—I use the word *apparently*, as little documentation on this scheme is available. Netscape Navigator 4, the only browser to understand this scheme, treats **castanet** URLs as equivalent to **http** URLs unless the special *Castanet Tuner* component is installed (which is rarely the case). In the absence of the *Castanet* software, the references

```
castanet://www.utoronto.ca
http://www.utoronto.ca
```

are equivalent. Authors should thus avoid **castanet** URLs, unless they are specifically targeting *Castanet* software.

8.2.2 Cid URLs

Cid URLs refer to a specific part of a MIME-encoded multipart message. Indeed, **Cid** URLs are designed for use within multipart HTML (M-HTML; see Appendix B on this book's companion Web site) messages. Such messages contain X/HTML documents and images as parts of the same multipart message body. The general form for a **cid** URL is

```
cid:content-id
```

where `content-id` is the URL-encoded version of the MIME Content-ID for the desired part of the message. The format for Content-IDs in a multipart message is defined in the MIME specifications, referenced at the end of Appendix B on this book's companion Web site. As an example, a typical ID might be

```
part3-12%d7f4@flopsy.org
```

which identifies the program that composed the message (`pine`) and the machine from which the message was sent (`flopsy.org`), and which contains a generated string (`part3-12%d7f4`) chosen to ensure that all ids in the message are unique. The corresponding **cid** URL would be:

```
cid:part3-12%25d7f4@flopsy.org
```

Note how the percent character (`%25`) in the Content-ID has been URL-escaped.

Cid URLs allow for links *between* parts of a multipart message. For example, a single message can contain multiple X/HTML documents, with links between them, or can contain an X/HTML document along with the associated image files. In this latter case, the images would be referenced from the X/HTML document using **img** elements of the form

```
<img src="cid:content-id" .../>
```

where `content-id` is the Content-ID for the image.

Cid URLs are supported by the Netscape Communicator 4 (and later) mail, news, and HTML authoring clients, but only within the mail or news viewing and authoring client (Netscape Messenger)—they are not understood by the browser. Indeed, if a user clicks in the Netscape Messenger mail client on a hypertext link referencing a **cid** URL, the resulting string displayed in the Navigator Location window is actually a **mailbox** URL. **Cid** URLs are not supported by Internet Explorer 4's default mail client (Microsoft Outlook), but they are supported by later versions of Outlook and Outlook Express, and are also apparently supported by recent versions of other mail clients, such as Eudora Pro.

An author would only rarely type a **cid** URL because such URLs are typically generated by the tools that assemble mail messages or newsgroup postings. **Cid** URLs are related to **mid** (Message Identifier) URLs, discussed later.

8.2.3 Data URLs

Data URLs allow for inclusion of small pieces of data within a URL—that is, instead of referencing an external resource, **data** URLs actually *contain* the data, encoded as part of the URL. This is useful for including small chunks of data within a document, such as **object** element parameter values or small, inline images.

The form for a data URL is rather complex, and you are referred to the specification document, listed in the references section, for details. In general, **data** URLs have the form

```
data:mime/type;base64,data-content
```

where `mime/type` gives the MIME type (and any optional parameters, such as the character set or encoding); the optional `;base64` parameter indicates that the data content is encoded following the base64 encoding (see RFC 2045, Section 6.8); and a comma separates the data URL parameters from the data content. Some typical forms are illustrated in the following, where `datastring` corresponds to the data content of the URL:

data:,*datastring*. A string of data, by default of type text/plain and in the US-ASCII character set.

data:image/gif;base64,*datastring*. A string of data that is base64-encoded and that corresponds to a GIF image.

`data:text/html;version=4.0;charset=utf8,`*`datastring`***.** A string of data that corresponds to HTML content, encoded using the Unicode UTF-8 character set, and is URL encoded.

Internet Explorer 3/4 and Netscape Navigator 4 and greater understand **data** URLs that specify data to be passed, via **object** elements, to Java or Active-X components. Netscape Navigator 4 and greater and Internet Explorer 4 and greater can handle **data** URLs in almost any context; for example, to encode small images (as an argument to an **img** element **src** attribute), or to encode small documents (as an argument to an **a** element **href** attribute).

8.2.4 File URLs

File URLs specify the location of resources relative to the local file system. Because such references are valid only for computers with direct access to the local file system (e.g., connected to the same Novell, UNIX, or Windows NT/2000 file server), **file** URLs should not be used in documents to be publicly accessed over the Internet.

NOTE DO NOT USE FILE URLs FOR INTERNET/INTRANET PUBLISHING **Because file URLs specify local files, and not network-accessible ones, file URLs should not be used for documents to be published on the Internet.**

The general form for a **file** URL is

```
file://int.domain.nam/path/file
```

where `int.domain.nam` is the domain name for the file server, and `path/file` is the locator of the file. Note that there is no specified port number, because local file access may be accomplished in many ways using many different protocols [e.g., directly from a local hard disk or remotely from a Network File System (NFS) file server, a Novell file server, or from a Windows file server]. All browsers allow local file access, often accessed by using a pull-down menu (or by dragging and dropping a document onto the browser), and represent the location using a **file** URL.

The domain name for local file access can either be the special string `localhost`, or an empty field (i.e., `file:///...`). For example, if you are using a UNIX system and are accessing the local file */big/web/docs.html*, the **file** URL could be either of the following

```
file://localhost/big/web/docs.html
file:///big/web/docs.html
```

where the file could be on a local disk or on a file system mounted on the local system from elsewhere. On a PC, the path portion of the URL—in particular, the portion that identifies the disk—is somewhat differently encoded. For example, if a file is located at *D:\betas\tests\example.html*, then the corresponding file URL is:

```
file:///D|/betas/tests/example.html
```

In this case the *D:* disk could be either a local hard drive, or it could be a remote file system mapped onto that virtual drive identifier.

8.2.5 Ftp URLs

Ftp URLs designate files and directories that can be accessed using the FTP protocol. In the absence of any username and password information in the URL, anonymous FTP access is assumed (implying a connection to the server as username *anonymous*, using the user's Internet mail address as the password). The general form for an anonymous **ftp** URL is

```
ftp://int.domain.nam:port/resource
```

where `int.domain.nam` is the domain name to access, `:port` specifies the optional port number (the default is 21), and `resource` is the local resource specification. Here is a typical example, referencing the file *splunge.txt*, which is located in the directory *stuff* at the Internet site *ftp.mysite.com* at the default port:

```
ftp://ftp.mysite.com/stuff/splunge.txt
```

You can specify FTP access of a directory using a URL such as

```
ftp://ftp.mysite.com/path/
```

in which case the server should return a listing of the directory contents. Browsers display this information as a menu, allowing the user to navigate through the file system or select particular files for downloading.

Special Characters in FTP URLs

The forward slash (/) and semicolon (;) characters are special in an **ftp** URL. The forward slash indicates directory or other hierarchical structures, and the semicolon is used to indicate the start of a *typecode string*. Typecode strings, discussed later in this section, must be the last string of the URL (not including any fragment identifier).

Nonanonymous FTP Access

You can log in to an FTP server as a regular (nonanonymous) user by specifying, within the URL, the username (and optionally the password) of the account you wish to access. For example, the URL

```
ftp://joe_bozo:bl123@internet.address.edu/dir1/Dir2/file.gz
```

references the indicated file on the machine *internet.address.edu*, accessible by logging in as user *joe_bozo* with password *bl123*. This URL form is obviously not a secure way of giving access, because anyone who reads the URL knows *joe_bozo*'s password. An alternative is to give only the username, as in:

```
ftp://joe_bozo@internet.address.edu/dir1/Dir2/file.gz
```

Most browsers (Navigator 2 and greater, Internet Explorer 3 and greater, most versions of Lynx and Opera) will connect to the remote machine using the indicated username and will prompt the user for an appropriate password. Note, however, that with some older browsers, both the username and the password entered by the user are displayed in the URL displayed in the browser's *location* text field, which again puts the password in plain view. Note also that the user will be logged into the Web server as long as the browser is active—the user must completely shut down the browser to ensure that subsequent users cannot access the FTP server.

> **TIP** TROUBLESHOOTING FTP URLs **At times, an ftp URL request will fail. This may occur because the network is down or because the machine being accessed is overloaded with FTP requests and refuses your connection. Alternatively, the remote server may be configured to limit access to a restricted set of Internet sites. Web browsers are often terse when handling FTP connections, and say very little when a connection fails. You can often diagnose the source of a problem by using an FTP program, independently of your Web browser. A stand-alone FTP session often provides more commentary on the state of the connection, which can help explain why a connection cannot be made.**

FTP Directory Paths

Directory locations during FTP accesses are defined relative to a well-defined *home directory*, with the actual location of this home directory depending on the identity of the user making the connection. A user who connects via an anonymous FTP is placed in a special anonymous FTP home directory and has restricted access to the server file system (generally, only to those files explicitly put in the area accessible to anonymous FTP accesses). This security feature permits making certain files publicly available without exposing the rest of the system to unauthorized users. On the other hand, if a visitor connects to the same machine as a regular (nonanonymous) user, the home directory will be that of the regular user, which in general is a directory entirely different from that attained via an anonymous FTP. Moreover, the user will then, in many cases, have unfettered access to the entire file system, including access to password and critical system files.

FTP File Transfer Modes

The FTP protocol supports several modes for transferring files. The most important is *image* or *binary* mode, which makes a byte-by-byte copy of the file. This is the safest mode to use and, in particular, must be used when transferring programs, compressed data, or image files. Also important is *ASCII* or *text* mode, which is designed for transferring plain, printable text files. This mode is useful because it corrects for the fact that PCs, Macintoshes, UNIX, and other operating systems use different characters to mark the end of a line of text. In particular, Macintoshes use the carriage-return character, CR; Unix computers use the line feed character, LF; and DOS/Windows computers use both CR and LF (often written CRLF). In ASCII mode, FTP automatically converts between these three end-of-line markers, to ensure that the received file has the new line codes appropriate to the local system. You cannot use this mode to transfer programs, however, because programs and data files contain bytes with the same codes as CR or LF characters—under ASCII mode, these codes are converted into the new-line codes appropriate to the local system, thereby corrupting the content of binary files.

The FTP protocol has no knowledge of the data content of a file and must be told what mode to use in a file transfer. Most browsers simply assume that all data is binary, and transfer the files without correcting the end-of-line character sequences. Alternately, the **ftp** URL syntax supports *typecode strings* to explicitly indicate the transfer mechanism that is appropriate for the indicated data.

FTP Typecode Strings

Typecode strings specify the desired transfer mode for an FTP transfer. For example, the following URL

```
ftp://ftp.mysite.edu/path/splunge.txt;type=a
```

indicates that the designated resource (the file *splunge.txt*) should be retrieved using ASCII mode. The semicolon character (special in **ftp** URLs) separates the end of the resource locator string from the type indicator. Other possible type indicators are `type=i` for image (binary) transfers and `type=d` for directory listings. Typecode strings are optional, the default being binary data transfers. Fragment identifiers, if used, must be placed after the typecode string—for example:

```
ftp://ftp.somesite.edu/path/goof.html;type=a#location
```

> **TIP** PROBLEMS WITH TYPECODE STRINGS? **Typecode strings are supported by Navigator 3.0 and Internet Explorer 3 and later but not by some other browsers, or by earlier versions of these programs. These older browsers assume the typecode string to be part of the file name. A workaround is to hand-edit the URL to remove the typecode string and to try reaccessing the resource.**

8.2.6 Gopher URLs

Gopher is a hypermedia protocol that predates the Web and that has largely been supplanted by HTTP. This section is thus most useful as a historical reference, as it will be rare that a user needs to enter a **gopher** URL into a document.

Gopher servers can be accessed via URLs in a manner that looks superficially similar to **ftp** or **http** URLs. However, the actual meaning of the URL is quite different. This is because Gopher resources are referenced using a combination of *resource identifier codes* and *selector strings*, and not using directory or file names. Resource identifiers are single-digit codes that specify the *type* of the Gopher resource—for example, that it is a text file, a directory, or a searchable index. The Gopher selector string is just a symbolic name associated with this resource. This can be a directory or file name, but it can also be a redirection to a database search procedure or to a Telnet session. Sometimes the selector string has, as its first character, a duplicate of the single-character resource type identifier. This can lead to hair-pulling confusion, with resource identifiers appearing alone or in pairs, seemingly at random. Table 8.4 summarizes the Gopher resource identifier codes.

General Form of a Gopher URL

The general form for a basic Gopher URL is

```
gopher://int.domain.nam:port/Tselector_string
```

where the port number is optional (the default value is 70), T is the Gopher type code from Table 8.4, and $selector\_string$ is the Gopher selector string. The root information of a Gopher server can be obtained by leaving out all type and selector string information. Thus, the root information of the Gopher server at *mr.bean.org* is available at:

```
gopher://mr.bean.org/
```

Table 8.4 Gopher Resource Identifier Codes

CODE	FILE OR RESOURCE TYPE
0	Text file
1	Directory
2	CSO name/phone book server
3	Error
4	Macintosh binhexed (*.hqx) file
5	DOS binary file of some type
6	Unix unencoded file
7	Full-text index search
8	Telnet session
9	Binary file

Hierarchical relationships are possible. For example

```
gopher://mr.bean.org/1stuff
```

indicates that *stuff* behaves like a directory, and that the request will retrieve the Gopher contents of *stuff*, whereas the URL

```
gopher://mr.bean.org/7stuff/index
```

indicates access to the *index* search in the directory *stuff*. Accessing this URL would cause the browser to ask the user for query string information to be used in the search.

Query Strings for Searches

Search information is sent to the Gopher server by appending the search strings to the URL, separated from the URL by a question mark. Thus, to pass the strings `tad`, `jill`, and `joanne` to the Gopher search index noted in the previous section, the URL is:

```
gopher://mr.bean.org/7stuff/index?tad+jill+joanne
```

Note that the URL syntax for Gopher queries uses a plus (+) sign to separate different search strings. Therefore, if you want to include a literal plus sign within a string, it must be encoded (the encoding for a plus sign is `%2B`).

The Gopher protocol supports additional features not discussed here. Please see the references at the end of this chapter for additional information.

8.2.7 Http URLs

Http URLs designate files, directories, or other server-side resources accessible using the HTTP protocol. An **http** URL must always point to a resource (text, data, or program) or a directory. The general form is

```
http://int.domain.nam:port/resource
```

where `int.domain.nam` is the Internet domain name of the server, `:port` is the optional port number (the default value is 80), and `resource` specifies the resource. Resources are usually (but not always) files or directories. A directory is indicated by ending the resource portion of the URL with a forward slash, as in:

```
http://www.utoronto.ca/webdocs/HTMLdocs/
```

Consequently, the following reference to this directory is an error, because it implies a reference to a file (or other resource) and not to a directory:

```
http://www.utoronto.ca/webdocs/HTMLdocs
```

HTTP servers can often detect this type of error and realize that the user wants to view the directory listing. In these cases, the server will return a *server redirect* HTTP response header, which contains the correct URL (complete with the trailing slash), and which instructs the browser to retry the request, this time using the corrected URL (server redirects are discussed in Chapter 9). Of course, this means that the actual retrieval takes two transactions with the server, which is inefficient and should be avoided. The moral is simple: Always put slashes on the end of URLs that reference directories.

Note, however, that you can omit the trailing slash when referencing the *root* of a Web site. Thus, the following two URLs are both equivalent and correct:

```
http://www.utoronto.ca/
http://www.utoronto.ca
```

Special ASCII Characters in Http URLs

The forward slash (/), question mark (?), hash (#), and semicolon (;) are special characters in the path and query string portions of an **http** URL. The slash denotes a change in hierarchy (such as a directory), and the question mark ends the resource location path and indicates the start of a query string. The hash denotes the start of a fragment identifier. The semicolon is reserved for future use (see later in this section) and should therefore be encoded in all cases where you intend a literal semicolon.

URL Encoding of Query Strings

Http URLs can contain query data to be passed to the server—these data are appended to the URL, separated from it by a question mark. Besides the character encodings required within URLs, query strings undergo additional levels of encoding to preserve information about the *structure* of the query data. This is necessary because certain characters in a query string are assigned special meanings as part of the query—for example, the plus character (+) is used to encode space characters. There are several different ways these encodings are done, depending both on the mechanism by which the data are input by the user and on the mechanism by which the data are sent to the server.

Document authors do not usually have to worry about the encoding phase; browsers take **isindex** or **form** data and do the encoding automatically. However, the person writing server programs that process this information must explicitly *decode* this data to recover the original information. Thus, he or she must understand the encoding to reverse the procedure. The following is a brief review of the encoding steps.

URL Encoding for Isindex and Form Data

The seven following steps outline the query string encoding process, elaborated to illustrate the important points. If the data is from an **isindex** query, these steps apply to the encoding of the entire query input string; if the data is from **form**-based input, the encoding steps apply to each name and value string from the **form**'s user-input elements.

1. Percent characters (%) are escaped (`%2f`).
2. Plus signs (+) are escaped (`%2b`).
3. Ampersands (&) are escaped (`%26`).
4. Equals signs (=) are escaped (`%3d`).
5. The possibly special characters—namely, #, ;, /, ?, :, &, !, ,, ', (, and)—are escaped.
6. Space characters are encoded as plus signs (+).
7. All non-ASCII characters are encoded and escaped as discussed in Section 8.1.4 (recall that this depends on the character set encoding being used).

At this point, all ASCII punctuation characters are encoded, except for the five characters: _, -, ., *, and @.

If the data is from an **isindex** query, the encoding is complete. If it is from a **form**, only the individual *name* and *value* strings from each **form** input mechanism are encoded as described in steps 1 through 7. These strings are then combined according to the two following rules, to form the complete query string:

1. Each *name* and *value* pair is combined into a composite ASCII string of the form *name=value*. Note that the first encoding phase (steps 1–7) encoded all equals signs in the *name* and *value* strings, so that the only *un*encoded equals signs in the string are those used to separate a name from its associated value.

2. The *name=value* strings from all the **form** elements are combined into a single string, separated by ampersand (&) characters. For example:

    name1=value1&name2=value2

Note that the first encoding phase (steps 1–7) encoded all ampersands in the *name* and *value* strings, so that the only *un*encoded ampersands in the query string are those that separate name/value pairs.

Query String Encoding MIME Type

Query string data encoded according to this algorithm is said to be *URL form–encoded.* In fact, this encoding mechanism is assigned its own MIME type, namely:

```
Content-type: application/x-www-form-url-encoded
```

Note that you can easily tell if the data comes from a **form** or **isindex** query just by checking for unencoded equals signs. For example, the first of the following two URLs is from an **isindex** query, the second from a **form** (the query string portion is in boldface):

```
http://some.site.edu/cgi-bin/foo?arg1+arg2+arg3
http://some.site.edu/cgi-bin/program?name1=value1&name2=value2
```

NOTE PROPOSED REPLACEMENT OF AMPERSAND (&) BY SEMICOLON (;) The form-encoding use of the ampersand (&) to separate name/value strings was an unfortunate choice, given the use of this character to denote character and entity references. The current URL specification recommends using an unencoded semicolon (;) in query strings instead of ampersands. Thus, strings would be combined as *name1=value1;name2=value2.* There are no current browsers that do this when processing **form** data. However, a gateway program author should write programs to interpret either the ampersand or semicolon character as the delimiting character, so that the program is compatible with next-generation browsers.

URL Encoding of Ismap Active Image Queries

A typical server-based active image is written in an X/HTML document as:

```
<a href="http://some.where.edu/prg-bin/program"><img
     src="funny_image.gif" ismap="ismap" />
</a>
```

The **ismap** attribute makes the **img** element active, and the surrounding anchor element gives the URL to which the image coordinates should be sent. **Ismap** active image queries are composed by taking the integer (x,y) pixel coordinates of the mouse click (when the user clicks the mouse on top of the image), with respect to the upper left-hand corner of the active image, and appending these coordinates to the URL of the enclosing anchor, using the format (query string in boldface italics):

```
http://some.where.edu/prg-bin/program?x,y
```

The only valid characters in the query string are the integer coordinates (x,y) and the comma separating the two values. An example is:

```
http://some.where.edu/prg-bin/program?56,312
```

Accessing Image Maps without Explicit Coordinates

Sometimes, however, a server-based image-mapped image link is accessed without the benefit of the actual image. This can happen in three ways:

1. By the user clicking on the box corresponding to the image, but where the image is not actually present (i.e., the user has disabled image loading or has clicked before the image is visible).

2. By the user using the Tab key to select the image and then pressing the Enter key to access the URL (and thus not selecting any specific coordinates).

3. By the user using a nongraphical browser that does not display images. This is equivalent to the preceding example, as the link is accessed by using a Tab (or other) key.

For all these cases, the formal X/HTML specifications state that the browser should access the URL without any appended coordinate data (i.e., without the question mark and the x and y coordinates). This form of the URL then serves as a signal to the program running on the server that the user did not see the image. Unfortunately, only Navigator 5 and Lynx get this right—all other browsers send incorrect coordinate data of some sort. The actual behavior is summarized in Table 8.5.

Server Issues: Server Processing of Queries

In general, HTTP servers do not handle queries themselves; instead, they pass query data on to other *gateway* programs for further processing—the path */cgi-bin/* in a URL often indicates that process is taking place. The name, however, need not be */cgi-bin/*—this is a configurable symbolic name, and other names (or many different names) may be used. This book generally uses the name cgi-bin to indicate this functionality.

The name following the path */cgi-bin/* is the name of the program to be run by the server. Any information following this name and preceding any query string data (i.e., after any slash following the program name and before a question mark) is known as *extra path* information. This is an additional parameter that, like the query string, is passed to the Common Gateway Interface (CGI) program.

When a server is contacted via a URL referencing a *gateway* program, the server launches the program and passes to it data sent from the client (if any) for further processing. In addition, it passes on any query string data, along with any extra path information. This is discussed in more detail in

Table 8.5 Data Appended to Image Map URL When the User Tabs to the Image or Clicks in a Box Corresponding to Missing Image Data

BROWSER	TAB TO IMAGE AND ENTER*	CLICK IN UNLOADED IMAGE BOX†
Lynx	no coordinate data	N/A (text-only browser)
IE 4	0,0	Selected coordinates
IE 5	0,0	Selected coordinates
IE 5.5	0,0	Selected coordinates
NN 3	N/A (cannot Tab to links)	Selected coordinates
NN 4	Coordinates of center of image	Selected coordinates
NN 5	No coordinate data	No coordinate data
OP 3.6	N/A (cannot Tab to links)	Selected coordinates

* User uses the Tab key (or other key sequence) to advance to the active image and presses the Enter (or other) key to access the link.
† User clicks the mouse button (or other pointer) inside the region occupied by the image—but does so before the image data is actually displayed in this region (e.g., when image loading is disabled on the browser).

Chapter 10. Here are two simple examples, with brief explanations—the part lying after the program specification is marked in boldface, with the query string portion also in italics:

`http://some.site.edu/cgi-bin/srch-example`. The server executes the program *srch-example* found in the *cgi-bin* directory. Any output from *srch-example* is sent back to the client.

`http://www.site.edu/cgi-bin/srch-example`**`/path/other?`*`srch_string`*. The server again executes the program *srch-example* found in the *cgi-bin* directory. The *extra path* information `path/other` is passed as a parameter to *srch-example*, as is the query information `srch_string`.

Server Issues: Personal User Directories

Users who have accounts on a machine running the Apache, Netscape/ iPlanet, and most other servers can have world-accessible documents in their own home directories. These personal HTTP document directories are indicated in a URL by a tilde (~) character prepended in front of the path information (the first item in the path hierarchy following the tilde must be the account name of the user). The tilde tells the server that this is not a regular directory, but a *redirection* to a personal document archive of the user with the indicated account. For example, if the user `iang` has a personal document directory, this could be accessed using the URL

```
http://site.world.edu/%7Eiang/
```

where `%7E` is the encoding for the tilde character. You will often see a real tilde in such URLs, as in

```
http://site.world.edu/~iang/
```

because the tilde character is safe in most situations.

8.2.8 Https URLs—Secure HTTP

Essentially all commercial Web browsers support **https** URLs. Such URLs are composed—and behave—in exactly the same way as **http** URLs, the only differences being the default port number (443 for **https**) and the fact that the connection between client and server is encrypted using the Secure Sockets Layer encryption technology. As a result, data can pass securely between client and server, without being intercepted and read by a third party. The URL used to access a Web server exporting files via a secure Web server is of the form:

```
https://int.domain.nam
```

Note that a single machine can run both secure and unsecure Web servers at the same time, because they use different ports. SSL is discussed in more detail in Chapter 9.

8.2.9 IMAP URLs

Internet Message Access Protocol (IMAP) is a protocol for accessing mail messages on remote message storage servers (commonly called post office machines). IMAP is in many ways a successor to the Post Office Protocol (POP) (see the section on **pop3** URLs), which was an earlier protocol designed for accessing post office servers. IMAP, however, offers many features not provided by the POP protocol, so that IMAP is more effective in large organizations with complex mail requirements. At present, both POP and IMAP are widely available.

An **imap** URL can reference IMAP servers, mailboxes on a server, specific messages on a server, MIME message parts on a server, or search programs accessible on an IMAP server. There are several general forms for these different types of queries. However, all **imap** URLs have a root URL of the form

```
imap://user;AUTH=authtype@int.domain.nam:port/
```

where `user` is the name of the account being accessed, `authtype` is the name of the authentication mechanism to use (the statement AUTH=* means that any authentication mechanism is acceptable), and `int.domain.nam` is the machine running the LDAP server at the indicated `port` (the default value is 143). All portions of this URL (`user,;AUTH=authtype,` and `:port`) except for the domain name are optional, so that the simplest possible IMAP URL is:

```
imap://int.domain.nam/
```

Mailboxes, messages, and mailbox queries are indicated by data that appears after the domain name of the server. For example, the URL

```
imap://;AUTH=KERBEROS_V4@imap.igraham.com/archive21?SUBJECT%20frogs
```

references an authenticated access to the indicated IMAP server, and a subsequent search in the indicated message archive (*archive21*) for messages that match the given query.

The syntax for the portion of the URL after the domain name (and for the valid values of the AUTH string) is complex, and is not discussed here (for details, please see RFC 2192, which specifies the **imap** URL syntax).

8.2.10 Lav URLs

Lav (and **lavs**) URLs reference a Liquid Audio (www.liquidaudio.com) streaming server resource via a proprietary Liquid Audio protocol. These resources provide streamed audio that can be played by the Liquid Audio player. The general form is

```
lav://int.domain.nam:port/resource
```

where `int.domain.nam` is the domain name for the server, `:port` is the port number, and `resource` is the path that specified the particular streaming resource. An example is:

```
lav://132.206.9.1:18888/213111/c,107017,137295886,liquid
```

8.2.11 Lavs URLs—Secure Lav

The **lavs** protocol specifier is equivalent to **lav** but references a commercial version of the Liquid Audio server that supports commerce transactions and (possibly) encryption of the data in transit (analogous to **https** URLs).

8.2.12 LDAP URLs

Lightweight Directory Access Protocol (LDAP) is a technology that provides simple access to corporate directory services. A directory service is a database of corporate resources (such as information about staff, resources, facilities, addresses, etc.) designed for quick searching and retrieval. LDAP URLs provide a syntax for accessing and querying directory databases using the LDAP protocol. The general form is

```
ldap://int.domain.nam:port/ldap-query
```

where `int.domain.nam` is the machine running the LDAP server at the indicated `port` (default value is 389), and `ldap-query` is a query string requesting information from the server. The syntax for such queries is complex and is not reproduced here—in general, a query is composed by the software creating the URL and not by the user. An example query is

```
ldap://ldap.utoronto.ca/o=University%20of%Toronto,c=CA
```

which requests directory information about the University of Toronto in Canada.

Ldap URLs are supported by Netscape Navigator 4 and Internet Explorer 4 and later, but are not supported by earlier versions of these (or other) browsers.

8.2.13 LDAPS URLs—Secure LDAP

Ldaps URLs are equivalent to **ldap** URLs, except that the request is addressed to port 636 instead of 389, and the connection to the LDAP server is encrypted. **Ldaps** URLs are supported by Netscape Navigator, but only via the conferencing and address book components of Netscape Communicator.

8.2.14 Mailto URLs

The **mailto** URL designates an Internet-format mail address to which mail can be sent. The format is

```
mailto:mail_address
```

where *mail_address* is the Internet mail address (as specified in RFC 822, the document that specifies the format for Internet mail) to which a message can be mailed. Typically, this is of the form *name@host*, where *name* is the user mail account name of the person, and *host* is the name of the machine at which the user receives mail. A browser that supports **mailto** will provide a mechanism for users to compose and send a letter to this destination.

Some mail addresses contain percent characters or slashes. These characters must be URL encoded, because they are otherwise interpreted as special (marking the beginning of a character encoding string or a hierarchical path). As an example, the e-mail address

```
jello%ian@irc.utoronto.ca
```

must be converted into the **mailto** URL:

```
mailto:jello%25ian@irc.utoronto.ca
```

A **mailto** URL does not indicate how the mail should be sent [this is why the URL syntax does not have two slashes (//) following the protocol specifier]. In general, a client mail program must contact a *mail server*—a program that validates the mail and forwards it to its destination. **Mailto** URLs do not specify a mail server—this information must be separately configured into the browser or mail client. Web browsers usually provide a configuration menu for this purpose.

Author-Specified Subject and Other Mail Information

When composing a URL to send a mail message, authors often want to include information beyond just the destination address. For example, the author may want to specify a default subject line, or perhaps give alternate (CC'd) mail destinations for the letter.

Netscape developers decided to include the information as query string information within the **mailto** URL itself—this approach is now widely adopted and is formally specified in RFC 2368. This mechanism works by appending required mail headers in URL-encoded format, using strings of the form *header=value*, where *header* is the mail header name (URL-encoded), and *value* is the (URL-encoded) string to associate with the name. For example, to send a message to the address *address*, specifying a given title and a list of CC recipients, the URL would be

```
mailto:address?subject=test%20mail%20message&cc=address1%2caddress2
```

which associates the subject line *test mail message* to the indicated address, as well as the two indicated CC'd addresses. Notice how the ampersand character separates the different values (as with **form** data encoding) and that all special characters in the fields are encoded via their URL-encoded values.

If a **mailto** URL appears in a hyperlink, then any headers that do not correspond to headers that can be edited in the mail authoring tool are ignored and are not added to the letter. On the other hand, if the **mailto** appears within a form that is using the POST method to send mail, then all headers present in the URL are generated, even if they are not understood by the mail client. However, headers that should not be altered (return address, content type, etc.) cannot be changed by the **mailto** URL, and in these cases the information in the URL is ignored. The list of mail headers that *cannot* be overridden is:

Apparently-to	BCC	Content-Encoding
Content-length	Content-transfer-encoding	Content-type
Date	Distribution	FCC
From	Lines	MIME-Version
Message-id	Newsgroup	Organization
Reply-to	Sender	X-UidL
XREF	Followup-to	

Netscape 4 and later also allow the inclusion of the actual message body in the URL, via the syntax

```
mailto:address@domain.com?subject=xxxx?body=body-of-message
```

where the special keyword *body* is assigned the content of the message. Netscape Navigator 3 or earlier does not support this extension.

This **mailto** extension syntax, now formalized in RFC 2368, is supported by Navigator 3 and later and by Internet Explorer 4 and later, but is not widely supported by other browsers. Note also that, to automatically send **form** data using a **mailto** URL value for the **action** attribute, you must use **method**="post" on the **form** element. In this case, Navigator 4 deletes any message body set by the *body=* parameter on the URL, and replaces it by the actual data gathered by the **form**. Internet Explorer 5, on the other hand, retains both pieces of data.

8.2.15 Mid URLs

Mid URLs reference specific mail or USENET messages, or can reference a specific body part of a specific message. Thus, **mid** URLs can be thought of as a generalization of **cid** URLs, which reference parts within a given message. A **mid** URL takes one of the following two forms:

```
mid:message-id
mid:message-id/content-id
```

The first form references an entire message (identified by the Message-ID), whereas the second form references a particular part (identified by the Content-ID) of a specific multipart message (identified by the Message-ID). Here, the `message-id` and `content-id` strings are the URL-encoded versions of the appropriate Message-ID and Content-ID headers, respectively, as defined by the MIME and USENET message protocols.

Mid URLs are supported by the Netscape Communicator mail and news message authoring clients and also by the mail or news viewing client (Netscape Messenger). However, the clients ignore the Message-ID portion of the URL and assume that the reference is internal within the displayed document. Essentially, then, Netscape treats **mid** URLs as equivalent to **cid** URLs. **Mid** URLs are not supported by Internet Explorer 4.

Following are two examples:

```
mid:12311-123124123@flopsy.org
mid:12411-123124123@flopsy.org/part3-12432-1212@flopsy.org
```

An author would only rarely type a **mid** URL, as they are typically created by the tool that assembles a mail message or newsgroup posting.

Mid URLs are related to **cid** (Content Identifier) URLs, discussed earlier in this chapter. **Cid** and **mid** URLs are apparently supported by several more recent mail clients, including Eudora Pro and Microsoft Outlook.

8.2.16 Mms URLs

Mms URLs reference streamed media that is produced by a Microsoft Media Services Server. Such servers support real-time streaming that lets a user rewind, stop, and fast-forward the medium (audio, video, or other) being played.

The general form for **mms** URLs is

```
mms:int.domain.nam:port/path_to_resource
```

where `int.domain.nam` is the domain name of a server, `:port` is the port number (usually omitted), and `path_to_resource` is the path to the desired streaming resource. An example is:

```
mms://netshow.microsoft.com/path/directory/file.asf
```

The extension *.asf* typically refers to an active streaming format resource. Certain media players, in particular Microsoft Media Player, currently understand this URL syntax.

8.2.17 News URLs

News URLs reference USENET newsgroups or individual USENET news articles. There are several ways to compose **news** URLs. Particular newsgroups are specified using the form

```
news:news.group.name
```

where `news.group.name` is the name of a particular newsgroup. The special form `news:*` references *all* available newsgroups. Note that this does not specify an NNTP server from which news can be accessed. This must be specified elsewhere, in a browser-specific manner. Most browsers let the user set the name of the news server using a pull-down menu, whereas on Unix systems it is set by defining the server domain name in an NNTPSERVER environment variable.

Referencing Specific News Articles

An alternative form is used to request particular news articles. The form is

```
news:message_id@int.domain.nam
```

where `message_id` is the unique ID associated with a particular article originating from the machine `int.domain.nam` (this is all discussed in gruesome detail in RFC 1036, referenced at the end of the chapter). The at (@) character is special in a **news** URL and indicates this alternative form of reference. This format is not generally useful, because most news servers delete articles after a few days or weeks, so that any referenced article is soon unavailable.

Referencing Both Server and Newsgroup

A third form, not part of the official URL standard, but nonetheless widely supported, references both the newsgroup and the server from which the articles should be retrieved, or both the server and a particular article. The two forms are

```
news://int.domain.nam:port/news.group.name
news://int.domain.nam:port/message_id@domain.name.edu
```

where `int.domain.nam` is the domain name of the server to be contacted, `:port` is the optional port number (the default value is 119), `news.group.name` is the desired newsgroup, and `message_id` and `domain.name.edu` form the message ID for a specific message posted from the machine at *domain.name.edu*.

8.2.18 Pop3 URLs

Pop3 URLs let the browser reference a POP3 mail server from which mail can be retrieved. The general form for such a URL is

```
pop3://user;AUTH=authtype@int.domain.nam:port
```

where `int.domain.nam` is the domain name of the server to be contacted, `port` is the optional port number (the default value is 110), `user` is the username of the account to access on the POP server, and `authtype` is a code indicating the preferred mechanism for authenticating the user. In practice, the `user`, `;AUTH=authtype`, and `:port` portions are optional, so that the simplest possible form for a **pop3** URL is:

```
pop3://int.domain.nam
```

> **NOTE** POP is short for *Post Office Protocol* and is a protocol, commonly used by mail clients, that connects to a central Post Office machine that holds their incoming mail. The IMAP protocol (see the **imap** URL section) is a more modern post office access protocol, also in wide use.

The supported `authtype` values will depend on the POP server being contacted. However, if a specific authentication method is specified in the URL, but the POP server does not support this method, then the browser should not try an alternate method without first asking the user for permission to do so. Alternatively, the special assignment `;AUTH=*` (which is the default, if no AUTH value is explicitly given) means that the browser can use any authentication mechanism supported by the POP server. For example, the URL

```
pop3://ray@mailbox2.grendel.org
```

will access the POP server at the indicated domain name, using the username `ray` and whatever user authentication mechanism is supported by that server.

8.2.19 Snews URLs—Secure News

Many commercial Web browsers support **snews** URLs. Such URLs are composed—and behave—in exactly the same way as **news** URLs, the only difference being the default port number (563 for **snews**) and the fact that the connection between client and server is encrypted using the SSL encryption technology. As a result, data can pass securely between client and server, without being intercepted and read by a third party. To access newsgroup listings summaries for a group accessible via a secure news server, the URL would be:

```
snews:news.group.name
```

The identity of the news server is in general set using browser Configure menus. SSL is discussed in more detail in Chapter 9.

8.2.20 Nntp URLs

In principle, the **nntp** URL scheme provides a way of explicitly referencing a news article from a particular NNTP news server. An example **nntp** URL might be

```
nntp://news.server.com/alt.rubber-chickens/12311121.121@foo.org
```

which references article number *12311121.121@foo.org*, in the newsgroup *alt.rubber-chickens*, from the NNTP server running on the machine *news.server.com* (at the default port number 119). The NNTP protocol is described in RFC 977, should you want additional details.

> **NOTE** NNTP FUNCTIONALITY USING NEWS URLS **Essentially all the functionality of nntp URLs has been added to news URLs by allowing server domain name specification in the news URL, as previously described. It is thus unlikely that nntp URLs will be widely implemented. At present, there are few browsers that support this URL scheme.**

8.2.21 Prospero URLs

This scheme references resources accessible using the Prospero Directory Service, which acts as a sophisticated caching and proxying service for directory, file, and other data. **Prospero** URLs take the form

```
prospero://int.domain.nam:port/string/stuff
```

which references a Prospero server running at the indicated machine and port (the default port is 1525), the remaining portion of the string indicating the desired resource.

> **NOTE** PROSPERO URLS ARE NOT WIDELY SUPPORTED **Very few Web browsers (i.e., practically none) support Prospero URLs, so this form is not discussed in detail here. Further information is found in the references at the end of this chapter.**

8.2.22 Rtsp and Rtspu URLs

Rtsp URLs reference streaming media resource accessible using Transmission Control Protocol (TCP) via the Real Time Streaming Protocol (RTSP), an Internet standard for streaming media over the Internet (RFC 2326). The standard form for such URLs is

```
rtsp://int.domain.nam:port/resource
```

where `int.domain.nam` is the name of the server, `:port` is the port number (the default is 554), and `resource` is the path and name that identify the resource. This URL syntax and the RTSP format are supported by the Real Audio RealPlayer G2 (and later) and the QuickTime 4 (and later) players, as well as by the Real Audio and Apple QuickTime streaming media servers.

Rtspu URLs are equivalent to **rtsp** URLs, except that they reference communication that uses User Datagram Protocol (UDP; see Chapter 7) instead of TCP.

8.2.23 Telnet URLs

Telnet URLs reference telnet connections to a remote machine. An example is

```
telnet://int.domain.nam:port
```

where `int.domain.nam` is the machine to which a connection should be made, and the optional `:port` specifies the desired port (the default value is 32). A more general form is

```
telnet://username:password@int.domain.nam:port/
```

to indicate the *username* and *password* that the user should employ (the *:password* is optional). The colon (:) and at (@) characters are special in a **telnet** URL. In general, the username and password information are not directly used by a browser to complete the connection. Rather, this information may be presented to users as a hint as to what they should do once the connection is made. Obviously, you do not want to use this more general form if you want to keep a password secret!

Tn3270 and Rlogin URLs

Some browsers support a variant of a **telnet** URL, called a **tn3270** URL, which references a connection requiring IBM 3270 terminal emulation on the part of the client. In general, this is only useful if the client computer supports a tn3270 client program (tn3270 clients are rarely built into Web browsers), and provided the browser knows about this program. If not, most browsers default to a regular Telnet connection.

A few browsers support rlogin connections via **rlogin** URLs. The specification is

```
rlogin://username@int.domain.nam
```

where `username` is the account name for the rlogin. The user will be prompted for a password in the resulting window unless one is not required. Most browsers that support this emulate **rlogin** URLs using a Telnet connection.

8.2.24 Wais URLs

Wide Area Information Server (WAIS) servers predate the World Wide Web, and are Internet-accessible text databases that can be automatically queried using WAIS client software. Early in the development of the Web, a **wais** URL syntax was developed to allow URLs that could express queries of a WAIS database. In a **wais** URL, the syntax indicates the domain name for the server, the desired search instructions, and information about the particular database component to be searched.

> **NOTE** WAIS servers were developed before the Internet evolved into today's Web. The company that developed WAIS was bought by PCDocs in 1997, which was subsequently purchased by Hummingbird Communication (www.hummingbird.com) in 1999. Unfortunately, a search for the string "WAIS" at the Hummingbird Web site produces no search results. So much for a sense of Internet history!

The standard form for accessing a WAIS server is

```
wais://int.domain.nam:port/database?search
```

where `int.domain.nam` is the Internet domain name of the host running a WAIS server at the indicated port (the default port is 210), `database` is the name of the WAIS database to be searched, and `search` is a list of search instructions to pass to the database. Another form is (leaving out the port number for brevity)

```
wais://int.domain.nam/database
```

which designates a particular searchable database. A browser will understand that this URL references a searchable database and will prompt for query string input.

Finally, **wais** URLs can reference individual resources on a WAIS database. The form for this URL is

```
wais://int.domain.nam/database/wais_type/resource_path
```

where *wais_type* is a type indicator, which gives the type of the object being accessed, and *resource_path* is the document ID used internally by the WAIS database. In general, these strings are generated by the WAIS server itself, and it is rare that a user (or document author) will actually compose the *wais_type* and *resource_path* fields.

Most browsers do not support **wais** URLs directly, and instead must forward WAIS queries through a WAIS proxy, identified via a browser's proxy configuration menu. However, WAIS servers are actually quite rare today, as their functionality has been supplanted by more sophisticated Internet search engines and databases, such as those provided by AltaVista, InfoSeek, and others.

8.2.25 Special Class ID URLs: Clsid, Java, and Javabean

There are several special URL formats that currently are only used as **classid** attribute values of **object** elements. These URLs define class ID values for special classes of executable objects so that the syntax of the URL schemes varies widely depending on the object code type (i.e., depending on the name space of the object classes). In addition, the URL syntax does not, in general, specify the location of the object—this must be obtained from an object catalog/directory service that is maintained by the browser, or from the **codebase** attribute. Indeed, these schemes are better described as Uniform Resource Names (URNs), as opposed to URLs.

There are three different URL schemes that fall into this category: **clsid**, **java**, and **javabean**, discused in the next three sections.

Clsid URLs

Clsid URLs were introduced by Microsoft and are used, within an **object** element, to reference an Active-X/COM object to be *instantiated* (loaded and run) when the object is created. The general form for a **clsid** URL is

```
clsid:class-id
```

where *class-id* is the identifier for the desired COM class. An example is

```
clsid:EFE6733J-1321-43Cf-J43B-08113F412501
```

where the string value is a COM CLSID (class id) value—these are Universally Unique Identifiers (UUIDs) defined by the OSF/DCE RPC.

Clsid URLs are only valid as the value of the **classid** attribute of an **object** element. They are currently only supported by Internet Explorer 3 and greater, but will likely also be supported by Navigator 6.

NOTE *OSF/DCE* stands for *Open Software Foundation/Distributed Computing Environment,* an industry standard for Open Software. *RPC* stands for *remote procedure call,* a specification by which one computer can contact another and request execution of remote code on the other machine. Information about the OSF/DCE is found at www.opengroup.org/dce/index.html.

Formally, **clsid**s are actually URNs, because they reference the resource by name and not by location. It is up to the browser (actually, a COM object handler that is integrated into the browser) to locate the desired code (either locally on the computer or from some remote location) and download and run it.

Java URLs

Java URLs were introduced by Netscape and are used, within an **object** element and on Navigator 4 (and greater) browsers, to reference a Java class to be instantiated and run. The general form is

```
java:package.location.packageobject
```

where `package.location` is the location of the package containing the desired class, and `packageobject` is the name of the class to be run. An example is

```
java:myjava.applet.start.class
```

which references an applet from the "myjava" personal applet collection. **Java** URLs are only valid as the value of the **classid** attribute of an **object** element. Like **clsid** URLs, these are actually URNs: It is up to the browser (and some code within the browser that understands the **java** class naming scheme) to locate the desired object.

Javabean URLs

Javabean URLs were introduced by Netscape to identify **java** objects compliant with the *JavaBean* specification, and designed for use with the JavaBean library (part of the standard Java 2 distribution). Thus, referencing a JavaBean tells the browser which other supporting classes will be required. The general form is

```
javabean:package.location.packageobject
```

where `package.location` is the location of the package containing the desired class, and `packageobject` is the name of the class to be run. An example is

```
javabean:netscape.application.Button
```

which references a Netscape Internet Foundation Class (IFC) button object. Note that **javabean** URLs are only valid as the value of **classid** attribute in an **object** element. They are only supported by Navigator 4.

8.2.26 Pseudo-URLs: About, Javascript, and Others

Last, there are several, often proprietary, pseudo-URLs often seen in a browser's Location window. The most common such schemes are **about**, **javascript**, **mailbox**, **res**, **view-source**, and **wysiwyg**. There are no formal specifications for these URLs: Indeed, the **about** URL was initially introduced—partly as a practical joke—by the Netscape development team, whereas the **javascript** URL was introduced to allow for easy testing of typed-in strings of JavaScript code. Many of these schemes are not of use to an author—although it is always nice to know what they mean! However, the special about:blank URL turned out to have several practical uses, such that this form is now supported by most browsers. Similarly, **javascript** URLs proved to be a simple (if not ideal) way of binding script programs to hypertext anchors, so that this URL form is also widely supported by browser vendors.

Addbook URLs (Navigator 4 Only)

Addbook URLs reference a vCard-format business card data file that should be added to the database of the browsers's Address Book application. This format URL is currently only understood by the Navigator 4 mail client, which internally uses **addbook** URLs to copy vCard attachments from e-mail messages to the address book.

About URLs

About URLs reference general information about the browser—this scheme was invented by Netscape as a tool for displaying information about the browser and for presenting personal information about the browser developers. For example, the URL about:mozilla references (but only on Netscape Navigator) a brief page that reflects the youthful enthusiasm of the Netscape developers (just try it!), and about:marca and about:ebina provided information about Marc Andreessen and Eric Bina, two of the cofounders of Netscape Inc. Needless to say, these three URLs do not work on Internet Explorer!

The following outlines the various **about** URLs and their (typically browser-specific) functions:

   about: (Navigator only). Provides some practical information about the browser, such as the version number and the list of software packages licensed for use with the browser. This is equivalent to the "Help . . . About" menu item.

about:blank (Navigator and Internet Explorer 3+ only). Requests that the browser display a blank page using the browser's default background color. This is useful for creating a blank window, or a blank frame within a frame document. The latter can be accomplished, for example, via a frame element of the form:

```
<FRAME SRC="about:blank" NAME="frame-name">
```

which creates an empty frame.

about:globalhistory (Navigator 4 and earlier only). Requests that the browser list all URLs that it has accessed in the recent past (i.e., list the contents of the global history cache).

about:cache (Navigator 4 and earlier, and Opera only). Requests that the browser list information about all files (text, images, and other) stored in the browser cache. Note that for large cache sizes, this can cause the computer (in particular, Windows 95 or Macintosh machines) to freeze for several minutes as the cache is processed.

about:memory-cache (Navigator 4 and earlier only). Requests that the browser list information about all files (text, images, and other) stored in the *in-memory* cache.

about:image-cache (Navigator 4 and earlier only). Requests that the browser list information about all image files currently stored in the in-memory cache.

about:document (Navigator 4 and earlier). Requests that the browser list information about the document currently being viewed (URL, MIME type, file name in cache, date last modified, etc.).

about:license (Navigator 4 and earlier). Requests that the browser display the text of the Netscape software license.

about:logo (Navigator 4 and earlier). Requests that the browser display the Netscape browser logo.

about:mozilla (Navigator only). Requests that the browser display a page from the book of Mozilla.

about:plugins (Navigator 4 and earlier, and Opera only). Requests that the browser list all the plug-ins installed on the Web browser. This lists the MIME types, the name of the company providing each plug-in, and the typical file name suffixes associated with the MIME type.

Javascript URLs

Javascript URLs encode JavaScript program code within a URL. The general form is:

```
javascript:javascript-statements
```

where `javascript-statements` is a semicolon-separated list of valid JavaScript statements. This URL can, on Navigator and Internet Explorer 4 and later (not Internet Explorer 3), be typed directly into the Open File or Location window, thereby providing an easy way to test simple JavaScript expressions. For example, typing the URL

```
javascript:alert('Hi Mom!')
```

into the browser's Location window will tell the browser to pop up a JavaScript alert window with the associated text.

With Netscape Navigator, the special URL `javascript:`—that is, a **javascript** URL without any JavaScript statements—causes the browser to display a special JavaScript type-in field at the bottom of the browser window. This is useful for testing small pieces of JavaScript code. The results of running the typed-in JavaScript commands are displayed in the portion of the browser window above the type-in field.

Javascript URLs can be used, within a hypertext anchor, to invoke a JavaScript program when the hypertext link is accessed. Example markup is

```
<a href="javascript:anchor_handler()">anchored text</a>
```

where the function `anchor_handler()` is a JavaScript function to run when the link is accessed. Similarly, the **src** element of an **img** element can take a **javascript** URL value—but note that the script must then pass an image to the **img** element object so that the element has something to display.

Of course, using **javascript** URLs in these contexts means that the documents will be improperly rendered—or will not function at all—if JavaScript is disabled or is not supported by the browser. A more reasonable approach is to use the **onclick** (or other) event-handling attributes for the **a** and **img** elements, as discussed in Chapter 3, and in Chapter 19 of *XHTML 1.0 Language and Design Sourcebook.*

> **NOTE** JAVASCRIPT URLs NOT FULLY SUPPORTED IN INTERNET EXPLORER 3 **Internet Explorer 3 does not support JavaScript URLs that are typed directly into the Location window of the browser. However, the browser does support JavaScript URLs that are present as values of hypertext anchor href attributes.**

Livescript URLs (Navigator 4 and Earlier Only)

Livescript URLs are equivalent to **javascript** URLs (Livescript was an early name for the JavaScript language). The `livescript:` prefix should be avoided, as it not supported by other browsers.

Mailbox URLs (Navigator 3+ Only)

Mailbox URLs reference the local mail client on the browser. With Netscape Navigator 4, a **mailbox** URL causes the browser to launch the mail client (usually Netscape Messenger) and open the mailbox defined in the body of the URL. For example, the URL

```
mailbox:inbox
```

will open the Inbox folder, which, with Netscape *Messenger,* is the default name for the folder containing incoming, unread mail. If no folder is specified (i.e., `mailbox:`), then the mail client is launched, and the user must choose a mailbox to open. If the URL specifies a mailbox that does not exist, then the mail client is not launched. Netscape Navigator 4 also uses **mailbox** URLs to display, on the Navigator browser, resources that are referenced, within mail or newsgroup messages, via **cid** or **mid** URLs.

Mocha URLs (Navigator 4 and Earlier Only)

Mocha URLs are equivalent to **javascript** URLs (*Mocha* was the code name for the JavaScript language during the early days of its development). The `mocha:` prefix should be avoided as it is not supported by other browsers.

Pnm URLs (Real Audio Players Only)

Pnm URLs are used in Real Audio metafiles (also called RAM files, as they typically end with the file name extension *.ram*) to indicate different streamed media resources. Such URLs take the general form

```
pnm://int.domain.nam/resource.ra
```

where `int.domain.nam` is the path to and name of the file containing the module, `resource` is the location of the resource, and where the extension `.ra` is found on all such resources and corresponds to a Real Audio streaming audio source. For example, a single document, such as *file.ram,* could contain the following three lines:

```
pnm://www.myserver.com/hello.ra
pnm://www.myserver.com/welcome.ra
pnm://www.myserver.com/coolstuff.ra
```

When a Real Audio player accesses *file.ram,* it will then play the three audio files, one after the other.

The RAM file format and the **pnm** URL syntax are obsolete—later versions of RealPlayer use the XML-format Synchronized Multimedia Interaction Language (SMIL) language to define media metainformation, and the RTSP protocol (referenced using **rtsp** URLs) to transmit the media. Thus, **pnm** URLs are only needed to support older, largely obsolete media players.

Res URLs (Internet Explorer 4+ Only)

Res URLs reference a local resource that can be retrieved from a software module, or Dynamic Load Library (DLL), accessible to the browser. The general form is

```
res://resource-file/res-type/res-id
```

where *resource-file/* is the path to and name of the file containing the module, *res-type/* is an optional string that defines the resource type, and *res-id* is the specific identifier for the resource within the module. An example is:

```
res://mymodule.dll/doc23.html
```

The use of **res** URLs requires a detailed understanding of the Active-X model for data storage within DLLs. More information is available at the Microsoft Web site, at msdn.microsoft.com/workshop/networking/ predefined/res.asp and msdn.microsoft.com/library/periodic/period99/ mindmsjold/0199/cutting/cutting0199.htm, although beware that Microsoft regularly reorganizes their site, so these documents may move. If you can't find the document, please visit the msdn.microsoft.com Web site, and search for the phrase "res://", or for "res protocol".

Internet Explorer 4 and greater implement **about** URLs as a particular instance of a **res** URL. For details, please see support.microsoft.com/ support/kb/articles/q183/9/78.asp.

View-Source URLs (Navigator 4 and Earlier, and Internet Explorer 4+ Only)

View-source URLs cause a Navigator 4 (and earlier) browser to render a source listing of the referenced resource. The value for the **view-source** URL must be the URL of the resource to be displayed, for example:

```
view-source:http://www.utoronto.ca/home.html
```

View-source URLs are used internally by the Navigator software to generate source listings and should not be used in HTML documents.

Wysiwyg URLs (Netscape Navigator 4 and Earlier Only)

Wysiwyg URLs are used internally by the Netscape Navigator 4 (and earlier) JavaScript engine and denote certain cases where JavaScript code produces the document content being displayed by the browser—they are sometimes displayed when such a document is printed. Authors themselves should never write (or need to write) **wysiwyg** URLs—but it is nice to know where they came from!

8.3 Coming Attractions

Several other special-purpose URL schemes were recently defined and are being deployed in a variety of applications. For example, the **nfs** URL scheme has been proposed as the foundation of a distributed, Web-based file system. Network File System (NFS) is a distributed file system architecture commonly used on Unix systems, and **nfs** URLs provide a way of referencing NFS-accessible resources. Netscape Navigator 4 supports **nfs** URLs, but only via specially equipped proxy servers.

Also of interest are the various **Z39.50** URL schemes. **Z39.50** is an information retrieval protocol commonly used by indexed databases such as those managed by libraries. **Z39.50** URLs would provide a standard syntax for encoding **Z39.50**-format database queries within a URL.

Other schemes, such as **irc** (for Internet Relay Chat sessions), **vemmi** (for a distributed multimedia/videotex standard), **whois++** (for referencing WHOIS++ servers), and **tv** (for referencing TV broadcasts), have also been proposed. These schemes are not discussed here—information about these proposals is found in the references at the end of the chapter.

8.4 Naming Schemes for the Web

The URL approach is the only addressing mechanism widely used on the Web, but it is not the only approach—several other approaches have been proposed, some of which are likely to be implemented in the near future. This brief section summarizes the names and general features of the different proposed mechanisms. Indeed, the Web standards actually have three different acronyms for defining *uniform* resource identification mechanisms. This short section helps clarify the meanings of these different acronyms.

8.4.1 Uniform Resource Identifier (URI)

Uniform Resource Identifiers (URIs) generically represent any naming or addressing scheme used to reference resources on the Internet. Thus, URLs and URNs (see Section 8.4.3) are types of URIs. The names *URI* and *URL* are often used synonymously, but this is only correct in the absence of a defined URN naming scheme.

The URI syntax specification, found in RFC 2396, defines the syntax rules for all URIs, including URLs and URNs. This document also explains how URL (and URN) strings should be encoded and is the basis of the character set encoding discussion found in Section 8.1.4.

8.4.2 Uniform Resource Locator (URL)

Uniform Resource Locators (URLs) are protocol- and location-specific schemes for referencing resources on the Internet. Thus, a URL references (1) a specific location for a resource (e.g., **http** or **ftp** URLs), (2) a specific mechanism for retrieving a resource (e.g., **news** or **imap** URLs), or (3) a specific mechanism for sending a resource somewhere else (e.g., a **mailto** URL). Almost all addressing schemes in current use are URLs, although a few (such as the **clsid** and **java** schemes) are more properly called *URNs*.

8.4.3 Uniform Resource Names (URN)

Uniform Resource Names (URNs) are intended to be a location-independent way of referencing an object. Thus, a URN neither specifies the location of the desired resource, nor does it even indicate how the resource should be located; instead, a URN specifies a generic name for it. The software processing the name would then locate the named object at the closest or most accessible location, using some sort of a name lookup service. For example, the proposed URN scheme

```
isbn:0-471-32753-0
```

references a printed (physical or electronic) volume by its International Standard Book Number (ISBN) code. It is then up to the software processing the ISBN number to find an appropriate location for the resource and to possibly retrieve it (if available in electronic format).

The specification of URNs is still being developed by the Internet Engineering Task Force's (IETF's) URN working group. The main difficulty in defining and using URNs is in developing a reliable scheme for looking up the location of a resource from the given name. Most current work is targeted at solving this problem.

Current draft documents under consideration are found on the URN working group's home page, at www.ietf.org/html-charters/urn-charter.html. You should visit this site for up-to-date information.

8.4.4 Uniform Resource Citation [URC (Obsolete)]

Uniform Resource Citations (URCs) were intended to be collections of attribute/value pairs that described a particular object (referenced using a

URI). Some of the values in these attribute/value pairs could also be URIs, thereby allowing for very rich descriptions of objects. The idea was that URCs could act in many ways—for example, as a cross-indexing resource for a large resource collection, or simply as a collection of references to related data.

The URC idea has largely fallen by the wayside. The current sentiment is to store citation and other metadata information about a resource in special XML documents [using the Resource Description Framework (RDF) syntax] designed expressly for that purpose. For details and a list of important standards, you can visit the metadata section of the W3C at www.w3.org/Metadata/.

8.5 References

The URI specifications originate from the various working groups currently developing Internet and Web standards. In most cases, the Internet protocols or standards are formalized in documents known as *Requests for Comments* (RFCs). Once approved by the appropriate IETF, these documents are officially numbered, giving rise to the referenced RFC numbers quoted here. For references related to character sets and character set encodings, please see the end of Appendix A on this book's companion Web site.

OVERVIEWS AND DEFINED URL SCHEMES

www.w3.org/Addressing/ Addressing.html	Overview of issues
www.w3.org/Addressing/schemes	List of proposed URL schemes
www.ietf.org/rfc/rfc1738.txt	Standard URL specification
www.ietf.org/rfc/rfc1808.txt	Relative URL specification
www.ietf.org/rfc/rfc2368.txt	Mailto URL (updates RFCs 1738, 1808)
www.ietf.org/rfc/rfc2396.txt	URI syntax (updates RFCs 1738, 1808)
www.w3.org/International/ O-URL-and-ident.html	Notes and working drafts on internationalized URLs
www.ietf.org/rfc/rfc2718.txt	Guidelines for new URL schemes
www.ietf.org/rfc/rfc2056.txt	Z39.50r and Z39.50s URLs
www.ietf.org/rfc/rfc2122.txt	VEMMI URLs
www.ietf.org/rfc/rfc2192.txt	IMAP URLs
www.ietf.org/rfc/rfc2224.txt	NFS URLs
www.ietf.org/rfc/rfc2255.txt	LDAP URLs

www.ietf.org/rfc/rfc2384.txt	POP URLs
www.ietf.org/rfc/rfc2392.txt	Cid and Mid URLs
www.ietf.org/rfc/rfc2397.txt	DATA URLs
www.ietf.org/rfc/rfc2717.txt	Registration procedure for URL name schemes

PROPOSED URL SCHEMES AND UPDATES

www.w3.org/Addressing/clsid-scheme	CLSID URLs
developer.netscape.com/docs/wpapers/ beanconnect/index.html	Javabean URLs
www.w3.org/Addressing/ draft-mirashi-url-irc-01.txt	IRC URLs
www.math.jyu.fi/~rjl/abouts.html	About URLs
www.ietf.org/html.charters/ urlreg-charter.html	URL registration working group charter

SOME PROTOCOL AND DATA FORMAT SPECIFICATIONS

www.ietf.org/rfc/rfc822.txt	Internet Mail messages
www.ietf.org/rfc/rfc1036.txt	Usenet messages
www.ietf.org/rfc/rfc2045.txt through / rfc2049.txt	MIME syntax
www.ietf.org/rfc/rfc2557.txt	Multipart messages; use of **cid** and **mid** URLs
www.ietf.org/rfc/rfc977.txt	NNTP protocol
www.sco.com/skunkprev/Skunk96/ src/Tools/freeWAIS-sf-2.1/doc/ original-TM-wais/	WAIS documentation
www.ietf.org/rfc/rfc1625.txt	WAIS protocol
www.isi.edu/gost/gost-group/products/ prospero/documentation/	Prospero documentation
www.ietf.org/rfc/rfc2279.txt	UTF-8 character set encoding
www.w3.org/Metadata/	Internet metadata mechanisms

URIs: UNIFORM RESOURCE IDENTIFIERS

www.ietf.org/rfc/rfc1630.txt	Historical issues
www.ietf.org/rfc/rfc2396.txt	Syntax specification (updates to RFCs 1738 and 1808)

URNs: UNIFORM RESOURCE NAMES

www.ietf.org/rfc/rfc1737.txt	Functional requirements for URNs
www.ietf.org/rfc/rfc2611.txt	Summary of current practice
www.ietf.org/rfc/rfc2141.txt	URN syntax
www.ietf.org/html.charters/ urn-charter.html	IETF URN working group information

CHAPTER 9

The HTTP Protocol

Topics/Concepts Covered: HTTP 1.0 overview, GET, POST, PUT, and HEAD methods, header fields and status codes, cookies, access control and authentication, proxy servers, data encryption, content negotiation

To develop interactive Web applications, a Web designer must understand how Web client programs, such as browsers, interact with a HyperText Transfer Protocol (HTTP) server. This interaction involves two distinct but related issues. The first issue is HTTP—the protocol by which a client program sends information to an HTTP server, and vice versa. HTTP supports mechanisms for communicating information about the transaction, such as the transaction status (successful or not) and the nature of the data being sent [i.e., what is the Multipurpose Internet Mail Extensions (MIME) type of the data], as part of the message sent from client to server or from server to client. The protocol also supports several communication *methods* (e.g., GET, POST, or HEAD) for specifying *how* message data is sent by the browser, or how the request should be handled by the server. This chapter presents a detailed discussion of these mechanisms and how they work.

The second issue is the manner in which servers *handle* a request. If the requested resource is a file, the server locates the file and sends it back to the client, or it sends an appropriate error message if the file is unavailable. However, the resource [specified by the Uniform Resource Locator (URL)] is often not a file, but rather a request for special processing at the server end of the transaction, such as a database query. In most cases, the Web server does not do this processing, because such tasks are specific to the applications running at the Web site, and do not reflect generic functionality that can be easily incorporated in a universal server. Instead, most servers hand off these application-specific tasks to other programs, traditionally called *gateway programs.*

These programs run independently of (but can communicate with) the HTTP server, and they are designed explicitly for the special processing required at a Web site. The *Common Gateway Interface* (CGI) specification, described in the next chapter, defines how HTTP servers communicate with these gateway programs.

> **NOTE** Most servers now support compiled modules that can be dynamically linked to the server and that support gateway functionality, with significant performance improvements over the CGI approach. These mechanisms, and the advantages and disadvantages of this approach, are discussed in Chapter 10.

This chapter first outlines the general principles of the HTTP protocol, and then illustrates its operation via example transactions that use Version 1.0 of the protocol. Of course, like all Web-related languages and protocols, HTTP is evolving, the most recent version being HTTP 1.1. This chapter primarily discusses HTTP 1.0, as this is the lowest-common-denominator version universally supported by today's browsers. However, Section 9.18 discusses some of the main changes associated with HTTP 1.1.

In general, all Web applications must be designed to work with both HTTP 1.0 and HTTP 1.1. This is because only the most recent browsers support HTTP 1.1, whereas all browsers support HTTP 1.0 (the protocol was designed to be backward-compatible, so that this would be possible). Table 9.1 summarizes the current level of support, by common browsers, for the two versions of HTTP.

Note, however, that a few HTTP 1.1 features, particularly important for controlling the client-server connection, were incorporated as extensions to HTTP 1.0 and are supported by most Web browsers and HTTP 1.0 Web servers. These extensions are also discussed here.

9.1 HTTP 1.0 Protocol Overview

HyperText Transfer Protocol (HTTP) is an Internet client-server protocol designed for the rapid and efficient delivery of hypertext materials. HTTP is said to be a *stateless* protocol, which means that once a server has delivered the requested data to a client, the client-server connection is broken, and the server retains no memory of the event that just took place.

All HTTP communication transmits data as a stream of eight-bit characters, or *octets.* This ensures the safe transmission of all forms of data, including images, executable programs, and eXtensible Markup Language (XML) or HyperText Markup Language (HTML) documents.

Table 9.1   Browser Support for Versions 1.0 and 1.1 of the HTTP Protocol

BROWSER	HTTP 1.0	HTTP 1.1
Navigator 2.x	Y	N
Navigator 3.x	Y	N
Navigator 4.x	Y	N
Navigator 6/Mozilla	Y	Y
Opera 3.6x	Y	N
Opera 4.x	Y	Y
Lynx 2.8.2	Y	N
Internet Explorer 2.x	Y	N
Internet Explorer 3.x	Y	N
Internet Explorer 4.x	Y	Y (partial)
Internet Explorer 5.x	Y	Y

A typical HTTP 1.0 session has four stages, described in the following list and illustrated in Figure 9.1:

1. *Client opens a Transmission Control Protocol/Internet Protocol (TCP/IP) connection to the server.* The client program (for example, a Web browser) contacts the server at the specified Internet address and port number (the default port is 80).

2. *Client sends a request for a resource.* The client sends a message to the server, requesting service. The request has either one or two parts. The first part is an HTTP *request header,* specifying the HTTP method to be used during the transaction and providing information about the capabilities of the client and about the data being sent to the server (if any). Example HTTP methods are GET (for getting an object from a server) and POST [for posting (sending) data to a resource (e.g., a gateway program) on the server]. The second part of the message consists of the data being sent by the client to the server—this part is absent if no data is being sent.

3. *Server sends a response.* The server sends a response message to the client. This consists of either one or two parts. The first part is the *response header* describing the state of the transaction (e.g., whether the transaction was successful, or not) and the type of data being sent (if any); the second part is the data being returned (if any).

4. *The server closed the TCP/IP connection.* The connection is closed; the server does not retain any knowledge of the transaction just completed.

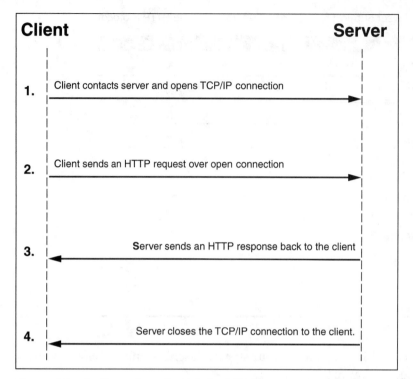

Figure 9.1 An illustration of a typical HTTP client-server transaction.

This procedure means that each connection processes a single transaction and can, therefore, only download a single data file to the client, while the stateless nature means that each connection knows nothing about previous connections. The implications of these features are illustrated in the following two illustrations.

9.1.1 Illustration: Single Transaction per Connection

Assume that HTTP is used to access an HTML document that contains, via **img** element references, 10 inline images. Displaying the document requires 11 distinct connections to the HTTP server—one to retrieve the HTML document itself and 10 others to retrieve the 10 image files.

9.1.2 Illustration: Stateless Transactions

Assume that a user retrieves, from a server, an X/HTML **form** containing a fill-in field for a username—by typing in a name, the user is able to access name-specific information in a personnel database. When the user submits the **form,** the name (and any other information gathered by the **form**) is sent to a gateway program residing on the server that processes the request; the URL that references this gateway program is specified as a **form** element attribute.

This gateway program processes the data and returns a second X/HTML document containing the results, along with another **form** allowing further requests of the database. In this case, however, the **form** does not contain a place to type a name. Because the server is stateless and, thus, has no memory of the first connection, how will it know the name of the person when data from this second form is sent to the server?

The answer is that the server does not know the name. Rather, the application designer must write software such that the programs on the server explicitly keep track of this information. One way to do so is to hide the name information *inside* the **form** returned to the user. This can be accomplished using special *hidden* input elements of the form `<input type="hidden" .../>`. In the case of this simple example, the element might be:

```
<input type="hidden" name="name_of_person" value="user_name" />
```

When the user submits the second **form,** the content of the hidden element is sent along with any new input, thereby returning the username to the server.

Information that tracks the history of a sequence of transactions is often called *state information.* Using hidden elements, state information can be passed back and forth between client and server as part of the message data, preserving knowledge of the name for each subsequent transaction. Alternatively, *HTTP cookies* can pass state information back and forth inside the actual HTTP header, as opposed to inside the message. This latter alternative is described in Section 9.12.

9.1.3 HTTP 1.0 Extension: HTTP Keep-Alive

Most HTTP 1.0-capable browsers and servers support an HTTP 1.0 extension known as *keep-alive,* which keeps the client-server connection open whenever a client requests multiple resources from the same server. In terms of the preceding model for HTTP transactions, this means that step 4 (the closing of the connection) is deferred—instead, the next request starts at step 2 and does not require the reopening of the connection. This can significantly increase the speed with which multiple files can be transferred, because it avoids the time (due to server processing and network negotiation between the client-server) costs associated with opening and closing connections. For example, if the transactions described in 9.1.2 are repeated using keep-alive, the browser still retrieves 11 distinct files, but the connection between browser and server is only broken after the last image has been downloaded. This significantly speeds up the downloading of composite documents, because the connection is only opened and closed once.

However, as far as the browser and server are concerned, each request is a single transaction, and the server does not retain knowledge of each transaction after it is completed, even if the connection to the client is still open.

The keep-alive mechanism, albeit implemented in a slightly different way, is a core feature of HTTP 1.1. The HTTP 1.1 keep-alive mechanism is briefly discussed in Section 9.18.

9.1.4 Example Client-Server Sessions

The easiest way to understand HTTP, and to illustrate the usage of the various header fields, is through simple examples. The next few sections present several examples covering the most common HTTP transactions. Each presentation shows both the data sent from the client to the HTTP server and the data returned from the server to the client. First, a few words about how this eavesdropping was accomplished.

Monitoring Client-Server Interaction

It is easy to monitor the interaction between HTTP servers and Web clients, because the communication is entirely in character data sent to (or received from) a particular port on a Web server (a port is a bit like a telephone extension to which data can be sent or received). Consequently, all you need do is *listen* at a port or *talk* to a port. The book's Web site provides several programs that can let you do this: Appendix C describes these programs in detail and explains how they are used. The following sections briefly summarize these uses.

Listening to Data Sent by a Browser

The *listen* program lets you find out what a Web client sends to a server. To do this, you run the *listen* program on a computer, and make a Web client talk to *listen*. As an example, suppose *listen* is started on the computer with domain name *leonardo.subnet.ca*. When started, *listen* indicates the port number it is listening at by printing a message such as:

```
listening at port 1743
```

It then falls silent, waiting to print any data that arrives at this port. The next step is to configure a Web client (such as a browser) to send HTTP requests to this port. With a browser, this is done by accessing a URL that *points* to port 1743 on *leonardo.subnet.ca.* An example is

```
http://leonardo.subnet.ca:1743/Tests/file.html
```

(the port number is marked in boldface). The browser dutifully sends the HTTP request headers to port number 1743 on *leonardo.subnet.ca,* whereupon *listen* receives the data and prints it to the screen.

Listing Data Returned by a Server

Determining what the server sends back to the client takes a bit more work. In this case, you can use Telnet to connect to the server, but you must now enter by hand the HTTP request headers that are sent by a real client (and which you fortunately intercepted using the *listen* program, using the procedure described in the previous section). Suppose, for example, that a server is running at port 80 on *leonardo.subnet.ca.* You can connect to this server by simply making a telnet connection to this port. On a Unix system, you would type (the typed command string is in boldface):

```
telnet leonardo.subnet.ca 80
Trying 128.100.121.33...
Connected to leonardo.subnet.ca
Escape character is '^]'.
```

Unix *telnet* clients typically give three lines of information to explain what they are doing and then fall silent. Whatever you now type is sent to the server running on *leonardo.subnet.ca,* so typically you now type in the required request headers. Whatever the server sends in response is sent to the *telnet* program and printed on the screen.

Mimicking a Web Server

The *backtalk* program is a derivative of *listen* that lets you both monitor the data sent by a browser, and also send data to the remote program talking to that port. This lets you mimic the actions of a Web server, because the data you type is returned to the browser. When launched, *backtalk* allocates a port and, like *listen,* prints out the port number, for example:

```
listening at port 1743
```

Thereafter, *backtalk* prints to the display anything that a remote program sends to port 1743, and anything typed into the console is sent out through port 1743 back to the remote program. Thus, you can use *backtalk* to mimic the response of an HTTP server, albeit by hand. This is useful for examining client response to special server response headers, such as a request for user authentication.

Monitoring the Client-Server Transactions

Finally, the program *monitor* lets you actually monitor (or store in a file) all the data sent between a client and an HTTP server. This program acts as an intermediary between a client and a remote server, and it *proxies* the data sent between them. That is, the client (e.g., a browser) sends data to *monitor*, which forwards this to a Web server, and the Web server sends a response to *monitor*, which then forwards the response to the browser. At the same time, *monitor* stores all this data in a file, which can be reviewed to examine the actual data that was exchanged.

The use of *monitor* is described in Appendix C, Section C.3 on this book's companion Web site. Like *listen* and *backtalk*, the source code (and executable versions) of *monitor* are found on the book's supporting Web site at www.utoronto.ca/ian/books/xhtml2/appc/.

9.2 Overview of Examples

The tools just described were used to determine the information passed between the client and server in several typical HTTP transactions. The examples that follow look at the following typical transactions:

- A simple GET method request, requesting an HTML document
- Another simple GET method request, illustrating some additional header fields
- A GET method request for a previously obtained document
- A HEAD method request for resource metainformation
- A GET method request with a query string within the URL
- A GET method request arising from an HTML **form** submission
- A POST method request arising from an HTML **form** submission
- Another POST method request arising from an HTML **form** submission
- A file access request requiring Basic user authentication
- Example POST and DELETE requests

To get the most out of these examples, you will need a basic understanding of URLs and of the way data is gathered by an HTML form and composed as a message for the server. These topics were covered in Chapter 8, as well as in Chapter 16 of *XHTML 1.0 Language and Design Sourcebook*.

9.3 A Simple GET Method Request

This example looks at how a client makes a GET request for a document resource from an HTTP server, and at how a server responds to the request.

In practice, this transaction could be invoked in two ways: (1) by the user typing the URL

```
http://smaug.java.utoronto.ca:13000/test.html
```

directly into the browser's location window, or (2) by the user selecting this URL from a bookmark or favorites list. The analysis is broken into the two basic parts: (1) the passing of the request to the server, and (2) the response sent by the server back to the client.

When a client contacts a server, it sends a *request header* defining the details of the request, followed by any data the client may be sending. In response, the server returns a *response header* describing the status of the transaction, followed in turn by any data being returned. The first example illustrates the basics of this flow of information.

9.3.1 The Client Request Header

Figure 9.2 shows the actual data sent by an old client (Navigator 3.02) to the server. Other clients send qualitatively the same information (we will look at some others later on).

This request message consists of a request header containing several *request header fields.* Each field is a line of ASCII text, terminated by a carriage-return line feed character pair (CRLF, not shown at the end of the lines). A blank line containing only a CRLF pair marks the end of the request header and the beginning of any *data* being sent from the client to the server. This example transaction does not send data to the server, so the blank line is the end of the request.

The request header contains two parts. The first part—the first line of the header—is called the *method* field. This field specifies the HTTP method to be used, the location of the desired resource on the server (as a URL), and the version of the HTTP protocol that the client program would like to use. This is followed by several HTTP *request* fields, which provide information to the server about the client, and about the nature of the data (if any) being sent by the client to the server.

```
GET /test.html HTTP/1.0
Connection: Keep-Alive
User-Agent: Mozilla/3.01 (Win95; I)
Host: smaug.java.utoronto.ca:13000
Accept: image/gif, image/x-xbitmap, image/jpeg, image/pjpeg, */*
[CRLF]
```

Figure 9.2 Data sent from a Navigator 3.02 client to an HTTP server during a simple GET request. The line at the bottom (denoted by *[CRLF]*) corresponds to an empty line containing only a carriage-return line feed character pair.

Client Request: Method

The method field contains three text fields, separated by white space (white space is any combination of space and/or tab characters). The general form for this field is

```
HTTP_method identifier HTTP_version
```

which, in our example, was:

```
GET /test.html HTTP/1.0
```

The three components of this method field are:

1. `HTTP_method`. The HTTP method specification—GET in this example. The method specifies what is to be done to the object specified by the URL. Some other common methods are HEAD, which requests header information about an object, and POST, which is used to send information to the object.

2. `identifier`. The identifier of the resource. In this example, the identifier,/test.html, is the URL stripped of the protocol and Internet domain name strings. If this were a request to a *proxy server,* it would be the entire URL. Proxy servers are discussed in Section 9.14.

3. `HTTP_version`. The HTTP protocol version used by the client—1.0 in this example. Table 9.1 lists the protocol versions supported by common browsers.

Client Request: Connection (HTTP 1.0 Extension)

The `connection` field is an extension to the HTTP 1.0 protocol that is widely supported by current browsers. This field is a signal to the server that it should keep open the connection to the browser, so that the browser can make additional requests using the already opened TCP/IP circuit. As described in the Note at the beginning of Section 9.1, opening and closing a TCP/IP connection is a time- and network-intensive process: Performance can be significantly improved if the browser and server can transfer multiple files over a single opened connection. If a browser sends an HTTP 1.0 `connection: keep-alive` header field, servers that understand this header will keep the connection open for a short time (typically, from 5 to 15 seconds) in preparation for the next request.

Older browsers (such as Navigator 2, Internet Explorer 3, and Lynx 2.8.2) do not support keep-alive. Similarly, not all servers support this feature and some simply ignore this field. Finally, an HTTP 1.0 server will use keep-alive *only if* it can return a `content-length` field for the data it returns—with keep-alive, the content-length field is the only way a client can determine if all the data have been sent by the server, whereupon it can make another request.

The connection field was introduced as an extension to HTTP 1.0, but the approach turned out to cause a number of problems that could only be resolved by significantly modifying the keep-alive mechanism. Thus, although HTTP 1.1 supports the `connection` field and the value `keep-alive`, the mechanism used is very different from that in HTTP 1.0. In HTTP 1.1, connections are kept alive by default and are explicitly closed by the server sending a `connection: close` header field in the response.

Client Request: User-Agent

There are several other common request header fields. The User-agent field, of the form `User-agent: ascii_string`, provides information about the client making the request. The example gave

```
User-Agent: Mozilla/3.01 (Win95; I)
```

to indicate the Netscape 3.01 browser (code-named *Mozilla*). Some other examples are:

```
User-Agent: Mozilla/2.02 (Windows 3.1)
User-Agent: Mozilla/4.03 [en] (Win95; I)
User-Agent: Mozilla/4.61 [en] (Win98; I)
User-Agent: Mozilla/5.0 [en-CA] (Windows_98; I)
User-Agent: Mozilla/2.0 (compatible; MSIE 3.0; Windows 95;1024,768
User-Agent: Mozilla/4.0 (compatible; MSIE 4.0; Windows 95)
User-Agent: Mozilla/4.0 (compatible; MSIE 5.0; Windows 98; DigExt)
User-Agent: Lynx/2.8.2rel.1 libwww-FM/2.14
```

The first four correspond to different versions of the Navigator browser, with the text inside the parentheses providing additional information about the platform (typically, the operating system) under which the browser is running—this is the accepted syntax for including such additional information. (Note, however, that some versions of Internet Explorer 3 omit the closing round bracket, as illustrated in the previous list.) Note, with Navigator 3 and up, use of text inside the square brackets to indicate the preferred language of the browser—this is a special extension supported only by Navigator that has been largely supplanted by the `accept-language` header described in Section 9.3.2. The fifth through seventh examples are from Microsoft Internet Explorer 3 through 5, respectively—note how these browsers claim to be Netscape equivalents and identify themselves as Internet Explorer only via the text inside the parentheses (*MSIE* stands for *Microsoft Internet Explorer*). The last example shows the identification string for the Lynx 2.8.2 browser.

Many server gateway programs use the browser identity string to select the type of data to return, and thus Microsoft uses the Mozilla name so that server software will treat the Microsoft product as equivalent to Netscape's.

Client Request: Accept

The example shows several additional request headers. The `accept` fields contain a list of data types, expressed as *MIME content-types,* which tell the server what type of data the client is willing to accept. MIME types are discussed in more detail later in this chapter and also in Appendix B on this book's companion Web site. The meanings for simple types are relatively straightforward. For example, `accept: text/plain` means that the client can accept plain text files, while `accept: audio/*` means that the client can accept any form of audio data. In our example from the Navigator 3.02 browser, this field was:

```
Accept: image/gif, image/x-xbitmap, image/jpeg, image/pjpeg, */*
```

Note how multiple MIME types can be provided in a single `Accept` header, provided commas separate them. Note in this case the last field—`*/*`—which indicates that this browser can accept any data at all!

In principle, this field can give the server an idea of the types of data the browser can accept, so that it can deliver data in the appropriate format, should multiple options be available. Please also see Section 9.3.2.

Client Request: Host

The `host` fields give the domain name (or numeric IP address) and port number to which the request was directed, using the format

```
host: domain.name:port
```

which, in the case of the example, was

```
host:smaug.java.utoronto.ca:13000
```

which indicates that this request was directed to the Web server running on port 13000 on the machine named smaug.java.utoronto.ca.

This is important because, as described in Chapter 7, Section 7.2.2, a machine can have many distinct names—and the `host` field is the only way a Web server can know which name is being referenced by the browser. Thus, if the same server machine has the domain names *www.shoeless.com* and *www.dogatemyfrog.com,* then requesting the home page from these two Web servers will produce the following different host fields in the HTTP request:

URL OF REQUEST	Host FIELD IN HTTP REQUEST
http://www.shoeless.com	Host: www.shoeless.com:80
http://www.dogatemyfrog.com	Host: www.dogatemyfrog.com:80

The Web server can use this information to return different data depending on which domain name was used in the request. This mechanism is often called *virtual hosting*.

9.3.2 Additional Request Fields: Accept-Charset, Accept-Encoding, and Accept-Language

Newer browsers include additional fields in the header when requesting a resource. An example is shown in Figure 9.3, which shows the header produced by the Navigator 4.61 browser. The extra fields are shown in boldface and are described in the following.

These additional fields are extensions upon accept and define additional information about the data that the browser prefers to receive. The Accept-Charset field defines the character sets and character encodings that the browser supports when downloading text resources, as opposed to binary data. Thus, the header

```
Accept-Charset: iso-8859-1,*,utf-8
```

means that browser accepts text encoded using the iso-8859-1 charset, the utf-8 charset—and any other charset (the * is a wildcard corresponding to any possible character set and character encoding). Character sets and encodings are discussed in Appendix A, which also lists charset strings that can appear in accept-charset headers.

```
GET /test.html HTTP/1.0
Connection: Keep-Alive
User-Agent: Mozilla/4.61 [en] (Win98; I)
Host: smaug.java.utoronto.ca:13000
Accept: image/gif, image/x-xbitmap, image/jpeg, image/pjpeg,
   image/png, */*
Accept-Charset: iso-8859-1,*,utf-8
Accept-Language: en,fr-CA
Accept-Encoding: gzip
```

Figure 9.3 Request headers from Navigator 4.61. Additional headers relative to Figure 9.2 are shown in boldface.

The `accept-language` field defines the human languages preferred by the browser user and, again, is relevant only for text documents. In Figure 9.3, the field

```
Accept-Language: en,fr-CA,fr
```

means that the user making this request prefers documents written in English, followed by documents written in Canadian French, followed by documents written in generic French. The user, using the browser's Preferences tool, typically defines this list of languages.

> **NOTE** Appendix C of the previous book in this series, *XHTML 1.0 Language and Design Sourcebook*, provides a detailed description of the special strings used to identify human (as opposed to computer) languages on the Internet. A detailed list of the substrings used to compose the language identifiers (two-letter language name, followed by an optional dash, followed by a country name for location-specific dialects) is found at www.utoronto.ca/ian/books/xhtml1/appc/index.html.

Last, the `accept-encoding` header gives the type of *data encoding* formats (typically data compression) that the browser can handle. Thus, the header

```
Accept-Encoding: gzip
```

means that this browser can download and decode on the fly data encoded using the GNU Zip program. Note that this can apply to any type of data, not just text. Compressed encoding is useful if the data file is large, as it will be much faster to download in compressed form.

The information in these three fields is used by the server to determine which data to return, should multiple versions of the data be available for the same URL. For example, suppose that the browser requests the following resource

```
http://smaug.java.utoronto.ca:13000/resource
```

and that this URL can reference the following different, but essentially equivalent, documents:

resource-en.html	XHTML, in English
resource-en-gzip.html	XHTML, in English, and also GZIP-compressed
resource-fr-gzip.html	XHTML, in generic French, and also GZIP-compressed

Because the browser prefers documents written in English, and as it also supports GZIP-compressed data, the server will choose to return the second of these resources.

At present, this feature, known as *content negotiation*, is implemented on several servers and is discussed in more detail in Section 9.17.

Request Header and Gateway Programs

In this example, the request headers are used by the server to determine whether a data file should be sent to the server and, if so, what type of data to send. If the request references a gateway program, then the server cannot make this decision. Instead, the server passes *all* the request header information to the gateway program (as a collection of environment variables) and lets the gateway program decide what to do. Thus, a gateway program author must understand the meanings of these header fields, because he or she will have to write gateway programs that interpret them.

9.3.3 The Server Response: Header and Data

When the server receives the request, it tries to apply the designated method (GET or POST, for example) to the specified object (file or program), and it passes the results of this effort back to the client. The returned data are preceded by a response header consisting of response header fields, which communicate information about the state of the transaction back to the client. As with the request header fields sent from client to server, these are single lines of text terminated by a CRLF, whereas the end of the response header is indicated by a single blank line containing only a CRLF. The data of the response follows the blank line. Figure 9.4 shows the data returned by an HTTP 1.0 Web server in response to the request of Figure 9.2 or 9.3.

The first eight lines are the response header—each line is ended by a CRLF (carriage return and a line feed). A single blank line (containing only CRLF) indicates the end of the header. The data response of the request (in this case, the requested document) follows this blank line.

Server Response: The Status Line

The first line in the response header is a status line that lets the client know what protocol the server uses, and whether the request was successfully completed or not. The general format for this line is

```
HTTP/version status_code explanation
```

```
HTTP/1.0 200 OK
Date: Sat, 29 Jan 2000 21:47:23 GMT
Server: Apache/1.1.1
Content-type: text/html
Content-length: 363
Last-modified: Fri, 28 Jan 2000 19:29:20 GMT
Connection: Keep-Alive
Keep-Alive: timeout=15, max=5
... (a blank line containing only CRLF)
<html> <head>
  <title>Simple Test XHTML document</title>
</head><body>
  <h1>Simple Test XHTML Document</h1>
  <p>This is a test. Please do not adjust your
     computer. Control of your computer will
     soon be returned to you. </p>
  <p>For more fun, why not try linking to
     another <a href="test2.html">test document</a>.!</p>
</body></html>
```

Figure 9.4   Data returned from the server to the client subsequent to the GET request of Figure 9.2 or 9.3. Comments are in italics.

which, in the example, was:

```
HTTP/1.0 200 OK
```

The three components of this status line are:

1. `HTTP/version`. The protocol version being used by the server, HTTP/1.0 in the example in Figure 9.4. If the client request uses the HTTP/1.1 syntax, but the server is only capable of HTTP/1.0, then the server will return HTTP/1.0 to indicate this fact.

2. `status_code`. The *status code* for the response, as a number between 200 and 599. Values from 200 through 299 indicate successful transactions, and values 300 through 399 indicate *redirection*—the resource at the requested URL has moved. In this case, the server must also send the new URL of the object, if it is known (sent within a `Location` response header field). Numbers 400 through 599 are error messages. When an error occurs, the server usually sends a small HTML document explaining the error, to help the user understand what happened and why.

3. `explanation`. A text string that provides descriptive information about the status. Explanation strings vary from server to server, whereas status codes and their meanings are explicitly defined by the HTTP specification. Here, the string `OK` simply means that everything was OK!

In this example, the code 200 means that everything went fine and that the server is returning the requested data.

The remaining response header fields contain information about the server and about the response being sent. The example in Figure 9.4 returns seven lines of response header information. The first two, date and server, describe the server and the time at which the response was made, and the content-type, content-length, and last-modified fields pass information specific to the document or data being returned. Finally, the connection and keep-alive fields (common extensions to HTTP 1.0) help control the connection between the browser and the Web server. The formats and meanings of these header fields are described in the following sections.

Server Response: Date

This field, of the format Date: *date_time,* contains the time and date when the message was assembled for transmission. Note that the time *must* be Greenwich Mean Time (GMT) to ensure that all clients and Web servers share a common time zone. In the example, this field was:

```
Date: Sat, 29 Jan 2000 21:47:23 GMT
```

Note that this is *not* the date at which the data being returned was created or last modified—that information is contained in the Last-modified field. Details about supported time formats for use with date values are given in Section 9.19.

Server Response: Server

This field, of the format Server: *name/version,* returns the name and version of the server software, with a slash character separating the two. Some examples are:

```
Server: Netscape-Enterprise/2.01
Server: Apache/1.1.1
Server: Apache/1.2.4
Server: Microsoft-IIS/4.0
```

Server Response: Content-Type

This field, of the form Content-type: type/subtype, indicates the *MIME content-type* of the data being sent from the server to the client. In this example, the returned data is HTML-format data (an XHTML document), so the field is:

```
Content-type: text/html
```

MIME types are discussed in Appendix B. If no data is being returned (the server does not always send data back), then this field is absent.

Server Response: Content-Length

This field, of the format `Content-length: length,` gives the length in bytes of the data portion of the message—this is the part that follows the blank line that ends the header. In Figure 9.4, this field is

```
Content-length: 363
```

which indicates that there are 363 bytes in the data portion of the message. This tells the browser exactly how much data it needs to read.

In some situations, the content-length is unknown (for example, if the data output of a gateway program, such that the length is not known ahead of time), in which case this field is absent. In this event, the client will continue to read data until the server breaks the connection, or until the server sends a special "data finished" signal. This field is also absent if no data is being returned.

Server Response: Last-Modified

This field, of the format `Last-modified: date_time,` gives the date and time at which the returned resource (here a document) was last modified. As with the `Date` field, the information must be given in GMT. In the example, this field was:

```
Last-modified: Fri, 28 Jan 2000 19:29:20 GMT
```

If the server does not know the date when the resource was last modified, this field is absent.

Server Response: Connection
(HTTP 1.0 Extension)

This field, of the format `connection: keep-alive,` directs the browser to keep the connection open after it has received the data being sent by the browser. This is equivalent in purpose to the connection header sent by the browser to the server. The `keep-alive` header (discussed next) then tells the browser how long it should keep the connection alive before giving up.

Server Response: Keep-Alive
(HTTP 1.0 Extension)

This field, of the format `keep-alive: timeout=nn, max=mm,` specifies how the server will actually handle the keep-alive mechanism. The parameter `timeout` specifies, in seconds, how long the Web server will wait for the next request before closing the connection. The parameter max specifies how many consecutive keep-alive requests the server will accept from the browser before it refuses any more. Thus, in Figure 9.4 the field

```
Keep-Alive: timeout=15, max=5
```

means that the server will accept 5 subsequent keep-alive requests from a given client before refusing to keep the connection alive any longer, and that it will wait at most 15 seconds before closing an unused keep-alive session.

This header is actually returned by older Apache servers (such as Apache 1.1.x).

NOTE PROBLEMS WITH HTTP 1.0 KEEP-ALIVE **The mechanisms for controlling** Keep-Alive **(and implemented by most Web browsers and HTTP 1.0 Web servers) have a number of problems, particularly when a browser connects to a Web server via a proxy server. As a result, the keep-alive mechanism was substantially modified for HTTP 1.1: the** Keep-Alive **header field was dropped entirely, and the meaning of** connection **was changed. The changes are summarized in Section 9.18.**

Server Generation of Response Header

How does the server generate the response header? If the requested resource is a file, the HTTP server constructs the header itself, based on knowledge of the file being requested and data contained in the Web server's configuration files. If the request is to a gateway program, then the gateway program must provide information about the details of the returned data, such as the content-type, since only this program knows what is to be returned.

There are two mechanisms used by gateway programs for providing response header information. In the first, the gateway program returns server directives to the server—used by the server to create appropriate header fields, which are included with the full response header generated by the server. In the second mechanism, the gateway program returns a complete response header, which is sent directly to the remote client, bypassing processing by the server. This is called the *nonparsed header* approach. Both methods are described in Chapter 10.

9.4 Linking to Another Document

The preceding example assumed that the URL request came upon the user's typing a URL into the browser's location or address window, or upon selecting a bookmarked URL. However, the situation is somewhat different if the browser accesses a resource because the user clicked on a link (or submitted a **form**) connecting one Web resource to another. For example, the document retrieved by the request shown in Figure 9.3 contains the markup

```
<p>For more fun, why not try linking to
    another <a href="test2.html">test document</a>.!</p>
```

which links this document at URL

```
http://smaug.java.utoronto.ca:13000/test.html
```

to an adjacent document, *test2.html.* Figure 9.5 shows the request header sent by the Navigator 4.61 browser when the user selects this link.

Note the new `referer` field in the request header (shown in boldface). When a user navigates from one page to another by selecting links or submitting forms, the request header contains a `referer` header giving the URL of the document from which the request was made—that is, where the link was *referred from.* Thus, this request (in Figure 9.5) contains the field

```
Referer: http://smaug.java.utoronto.ca:13000/test.html
```

to indicate that this request for the document *test2.html* originated from the document *test1.html.*

A `referer` is also added whenever a browser retrieves images, script programs, or other data referenced by **img**, **link**, **script**, **embed**, **object**, **iframe**, or **frame** elements inside an already-retrieved document.

As noted in Section 9.3, a `referer` field is *not* included if a request is made by directly typing a URL into the browser's location or address window. It is also not generally included if the document containing the link was accessed from the local computer (i.e., if it shows up as having a **file** URL), for example by dragging a file from the desktop onto the browser. However, some earlier browsers (Navigator 3 and earlier, and Lynx 2.8.2) do include referer data in this latter case.

9.5 Linking to an Already-Retrieved File

The document *test2.html* retrieved in Figure 9.5 contains the following markup

```
<p> Here is a link back to the
    <a href="test.html">previous document</a>.</p>
```

Browser Request

```
GET /test2.html HTTP/1.0
Referer: http://smaug.java.utoronto.ca:13000/test.html
Connection: Keep-Alive
User-Agent: Mozilla/4.61 [en] (Win98; I)
Host: smaug.java.utoronto.ca:13000
Accept: image/gif, image/x-xbitmap, image/jpeg, image/pjpeg,
   image/png, */*
Accept-Encoding: gzip
Accept-Language: en,fr-CA
Accept-Charset: iso-8859-1,*,utf-8
... (a blank line containing only CRLF)
```

Server Response

```
HTTP/1.0 200 OK
Date: Sat, 29 Jan 2000 21:47:24 GMT
Server: Apache/1.1.1
Content-type: text/html
Content-length: 332
Last-modified: Fri, 28 Jan 2000 23:07:22 GMT
Connection: Keep-Alive
Keep-Alive: timeout=15, max=5
... (a blank line containing only CRLF)
<html><head>
  <title>Another Simple Test XHTML document</title>
</head><body>
  <h1>Another Simple Test XHTML Document</h1>
  <p>This is a second test document. Boy, it just
     doesn't get more exciting than this! </p>
  <p> Here is a link back to the
     <a href="test.html">previous document</a>.</p>
</body> </html>
```

Figure 9.5   Request header sent by Navigator 4.61 browser when the user clicks on the hypertext link in the document returned in Figure 9.4, and the subsequent server response. The new header field (relative to Figure 9.3) is shown in boldface.

that links back to the document *test.html*, which is of course the document we started with in this example. Figure 9.6 shows the request sent by the browser when this link is accessed, and it also shows the data returned by the server in the response header.

The `referer` field in the request header (shown in boldface) now indicates that the request came from the file *test2.html*. However, there is also a new `if-modified-since` field:

```
If-Modified-Since: Fri, 28 Jan 2000 19:29:20 GMT; length=363
```

Browser Request

```
GET /test.html HTTP/1.0
If-Modified-Since: Fri, 28 Jan 2000 19:29:20 GMT; length=363
Referer: http://smaug.java.utoronto.ca:13000/test2.html
Connection: Keep-Alive
User-Agent: Mozilla/4.61 [en] (Win98; I)
Host: smaug.java.utoronto.ca:13000
Accept: image/gif, image/x-xbitmap, image/jpeg, image/pjpeg,
   image/png, */*
Accept-Encoding: gzip
Accept-Language: en,fr-CA
Accept-Charset: iso-8859-1,*,utf-8
... (a blank line containing only CRLF)
```

Server Response

```
HTTP/1.0 304 Not Modified
Date: Sun, 30 Jan 2000 00:17:48 GMT
Server: Apache/1.1.1
Connection: Keep-Alive
... (a blank line containing only CRLF)
```

Figure 9.6 Request header sent by Navigator 4.61 browser when the user clicks on the hypertext link in *test2.html* linking back to the already-accessed *test.html*. The headers different from Figure 9.5 are shown in boldface. Note how the response message does not return any data.

This field is included when the browser already has a locally cached copy of the file, and where this local copy was retrieved with a well-defined last-modified field. With subsequent requests to the server, the browser can retrieve this file conditionally—that is, it can request that the server only send back a copy if the file has been modified since the last-modified date of the cached copy.

When a server receives a request containing an if-modified-since field, it compares the date in this field with the time at which the requested resource was last modified. If the resource has not been modified since the indicated date, then the server does not return the data. Instead, it returns the special status line:

```
HTTP/1.0 304 Not Modified
```

Status code 304 means that the resource has not been changed since it was last retrieved, and is an indication, to the browser, that it should simply redisplay the copy it already has.

9.5.1 Browsers and Browser Cache Verification

Browsers do not always contact a server to check for more recent versions of locally cached data files. Instead, this behavior is often configurable on the browser. For example, Internet Explorer 4 and Mozilla/Navigator 6 (and earlier) offer the following three configuration options, available from the Preferences tool:

- Every time/Every visit to the page
- Once per session/Every time you start Internet Explorer
- Never/Never

(Internet Explorer 5 and greater offer *Automatically* as a cryptic fourth choice.) If the third of these is selected, then the browser will never contact a remote server to verify that it has the most recent version of a cached file, whereas if the second option is enabled, it will check only once during a session.

This, of course, makes loading pages faster and is not a problem with regular inline images (or HTML documents) that do not change. However, it can be a problem if the resource changes on a regular basis, such as with dynamically generated content. Fortunately, there are several mechanisms for controlling a browser's handling of locally cached data, discussed in the next section.

9.5.2 Disabling Resource Caching on a Browser

A browser will only cache a resource if it knows the date at which the resource was last modified. If this information is not provided in the response HTTP header, then the browser will assume that the resource changes on each request, and it will not store a local copy of the data in the browser's cache. In this case, the browser must always contact the server to obtain the resource, which bypasses the possible problems caused by the browser-selectable options discussed in the previous section. An example of such a response is found in Figure 9.7A.

Alternatively, if the server knows when a resource is going to *expire* (that is, when it will next be updated and need to be refreshed), it can return a special expires field to indicate this fact. An example of such a response is shown in Figure 9.7B. Upon receiving this response message, a browser will cache the resource until the time indicated by the Expires header. At that time, it will delete the file from the cache, and it will be forced to return to the Web for a fresh copy when the resource is next requested by the browser.

A) Data Never to Be Cached

```
HTTP/1.0 200 OK
Date: Sat, 29 Jan 2000 21:47:24 GMT
Server: Apache/1.1.1
Content-type: text/html
Content-length: 332
Connection: Keep-Alive
Keep-Alive: timeout=15, max=5
... (a blank line containing only CRLF)
<html><head>
    ... (the data in the document) ...
```

B) Data to Be Cached Until It Expires

```
HTTP/1.0 200 OK
Date: Sat, 29 Jan 2000 21:47:24 GMT
Server: Apache/1.1.1
Content-type: text/html
Content-length: 332
Last-modified: Fri, 28 Jan 2000 23:07:22 GMT
Expires: Fri, 28 Jan 2000 23:45:00 GMT
Connection: Keep-Alive
Keep-Alive: timeout=15, max=5
... (a blank line containing only CRLF)
<html><head>
    ... (the data in the document) ...
```

Figure 9.7 Data sent by a server: the data in response (*A*) will never be cached, as there is no `last-modified` field, whereas the data in response (*B*) will be cached until the date specified by the expires field.

9.6 Requesting a Moved Resource

In some cases, a URL request can reference a resource that does not exist at the indicated URL, but that has been moved to another location known to the Web server. There are two common cases where this occurs:

1. The request URL references a directory, but the URL does not end with a trailing slash character.

2. The request URL references a standard resource, but the server has been configured to know that this resource has moved to a different URL.

Figure 9.8 illustrates the first of these cases. In this example, the user has typed in the URL

```
http://smaug.java.utoronto.ca:13000/Tmp
```

but the requested resource is actually a directory and not a file. The server, however, can detect this error, and it returns a special response header to indicate this fact and to provide the correct location. The status field

```
HTTP/1.0 301 Moved Permanently
```

means that the server knows the new, permanent location of the resource and is returning information to the browser *redirecting* it to the new location. The new location is included in a `location` field, which in this figure is:

```
Location: http://smaug.java.utoronto.ca:13000/Tmp/
```

This field gives the new location of the resource—the correct URL, complete with the trailing slash character.

Upon receiving a 301 response, a browser automatically accesses the location given in the `location` field (in this case, the same URL corrected to include a trailing slash character) and will access the directory listing. Note also, in Figure 9.8, how any other header field in the original request (such as `referer`) is included in the second request. Furthermore, if additional fields (such as `if-modified-since`) are relevant to the redirected URL, these are added to the second request.

This process is largely transparent to the browser user. The only obvious effect will be a slight delay in retrieving the resource due to the need for a second request, combined with a modification of the URL shown in the Location window to correct the URL to reference the new location.

If actual files are moved to new locations, this information can be added to a server's configuration files. Then, if a request comes in for the resource at its old location, the request will be automatically redirected to the new location.

9.6.1 Temporarily Moved Resources

HTTP 1.0 also supports a 302 response status code, which is used when a resource is moved *temporarily.* In all other ways, a response with a 302 status message is identical to a 301 response (such as in Figure 9.8). Indeed, browsers handle a 302 response in the same way as a 301—they automatically redirect their request to the resource specified by the `location` field.

A Web indexing robot, on the other hand, will take special note of the 302 status, and will mark the new location as temporary. It can then monitor the original URL (before the redirection) and check for any changes in the relocated position of the desired resource.

Note that some earlier HTTP 1.0 servers (such as Apache 1.1.1) erroneously return the 302 status code for resources that have actually been permanently moved.

Browser Request

```
GET /Tmp HTTP/1.0
Referer: http://smaug.java.utoronto.ca:13000/start.html
Connection: Keep-Alive
User-Agent: Mozilla/4.61 [en] (Win98; I)
Host: smaug.java.utoronto.ca:13000
Accept: image/gif, image/x-xbitmap, image/jpeg, image/pjpeg,
    image/png, */*
Accept-Encoding: gzip
Accept-Language: en,fr-CA
Accept-Charset: iso-8859-1,*,utf-8
... (a blank line containing only CRLF)
```

Server Response

```
HTTP/1.0 301 Moved Permanently
Date: Sun, 30 Jan 2000 20:20:03 GMT
Server: Apache/1.2.1
Location: http://smaug.java.utoronto.ca:13000/Tmp/
Content-type: text/html
... (a blank line containing only CRLF)
<html><head><title>Document moved</title></head>
<body><h1>Document moved</h1>
    <p>The document has moved <a
href="http://smaug.java.utoronto.ca:8000/Tmp/">here</a></p>
</body></html>
```

Subsequent Browser Request (Note correction of URL)

```
GET /Tmp/ HTTP/1.0
Referer: http://smaug.java.utoronto.ca:13000/start.html
Connection: Keep-Alive
User-Agent: Mozilla/4.61 [en] (Win98; I)
Host: smaug.java.utoronto.ca:13000
Accept: image/gif, image/x-xbitmap, image/jpeg, image/pjpeg,
    image/png, */*
Accept-Encoding: gzip
Accept-Language: en,fr-CA
Accept-Charset: iso-8859-1,*,utf-8
... (a blank line containing only CRLF)
```

Figure 9.8 Client-server transaction when a browser incorrectly requests a data resource that is, in fact, a directory. The server returns a redirect response, providing the corrected URL. The important portions of the request and response are noted in boldface. Comments are in italics.

9.7 HEAD Method: Information about a Resource

In some cases, it is useful to gather information about a resource without retrieving it. For example, a link-checking program does not always need to retrieve a resource to verify that it exists, whereas an indexing package may only want to know if a resource has changed since it was last cataloged.

This role is provided by the HTTP HEAD method, which requests that a server send only the response header relevant to the requested URL, but not the content of the referenced object. As the following example indicates, this is a quick way of seeing if a document or gateway program is actually present and of obtaining some general information about it, such as its content type or the date it was last modified, without downloading the entire resource.

In this example, we suppose that the user (or some automated program, such as a robot or spider) wants to access HEAD information about a document. The request that would be sent to the server is simply:

```
HEAD /test.html HTTP/1.0
User-Agent: Ian's_HEAD_Test_Agent (by-Hand)
From: name@domain.name.edu
```

The request does not need `accept` fields, because no data is being retrieved. The `From` field gives the server the electronic mail address of the person managing the file and making the HEAD request—it is important to give this information if the request comes from an automated program. A typical response (in this case, from an Apache 1.1.1 HTTP server) is:

```
HTTP/1.0 200 OK
Date: Sun, 30 Jan 2000 19:59:12 GMT
Server: Apache/1.1.1
Content-type: text/html
Content-length: 363
Last-modified: Fri, 28 Jan 2000 19:29:20 GMT
```

This indicates that the document exists (the status code 200 means the request was successful) and provides information about the document type, size, and the date it was last modified. If the URL instead referenced a dynamic resource, such as a program, the `content-length`, `last-modified`, and `content-type` headers would be absent, to indicate that this information is unknown a priori, and that the document is essentially new every time it is accessed.

The HEAD method is not implemented by browsers, but it is used by most Web indexing robots.

9.8 Sending Data to a Server Using GET

The HTTP protocol supports several HTTP methods for sending data from the client to the server. The most common are GET and POST, typically used to connect HTML **form**s or **isindex** queries with server-side processing programs. The PUT method, on the other hand, is used to create new resources (such as a file) on a server. PUT is described later in this chapter.

This section illustrates a GET method request arising from an XHTML **form**. Figure 9.9 shows the **form** markup for this example. Figure 9.10 shows the browser rendering of the **form** just before the Submit button is pressed (the actual document, *form-get.html,* available from the book's supporting Web site, uses **table** and other markup to elegantly lay out the form content). Figure 9.10 shows the data sent to the server by the browser and the response that is returned by the server.

```
<form action="http://smaug.java.utoronto.ca:13000/cgi-bin/dummy"
      method="GET">

Search string: <input type="text" name="srch" value="dogfish" />

Search Type: <select name="type">
                <option value="1"> Insensitive Substring </option>
                <option value="2" selected="selected"> Exact Match
   </option>
                <option value="3"> Sensitive Substring </option>
                <option value="4"> Regular Expression </option>
             </select>

Search databases in:
    <input type="checkbox" name="sr" value="CA"
        checked="checked" /> Canada <br />
    <input type="checkbox" name="sr" value="RU" /> Russia <br />
    <input type="checkbox" name="sr" value="SW"
        checked="checked" /> Sweden <br />
    <input type="checkbox" name="sr" value="US" /> U.S.A. <br />
    <em>(multiple items can be selected.)</em>

    <input type="submit" name="sub" value="Submit" />
    <input type="reset" name="reset" value="Reset Form"></td>

</form>
```

Figure 9.9 Simple **form** document, *form-get.html,* that uses the GET method to submit data to a server. Only the form-related markup is shown; the actual document, rendered in Figure 9.10 (and available from the book Web site), uses additional markup to control the form layout.

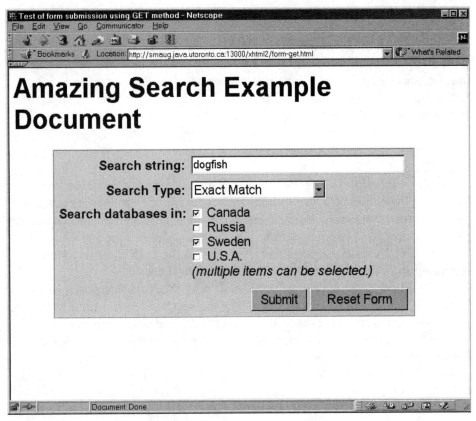

Figure 9.10   Navigator 4.7 rendering of the **form** example document, *form-get.html.* The form-related elements (but not the table layout and other markup) are outlined in Figure 9.9.

The **form** element defines where the data is to be sent, and the HTTP method to use when sending it. Thus, the form in Figure 9.9 begins with:

```
<form action="http://smaug.java.utoronto.ca:13000/cgi-bin/dummy"
      method="GET">
```

The **action** attribute defines the URL to which the form data should be sent when the user presses the Submit button, and the **method** attribute defines the HTTP method to use. If **method** is not specified, browsers will default to the GET method.

NOTE If the form **action** attribute specifies a **mailto** URL, most browsers will default to the POST method and will send the form data as the body of the mail message.

With the GET method, any data sent to the server must be appended to the URL as a query string, as described in Chapter 8, Section 8.2.7. Thus, when the user presses the form's Submit button, the browser gathers the form data selected by the user, composes a query string (according to the URL escaping mechanisms discussed in Chapter 8), and appends this query string to the URL specified by the action attribute. Thus, in the HTTP request sent to the server (shown in Figure 9.11), the method field is

```
GET /cgi-bin/dummy?srch=dogfish&type=2&sr=CA&sr=SW&sub=Submit HTTP/1.0
```

where the text in boldface is the query string data gathered from the **form**. Note how the names and values from each form input element are encoded and composed into strings of the form *name=value*, with ampersand characters (&) separating the composite strings (e.g., *name1=value1&name2=value2* . . .). With the GET method, this string is appended to the URL as a *query string*, separated from the base of the URL by a question mark.

Figure 9.11 shows the request headers sent by the Netscape Navigator 4.61 browser when this form is submitted. The request header is similar to the one produced by a simple hypertext link (Figures 9.3 and 9.5). The only real difference is in the query string appended to the locator string in the method field at the start of the header.

The URL given in the **form** element's **action** attribute references a simple CGI program, named *dummy:* Figure 9.12 shows the (perl5) source code listing for *dummy.* When the Web server receives the request, it starts the CGI program, and passes to it information about the request. In the case of GET method requests, all this information is passed to the CGI program inside a so-called *environment variables* program. To a perl program, these environment variables are accessible using a special hash table named ENV. In fact, the purpose of *dummy* is to print out the different environment variables and display them on the browser.

In fact, the CGI program in Figure 9.12 does three things. First, it prints out a single line

```
print "Content-type: text/plain\r\n\r\n";
```

which is a directive to the Web server indicating the type of data the CGI program is returning—all data printed by the CGI program is sent back to the Web server. The extra blank line after the header (the extra \r\n) is a CRLF pair, and marks the end of the server directives and the start of the actual data being returned.

The response data produced by *dummy* arises from the subsequent code. The first block:

Browser Request

```
GET /cgi-bin/dummy?srch=dogfish&type=2&sr=CA&sr=SW&sub=Submit HTTP/1.0
Referer: http://smaug.java.utoronto.ca:13000/form-get.html
Connection: Keep-Alive
User-Agent: Mozilla/4.61 [en] (Win98; I)
Host: smaug.java.utoronto.ca:13000
Accept: image/gif, image/x-xbitmap, image/jpeg, image/pjpeg,
   image/png, */*
Accept-Encoding: gzip
Accept-Language: en,fr-CA
Accept-Charset: iso-8859-1,*,utf-8
... (a blank line containing only CRLF)
```

Server Response

```
HTTP/1.0 200 OK
Date: Thu, 03 Feb 2000 17:00:52 GMT
Server: Apache/1.1.1
Content-type: text/plain
... (a blank line containing only CRLF)
Environment Variables and their Values
--------------------------------------
DOCUMENT_ROOT = /home/web
GATEWAY_INTERFACE = CGI/1.1
HTTP_ACCEPT = image/gif, image/x-xbitmap, image/png, */*
HTTP_ACCEPT_CHARSET = iso-8859-1,*,utf-8
HTTP_ACCEPT_ENCODING = gzip
HTTP_ACCEPT_LANGUAGE = en
HTTP_CONNECTION = Keep-Alive
HTTP_HOST = smaug.java.utoronto.ca:13000
HTTP_REFERER = http://smaug.java.utoronto.ca:13000/xhtml2/form-
   get.html
HTTP_USER_AGENT = Mozilla/4.61 [en] (Win98; I)
PATH = /usr/sbin:/usr/bsd:/sbin:/usr/bin:/usr/java/bin:/bin
QUERY_STRING = srch=dogfish&type=2&sr=CA&sr=SW&sub=Submit
REMOTE_ADDR = 132.206.43.21
REMOTE_HOST = test.java.utoronto.ca
REQUEST_METHOD = GET
SCRIPT_FILENAME = /home/Servers/apache_1.1.1/cgi-bin/dummy
SCRIPT_NAME = /cgi-bin/dummy
SERVER_ADMIN = ig@test.utoronto.ca
SERVER_NAME = smaug.java.utoronto.ca
SERVER_PORT = 13000
SERVER_PROTOCOL = HTTP/1.0
SERVER_SOFTWARE = Apache/1.1.1
TZ = EST5EDT
```

Figure 9.11 Data sent from the Navigator 4.7 browser to an HTTP server during a GET request arising from submitting the form listed in Figure 9.9. Note the query data (in boldface) appended to the URL. Comments are in italics. Note that some of the environment variable values have been shortened to reduce the line lengths.

```
#!/usr/sbin/perl -w

use strict;
&| = 1;                         # flush standard output
my &data;
my &key;
my &val;


print "Content-type: text/plain\r\n\r\n";
print "Environment Variables and their Values \r\n";
print "----------------------------------- \r\n";
while ((&key, &val) = each %ENV) {
        print "&key = &val\n";
}
&val = &ENV{CONTENT_LENGTH}; # set buffer size for reading data

if( defined (&val) ) {          # do only if there is POSTed data
    print "\r\n";
    print "Data sent from Browser to Server\r\n";
    print "-----------------------------\r\n";
    while( read(STDIN, &data, &val) ) { #read in &val bytes
        print &data;
    }
}
```

Figure 9.12   Source listing for the perl CGI program *dummy*.

```
print "Environment Variables and their Values \r\n";
print "----------------------------------- \r\n";
while ((&key, &val) = each %ENV) {
        print "&key = &val\n";
}
```

prints a list of all the environment variable names and values—that is, a list of all the environment variable data available to the CGI program. The next block tests to see if there is any POSTed data sent by the browser—if there is such data, it too is printed out. In this case, of course, there is no such data.

As mentioned, the data printed by the CGI program is sent back to the Web server. The Web server, in turn, takes the server directives sent by the CGI program and uses them to construct a complete HTTP response header (using the correct content-type indicated by the directive that is returned by the CGI program). The other data returned by the CGI program is then sent back to the browser as the returned data. The resulting server response is listed at the bottom of Figure 9.11. Note that the header *does not* give the content-length of the message, because the CGI program did not provide this information in a server directive.

Finally, Figure 9.13 shows the returned data as rendered by the browser. Note, in particular, that the displayed *Location* URL (in the browser's location window) includes the encoded URL data. Thus, this page is bookmarkable, as all the data needed to create this document is stored in the URL.

9.9 Sending Data to a Server Using POST (1)

Alternatively, **form** data can be sent to the Web server using the HTTP POST method. This is done simply by changing the **method** attribute value to POST. A form that does this is available at the book's supporting Web site, under the name *form-post1.html.* This document is identical with that used in Section 9.9, except that the form element start tag is:

```
<form action="http://smaug.java.utoronto.ca:13000/cgi-bin/dummy"
      method="POST">
```

Figure 9.14 shows the resulting client-server messages. Relative to the otherwise equivalent GET request in Figure 9.12, the POST request is different in the following four ways:

- The status line (first line in the request) indicates the POST method and not GET. Also, there is no query data appended to the location string in the status line.

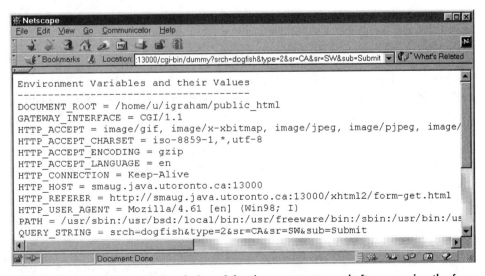

Figure 9.13   Navigator 4.61 rendering of the document returned after accessing the form in Figure 9.10. Note the query string in the URL.

- There is a content-type field, indicating that data is being sent after the header. The MIME-type application/x-www-form-urlencoded means that the data will be encoded just as if it were appended to a URL.

- There is a content-length field giving the length of the data message being sent after the header.

- There is a data message after the header, separated from the header by a single blank line.

These four differences are also reflected in the environment variables available to the CGI program, and in the way data is passed to the CGI program. Again, the lines in boldface in Figure 9.14 show the differences in the server response relative to those of the GET request in Figure 9.12. Note how the QUERY_STRING environment variable is empty, and there are two new environment variables (CONTENT_TYPE and CONTENT_LENGTH). Most important, the CGI program now reads input data—when data is POSTed to the server, this is passed on to the CGI program, which simply reads in the data. Thus, the last block of dummy is executed

```
print "Data sent from Browser to Server\r\n";
    print "----------------------------\r\n";
    while( read(STDIN, &data, &val) ) { # read in &val bytes
    print &data;
}
```

which reads in the data sent to dummy, and simply prints it out again for return to the browser. This appears as the string:

```
srch=dogfish&type=2&sr=CA&sr=SW&sub=Submit
```

Note, by comparison with the URL in Figure 9.11, that this is encoded in the same way as when the data was appended to a URL. Indeed, the MIME content-type application/x-www-form-urlencoded means that the data sent in the POST message is encoded according to the form URL encoding mechanisms. If no other encoding is indicated in the form element, form data is typically encoded in this way.

Of course, if the form data is not encoded in the URL, then the page *cannot be bookmarked.* If a user tries to bookmark this page, and accesses it sometime in the future, then the page is accessed without any of the required form data, as POST data is discarded by the browser.

9.10 Sending Data to a Server Using POST (2)

Browsers support two encoding mechanisms for POSTing data to a Web server. The default encoding (MIME-type application/x-www-form-

Browser Request

```
POST /cgi-bin/dummy HTTP/1.0
Referer: http://www.java.utoronto.ca:13000/xhtml2/form-post1.html
Connection: Keep-Alive
User-Agent: Mozilla/4.61 [en] (Win98; I)^
Host: smaug.java.utoronto.ca:13000
Accept: image/gif, image/x-xbitmap, image/jpeg, image/pjpeg,
    image/png, */*
Accept-Encoding: gzip
Accept-Language: en
Accept-Charset: iso-8859-1,*,utf-8
Content-type: application/x-www-form-urlencoded
Content-length: 42
... (a blank line containing only CRLF)
srch=dogfish&type=2&sr=CA&sr=SW&sub=Submit
```

Server Response

```
HTTP/1.0 200 OK
Date: Thu, 03 Feb 2000 16:59:07 GMT
Server: Apache/1.1.1
Content-type: text/plain
... (a blank line containing only CRLF)
Environment Variables and their Values
-------------------------------------
CONTENT_LENGTH = 42
CONTENT_TYPE = application/x-www-form-urlencoded
DOCUMENT_ROOT = /home/web
GATEWAY_INTERFACE = CGI/1.1
HTTP_ACCEPT = image/gif, image/x-xbitmap, image/png, */*
HTTP_ACCEPT_CHARSET = iso-8859-1,*,utf-8
HTTP_ACCEPT_ENCODING = gzip
HTTP_ACCEPT_LANGUAGE = en
HTTP_CONNECTION = Keep-Alive
HTTP_HOST = smaug.java.utoronto.ca:13000
HTTP_REFERER = http://smaug.java.utoronto.ca:13000/xhtml2/form-
    get.html
HTTP_USER_AGENT = Mozilla/4.61 [en] (Win98; I)
PATH = /usr/sbin:/usr/bsd:/sbin:/usr/bin:/usr/java/bin:/bin
QUERY_STRING =
REMOTE_ADDR = 132.206.43.21
REMOTE_HOST = test.java.utoronto.ca
REQUEST_METHOD = GET
SCRIPT_FILENAME = /home/Servers/apache_1.1.1/cgi-bin/dummy
SCRIPT_NAME = /cgi-bin/dummy
SERVER_ADMIN = ig@test.utoronto.ca
```
continues

Figure 9.14 Data sent from a client to an HTTP server during a form-based POST request from the document *form-post1.html*. Differences relative to the equivalent GET request in Figure 9.11 are shown in boldface.

```
SERVER_NAME = smaug.java.utoronto.ca
SERVER_PORT = 13000
SERVER_PROTOCOL = HTTP/1.0
SERVER_SOFTWARE = Apache/1.1.1
TZ = EST5EDT


Data sent from Browser to Server
--------------------------------
srch=dogfish&type=2&sr=CA&sr=SW&sub=Submit
```

Figure 9.14   *(Continued)*

urlencoded) was illustrated in the previous example. Alternatively, **form** data sent via the POST method can be encoded as a MIME *multipart/form-data* message. On a browser, this encoding is selected by changing the first two lines in Figure 9.9 (the changes are noted in boldface) to

```
<form action="http://smaug.java.utoronto.ca:13000/cgi-bin/dummy"
      enctype="multipart/form-data"
      method="POST">
```

where the new **enctype** attribute specifies the desired content-type encoding for the data. The only supported values are multipart/form-data and application/x-www-form-urlencoded. Note that, if multipart/form-data is selected, then the **method** must be POST, because this encoding type is not supported by the GET method.

Figure 9.15 shows the data sent to the server by the Navigator 4.61 browser. The important changes from Figure 9.14 are noted in boldface. Once again, the method is POST—content-type and content-length header fields are again present, and data is sent following the header. Note, however, the encoding of the data: The form data are encoded as a special multipart/form-data MIME type, so that each block of the message corresponds to a different **form** input element. Indeed, the content-type header now also gives the boundary string used to separate the different parts of the message.

This encoding has several advantages. First, you can use multipart/form-data to upload data files from a client to a server—indeed, if a form contains **input type**="file" elements (for selecting a file to upload), then multipart/form-data is the only supported encoding. Second, the multipart/form-data easily allows for text input that is not coded in the ISO Latin-1 character set.

```
Browser Request
    POST /cgi-bin/dummy HTTP/1.0
    Referer: http://www.java.utoronto.ca:13000/xhtml2/form-post2.html
    Connection: Keep-Alive
    User-Agent: Mozilla/4.61 [en] (Win98; I)
    Host: smaug.java.utoronto.ca:13000
    Accept: image/gif, image/x-xbitmap, image/jpeg, image/pjpeg,
      image/png, */*
    Accept-Encoding: gzip
    Accept-Language: en
    Accept-Charset: iso-8859-1,*,utf-8
    Content-type: multipart/form-data; boundary=-------------4494255837560
    Content-Length: 440
    ... (a blank line containing only CRLF)
    ---------------4494255837560
    Content-Disposition: form-data; name="srch"

    dogfish
    ---------------4494255837560
    Content-Disposition: form-data; name="type"


    2
    ---------------4494255837560
    Content-Disposition: form-data; name="sr"


    CA
    ---------------4494255837560
    Content-Disposition: form-data; name="sr"


    SW
    ---------------4494255837560
    Content-Disposition: form-data; name="sub"


    Submit
    -------------4494255837560--

Server Response
    HTTP/1.0 200 OK
    Date: Thu, 03 Feb 2000 16:59:07 GMT
    Server: Apache/1.1.1
    Content-type: text/plain
    ... (a blank line containing only CRLF)
    Environment Variables and their Values
    -----------------------------------
    CONTENT_LENGTH = 440
    CONTENT_TYPE = multipart/form-data; boundary=-------------
      4494255837560                                              continues
```

Figure 9.15 Data sent from a client to an HTTP server during a **form**s-based POST request using the multipart/form-data encoding mechanism.

```
DOCUMENT_ROOT = /home/web
GATEWAY_INTERFACE = CGI/1.1
HTTP_ACCEPT = image/gif, image/x-xbitmap, image/png, */*
HTTP_ACCEPT_CHARSET = iso-8859-1,*,utf-8
HTTP_ACCEPT_ENCODING = gzip
HTTP_ACCEPT_LANGUAGE = en
HTTP_CONNECTION = Keep-Alive
HTTP_HOST = smaug.java.utoronto.ca:13000
HTTP_REFERER = http://smaug.java.utoronto.ca:13000/xhtml2/form-
   get.html
HTTP_USER_AGENT = Mozilla/4.61 [en] (Win98; I)
PATH = /usr/sbin:/usr/bsd:/sbin:/usr/bin:/usr/java/bin:/bin
QUERY_STRING =
REMOTE_ADDR = 132.206.43.21
REMOTE_HOST = test.java.utoronto.ca
REQUEST_METHOD = GET
SCRIPT_FILENAME = /home/Servers/apache_1.1.1/cgi-bin/dummy
SCRIPT_NAME = /cgi-bin/dummy
SERVER_ADMIN = ig@test.utoronto.ca
SERVER_NAME = smaug.java.utoronto.ca
SERVER_PORT = 13000
SERVER_PROTOCOL = HTTP/1.0
SERVER_SOFTWARE = Apache/1.1.1
TZ = EST5EDT
... (rest omitted from figure) ...
```

Figure 9.15   *(Continued)*

9.11 Managing Data on a Server: PUT and DELETE

The methods PUT and DELETE are designed for managing data via an HTTP server—PUT is used to *put* a file onto a server, and DELETE is used to *delete* a file from a server. This mechanism is supported by the Netscape Composer (and other) Web page editing clients, which use PUT and DELETE to copy files up to a Web server, or to delete files from a Web server. An example transaction is shown in Figure 9.16, wherein the Composer client is uploading a file to the Web server using the POST method.

The request header is much like that from the browser, except that it requests the POST method and has a new monospace field (this field is related to proxy servers, and is discussed in Section 9.14.2). If configured to accept PUT requests, the server interprets this to mean that it should take the data sent in the message and store it in a new resource at the location */dir/test-file.html* (the root location is determined by the server's configuration files). If

Browser Request

```
PUT /dir/testfile.html HTTP/1.0
Connection: Keep-Alive
User-Agent: Mozilla/4.61 [en] (Win98; I)
Pragma: no-cache
Host: smaug.java.utoronto.ca:13000
Accept: image/gif, image/x-xbitmap, image/jpeg, image/pjpeg,
   image/png, */*
Accept-Encoding: gzip
Accept-Language: en,fr-CA
Accept-Charset: iso-8859-1,*,utf-8
Content-Length: 369
... (a blank line containing only CRLF)
<!doctype html public "-//w3c//dtd html 4.0 transitional//en">
<html><head>
   <meta http-equiv="Content-Type" content="text/html; charset=iso-
      8859-1">
   <meta name="Author" content="Ian Graham">
   <meta name="GENERATOR" content="Mozilla/4.61 [en] (Win98; I)
      [Netscape]">
   <title>My page</title>
</head>
<body>
<p>This is a test page</p>
</body></html>
```

Server Response

```
HTTP/1.0 201 Resource Created
Date: Thu, 03 Feb 2000 21:03:35 GMT
Server: Apache/1.1.1
Content-type: text/html
Content-length: 215
... (a blank line containing only CRLF)
<html> <head><title>Resource Succesfully Created</title></head>
<body><h1>Resource Succesfully Created</h1>
<p>The Resource <em> dir/testfile.html</em> was
   succesfully created on this server.</p>
</body></html>
```

Figure 9.16 Example PUT method for creating a resource on a Web server.

successful, the response status field line (as shown in the response header in Figure 9.16) should read as

```
HTTP/1.0 201 created
```

to indicate that the resource was successfully created.

Note also in Figure 9.16 that the PUT request does not give the content-type for the data. The assumption here is that the resource type is *implied* by the file name extension.

The DELETE method is the converse of PUT. A typical DELETE request, and an appropriate response, is illustrated in Figure 9.17. If the deletion request is successful, the server should then return a 200 response.

Some servers directly support PUT and DELETE methods, whereas others support them only via gateway programs or application-specific server plug-ins. Also, it is pretty obvious that PUT and DELETE are not terribly practical without mechanisms for controlling user access, and for controlling how objects are put onto, modified, or deleted from a server. In this regard, there are several document management systems (e.g., Netscape Composer or MKS Web Integrity) that use PUT and DELETE to manage document archives on Web servers.

However, shared management and editing of documents is in itself a very complex issue, and one that cannot be solved solely using two simple HTTP

Browser Request

```
DELETE /dir/testfile.html HTTP/1.0
Connection: Keep-Alive
User-Agent: Mozilla/4.61 [en] (Win98; I)
Host: smaug.java.utoronto.ca:13000
Accept: image/gif, image/x-xbitmap, image/jpeg, image/pjpeg,
   image/png, */*
Accept-Encoding: gzip
Accept-Language: en,fr-CA
Accept-Charset: iso-8859-1,*,utf-8
... (a blank line containing only CRLF)
```

Server Response

```
HTTP/1.0 200 OK
Date: Thu, 03 Feb 2000 21:13:35 GMT
Server: Apache/1.1.1
Content-type: text/html
Content-length: 217
... (a blank line containing only CRLF)
<html> <head><title>Resource Succesfully Deleted</title></head>
<body><h1>Resource Succesfully Deleted</h1>
<p>The Resource <em> dir/testfile.html</em> was
   succesfully deleted from this server.</p>
</body></html>
```

Figure 9.17 Example HTTP transaction invoking an HTTP DELETE method.

methods. Indeed, there is an entire project, known as *Web-based Distributed Authoring and Versioning* (WebDAV), that is developing a whole set of HTTP (and other) Web extensions to support document management. WebDAV is discussed briefly in Section 9.18.

9.12 Cookies and Cookie Data

With Navigator 2, Netscape introduced an HTTP 1.0 extension often called either *Netscape* or *HTTP cookies.* The idea was to create a way for the server to store small pieces of information (called *cookie data*) on a remote browser, such that the browser returns this data in subsequent requests to the server. The *cookie* can then contain information about the session (such as the login identity of the user or some other Preference settings chosen by the user), which would be returned with every browser request.

Cookies are sent to a browser using a `Set-Cookie` HTTP field (or fields—a server can send more than one cookie in a single transaction, using multiple `Set-Cookie` fields). In turn, the browser sends cookie data back to a server using a single `Cookie` field.

9.12.1 Putting a Cookie on the Browser

An HTTP server places cookie information on a browser by sending a `Set-Cookie` HTTP header field—this is often returned by CGI programs within a server directive. The `Set-Cookie` field contains the cookie data as a name/value pair. The field can also contain information explaining when the cookie ceases to be valid (`expires`), the Internet domain for which the cookie is valid (`domain`), and the path portion of the URL within this domain for which the cookie is valid (`path`). The general form of a `Set-Cookie` field is:

```
Set-Cookie: name=val; domain=dnam; expires=date; path=val_path; secure
```

Note that semicolons separate the different parts of the field. Most of these parameters are optional. The meanings and uses of the parameters are described in Table 9.2.

> **TIP**   NO QUOTATION MARKS IN PARAMETER FIELDS   Unlike with XHTML attributes, cookie parameter values must not have surrounding quotation marks. Thus, you must type `domain=.sub.domain.edu` and not `domain=".sub.domain.edu"`—the latter will not work. Similarly, you must not surround the `name=value` portion with quotes, as the quotation marks will be taken as the first character of the name and the last character of the value.

Table 9.2 Definition of Parameters for `Set-Cookie` Fields

PARAMETER	MEANING AND USE
`name=val` (mandatory)	This mandatory parameter specifies the name and value for the cookie data. Both name and value must be strings of printable ASCII characters and cannot contain semicolons (;), commas (,), or space characters. There is no encoding mechanism specified for cookies. Both the name and value are arbitrary, given the above restrictions. The similarity to the name and value portions of a form **input** element is intentional.
`domain=dnam` (optional)	This parameter specifies the Internet domain for which the cookie is valid and to which the cookie content can be sent. This can be a *subdomain* (e.g., `.java.utoronto.ca`) in which case any domain name ending with this string is valid. For domain names ending in country codes (e.g., .ca, .us—see Appendix C of *XHTML 1.0 Language and Design Sourcebook,* and also www.utoronto.ca/ian/books/ xhtml1/appe/), the *subdomain* specification must contain at least three periods, as in the above example. In the case of the special top-level domains (i.e., .com, .edu, .net, .org, .gov, .mil, and .int), only two periods are needed (e.g., .netscape.com). The server sending the `Set-Cookie` request must reside in the domain specified by the domain parameter. Thus, the machine home.netscape.com can specify `domain=.netscape.com`, whereas the machine smaug.java.utoronto.ca cannot. If not specified, the default value is taken to be the full domain name for the server sending the `Set-Cookie` request. Note that you *cannot* append port numbers to the domain name string.
`expires=date` (optional)	Sets the date at which the cookie data expires and should be deleted. The value must be a date string of the format `Day, dd-Mon-yyyy hh:mm:ss GMT` (see Section 9.19). If this field is absent, the cookie is deleted when the user exits the browser session.
`path=val_path` (optional)	Specifies the set of URLs at the allowed domain(s) for which the cookie is valid. If not specified, the default value is the path to the resource being returned with the `Set-Cookie` header.
`secure` (optional)	Indicates that the cookie content should only be communicated down a secure HTTP connection (i.e., **https**). If this parameter is present and the connection is not secure, then the cookie content is not sent. If this parameter is absent, the cookie is sent regardless of security issues.

9.12.2 Returning Cookies to a Server

When a browser that supports cookies accesses a URL, it checks in its database of cookies for all cookies that are appropriate to the domain and path of the URL. If there are no relevant cookies, the transaction proceeds normally, and no cookie data is sent. However, if there are relevant cookies, then the browser combines all the cookie *name=value* strings together, separated by semicolons, and modifies the request to include an HTTP request header field of the form:

```
Cookie: name1=value1; name2=value2; ...
```

A gateway program parsing this request will find the cookie data in the HTTP_COOKIE environment variable and extract the cookie information.

9.12.3 Example Cookie Transactions

In this example, we use the small perl program *dummy2* (available from the book's supporting Web site) to demonstrate how cookies work. Figure 9.18 shows an initial request to a server, before cookies values are sent to the browsers—to reduce the size of the figures, the data content of the response (plus all the accept headers in the request) has been omitted. In this case, we are requesting resources from the server *test.uto.ca* via port 13000.

Browser Request

```
GET /test.html HTTP/1.0
Connection: Keep-Alive
User-Agent: Mozilla/4.61 [en] (Win98; I)
Host: test.uto.ca:13000
... (a blank line containing only CRLF)
```

Server Response

```
HTTP/1.0 200 OK
Date: Fri, 04 Feb 2000 16:32:44 GMT
Server: Apache/1.1.1
Content-type: text/html
Content-length: 363
Last-modified: Fri, 04 Feb 2000 16:30:17 GMT
Connection: Keep-Alive
Keep-Alive: timeout=15, max=5
... (a blank line containing only CRLF)
   ... data returned from server ....
```

Figure 9.18 Request for the file *test.html,* from the server's root directory, before cookies values are set.

We next access the CGI program at */cgi-bin/dummy2.* This returns the following header data

```
HTTP/1.0 200 OK
Date: Fri, 04 Feb 2000 17:00:55 GMT
Server: Apache/1.1.1
Content-type: text/plain
Set-cookie: name=cook1; domain=.uto.ca; expires=Tue, 08-Feb-2000
   12:00:00 GMT
Set-cookie: name=cook2; domain=.uto.ca; path=/xhtml2/
Set-cookie: name=cook3; domain=.uto.ca; path=/
```

which sets three cookies. The cookie with name `cook3` will be valid for any document or directory on the Web server, as the path parameter is `path=/`. The cookie with name `cook2`, on the other hand, will be valid only for the directory */xhtml2/* (and below), and `cook1` will be valid only for the location path */cgi-bin/* and below, because a `path` is not specified for this cookie. Thus, subsequent requests to the following three resources on this server will have the corresponding `cookie` fields in the request header:

PATH ON SERVER	COOKIE FIELD IN REQUEST HEADER
`/test.html`	`Cookie: name=cook3`
`/cgi-bin/dummy`	`Cookie: name=cook1; name=cook3`
`/xhtml2/`	`Cookie: name=cook2; name=cook3`
`/xhtml2/test.html`	`Cookie: name=cook2; name=cook3`
`/xhtml1/`	`Cookie: name=cook3`

Now, if the browser session ends (the user quits the browser), then `cook2` and `cook3` are destroyed, as no value was specified for `expires`. If the browser is then restarted, then the `cookie` fields sent with the requests for these same resources will be:

PATH ON SERVER	COOKIE FIELD IN REQUEST HEADER
`/test.html`	*None*
`/cgi-bin/dummy`	`Cookie: name=cook1`
`/xhtml2/`	*None*
`/xhtml2/test.html`	*None*
`/xhtml1/`	*None*

9.12.4 Browsers and Cookie Management

As noted, a browser does not keep cookie data forever. Also, browsers support only a finite number of cookies and limit individual cookies to some maximum size. For example, Navigator 4 supports at most 300 cookies, each no longer than 4 kB. It also allows no more than 20 cookies per server or per domain. If these limits are exceeded, the client will delete surplus cookies, starting with the ones least recently used.

A server (or gateway program) can delete unneeded cookies by sending a new `Set-Cookie` field that references an existing cookie *name,* but that contains an *expires* value that has already expired. This is a useful way of cleaning up cookies that are no longer required. Note that this will only work if the replacement header uses the same `name` for the cookie value.

Cookies and cookie content can also be modified, created, or destroyed by JavaScript programs in HTML X/HTML documents. However, a JavaScript program can only modify cookies that arrived from the same server as the JavaScript program. This prevents a user from writing a JavaScript program that modifies cookies destined for another person's Web site.

Cookies would seem an ideal way to preserve state during a transaction. This would be true—if one could guarantee that they work. However, not all browsers support cookies, while browsers that do support cookies let the user disable cookie storage. In addition, almost all browsers can be configured to prompt the user whenever a server tries to send a cookie and to give the user the option of refusing the cookie data. Thus, a well-designed Web application must first check to see if a browser supports cookies before actually counting on this mechanism.

The `cookie` and `set-cookie` fields are not defined in the HTTP 1.0 or HTTP 1.1 standards, but are instead defined in a separate specification (RFC 2109; www.ietf.org/rfc/rfc2109.txt). This mechanism is supported by essentially all Web browsers and servers.

9.13 Access Control and User Authentication

So far, we have not discussed the control of access to an HTTP server. There are several mechanisms for doing this. This section briefly discusses those that are supported by most Web servers.

For low-level access control, servers can be configured to restrict access to machines in an authorized Internet domain or subdomain. For example, servers can be configured so that only machines inside a particular domain (for example, all machines with domain name ending in *.middle.earth.com*) are permitted access. In general, this restriction can be applied only to a directory (and all subdirectories), although some servers can apply restrictions file by file. Note that this is not a terribly secure method of access control, however, because a clever cracker can *spoof* (mimic) a domain name, bypass the restrictions, and access the server. It is also not very specific, because anyone who can use a machine inside the domain can access the restricted material.

Finer access control is possible via *user authentication.* The Basic user authentication scheme is defined as part of the HTTP 1.0 protocol, and it lets a server restrict access to users who can provide verifiable usernames and passwords. When users request a password-protected file, the browser prompts them for username and password information, which is sent to the server with the request, as part of the request header. The server then checks the name and password against a designated password file or database. However, in the Basic user authentication scheme, the username and password are sent over the Internet in an essentially unencrypted format, so that it is easy for anyone sniffing the network traffic to extract the username and password. Thus, the Basic scheme is not very secure, unless the underlying HTTP messages are also encrypted in some way. And, of course, you need some other mechanism for getting the usernames and passwords onto the server in the first place.

A second method, known as *digest authentication*, is implemented experimentally by some HTTP 1.0 servers. The mechanism is similar to that of the Basic scheme, except that the usernames and passwords are passed in an encrypted string. Although experimental in HTTP 1.0, digest authentication is formalized in RFC 2617 and is an integral part of most current servers. It is not, however, supported by older browsers (Navigator 4 and earlier, Internet Explorer 4 and earlier).

Fully secure communication and user authentication requires encryption of the data being sent between client and server. The most common mechanisms for doing so employ *negotiated encryption.* Negotiated encryption means that the server and client exchange information, usually encryption keys, that allows each to send encrypted information that can only be decoded by the other. This requires that both client and server support the same encryption and decryption software, and that they both understand the encryption protocol used to send messages between the two. We briefly discuss encryption in Section 9.16.

9.13.1 The Basic Authentication Scheme

The Basic authentication scheme is the only user authentication scheme universally supported on the Web. This scheme is *not* secure, as username and password information are not encrypted when sent from client to server (they are encoded, however, which at least hides them from nonexperts). Consequently, you should not think of this as a secure authentication scheme, unless it is combined with an encryption mechanism such as the Secure Sockets Layer (SSL) technology, discussed later.

The Basic scheme uses special HTTP request (`Authorization`) and response

(WWW-authenticate) header fields. To illustrate how these work, the example in this section follows a request for a resource that requires user authentication and illustrates how these fields negotiate the request for—and exchange of—authentication information.

Step 1: Client Requests the Resource

Initially, the client makes a regular request for the resource—in Figure 9.19 this is for a listing of the resource *xhtml2/secure/* (a directory). At this point, the browser has no idea that authentication is needed for this resource and simply proceeds as if authentication was not required.

Browser Request

```
GET /xhtml2/secure/ HTTP/1.0
Referer: http://smaug.java.utoronto.ca:13000/xhtml2/
Connection: Keep-Alive
User-Agent: Mozilla/4.61 [en] (Win98; I)
Host: smaug.java.utoronto.ca:13000
Accept: image/gif, image/x-xbitmap, image/jpeg, image/pjpeg,
    image/png, */*
Accept-Encoding: gzip
Accept-Language: en,fr-CA
Accept-Charset: iso-8859-1,*,utf-8
... (a blank line containing only CRLF)
```

Server Response

```
HTTP/1.0 401 Unauthorized
Date: Fri, 04 Feb 2000 01:26:15 GMT
Server: Apache/1.1.1
WWW-Authenticate: Basic realm="SecRealm1@smaug.java.utoronto.ca"
Content-type: text/html
... (a blank line containing only CRLF)
<HEAD><TITLE>Authorization Required</TITLE></HEAD>
<BODY><H1>Authorization Required</H1>
This server could not verify that you
are authorized to access the document you
requested. Either you supplied the wrong
credentials (e.g., bad password), or your
browser doesn't understand how to supply
the credentials required.<P>
</BODY>
```

Figure 9.19 Typical GET request and server response when initially requesting a password-protected resource.

Step 2: Server Response—Authentication Required

The response message is shown at the bottom of Figure 9.19, with the authentication-specific lines in boldface. The server status message

```
HTTP/1.0 401 Unauthorized
```

tells the client that the resource was not returned because user authentication is needed. In this regard, the server also sends the additional header field:

```
WWW-Authenticate: Basic realm="SecRealm1@smaug.java.utoronto.ca"
```

This tells the client which authentication scheme to use (Basic), and also what *realm* is involved (realms are discussed a bit later on). On browsers, this field (and the 401 status message) causes the browser to produce a Login pop-up window that states the name of the realm for which the login is valid (here, *SecRealm1@smaug.java.utoronto.ca*) and that provides input boxes for the user to enter his or her name and password.

The response message includes a short HTML document, displayed by a browser if the user chooses not to provide authentication information (i.e., presses cancel on the login window), or if the browser does not understand WWW-Authenticate headers.

Step 3: Client Requests Resource Again

After the user enters the username and password information, the browser takes this information and forms the string:

```
username:password
```

This string is then *base64*-encoded into a pseudoencrypted string (I say pseudoencrypted, because it is trivial to undo the base64 encoding to get the data back again). The client then tries, once again, to access the resource, this time passing the encoded username and password information within an Authorization request header field of the form

```
Authorization: Basic dGVzdHVzZXI6dGVzdHVzZXI=
```

where the string dGVzdHVzZXI6dGVzdHVzZXI= is the encoded username and password. Figure 9.20 shows a typical request containing this authentication information and the subsequent response (assuming the username and password are correct).

The server takes the contents of the Authorization field and checks the username/password string against its own list of usernames and passwords.

Browser Request

```
GET /xhtm12/secure/ HTTP/1.0
Referer: http://smaug.java.utoronto.ca:13000/xhtml2/secure/
Connection: Keep-Alive
User-Agent: Mozilla/4.61 [en] (Win98; I)
Host: smaug.java.utoronto.ca:13000
Accept: image/gif, image/x-xbitmap, image/jpeg, image/pjpeg,
   image/png, */*
Accept-Encoding: gzip
Accept-Language: en,fr-CA
Accept-Charset: iso-8859-1,*,utf-8
Authorization: Basic dGVzdHVzZXI6dGVzdHVzZXI=
... (a blank line containing only CRLF)
```

Server Response

```
HTTP/1.0 200 OK
Date: Fri, 04 Feb 2000 01:26:23 GMT
Server: Apache/1.1.1
Content-type: text/html
Content-length: 363
Last-modified: Fri, 04 Feb 2000 01:24:01 GMT
Connection: Keep-Alive
Keep-Alive: timeout=15, max=5
... (a blank line containing only CRLF)
<html> <head>
  <title>Directory Listing</title>
  .. remaining data omitted to reduce size of this figure ..
```

Figure 9.20 Typical client request for a resource protected by the Basic authentication scheme—the `Authorization:` field indicates the authentication scheme being used (Basic) along with the encoded username and password. The authentication-related fields are shown in boldface (comments in italics).

If there is a match, then the user is authenticated and the server returns the resource, just as per a regular GET request. If there is no match, then the server again returns a 401 not authorized status message and a `WWW-Authenticate` header, so that the browser will once again prompt the user for a username and password.

The Meaning of a Realm

A realm is simply a way of grouping username and password information, so that the browser need not prompt the user for this information if subsequent requests access the same realm. Consider, for example, Figure 9.21, in which the server administrator has created two different secure areas, *SecDir1* and

Stuff/SecDir2, and controls access to these using the password files *pass1* and *pass2,* respectively. The administrator must also assign realm names to these directories so that, in communicating with a client, the server can inform the client which realm is involved, without giving away the name of the password file. In this example, we assume the administrator assigned the name "Lock1@server.dom.edu" to the directory *SecDir1* and the name "Lock2@server.dom.edu" to the directory *Stuff/SecDir2.*

The first time a user accesses a document in *SecDir1,* he or she is prompted for a username and password. The browser stores this name/password string under the realm name *Lock1@server.dom.edu.* On subsequent accesses to this directory or to any subdirectory of this directory, the browser automatically returns the authentication username and password already stored under this realm name.

If, on the other hand, the user requests a document from *SecDir2,* the browser does not send an `authorization` field, because this directory is not in the Lock1 realm. Thus, the server sends back the header

```
WWW-Authenticate: Basic realm="Lock2@server.dom.edu"
```

to tell the browser that authentication is required for this new, as yet unentered, realm. As the browser has never accessed this realm, it has no record of an appropriate username and password, and therefore prompts the user for this information. This information is then stored on the browser under the second realm keyword.

Note how all the realm names in these examples contained the domain name of the server housing the access-controlled documents. This is recommended practice, as it ensures that realm names created for one server will not conflict with realm names created for another.

> **NOTE** SECURITY ISSUES WITH THE BASIC PASSWORD SCHEME **With most browsers, usernames and passwords are preserved until the user exits the browser. This can create security concerns when browsers are running on public-area facilities, because once a user has entered his or her username, the next user of the machine can reuse this information.**

9.13.2 The Digest Authentication Scheme

The digest authentication mechanism works in essentially the same way as Basic authentication: the `WWW-authenticate` response header field indicates the name of the realm the user needs to authenticate for, while the `authorization` request header field provides the needed authorization data. However, the data in these fields is more complex to allow for encryption of the data and

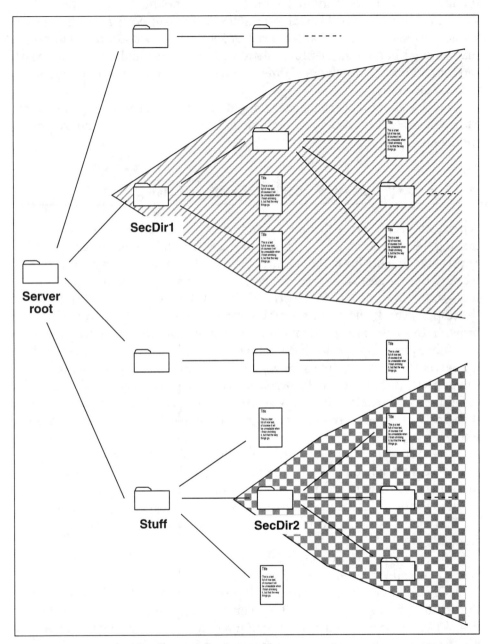

Figure 9.21 An illustration of the two realms described in the text. The realm "Lock1@server.dom.edu" encompasses the directory *SecDir1/* and its contents, and the realm "Lock2@server.dom.edu" encompasses the directory *Stuff/SecDir2/* and its contents.

for additional data to verify that a third party has not modified the data in the `authentication` field. Also, digest authentication supports an additional `Authentication-info` field that lets a server send a browser additional information regarding the successful authentication that just took place, such as a random number to use the next time an encrypted username and password pair are generated.

We won't go into the (rather complex) details of digest authentication here: Please see RFC 2617 (listed in the reference section at the end of the chapter) for details.

9.14 Proxy Servers and Server Caching

A *proxy server* is a server that acts as an intermediary between the browser making the request for a resource and the server (often called the *origin server*) that actually hosts the resource. Then, when a browser makes a request, this request is first sent to the proxy server, which proxies the request, forwarding it on to the origin server. When the origin server sends the response back, the proxy server forwards the response back to the browser. In some cases, the proxy server may *cache* a copy of the resource, so that subsequent requests for it do not have to go all the way back to the origin server. This is much like a browser's own cache, except that the proxy server cache is shared by all browsers sharing the proxy server.

Figure 9.22 illustrates the proxy server mechanism. Note that, in principle, there can be a whole series of proxy servers between the browser and the origin server.

Proxy Web servers are often used to protect local area networks (LANs) from access by outside users. Such protection can be accomplished by installing *firewall* software on the gateway machine that links the local network to the outside world. A firewall keeps TCP/IP packets from entering the local network from outside, and it thereby protects the internal network from intruders.

Unfortunately, this also means that users inside the LAN often cannot access external Web resources, because incoming data is blocked at the firewall. One solution is to install an HTTP proxy server on the firewall (i.e., in the demilitarized zone between the inner and outer networks) and configure users' Web browsers to refer all outgoing requests via the proxy server. A proxy server can be set up to have access to both the inside and outside worlds, and it can safely pass information back and forth across the firewall.

A second reason to use a proxy is to speed up service within a local network, by using the proxy server as a shared cache for external files. For example, the first time a user requests a given resource, the server can go to the outside world and fetch it. However, the proxy server can also (if appro-

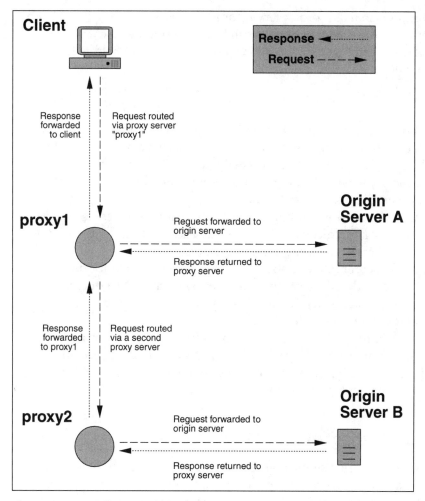

Figure 9.22 An illustration of proxy servers and proxied HTTP requests.

priate) keep a copy of the file on its own disk cache. If another user requests the same file, the proxy server returns the locally cached copy and does not need to access the origin server to refetch it. This both saves time for the user and can significantly reduce the load on the network connection.

This can be a problem, however, if the file changes with time. This is the case for pages containing periodically updated data, or for documents created dynamically by CGI programs: Obviously, such files should not be cached, or they should be removed from the cache at some predetermined time. With HTTP 1.0, these problems are mitigated somewhat by using Expires and Pragma fields in the server response coming from the origin server (the server from which the data originates). Expires contains an expiry time and date (in one of the standard time/date formats described at the end of this chapter), which tells a proxy server (or a browser) how long it can keep a cached copy of a document before it expires and should be discarded or replaced. An even stronger statement is made by the `Pragma` field, which in HTTP 1.0 takes the form:

```
Pragma: no-cache
```

When a client (or a proxy server) sends a request header containing this field to a server, the targeted server must always access a new copy of the requested URL and can never use a cached version. This ensures that the requesting client always gets the most up-to-date version, regardless of which proxy server(s) the requests pass through.

Similarly, if a browser is sending time-sensitive or noncacheable data to a server, the request should contain a `pragma: no-cache` field to ensure that no proxy server will cache the information in the request.

Finally, origin servers should not send a `last-modified` field for data that should not be cached. A browser (or proxy server) retrieving a document that does not contain a `last-modified` field will assume that the document is not cacheable and will not save a local copy.

For a variety of reasons, HTTP 1.0 is poor at handling proxy transactions and the proper maintenance of cached files. Indeed, HTTP 1.1 contains a number of protocol enhancements designed to make proxy server caching more effective, efficient, and reliable.

9.14.1 Configuring a Browser

Browsers such as Navigator or Internet Explorer provide a Preferences menu for selecting a proxy server. Note that proxy server support can be provided for any Internet protocol, not just HTTP. Typically, proxy support would be needed for FTP, HTTP, and NNTP transactions if the internal network is strongly protected from the outside world. Note too that the menu typically lets the user select root URLs (such as http://www.mydomain.com) that do not require the proxy. This lets the user configure the browser to use the proxy server for external domains, but bypass the proxy server if the request is to an internal Web server.

Alternatively, both Navigator and Internet Explorer support a feature known as *proxy autoconfiguration*. With proxy autoconfiguration, the browser, on start-up, contacts a specific URL and downloads a proxy autoconfiguration file, of MIME type *application/x-ns-proxy-autoconfig*. This data defines rules for configuring the browser and can automatically configure the browser. The file actually contains a set of special JavaScript functions that the browser calls whenever it retrieves a URL. After retrieving the file, if the browser wishes to access the URL

```
http://zool.div.com/ian/
```

it will first run the JavaScript function `FindProxyForURL()` defined in this file, as follows

```
ret = FindProxyForURL("http://zool.div.com/ian/", "zool.div.com");
```

with the return value `ret` defining how the resource should be retrieved (either directly or via a defined proxy server).

The advantages are significant. Within a network, the administrator can configure all browsers to reference a single proxy autoconfiguration file, guaranteeing that all browsers will share the same configuration properties. Also, if the administrator needs to change the configuration properties, he or she needs only change this configuration file. The next time the browsers start up, they will download the new configuration file and reconfigure themselves automatically.

9.14.2 Example Proxy Transactions

A browser sends somewhat different information to a proxy server than when communicating directly with the server hosting a resource. For example, if the Navigator 4.61 browser is requesting the resource at http://www.w3.org/Style/CSS/, but via a proxy server, then the message sent to the proxy server is of the form:

```
GET http://www.w3.org/Style/CSS/ HTTP/1.0
Proxy-Connection: Keep-Alive
User-Agent: Mozilla/4.61 [en] (Win98; I)
Host: www.w3.org
Accept: image/gif, image/x-xbitmap, image/jpeg, image/png, */*
Accept-Encoding: gzip
Accept-Language: en,fr-CA
Accept-Charset: iso-8859-1,*,utf-8
(blank line containing CRLF)
```

The differences from a standard request header are noted in boldface. First, we note that the location portion of the method field contains the full URL for the desired resource—obviously, the proxy server needs this information if it is to know which server to eventually contact. Also, the browser now also sends a new `proxy-connection` header. This is a nonstandard header, which was introduced experimentally in HTTP 1.0 but dropped in HTTP 1.1. The purpose was to indicate that proxy server–to–proxy server connections should be kept alive, so that the entire chain of connections between the client and the origin server could be kept open for the duration of the transaction. Some servers do this correctly, but most do not.

The response received from a proxy server will consist of some headers produced by the proxy server, plus the resource information headers returned by the origin server. For example, Table 9.3 shows on the left the response to the proxied request (via the Apache 1.1.1 proxy server), and on the right the response for a nonproxied request. Note how the proxy server has essentially transparently delivered the resource.

The Pragma: No-Cache Field

In subsequent requests by the browser for a resource previously accessed via a proxy server, most browsers will add a `pragma:no-cache` field in the request header. This directive tells the proxy server (and any other proxy server in the sequence) to bypass any cached copies of the desired resource, and it forces the proxy server to get a definitive copy of the resource from the origin server. This field is sent by Navigator 4 (and greater), Internet Explorer 4 (and greater), and by Opera 3.6 (and greater).

HTTP 1.1 adds several new features to better support proxy servers and appropriate caching of data. For details, please see the HTTP protocol specification documents.

Table 9.3 Data Returned to a Browser upon Directly Requesting a Resource (Right Column) and Requesting the Same Resource via a Proxy Server*

RESPONSE VIA HTTP 1.0 PROXY	DIRECT RESPONSE
`HTTP/1.0` 200 OK	`HTTP/1.1` 200 OK
Date: Fri, 04 Feb 2000 21:53:32 GMT	Date: Fri, 04 Feb 2000 23:17:00 GMT
Server: Apache/1.3.6 (Unix) PHP/3.0.11	Server: Apache/1.3.6 (Unix) PHP/3.0.11
Last-Modified: Wed, 26 Jan 2000 17:16:11 GMT	Last-Modified: Wed, 26 Jan 2000 17:16:11 GMT
ETag: "3e24132-71d9-388f2bdb"	ETag: "3e24132-71d9-388f2bdb"
Accept-Ranges: bytes	Accept-Ranges: bytes
Content-Length: 29145	Content-Length: 29145
Connection: close	Connection: close
Content-Type: text/html; charset=iso-8859-1	Content-Type: text/html; charset=iso-8859-1
... message data	... message data...

*Note how the proxy server transparently delivers the data and header fields sent by the origin server.

9.15 Other Common Status Messages

The previous sections discussed several different possible status message responses from a server, ranging from 200 (for successful response to a GET request for a file) to 401 (not authorized because no authentication data was provided).

However, HTTP 1.0 provides several additional status responses used in a number of important situations. For example, a 404 (not found) response is returned if the request was to a nonexistent URL. The next three sections discuss these additional status codes and explain when they are used.

9.15.1 Successful Transaction Status Responses

Successful transactions are indicated by status codes in the range 200 to 299. We previously discussed the 200 (when successfully retrieving a resource) and 201 (successfully creating a resource, typically using a POST request). However, there are several other ways that a transaction can proceed with apparent success. HTTP 1.0 defines two additional level-200 status messages corresponding to the case where the processing of the request is deferred (202) and to the case where the server is not returning any data (204).

Accepted but Not Completed (202)

Sometimes a browser (or a CGI program) will return a response before the requested action has been completed on the server. For example, a request could ask that a back-end program on the server begin analyzing some data—with the results to be e-mailed to users when the analysis is completed. In this case, a 200 response is not appropriate, because it is not clear that the task will succeed. To handle this case, HTTP defines a status message of 202, which corresponds to a request that was accepted, but which is not yet completed. An example of such a response, in this case from a CGI program, is:

```
HTTP/1.1 202 Accepted
Date: Sat, 05 Feb 2000 00:19:34 GMT
Server: Apache/1.1.4 (Unix)
Connection: close
Content-Type: text/html
(blank line containing CRLF)
.... HTML data returned as message ...
```

Browsers handle 202 responses in the same manner as 200 and 201—the returned data is displayed to the user, but no special messages are provided.

The status messages are more useful to automated client programs, which can use this information to determine whether the transaction proceeded as expected.

No Data Being Returned (204)

In some cases, the server does not need to return any data upon completing the request. If it is a browser that made the request, then the server must be able to tell the browser two things:

- That no data is being returned
- That the browser should continue displaying the document currently in view

This is the purpose of the 204 status message. A typical 204 response is:

```
HTTP/1.0 204 No Content
Date: Sat, 05 Feb 2000 00:09:14 GMT
Server: Apache/1.1.5 (Unix)
Connection: close
(blank line containing CRLF)
```

Of course, no data is returned. A browser receiving this response will close the connection and will simply continue displaying the document already in view. Server-side image map handlers typically return this response when the user clicks inside a region of the image that was not mapped onto a URL.

9.15.2 Diagnosable Problem Status Responses

Status codes in the range 400 to 499 indicate errors that occurred as a result of properly processing the request. For example, the request could be garbled in some way, could be for a forbidden resource, or could be directed at a resource that does not exist. The 400-level status codes are designed to explain the type of client-derived error and provide suggestions to the client as to how to proceed next.

Bad Syntax (400)

Sometimes, the HTTP request header is garbled and makes no sense. This would most often be the case if the request header is missing a header field that is required by the server or by the CGI program processing the request. In any of these cases, the response should return a status 400 message. An example response is:

```
HTTP/1.0 400 Bad Request
Date: Sat, 05 Feb 2000 00:09:14 GMT
Server: Apache/1.3.4 (Unix)
Connection: close
Content-Type: text/html

.... short HTML explanation of problem...
```

A server automatically returns this message if the browser (or other program) was sending data to the server, but the request did not give the content-length for the data being sent.

Forbidden Access (403)

If a request is to a resource, but access is forbidden to that resource (for example, the server has been configured to allow access only to users coming from specific domain names or IP addresses), then the server will return a 403 status message, to indicate that access is forbidden. An example is:

```
HTTP/1.1 403 Forbidden
Date: Sat, 05 Feb 2000 00:19:34 GMT
Server: Apache/1.1.4 (Unix)
Connection: close
Content-Type: text/html

.... short HTML explanation of problem...
```

This can be returned whenever access is forbidden. Thus, if requesting access to a restricted directory, the server will return "403 forbidden" messages for all requests, even if the requests refer to files or directories that don't exist. That way, the remote software cannot randomly explore the server and identify the internal file structure.

Resource Not Found (404)

If the URL requests a resource that does not exist on the server, then the server will return a status code 404 response, which means that the resource does not exist. A typical response is:

```
HTTP/1.0 404 Not found
Date: Fri, 04 Feb 2000 23:42:13 GMT
Server: Apache/1.1.1
Content-type: text/html

.... short HTML explanation of problem...
```

9.15.3 Server-Centric Error Responses

A server can fail to process a request for other reasons as well—for example, it may simply be too heavily loaded, or it may have encountered some fatal internal error of unknown origin. In any of these cases, the server will return a status code in the range 500 to 599.

Fatal Server Error (500)

If the server failed to process the request but has no idea why, then it should return a status 500 error. This is essentially the last-gasp error response and means that something went wrong, but the server did not understand what the problem was. A typical response message would be:

```
HTTP/1.0 500 Internal Server Error
Date: Fri, 04 Feb 2000 23:37:20 GMT
Server: Apache/1.1.1
Content-type: text/html

.... short HTML explanation of problem...
```

Of course, because the server itself does not know what went wrong, the short explanation document that follows the header will not be very useful!

Ideally, the server should return one of the other level-500 status messages, outlined in the following sections.

HTTP Method Not Implemented (501)

It is possible to request a resource on a server using a method that is not supported by that resource. For example, a **form** may try to use the POST method to send data to a CGI program that does not support POST requests (in general, this type of information is defined in a server's configuration files). In that case, an HTTP 1.0 server should return a response of the form

```
HTTP/1.0 501 Not Implemented
Date: Sat, 05 Feb 2000 00:00:13 GMT
Server: Apache/1.1.1
Content-type: text/html

... brief HTML explanation of problem ...
```

where the 501 message means that the method is not implemented or supported at that URL. Note that, in this case, HTTP 1.1 servers provide far more useful information and, indeed, return a different error message. For example, the HTTP 1.1 response to this request might be

```
HTTP/1.1 405 Method Not Allowed
Date: Sat, 05 Feb 2000 00:00:40 GMT
Server: Apache/1.3.4 (Unix)
Allow: GET, HEAD, OPTIONS, TRACE
Connection: close
Content-Type: text/html

.. brief HTML explanation of problem ...
```

where the 405 status code more directly corresponds to the problem, and the `Allow` field provides a list of methods that are supported on the requested resource.

Proxy Server Errors (502)

Errors can also happen when requesting resources from a proxy server. For example, the domain name in the URL could be incorrect, in which case the proxy server cannot find the origin server. Alternatively, the proxy server might not be able to contact the server, because the connection is down. In these cases, the server should return a 502 status code, in a message such as:

```
HTTP/1.0 502 Bad Gateway
Date: Fri, 04 Feb 2000 23:37:20 GMT
Server: Apache/1.2.5
Content-type: text/html

.... short HTML explanation of problem...
```

However, many early HTTP 1.0 servers (such as Apache 1.1.1) instead return a 500 status code message, typically of the form

```
HTTP/1.0 500 Proxy Error
Date: Fri, 04 Feb 2000 23:37:20 GMT
Server: Apache/1.1.1
Content-type: text/html

.... short HTML explanation of problem...
```

where the text in the status line (Proxy Error) explains the type of problem encountered.

Server Temporarily Unavailable (503)

In some cases, a server can be running, but can decline to handle the request—for example, if it is too heavily loaded or if the server is temporarily disabled (e.g., for maintenance). In these cases, the implication is that the server at some point in the future will be able to receive requests, but for now it cannot.

If this is the case, then the server should return a 503 status code, typically of the form:

```
HTTP/1.0 503 Service Unavailable
Date: Fri, 04 Feb 2000 23:37:20 GMT
Server: Apache/1.1.1
Content-type: text/html

.... short HTML explanation of problem...
```

A browser, upon receiving this response, will simply display the returned data to the user. More complex client applications can use this response more intelligently, for example, by choosing to wait for some period of time before reattempting the request.

9.16 Client-Server Data Encryption

As mentioned in the previous section, any authentication scheme is insecure if the messages and data passed between client and server are unencrypted. If the username and password are not encrypted, then they can be copied and used by someone else, while if the transported data is not encrypted, then it can be intercepted and read. This section briefly describes encryption schemes used on the Web to solve these security problems. More detailed information is found in the references at the end of this chapter.

9.16.1 Netscape's Secure Sockets Layer

The *Secure Sockets Layer* (SSL) protocol is designed as an encryption layer *below* the HTTP protocol. Thus, HTTP messages are unaffected, with encryption occurring just prior to converting the messages into TCP/IP packets for transmission over the Internet. To indicate the special nature of this connection, Netscape created the new URL **https** (HTTP-Secure) scheme, identical to **http** URLs save for the initial string https. The default port for **https** URLs is 443, and not 80, so that a single machine can run secure and nonsecure HTTP servers at the same time.

In principle, SSL can be used for any Internet tool that uses the underlying TCP/IP protocol for data communications. For example, Netscape (and others) market NNTP news and LDAP directory servers employing SSL.

SSL works at several levels. At the encryption level, SSL employs a sophisticated security handshake protocol: When a client contacts a secure server, they exchange encryption keys, which are subsequently used to encrypt all data passed between the server and client. Encryption keys are never reused, to ensure that keys cannot be intercepted and used by an unauthorized party. The server also sends the client a cryptographic certificate that tells the client which server it is in contact with, and that is used to validate that the server is indeed who it claims to be. Finally, the client and server send, ahead of the transmitted data, a message digest calculated from the data; the receiving party uses this message digest to ensure that an intervening party has not modified the data content.

Version 3 of the SSL protocol includes mechanisms for client certificates, which allow users to authenticate themselves using digital signatures, just as servers are currently authenticated.

At present, almost all commercial browsers and servers support SSL.

9.17 HTTP Content Negotiation

The last topic for this chapter is *content negotiation.* As mentioned in the discussion of accept request headers, a client can send information to a server explaining the types of data it prefers and the order of this preference. This content can be negotiated in terms of four factors: (1) the type of data, (2) the charset used to encode the data (if it is text), (3) the human language of the data (if it is text), or (4) the content-encoding (typically compression) of the data. For example, suppose that a browser request contains the following fields:

```
Accept-Charset: iso-8859-1,utf-8,*
Accept-Language: en,fr-CA
Accept-Encoding: gzip
Accept: image/jpeg; q=0.7
Accept: image/gif;
```

These headers make the following statements:

- The browser will accept text document encoded using any charset, but with the indicated order of preference (ISO-8859-1 over UFT-8 over any other charset).

- The browser prefers text documents written in English or Canadian French, with English being the preferred language.

- The browser will accept data encoded using the *gzip* content encoding (the response message has the field content-encoding: gzip). By default, a browser always accepts data that is not content-encoded.

- The browser will accept the two listed image data types. The q factor defines the degree of preference, and is an extension commonly supported on HTTP 1.0 servers, and defined in the HTTP 1.1 specification. The value q=0.7 means that the browser will prefer JPEG-format images if, after a 30 percent degradation in quality, these images are qualitatively better than the corresponding GIF image.

The Apache Web server provides two ways of delivering different data, depending on the information provided in these headers. The first requires that the Web or document administrator create a special map file containing information about the different data variants of the same resource. As an example, consider the map file *monty_python.image*, illustrated in Figure 9.23.

The content of this file indicates that there are three different image variants for this resource (the locations of the different resources are indicated by the URI field) and describes the relative qualities of the images (through the parameter *qs*, with lower qs values implying a resource of lower quality). A URL referencing the file *monty_python.image*, for example

```
http://www.testserver.org/path/dir/monty_python.image
```

will retrieve the appropriate image file from among the three possible formats, depending on the accept headers sent by the client.

The map file can also contain content-language, content-encoding, and content-length fields to define the language, encoding, and length of each resource variant. For example, the map file *albatross*

```
URI: albatross

URI: albatross.en.html
Content-type: text/html; charset=utf-8
Content-language: en;

URI: albatross.en.gz.html
Content-type: text/html; charset=utf-8
Content-language: en;
Content-encoding: gzip;
```

```
URI: monty_python

URI: monty_python.jpeg
Content-type: image/jpeg; qs=0.85

URI: monty_python.gif
Content-type image/gif; qs=0.5

URI: monty_python.xpm
Content-type: image/xpm; qs=0.2
```

Figure 9.23 An example Apache map file providing three different image alternatives for the same resource.

```
URI: albatross.fr.html
Content-type: text/html; charset=utf-8
Content-language: fr;
```

implies three different variants of the resource, with the indicated charsets, content-encodings, and languages.

The Apache server also provides a special *Multiviews* feature that lets the server automatically generate a list of options based on the file names of the resources in a directory. Please see the Apache documentation for details.

9.17.1 Content Negotiation and Proxy Servers

Content negotiation presents a problem with proxy servers. In particular, HTTP 1.0 proxy servers can't tell which content-negotiated variant is being returned by the origin server, as the HTTP 1.0 protocol does not provide this information in the response. To avoid inappropriate caching in this case, most HTTP 1.0 servers return headers that disable caching on proxies, typically `pragma: no-cache`.

HTTP 1.1, on the other hand, provides several additional HTTP response header fields to help manage caching of data on proxy servers. For example, the `vary` field provides information about which requests header fields led to the returned data; `cache-control` controls whether the data can or cannot be cached by proxy servers; and the `Etag` header defines a unique entity tag for the data, which is different for each possible variant of a given resource. Thus, HTTP 1.1 servers can reliably cache content-negotiated data, and will recontact the origin server if they do not have an appropriate version for the client making a request.

9.18 HTTP 1.1 and Extensions

HTTP 1.1, defined in RFC 2616, is a backward-compatible upgrade to HTTP 1.0 that was designed to fix several known problems with the HTTP 1.0 protocol. However, this upgrade was done such that browsers that only speak HTTP 1.0 can safely communicate with HTTP 1.1 servers. Thus, an HTTP 1.1 server will return a response that is acceptable to an HTTP 1.0 browser, whereas an HTTP 1.1 proxy server will disable all proxy caching features that are not possible given the limited information provided by the HTTP 1.0 browser or an HTTP 1.0 origin server.

The main issues addressed by the changes in HTTP 1.1 are:

- Better support for keep-alive connections, so that the connection between browser and server can remain open while multiple files are being transferred. Indeed, with HTTP 1.1, the default is to keep a connection open. With HTTP 1.1, a connection is only closed when the server returns a `connection: close` header field. Note that this is entirely different from the mechanism used in HTTP 1.0.

- Better support for proxy servers, so that proxy servers can accurately cache data, so that user authentication can be safely proxied by proxy servers, and so that users can authenticate themselves to proxy servers.

- New ability to send chunked data, so that resources can be transferred in multiple chunks, each with its own set of trailing fields describing the content of the chunk. This allows for more reliable transmission of dynamically generated data, because the accurate receipt of each chunk can be verified by receipt of the trailing fields.

To support these changes, HTTP 1.1 defines some 25 additional header fields, in addition to several new HTTP methods and status codes. However, subsequent to the release of the first version of the HTTP 1.1 standard, additional HTTP-related specifications were released to define mechanisms for doing transparent content negotiation between client and server (RFC 2295) and for the more secure Digest method of user authentication (RFC 2617). These, again, added new header fields for HTTP response and request messages and redefined the syntax of some of those fields.

Also of interest are the WebDAV extensions to HTTP (RFC 2518). WebDAV is an extension that lets clients perform remote web content authoring operations and resource management on Web servers. The WebDAV extensions define additional methods and HTTP header fields, in addition to special message body formats (dialects of XML) for defining such management tasks.

If you are interested in knowing more about HTTP 1.1, the various extensions to HTTP 1.1, or in particular the WebDAV extensions and document management environment, please see the references at the end of the chapter.

9.19 Time and Date Format Specifications

The HTTP protocol defines a preferred format for specifying times and dates: All new HTTP software must *provide* time and date information in this format. However, HTTP-aware software must be able to recognize and *understand* two other formats used by older Web servers and browsers. These same requirements also apply to server-side gateway applications, which often return time and date information to a browser, or which often use time and date information sent by a browser to control data processing.

The specified format is defined in RFC 1123. The general form is

```
WDY, DD MMM YYYY HH:MM:SS GMT
```

where *WDY* (followed by a comma) gives the day of the week (Mon, Tue, Wed, Thu, Fri, Sat, or Sun), *DD* is the day of the month (two digits, 01 through 31), *MMM* gives the month (Jan, Feb, Mar, Apr, May, Jun, Jul, Aug, Sep, Oct, Nov, or Dec); *HH* gives the hours, (00 through 24), *MM* the minutes (00 through 59), and *SS* the seconds (00 through 59). The time must be in Greenwich Mean Time (GMT), so that all Web applications share a common time zone. A simple example is:

```
Thu, 23 Dec 1999 07:49:37 GMT
```

9.19.1 Other Time and Date Formats

An older (and essentially obsolete) format is defined in RFC 850. An example is

```
Wednesday, 09-Aug-94 07:49:37 GMT
```

where the first field is the day of the week (Monday, Tuesday, Wednesday, Thursday, Friday, Saturday, or Sunday), the second is the day of the month (01 through 31), the third is the month (as given in the preceding format description), the fourth field is the final two digits of the year, and the remaining fields are obvious. This second format presents obvious Y2K problems, and was thus dropped as a formal standard long ago. However, some older Web servers and browsers deliver date information in this format, so that software should be able to recognize such date strings and be able to make sense out of a value such as Tuesday, 18-Jan-00 12:21:43 GMT.

Another format is defined by the ANSI C language asctime() function. An example date is

```
Wed Aug 9 07:49:37 1994
```

Note that this format does not specify a time zone—for Web applications, the assumption is that times are given in GMT. There are very few Web applications that deliver time using these alternate formats, but Web applications should still be able to recognize these formats, should they end up communicating with an older pieces of software delivering HTTP headers that use these forms.

9.20 References

BOOKS ON HTTP

Web Proxy Servers, by Ari Luotonen, Prentice-Hall (1998)—A detailed review of Web server operation and management, with a focus on proxy servers.

HTTP OVERVIEWS AND SPECIFICATIONS

www.w3.org/Protocols/	Overview
www.jmarshall.com/easy/http/	Tutorial on HTTP
www.ietf.org/rfc/rfc1945.txt	HTTP 1.0 specification
www.ietf.org/rfc/rfc2616.txt	HTTP 1.1 specification
www.ietf.org/rfc/rfc2617.txt	Basic and Digest authentication
www.ietf.org/rfc/rfc2295.txt	HTTP Transparent content negotiation
www.ietf.org/rfc/rfc2774.txt	HTTP 1.x extension framework
www.ietf.org/rfc/rfc2291.txt	WebDAV requirements
www.ietf.org/rfc/rfc2518.txt	WebDAV extensions to HTTP
www.webdav.org	WebDAV resources
www.ics.uci.edu/~ejw/authoring/	WebDAV working group notes
www.ietf.org/html.charters/ http-charter.html	HTTP protocol working group
www.ietf.org/rfc/rfc1867.txt	multipart/form-data MIME type

DATA ENCRYPTION AND SECURITY

www.w3.org/Security/	Overview
www.netscape.com/info/ security-doc.html	SSL
www.genome.wi.mit.edu/WWW/ faqs/www-security-faq.html	Web security FAQ
ganges.cs.tcd.ie/mepeirce/project.html	Digital cash overview
www-s2.visa.com/nt/ecomm/set/ main.html	Security Enhanced Transactions (SET)

BROWSER PROXY AUTOCONFIGURATION

home.netscape.com/eng/mozilla/ 2.0/relnotes/demo/proxy-live.html	Specifications
developer.netscape.com/docs/manuals/ proxy/adminux/autoconf.htm	

CONTENT NEGOTIATION

www.apache.org/docs/ content-negotiation.html	Apache server documentation
www.ietf.org/rfc/rfc2295.txt	HTTP Transparent content negotiation
www.ietf.org/rfc/rfc2296.txt	Remote variant selection algorithm

TIME AND DATE FORMATS

www.ietf.org/rfc/rfc1123.txt

www.ietf.org/rfc/rfc850.txt

BROWSER AND SERVER COMPARISONS

serverwatch.internet.com	Server comparisons and benchmarks
browserwatch.internet.com/ browsers.html	Browser comparisons
directory.google.com/Top/Computers/ Software/Internet/Servers/WWW/	Google list of Web servers
www.apache.org/docs/misc/ known_client_problems.html	Known browser problems with HTTP

CHAPTER 10

Data Processing on an HTTP Server

Topics/Concepts Covered: The common gateway interface, CGI examples; CGI and HTML forms, state preservation, cookies, server APIs, servlets, CGI accelerators

Chapter 9 described in some detail how the HTTP protocol communicates both data and session control messages between a Web client and a Web server. However, a Web server on its own performs only a limited number of functions, typically delivering data files to browsers and providing limited forms of access control over those files. Indeed, it would be impossible to write a server that came prepared to do all the special processing everyone would want. Some general-purpose extensions to the HTTP protocol [such as Web-based Distributed Authoring and Versioning (WebDAV), discussed briefly in Section 9.18] have been introduced and are supported on some servers. These extensions, however, provide a very specific set of services and do not provide the general, customized functionality that most Web-based applications require.

Building Web applications, however, generally means adding custom functionality to the Web site. In practice, this means you will need to add functionality to the server, and adding functionality means adding programs that can interact with the data sent by a client. The HTTP protocol, through the GET, POST, and PUT methods, provides many mechanisms for sending user-defined data (from HTML **form**s; data encoded in URLs; HTTP header data, including cookies) to the server. The issues to be addressed in this regard are twofold:

- How to add extra programs onto a Web server.

- How to get the data sent by a Web client to these programs, and how to return the data produced by these programs back to the client.

The traditional mechanism for accomplishing these two goals is called the *common gateway interface* (CGI). When the CGI mechanism is invoked (for example, by referencing a CGI-accessible resource using an appropriate URL), the server launches a gateway program *as a separate running process.* The server then passes to this program any **isindex**, **form**, or other data sent by the client in the HTTP request, along with server-specific information provided by the server itself. When the gateway program finishes processing the data, it sends the results back to the server, which, in turn, forwards this data to the client that made the initial request. The CGI specifications define how these data are passed from the server to the gateway program, and vice versa.

This data flow is schematically illustrated in Figure 10.1. Note how the gateway program acts as a gateway between the Web server and back-end software such as databases, document repositories, legacy software tools, and so on. Such programs are also often called *CGI programs*, to reflect the mechanisms that connect the programs to the Web server.

This chapter begins by reviewing how data is communicated between a client and server (using the HTTP protocol) and then discusses how data is communicated (using the CGI mechanisms) between a server and a gateway program launched by a Web server. Sections 10.2 through 10.6 provide some simple gateway program examples that illustrate the details of the CGI mechanisms for the GET and POST HTTP methods and for different HTML user input tools, namely **isindex** and **form** elements. Section 10.7 discusses how the various HTML, HTTP, and gateway program tools can be used to track information from request to request, letting you write CGI-based applications that preserve the state of the transaction over time. If you want a quick, nontechnical summary, you can read Section 10.1 (and perhaps 10.2), and then skip to Sections 10.7 and 10.8.

The next chapter follows up with a few simple CGI programming examples. Chapter 11 also discusses some practical issues associated with CGI program design and describes some useful tools and libraries that can speed up and simplify the design of CGI-based applications.

Gateway programs can be compiled programs written in languages such as C, C++, or Pascal, or they can be executable scripts written in languages such as perl, tcl, or python. In fact, many gateway programs are written in perl, because perl scripts are easy to write and modify and are easily portable from machine to machine. In addition, execution speed is often not an important factor with gateway programs (scripts programs are generally slower than compiled ones), because the slowest component is often the resource to which the gateway connects, and not the gateway program itself. After all, if

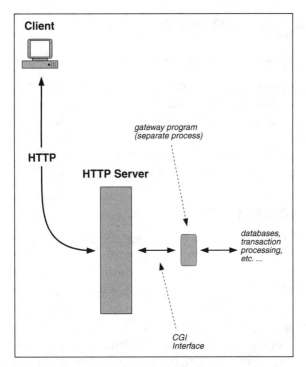

Figure 10.1 Schematic diagram illustrating the data flow between a client, an HTTP server, and a server-side gateway program. The CGI program then acts as a gateway to other resources on the server.

a database takes many seconds to complete a query, it does not matter if the gateway program takes an extra millisecond to start up. Even when this is not the case, speed is usually not an issue, because most CGI programs are actually quite small and fast to start.

However, in some cases speed and scalability are important issues. Fortunately, there are other mechanisms, such as compiled server modules, Java servlets, and others, that allow for faster and more scalable tools for extending a server's functionality. These mechanisms are briefly reviewed in Section 10.8: Some common commercial and open source tools are discussed in Chapter 12.

At the same time, the CGI (or other, equivalent) approach generally implies writing a program that produces HTML data as output. An alternative approach is to write *scripted* X/HTML documents that include the output of server-side programs into the X/HTML document. Section 10.8 briefly discusses this approach, and the next chapter (Section 11.5) briefly describes one way of providing this functionality. Chapter 12 then describes some open source and commercial packages that support this model of Web application design.

10.1 Communication with Gateway Programs

The CGI mechanisms describe what data is passed from a server to a server-side gateway program, and vice versa, and how this communication takes place. In general, all of the data that a client sends to an HTTP server is made available to a referenced gateway program using *three* CGI mechanisms. In turn, a gateway program has two CGI mechanisms for returning data to the server and from there to the client. A discussion of these mechanisms follows.

10.1.1 Client Sends to Server (HTTP)

There are four ways in which data can be sent from a client to a server. These are:

As a URL query string. An example URL is:

```
http://some.site.edu/cgi-bin/ex_prog?query_info
```

This passes the query string query_info to the server. The server, in turn, places the query string data in an *environment variable,* and then launches the gateway program *ex_prog,* which, in turn, obtains the query string from the environment variable.

As *extra path* information in the URL. Extra path information is placed in the URL by adding directory-like information to the URL just after the name of the gateway program. An example is (extra path in boldface):

```
http://some.site.edu/cgi-bin/ex_prog/dir/file?query_info
```

If the server knows that /cgi-bin/ex_prog references a gateway program, then the string /dir/file is interpreted by the server as extra path information, while query_info is again the query string. When the server launches the gateway program ex_prog, it passes both the query string query_info and the extra path string /dir/file to *ex_prog.* In both cases, this data is passed to the gateway program within environment variables.

As data sent to the server in a message body. This is possible with the HTTP POST method and is commonly used with X/HTML forms. When a server receives a POST method message from a form, it sends the POSTed data to the designated gateway program. The gateway program reads the data from its standard input.

As HTTP request header data. The HTTP request contains a whole collection of header fields providing information about the client making the request, the resource being requested, authentication information, and so on. Essentially all of this information is passed on to a CGI program using environment variables.

10.1.2 Server Sends to Gateway (CGI)

The CGI specifications define three mechanisms by which data can be forwarded from a Web server to a gateway program:

Command-line arguments. The server launches the gateway program and passes data to the program as command-line arguments. This mechanism is only used following a GET method request arising from an **isindex** query.

Environment variables. The server puts information in *environment variables* before starting the gateway program—the gateway program can then access these variables and obtain their contents. Everything contained in the HTTP header fields sent by a Web client (with a few exceptions) is placed in a set of environment variables. Thus, environment variables contain the query string and the extra path information discussed previously, as well as the content of every request header field sent by the browser. There are also environment variables containing local server-specific information, such as the home directory for the documents, the type of server, and the server's domain name. Some of these may be specific to the type of server.

Standard input. The server writes data to an output stream. A gateway program can read in this data from standard input. This is how message data sent by a browser using the POST or PUT method is passed to the gateway program.

The mechanisms that are relevant during a particular transaction depend on the HTTP method used (GET or POST), and on the nature of the query string appended to the URL (**isindex** versus non-**isindex** queries). Examples illustrating typical cases are given later in this chapter.

10.1.3 Gateway Sends to Server (CGI)

There are two mechanisms by which a CGI program sends information back to the server:

By writing to standard output. A gateway program passes results back to the server by writing to standard output—this is the *only* way a gateway program can return data. In general, the returned data comes in two parts. The first part is a collection of *server directives*, which are parsed by the server and are used by the server to compose the response header that the server sends ahead of the returned data. The second part is the actual data being returned by the gateway program. The two parts are separated by a blank line containing only a CRLF (carriage return line feed) pair.

By the *name* **of the gateway program.** Gateway programs with names beginning with the string *nph-* are called *nonparsed header* programs and are treated specially by the server. As just described, the server usually parses the output of a gateway program and uses the *server directives* to create the HTTP response header that is sent to the client ahead of the returned data. If a gateway program name begins with *nph-*, the server sends the gateway program output directly to the client without this extra processing, which means the server does *not* add any header information. In this case, a gateway program must itself provide *all* of the required HTTP response header fields.

These methods are illustrated in the next five sections. Section 10.2 looks at an HTML **isindex** document request and illustrates the basic CGI mechanisms. Section 10.3 then demonstrates nonparsed header gateway programs, which send data directly back to the client, bypassing any server processing. Section 10.4 shows how environment variables are passed to the gateway program and explains the contents of these variables. Sections 10.5 and 10.6 illustrate how data from HTML **forms**—using the GET and POST methods, respectively—are passed to a gateway program. These examples also illustrate how a gateway program can decode **form-**based data. Section 10.7 then discusses how CGI programs can use cookies, hidden-form data, or other means to preserve state about a session. Last, Section 10.8 reviews important alternatives to the gateway program approach, such as compiled server modules, Java servlets, or page scripting environments.

10.2 Simple Example: Isindex Searches

An X/HTML **isindex** element is the *only* query method that passes data to a gateway program using command-line arguments. And as mentioned in the *XHTML 1.0 Language and Design Sourcebook,* this element is in fact deprecated—so you should avoid using it in any Web applications you design. However, the **isindex** mechanism is particularly simple to describe, and thus is a useful starting point for understanding client-server-gateway interactions.

This example accesses the gateway program *srch-example* listed in Figure 10.2, which is a Bourne-shell script program designed to search a phone number database via the search program *grep*. The script searches for names in a phone number database, and uses the **isindex** element to prompt the user for a search string. In this example, the search string is just the list of names you want to search for. When the script receives the data, it searches the database for the indicated names and returns the names and phone numbers of any matches. The script is designed both to prompt for search strings and return the results of the search.

```
01 #!/bin/sh
02 echo Content-TYPE:   text/html
03 echo
04
05 if [ &# = 0 ]        # is the number of arguments == 0 ?
06 then                 # do this part if there are NO arguments
07     echo "<html><head>"
08     echo "<title>Local Phonebook Search</title>"
09     echo "<isindex />"
10     echo "</head>"
11     echo "<body>"
12     echo "<h1>Local Phonebook Search</h1>"
13     echo "<p>Enter your search in the search field.</p>"
14     echo "<p>This is a case-insensitive substring search: thus"
15     echo "searching for 'ian' will find 'Ian' and Adriana'.</p>"
16     echo "</body></html>"
17 else                 # this part if there ARE arguments
18     echo "<html><head>"
19     echo "<title>Result of search for \"$*\".</title>"
20     echo "</head>"
21     echo "<body>"
22     echo "<h1>Result of search for \"$*\".</h1>"
23     echo "<pre>"
24     for i in $*
25     do
26          grep -i $i /vast/igraham/Personnel
27     done
28     echo "</pre>"
39     echo "</body></html>"
40 fi
```

Figure 10.2 Bourne-shell script CGI gateway program *srch-example.*

On a browser, an **isindex** element produces a simple type-in box into which the user can enter a single line of typed text. When the user then presses the Enter key, this data is URL-encoded as described in Chapter 8 and is appended as query data to the URL of the document already being viewed. The browser then accesses this URL as an HTTP GET request. An example of such a URL is:

```
http://some.where.edu/cgi-bin/srch_program?string1+string2
```

In this case, we assume that *srch_program* is a CGI program (the directory name *cgi-bin/* is a dead giveaway). When this request reaches the server, and if the request is one coming from an **isindex** query (and not from an X/HTML **form**), the server does the following three things:

- Decodes the URL [converts plus (+) signs back into spaces and converts URL character encodings back into the correct characters].

- Uses the space characters to break the query string into individual words.

- Passes these words to the referenced gateway program (*srch_program*) as a collection of command-line arguments.

10.2.1 Detecting Isindex Queries

How does the server know if a GET method request comes from an **isindex** query, and not from a **form**? The answer is that an **isindex** query string *never* contains unescaped equals signs (=). As pointed out in Chapter 8 (Section 8.2.7), **form** data are encoded as a collection of strings of the form *name=value*, which always contain at least one unescaped equals sign (any equals signs originally present in the name or value strings are escaped as %3d). Therefore, the presence of a real equals sign in the query string means that the data came from a **form**, and not from an **isindex**.

10.2.2 Step 1: Initial Access of the Program

In this example, the script *srch-example* is initially accessed via the URL:

```
http://leonardo.utirc.utoronto.ca:8080/cgi-bin/srch-example
```

Note that there is no query information attached to the URL; this is an important factor in the initial behavior of the script.

Line 1 tells the computer to interpret this script using the */bin/sh* program, which is the traditional location and name for the Bourne shell. Lines 2 and 3 echo information to standard output (echo is the Bourne-shell command that prints to standard output). Standard output is sent back to the server and from there back to the client.

Server Directives in Gateway Programs

The first line prints an HTTP *server directive*, which gives the server information about the data to come. This is absolutely necessary, as the server has no other way of knowing what type of data the program will return. This line prints the header

```
Content-TYPE: text/html
```

to tell the server that the data to follow is an HTML document. The next line prints a blank line. This denotes the end of the header—subsequent output is the actual data being returned.

Many other server directives are possible—the most important ones are summarized in Table 10.1.

Line 5 tests the *number* of command-line arguments. In this case, there was no query string, so there are no command-line arguments and the first branch of the `if` statement is executed. This branch of the program prints, to standard output, a simple HTML document explaining the nature of the search; this is shown in Figure 10.3. This document contains an **isindex** element, to tell the browser to prompt for search information—this element produces the text-input box shown in Figure 10.3. I have typed the names *ian* and *bradley* into this box (I always like to look for my own name), separated by a single space. These are the names that will be used in the search.

10.2.3 Step 2: Second Access of the Program

Submitting this **isindex** search information accesses the same URL, but appends the names *ian* and *bradley* to the URL as a query string. Thus, in this second phase, the accessed URL is:

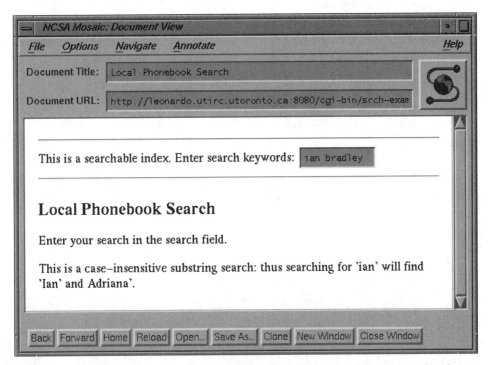

Figure 10.3 Document returned from the script *srch-example* when accessed *without* a query string, as rendered by the Mosaic 2.4 browser.

```
http://leonardo.utirc.utoronto.ca:8080/cgi-bin/srch-example?ian+bradley
```

where the space between *ian* and *bradley* has been encoded as a plus sign, as required by the URL query string encoding scheme described in Chapter 8, Section 8.1.3.

When the HTTP server receives this URL, it parses the query string and finds that there are no unencoded equals signs, so it knows that this is an **isindex** query. It therefore takes the query string, decodes it, and breaks it into individual strings using the plus signs (the escaped space characters) as the word separators. This yields the two strings *ian* and *bradley*. The server next launches the gateway program *srch-example,* using the names *ian* and *bradley* as command-line arguments. The equivalent command, typed by hand and the command prompt, would be:

```
srch-example ian bradley
```

Figure 10.4 shows the results of this second access to the Bourne-shell program; by following Figure 10.2, you can see how it was generated. As before, the first two lines print the MIME content-type of the message and the blank line separating the HTTP headers from the data. At line 5, the program checks

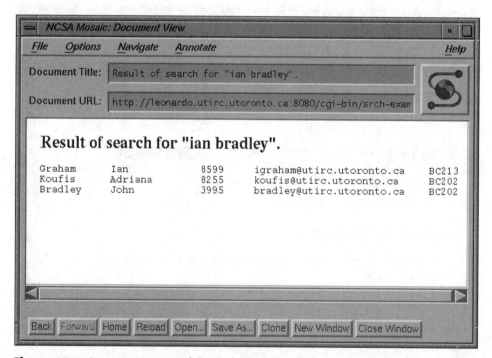

Figure 10.4 Document returned from the script *srch-example* when accessed *with* a query string appended to the URL, as rendered by the Mosaic 2.4 browser.

for command-line arguments. This time there are two such arguments, so the second branch of the script is executed, starting at line 18. This section prints a different HTML document, this time including output from the program *grep*. Lines 24 through 27 loop the variable i through all the command-line arguments. The content of the variable i (denoted by $i) is used as an argument to the program *grep*, which scans the file */vast/igraham/Personnel* for names matching the pattern given by $i. Grep prints the matches to standard output. The result of the searches is shown in Figure 10.4. Note that there is no query box, as the document printed out by the second branch of the script in Figure 10.2 did not include an **isindex** element.

10.3 Gateway Program Server Directives

The second example looks at how HTTP servers compose a response header for data returned by a gateway program. Consider first the actual data that is sent by a server (here, the Apache 1.1.1 server) upon the client's first access of the program *srch-example* (Figure 10.5; this is the data that produced Figure 10.3).

Comparing Figure 10.5 with Figure 10.2, you will see that the headers are *not* those returned by the script—note how the content-type headers are typographically different (Content-TYPE versus Content-type). In fact, the HTTP server generated the response header fields returned to the client, with help from server directives returned by the gateway program.

```
HTTP/1.0 200 OK
Server: Apache/1.1.1
Date: Thu, 01 Aug 1996 16:43:53 GMT
Content-type: text/html

<html><head>
<title>Local Phonebook Search</title>
<isindex />
</head>
<body>
<h1>Local Phonebook Search</h1>
<p>Enter your search in the search field.</p>
<p>This is a case-insensitive substring search: thus
searching for 'ian' will find 'Ian' and Adriana'.</p>
</body> <html>
```

Figure 10.5 Data returned to the client upon accessing the URL: http://leonardo.utirc .utoronto.ca:8080/cgi-bin/srch-example. This is the data that produced Figure 10.3.

10.3.1 Server Directives

The server takes the header data returned by the gateway program and parses each of the header fields. Most of these headers are passed through unaltered and are included as part of the server response header returned to the client. Some, however, are treated as *server directives* and are used by the server to *modify* the HTTP response header fields that the server normally returns in the response. The three valid server-directive headers are listed and described in Table 10.1.

In addition to these special server directives, a gateway program can return most regular server response header fields—they are simply forwarded to the client as part of the response header following those headers generated by the server itself. For example, if a gateway program returns results from a database that is updated on a regular basis, the program could return an Expires header as part of the server directives to indicate when the data will be stale, thereby allowing clients to reliably cache copies until the specified expiration date.

Limitations of Server Directives

Although a CGI program can return a wide variety of server directives for use in the actual server response, they *must not* return server directives that

Table 10.1 CGI Server Directives and Their Allowed Content

SERVER-DIRECTIVE HEADER	DESCRIPTION
Content-type: type/subtype (; parameters)	Gives the MIME type for the data being returned by the gateway program. The server will use this value to compose the content-type header field returned with the HTTP response header. An example is content-type: text/html; charset=utf-8
Location: URL	Specifies a URL to which the client should be *redirected*. A server will add this Location: field to the server response header and will also modify the server response status line to be HTTP/1.0 302 Redirection
Status: code string	Contains an HTTP status code (code) and arbitrary descriptive status string (string) to be used by the server in place of the standard response. A server will modify its default status field to return the server response header field: HTTP/1.0 code string

override headers ordinarily returned by the server. For example, CGI programs cannot use server directives to override the Server, and Date header fields, because these fields are considered to be server-specific. Obviously, you don't want a CGI program to be able to override the name of the server software (server), nor should it be able to set the actual time when the response was sent (date) by the server (because there may be a delay between the time when the gateway program sends data to the server and when the server returns this data to the client).

But, as with spelling, there is an exception to every rule—and the exception here is for *nonparsed header* gateway programs. Nonparsed header programs let a CGI program completely bypass processing by the server, and return data directly to the client that initiated the request.

10.3.2 Nonparsed Header Gateway Programs

It is possible to return gateway program output directly to the client without any processing by an HTTP server; in this case, the gateway can return any header fields it wants regardless of the rules described above. This is accomplished by appending the string *nph-*, for *nonparsed header,* to the beginning of the name of the script. When the server sees a gateway program name beginning with *nph-*, it passes the gateway program output directly to the client, without any processing. For example, Figure 10.6 shows the data returned from the gateway *program nph-srch-example:* This is an exact duplicate of the program *srch-example* listed in Figure 10.2, the only change being the string *nph-* added to the front of the file name.

```
Content-TYPE: text/html

<html><head>
 <title>Local Phonebook Search</title>
<isindex />
</head>
<body>
<h1>Local Phonebook Search</h1>
<p>Enter your search in the search field.</p>
<p>This is a case-insensitive substring search: thus
searching for 'ian' will find 'Ian' and Adriana'. </p>
</body> </html>
```

Figure 10.6 Nonparsed header output returned upon accessing the URL http://leonardo.utirc.utoronto.ca:8080/cgi-bin/nph-srch-example. The response header fields are shown in boldface.

Comparing Figure 10.6 with the program listing in Figure 10.2 shows that the response now contains just the data printed by the gateway program, with nothing added or modified by the server.

The advantages of a nonparsed header gateway program are speed and flexibility. It is faster as the server is not required to parse the returned data and generate appropriate headers, and it is more flexible because the programmer is not limited to the types of information that can be returned in response header. In exchange, the gateway program itself must produce *all* of the required headers fields. Note how the data in Figure 10.6 is an *invalid* server response, as it does not contain a status line nor does it indicate the date or server type. Thus, an *nph-* script *must,* at a minimum, return the following response headers with values appropriate to the script and the data being returned (the portions that must be customized to the situation are shown in italics; these are just example values):

```
HTTP/1.0 200 OK
Date: Thu, 01 Aug 1996 16:50:57 GMT
Server: Apache/1.4.2 Ians-test-nph-cgi-program
Content-type: text/x-babelfish
```

10.3.3 Custom Fields: Content-Disposition

Of course, a CGI program can return any manner of response fields—with nonparsed header scripts, these are passed right through to the client, whereas if the server parses the response, it will generally pass along any well-formed field that does not conflict with a field that the server normally returns.

This can be useful, as some browsers understand nonstandard fields in the response header. For example, Navigator understands *content-disposition* fields of the form:

```
content-disposition: attachment; filename=name-of-file
```

Such fields tell the browser that the downloaded data is a file and that the user should be given the choice of saving the file to disk using the indicated file name. For example, the message

```
content-type: application/x-gzip
content-length: 1232123
content-disposition: attachment; filename=archive.gz
```

tells the browser that the downloaded file (a GZIP archive) has the name *archive.gz*. Because Netscape cannot view this type of file, it will prompt the user to save the file and will offer to save it under the name *archive.gz*.

If the content-disposition field is not present, the browser generally uses the last part of the URL (minus the query string) as the default file name, which in this case would likely be the name of the program that generated the response. Thus, the content-disposition field lets you change the name under which returned data should be saved.

This is a convenient way to use a single CGI program for downloading a variety of stored archive files. However, there are two important caveats you should know before embracing this approach wholeheartedly:

- Internet Explorer 4 and earlier do not support this header field. This field is supported by Navigator 2 (and greater), Opera 3.6 (and greater), and Internet Explorer 5 (and greater).

- Navigator 2 and greater only support content-disposition for resources that cannot be displayed by the browser (e.g., compressed data files or nonsupported image file formats). Thus, if the CGI program returns an HTML document, and the user attempts to save the HTML document to disk, the Save File tool will offer the last string portion of the URL as the default file name.

10.4 Environment Variables

The preceding examples would imply that the server passes very little information to a gateway program. In fact, the server is not so ungenerous. Before launching a gateway program, the server initializes several *environment variables* that subsequently are accessible in the program. In particular, this mechanism passes any extra path and query string information to a gateway program. Table 10.2 lists the environment variables defined as part of the CGI standard, and Figures 10.7 and 10.8 illustrate the most common variables in an example application. Figure 10.7 shows the gateway script *srch-example-2;* this is the same **isindex** script that is listed in Figure 10.2, modified to print out environment variable contents. The HTML document generated upon accessing this script at the URL

```
http://leonardo.utirc.utoronto.ca:8080/cgi-bin/srch-example-
2/dir/file?ian+bradley
```

is shown in Figure 10.8. Accessing this URL passes both query string (ian+bradley) and extra path information (/dir/file) to the referenced gateway program.

Most of the environment variables in Figure 10.8 are easy to understand. Some are set by default and do not depend on the nature of the request, and others are set only when particular client-server-gateway interactions are involved.

Table 10.2 Environment Variables Available within a Gateway Program

STANDARD ENVIRON-MENT VARIABLE	DESCRIPTION
	Server Properties
SERVER_SOFTWARE	The name and version of the server software answering the request, in the format *name/version,* followed by a text string describing any extra modules installed on that server. Some examples are `Apache/1.3.11 (Unix) PHP/3.0.14 Netscape-Enterprise/3.6,` and `Microsoft-IIS/5.0.`
SERVER_NAME	The Internet domain name of the server; if the domain name is not known, this is the numerical IP address.
GATEWAY_INTERFACE	The version of the CGI specification used by the server, in the format CGI/*version.* The current version is 1.1, so this should be CGI/1.1.
SERVER_PROTOCOL	The protocol being used and the version number, in the format *protocol/version.* This permits gateway programs that support different versions of the HTTP protocol, as the program can use this variable to select appropriate code sections. The values will typically be `HTTP/1.0` or `HTTP/1.1.`
SERVER_PORT	The server port number used in a transaction (typically 80).
	Client Properties
REMOTE_HOST	The Internet domain name of the host making the request. If the domain name is unavailable, this variable is undefined. The numerical IP address is always available in the `REMOTE_ADDR` variable.
REMOTE_ADDR	The numeric IP address of the remote host accessing the server. This is always defined.
HTTP_*NAME*	The contents of essentially all the request header fields sent by the client. The environment variable name is composed of the string `HTTP_NAME`, where *NAME* is capitalized *header field name,* with all dashes in the name converted to underscores; for example, `HTTP_USER_AGENT` for the `User-Agent` field. Note, however, that many servers do not forward user authentication information sent in `authorization` headers.
	Request Properties
REQUEST_METHOD	The method associated with the request. This will be GET, HEAD, POST, PUT, and so on.

STANDARD ENVIRON-MENT VARIABLE	DESCRIPTION
PATH_INFO	Extra path information present in the URL (after the reference to the CGI program). This variable is empty or undefined if there is no such information in the URL.
PATH_TRANSLATED	The `PATH_INFO` path translated into an *absolute path* on the server's filesystem; undefined if `PATH_INFO` is undefined. For example, if the server document directory is */vast/igraham/WebDocs,* and `PATH_INFO=dir/file`, then `PATH_TRANSLATED=/vast/igraham/WebDocs/dir/file`. This is often used to reference gateway program configuration files. Note that this is *not* related to the location of the gateway program.
SCRIPT_NAME	The *path* and *name* of the script being accessed as it would be referenced in a URL; for example, `/cgi-bin/prog.pl`. This can be used to construct URLs that refer back to this same gateway program, for insertion in script-generated HTML documents. For example, the string `http://$SERVER_NAME:$SERVER_PORT$SCRIPT_NAME` generates the full URL to the program using information contained in the environment variables (where `$NAME` refers to the *content* of the environment variable `NAME`).
QUERY_STRING	The query string portion of the URL, in encoded form. A gateway program must decode this string to extract the data sent by the client. If this string results from an **isindex** search request, then the query string data are also passed to the program as *decoded* command-line arguments.
Authentication Information	
AUTH_TYPE	The *authentication method* required to authenticate the user requesting access. This is defined only for scripts that are access protected. The value will be either `Basic` (Basic authentication) or `Digest` (for digest authentication).
REMOTE_USER	The *authenticated name* of the user, defined only when authentication is required. This is undefined if authentication is not required.
REMOTE_IDENT	The remote username, retrieved by the server from the client machine using the *identd* protocol and the remote identification daemon. Most remote clients do not support the *identd* protocol, so this is largely unused.

continues

Table 10.2 Environment Variables Available within a Gateway Program *(Continued)*

STANDARD ENVIRON- MENT VARIABLE	DESCRIPTION
Client Data Properties	
CONTENT_TYPE	The MIME content-type of the data sent by the client to the server (POST or PUT method). This is undefined if no data is sent. The actual data is available to the gateway program by reading from standard input. The currently implemented types for POST requests are *application/x-www-form-urlencoded* and *application/form-data.*
CONTENT_LENGTH	The length, in bytes, of the data message sent to the server by the client (POST or PUT methods). If no data is being sent, this is undefined. A gateway program does not have to read all the data before returning a response or before exiting.

```sh
#!/bin/sh
echo Content-TYPE:  text/html
echo
 if [ $# = 0 ]    # is the number of arguments == 0 ?
 then             # do this part if there are NO arguments
      echo "<html><head>"
      echo "<title>Local Phonebook Search</title>"
      echo "<isindex />"
      echo "</head>"
      echo "<body>"
      echo "<h1>Local Phonebook Search</h1>"
      echo "<p>Enter your search in the search field.</p>"
      echo "<p>This is a case-insensitive substring search: thus"
      echo "searching for 'ian' will find 'Ian' and Adriana'.</p>"
      echo "</body></html>"
 else             # this part if there ARE arguments
      echo "<html><head>"
      echo "<title>Result of search for \"$*\".</title>"
      echo "</head>"
      echo "<body>"
      echo "<p> Number of Command-line Arguments = $#. They are: </p>"
      for i in $*
      do
            echo " <code> $i </code> "
      done
```

Figure 10.7 Bourne-shell script *srch-example-2*. This is essentially the same script that is shown in Figure 10.2, but modified to explicitly print out the command-line arguments and some of the environment variables.

```
         echo "<h2> The Environment Variables </h2>"
         echo "<pre>"        # print the environment variables
         echo " SERVER_SOFTWARE = $SERVER_SOFTWARE"
         echo " SERVER_NAME = $SERVER_NAME"
         echo " GATEWAY_INTERFACE = $GATEWAY_INTERFACE"
         echo " SERVER_PROTOCOL = $SERVER_PROTOCOL"
         echo " SERVER_PORT = $SERVER_PORT"
         echo " REQUEST_METHOD = $REQUEST_METHOD"
         echo " HTTP_ACCEPT = $HTTP_ACCEPT"
         echo " PATH_INFO = $PATH_INFO"
         echo " PATH_TRANSLATED = $PATH_TRANSLATED"
         echo " SCRIPT_NAME = $SCRIPT_NAME"
         echo " QUERY_STRING = $QUERY_STRING"
         echo " REMOTE_HOST = $REMOTE_HOST"
         echo " REMOTE_ADDR = $REMOTE_ADDR"
         echo " REMOTE_USER = $REMOTE_USER"
         echo " AUTH_TYPE = $AUTH_TYPE"
         echo " CONTENT_TYPE = $CONTENT_TYPE"
         echo " CONTENT_LENGTH = $CONTENT_LENGTH"
         echo "</pre>"
         echo "<h2>Result of search for \"$*\".</h2>"
         echo "<pre>"
         for i in $*
         do
             grep -i $i /vast/igraham/Personnel
         done
         echo "</pre>"
         echo "</body></html>"
    fi
```

Figure 10.7   *(Continued)*

10.4.1 Standard Environment Variables

Table 10.2 lists the standard environment variables that are passed to a gateway program by an HTTP server. Not all variables are defined in all cases; for example, the variables associated with user authentication are only defined when authentication is being used.

10.4.2 Request Header-Based Environment Variables

As noted in Table 10.2, *every* piece of information in the HTTP request header (the headers sent from the client to the server) that is not contained within a standard CGI environment variable is passed to the gateway program in an

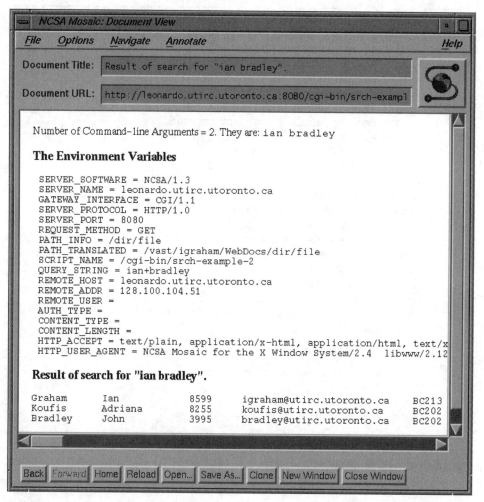

Figure 10.8 Document returned from the script in Figure 10.7 after accessing the URL http://leonardo.utirc.utoronto.ca:8080/cgi-bin/srch-example-2/dir/file?ian+bradley.

environment variable of the form HTTP_*NAME*, where *NAME* is related to the *name* of the request header fields. These environment variable names are constructed by:

- *Capitalizing* the name in the request header field (e.g., User-agent to USER-AGENT)

- *Converting* dash (-) characters into underscores (_) (e.g., USER-AGENT to USER_AGENT)

- *Adding* the prefix HTTP_ (e.g., USER_AGENT to HTTP_USER_AGENT)

Some of the more common environment variables of this type are listed in Table 10.3. Note, in particular, the construction of the HTTP_ACCEPT header.

Table 10.3 Common Gateway Environment Variables Derived from HTTP Request Header Fields

VARIABLE	CONTENT
HTTP_ACCEPT	A comma-separated list of all MIME types acceptable to the client, as indicated by the Accept headers sent to the server. An example is shown in Figure 10.8. Gateway programs can use this to determine which type of data to return to the client.
HTTP_COOKIE	A semicolon-separated list of HTTP cookie values.
HTTP_IF_MODIFIED_SINCE	Gives the time and date, in the standard format described at the end of Chapter 9, of data held by the client. The gateway program can then decide if the server has data that are newer than this, and if it should forward updated data or not.
HTTP_REFERER	Contains the URL that referred the user to the current request; undefined if there is no Referer header field.
HTTP_USER_AGENT	The contents of the User-Agent request header field. An example is shown at the bottom of Figure 10.8.

10.4.3 Extended/Custom Environment Variables

Some HTTP servers provide additional bonus CGI-environment variables not described previously. If your HTTP server supports *perl,* then you can use the following simple CGI program to list all the environment variables defined on your server:

```perl
print "Status: 200 Okey Dokey\r\n";
print "Content-type: text/html\r\n\r\n";
# Loop over all environment variables
# and print them out --
print <<EOF;
<html> <head>
<title> Environment Variables on this server </title>
</head><body>
<h1>Defined Environment Variables are:</h1><p>
EOF

while (($key, $val) = each %ENV) {
        print "$key = $val<br />\n";
}
print "</p><hr /></body></html>\n";
```

Also, as mentioned earlier, several servers support parsed HTML documents. Such documents contain special server directives that are processed by a special page parser (integrated into the server) and which are replaced by output from the parser or by output from CGI programs referenced via the parser. These parser approaches (e.g., server-side includes PHP, ASP, etc.) often define additional environment variables not mentioned in Tables 10.2 and 10.3. Chapter 11 contains a thorough discussion of the server-side include (SSI) mechanism, and Chapter 12 reviews some of the other, richer scripting environments.

NOTE   CUSTOMIZED ENVIRONMENT VARIABLES   **Most HTTP servers permit local customization of CGI environment variables. You should check with your local server administration, or with any specially installed server software, to find out about any special-purpose CGI environment variables available at your site.**

10.5 HTML Forms via a GET Request

This example examines the data passed by an HTML **form** to the program shown in Figure 10.9. The **form** used is the same one employed in Chapter 9, which uses the GET method to send the data to the program (the **form** document is shown in Figure 9.9 and, as rendered by a browser, in Figure 9.10). The perl script in Figure 10.9 prints out the relevant environment variables, and also reads in data from standard input (the `while (<STDIN>)` command, on the ninth line from the bottom) and prints this input data to standard output.

The data sent to the server (and to the gateway program listed in Figure 10.9) by the **form** listed in Figure 9.9 and using the Internet Explorer 5 browser is:

```
GET /cgi-bin/form1?srch=dogfish&srch_type=Exact+Match&srvr=Canada&srvr=
Sweden HTTP/1.1 Accept: image/gif, image/x-xbitmap, image/jpeg,
image/pjpeg, application/vnd.ms-excel, application/msword, application/
vnd.ms-powerpoint, */* Referer: http://smaug.java.utoronto.ca:8008/
xhtml2/chap10/form.html Accept-Language: en-ca, fr-ca; q=0.7, fr;q=0.3
Accept-Encoding: gzip, deflate User-Agent: Mozilla/4.0 (compatible; MSIE
5.0; Windows 98; DigExt) Host: www.java.utoronto.ca:80 Connection: Keep-
Alive
    [a blank line, containing only CRLF ]
```

Figure 10.10 shows the document returned by the script listed in Figure 10.9. You will note that there are no command-line arguments. In parsing the URL, the server detected real equals signs in the query string. This indicates a non-**isindex** query, so the server does not parse the string to create command-line arguments. The remaining quantities are obvious. The REQUEST_METHOD

```perl
#! /usr/sbin/perl  -w
use strict;

# 1. Header data
#
print "Staus: 200 Okey-dokey\r\n";
print "content-TYPE: text/html\r\n";
print "\r\n";
# Initialize variables and print HTML document header
#
my $num = $#ARGV+1;  # Number of command line arguments
my $i = 0;
my $key = 0;
my $val = 0;

print <<EOF;
<html><head>
<title>Forms Test Page </title>
</head><body>
<h2>1. Number of Command Line Arguments = $num</h2>
EOF

if($#ARGV > 0) {
  print "<p>Command Line Arguments are: <br />";
  my $i = 0;
  for($i=0; $i<=$#ARGV; $i++) {
     print "Arg $i = $ARGV[$i] <br /> \n";
  }
  print "</p>\n";
}
else {
  print "<p>There are no command line arguments.\n";
}
print "</p>\n";
print "<h2>2. Environment Variables are:</h2>\n<p>";
while (($key, $val) = each %ENV) {
        print "$key = $val<br />\n";
}
print "</p>\n";
print "<h2>3. Data at Standard Input </h2>\n<p>";
if ($ENV{"CONTENT_LENGTH"} ne "" ) {
   while( <STDIN> ) {
        print "$_<br />";
   }
   print "</p><hr />\n";
}
else {
   print "<i>No data at standard input... </p><hr />\n";
}
print "</body></html>\n";
```

Figure 10.9 Test program *form1* accessed by the HTML form in Figure 9.9. This script returns an HTML document listing the script command-line arguments (if there are any), the contents of all the environment variables, and any data read from standard input (if any exists).

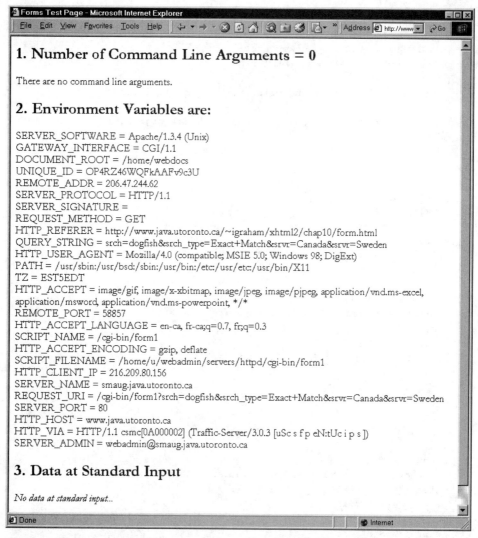

Figure 10.10 Data returned from the script shown in Figure 10.9 when accessed, using the GET method, by the form shown in Figure 9.9.

environment variable is set to GET, and the query string is placed in the QUERY_STRING environment variable. The CONTENT_TYPE and CONTENT_LENGTH variables are empty, because there is no data sent in a GET method, and the PATH_INFO and PATH_TRANSLATED variables are also empty, because there was no extra path information in the query.

Further processing requires code to parse the QUERY_STRING and break it into its component parts. This is not difficult, recalling that the ampersand character divides the different segments; the equals sign relates form variable names to the assigned values; and spaces in the query strings are encoded as plus signs. Finally, you must decode all the special characters that may have been encoded using the URL escaping and encoding schemes discussed in Chapter 8. The perl code extract in Figure 10.11 illustrates how this decoding can be done, under the assumption that the original text was encoded using ISO-8859-1.

The `pack()` functions convert the *%xx* escape sequences back into their ISO Latin-1 character positions. This, of course, is only correct if the URL text was built from text originally encoded using ISO 8859-1. If the original text was encoded using UTF-8 (see Section 8.1.4), then this algorithm won't work.

10.6 HTML Forms via a POST Request

This is slightly different if the **form** sends data using a POST request. This example again accesses the program shown in Figure 10.9 using a **form** equivalent to the one in Figure 9.6, but this time, using the POST method. The data sent to a server (again using the Internet Explorer 5 browser) is

```
POST /cgi-bin/form1 HTTP/1.1
Accept: image/gif, image/x-xbitmap, image/jpeg, image/pjpeg,
application/vnd.ms-excel, application/msword, application/vnd.ms-
powerpoint, */*
Referer: http://www.java.utoronto.ca/~igraham/xhtml2/chap10/form2.html
Accept-Language: en-ca,fr-ca;q=0.7, fr;q=0.3
Content-Type: application/x-www-form-urlencoded
Accept-Encoding: gzip, deflate
User-Agent: Mozilla/4.0 (compatible; MSIE 5.0; Windows 98; DigExt)
Host: www.java.utoronto.ca:1939
Content-Length: 58
Connection: Keep-Alive
[a blank line, containing only CRLF ]
srch=dogfish&srch_type=Exact+Match&srvr=Canada&srvr=Sweden
```

where the differences from the data sent by the equivalent GET request are shown in boldface. Note how the data is sent to the server as an encoded message following the headers. There are two extra fields: `content-length` (giving the length of the message) and `content-type` (giving the message data type). Here, the type is *application/x-www-form-urlencoded*—this MIME type implies **form** data that have been encoded using the URL encoding scheme.

Figure 10.12 shows the results returned by the script in Figure 10.9 and displays the data that arrived at the script. There are no command-line arguments—this time, because there is no query string. Most of the environment variables are the same as with the GET request shown in Figure 10.10. Obvious differences are the `REQUEST_METHOD` variable, which is now POST instead of GET, and the null `QUERY_STRING`. In addition, the `CONTENT_TYPE` and

```
    if( !defined($ENV{"QUERY_STRING"})) { # Check for Query String
                                          # variable
        $pk_error("No Query String\n");   # variable: if absent, then
                                          # error.
    }
    $input=$ENV{"QUERY_STRING"}            # get form data from query
                                          # string
                                          # Check for unencoded equals
                                          # sign.
                                          # If there are none, the string
    if( $input !~  /=/ ) {                 # didn't come from a form, which
                                          # is an error.
        &pk_error("Query String not from form\n");
    }
                                          # If we get to here, all is OK.
    @fields=split("&",$input);            # Now split data into separate
    name=value                            # fields(@fields is an array)

    #   Now loop over each of the entries in the @fields array and break
    #   them into the name and value parts. Then decode each part to get
    #   back the strings typed into the form by the user

    foreach $one (@fields) {
       ($name, $value) = split("=",$one); # split, at the equals sign,
                                          # into the name and value
                                          # strings.
                                          # Next, decode the strings.
       $name =~ s/\+/ /g;                 # convert +'s to spaces
       $name =~ s/%(..)/pack("c",hex($1))/ge;
                                          # convert hex codes to Latin-1
       $value =~ s/\+/ /g;                # convert +'s to spaces
       $value =~ s/%(..)/pack("c",hex($1))/ge;
                                          # convert hex codes to Latin-1

    # What you do now depends on how the program works. If you know that
    # each name is unique (your FORM does not have checkbox or SELECT
    # items that allow multiple name=value strings with the same name)
    # then you can place all the data in an associative array (a useful
    # little perl feature!):

       $array{"$name"} = $value;

    # If your form does have select or <input type=checkbox../> items,
    # then you'll have to be a bit more careful...


    }
```

Figure 10.11 Perl code extract for decoding form data passed in a query string. Note that this is not a functional piece of code and that the extracted name and value strings must be placed in a permanent storage location (such as an associative array) for subsequent processing.

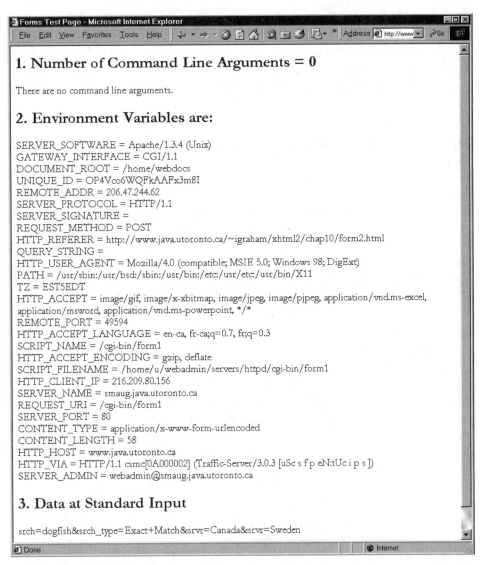

Figure 10.12 Data returned from the script shown in Figure 10.9 when accessed by the form shown in Figure 9.9 and modified to use the POST HTTP method.

CONTENT_LENGTH are not empty but contain the length of the message and the content-type, as indicated in the fields sent by the client.

With the POST method, the form data is sent to the gateway program as an input stream, which the program reads from standard input. The script in Figure 10.9 reads data from standard input, and prints the results back to standard output. The result is printed at the bottom of Figure 10.12, which clearly shows the query data sent by the client. This data is encoded using the same URL encoding mechanisms employed with the GET query in Figure 10.10. To further process this data, you must parse it and separate the fields. Figure 10.13 shows an extract of a perl program that illustrates how this decoding can be done. This is equivalent to the code in Figure 10.11—the differences occur only at the beginning of the script and are marked in boldface italics.

10.6.1 Relative Advantages of GET and POST

The POST mechanism may seem similar to GET, but, in fact, it offers some important advantages—and a few disadvantages. First, many computer operating systems limit the size of environment variables or the length of data that can be sent in a query string, so that large messages passed via GET URLs may be truncated. In addition, the POST method lets you send complex MIME-encoded data messages to a server, something that is impossible, with the GET method. In particular, **form** data can be POSTed to a server using the *multipart/form-data* encoding scheme, discussed in Section 9.10. This mechanism allows for HTTP-based file uploads (the ability to upload arbitrary data files from the client to the server)—something that is not possible using GET requests. Moreover, each block in a *multipart/form-data* message can indicate the charset used within it, eliminating the possibility of confusion over the charset used to encode text-based data.

The GET and POST methods for handling **form** data have different strengths and weaknesses. POST is clearly superior if you are sending large quantities of data to the server or data encoded in character sets other than ISO Latin-1. If you are sending small quantities of data, the choice is less clear. One useful criterion is to ask if you want the user to be able to store (i.e., to bookmark or to write down as a hypertext reference) a URL that will return the user to this particular resource. If the answer is yes, then you must use the GET method, because the relevant data will be placed in the query string portion of a URL, which is stored when a URL is recorded. If, on the other hand, you do not want the user to be able to quickly return to this resource, or if you want to hide the **form** content as much as possible, then you should use POST.

10.6.2 Encoding of Data in a Form

With gateway programs, you often need to place data inside the **form** that is sent to the client. This might be initial values assigned to the **value** attributes of **input** or **option** elements, or it might be *state information* (information describing the state of the interaction between the user and the server-side application) preserved within the **value** attributes of **type**="hidden" **input**

```perl
$input=<STDIN>;                       # read form data from stdin
$input =~ s/\s*$//;                   # chop trailing CR/LF/space
characters:
                                      # recall that the data sent by a
                                      # client
                                      # is always terminated by a single
                                      # line
                                      # containing only a CRLF pair. This
                                      # must be removed, since it is not
                                      # part of the message body.
                                      # Check for unencoded equals sign --
                                      # if
                                      # there are none, the string didn't
if( $input !~ /=/ ) {                 # come from a form, which is an error.
    &pk_error("Query String not from form\n");
}
                                      # If we get to here, all is OK. Now
@fields=split("&",$input);            # split data into name=value
                                      # fields(@fields is an array)


#   Now loop over each of the entries in the @fields array and break
#   them into the name and value parts. Then decode each part to get
#   back the strings typed into the form by the user

foreach $one (@fields) {
    ($name, $value) = split("=",$one);     # split,at equals sign,into
                                           # name and value strings.
                                           # Then decode the strings.
    $name =~ s/\+/ /g;                      # convert +'s to spaces
    $name =~ s/%(..)/pack("c",hex($1))/ge; # convert hex to Latin-1
    $value =~ s/\+/ /g;                     # convert +'s to spaces
    $value =~ s/%(..)/pack("c",hex($1))/ge; # convert hex to Latin-1

# What you do now depends on how the program works. If you know that
# each name is unique (your FORM does not have checkbox or SELECT
# items that allow multiple name=value strings with the same name)
# then you can place all the data in an associative array (a useful
# little perl feature!):

    $array{"$name"} = $value;

#   If your form does have select or <input type=checkbox../> items,
#   then you'll have to be a bit more careful...


}
```

Figure 10.13 Perl code extract for decoding form data passed to the program via standard input. Differences from the extract in Figure 10.11 are shown in italics. Note that this is not a functional piece of code, and that the extracted name and value strings must be placed in a permanent storage location (such as an associative array) for subsequent processing.

elements. However, in doing so, you must remember that the HTML processor that displays the page will parse the text it receives. This means that any entity or character references placed in the **value** (or **name**) strings, or within the body of a **textarea** element, will be automatically expanded into the correct character. For example, if a document sent to a client contains the hidden element

```
<input TYPE="hidden" name="stuff" value="&lt;BOO&quot;&gt;" />
```

the client will *parse* the **value** string and convert it into the string `<BOO">`. When the **form** containing this hidden element is submitted, the string `<BOO">` will be URL encoded and sent to the server, so that the entity references in the original data are lost.

This is obvious if you recall that, as far as the browser is concerned, entity references and character references are little different from the characters they represent. This can be a problem, however, if the data within the hidden form contains HTML markup that you want to pass back and forth from the browser to the server, because you will then need to *preserve* entity references distinct from the characters they represent; for example, so that simple character strings (`&lt;tag&gt;`) do not get converted into markup tags (`<tag>`) by the conversion process. Thus, if you need to preserve entity references in form-submitted data, you must do the following three encodings of the string prior to placing it within a **value** or **name** attribute, or inside a **textarea** element:

1. Encode all ampersand characters in the text string as `&amp;`.

2. Encode all double quotation symbols as `&quot;`.

3. Encode all right angle brackets as `&gt;`.

The second and third steps are necessary, as any raw double quote characters (") will prematurely terminate a **value** or **name** string, and some browsers mistakenly use an unencoded greater-than symbol (>) to prematurely end **input** elements. The first step encodes the leading character of each entity or character reference: For example, the original string `&eacute;` becomes `&amp;eacute;`. This is converted by the client browser into the string `&eacute;`, which brings you full circle when the data are returned to the server.

10.7 State Preservation in CGI Transactions

With most Web server–based applications, a complete user session involves many Web pages exchanged between the client and server. Because the HTTP protocol is stateless, the server—and any gateway program on the server—

retains no knowledge of any previous transaction unless this need is explicitly accounted for in the program design. Thus, the gateway program designer must include mechanisms for keeping track of what happened in any previous stage.

This problem goes under two names: (1) *state preservation* or (2) *session management.* On the Web, there are three strategies for handling this problem. One way is to use **type**="hidden" **input** elements within HTML forms to pass state information back and forth between client and server—when the form is submitted, any state information stored in the hidden elements is submitted along with new information provided by the user. A second approach is to encode state information in some way as part of the base path in the URL—this approach was discussed briefly in Chapter 4, Section 4.3.2. A third alternative is to use HTTP cookies to store state information on the client, for automatic return when the client recontacts the server.

10.7.1 State Preservation Using Hidden Input Elements

There are two ways to use **type**="hidden" **input** ("hidden," for short) elements to preserve state information. First, the gateway program can place all the data received from the client inside "hidden" elements returned with the **form** used for the next stage of a transaction. Then, the subsequent access to a server resends the data from the previous interaction(s), because all the data is preserved in the "hidden" elements. This works well but can be cumbersome if there is a lot of information to be passed back and forth—the document gets big and slow to download, and the risk of introducing programming errors gets greater and greater. This approach also poses some security risks, because the information can be easily seen by anyone who can view the source listing for the Web page, making it easy for someone to fake a request. This problem can be mitigated somewhat by encrypting the data in the hidden fields so that the content is not understandable to the reader.

The second method is to create a temporary file or database entry on the server to store the transaction data. In this case, the gateway program need only return a single hidden element containing the *name* of this resource so that the gateway program, on subsequent requests, is told where to find the state information. This reduces the amount of data that must be sent from client to server (and back again), and also means that the data remains stored on the server, hidden from any interlopers who might want to hack into an ongoing transaction. On the other hand, this approach also means that the gateway programs must manage these temporary files or database entries. For example, many remote users may not complete the transaction, which will leave temporary data in place unless there are auxiliary routines for deleting stale entries.

10.7.2 State Preservation Using URL Data

Of course, the form-based approach will only work when each stage in the user session is a result of the user pressing **form** submit buttons, because it is the form that carries information about the session. A useful alternative is to encode session information in the URL strings used in the **href** attribute of anchor elements or the action attribute of a **form.** This encoded information might consist of a session id key that references a database entry (or file) on the server containing session-specific data.

As an example, consider the following URL:

```
http://www.foo.org/cgi-bin/do_stuff/x23-13121:312
```

Here, `do_stuff` is the CGI program being referenced, and the extra path information `x23-13121:312` is a session key that references information about the current session. Such a URL could be used in a regular anchor element or as the value of an action attribute in a **form**—if the **form** uses the GET method, the form data query string is appended after the extra path data.

Of course, this means that every URL in the document must be dynamically generated, because they must be customized for each user and each session.

10.7.3 State Preservation Using Cookies

The hidden form element mechanism works but is not ideal. Problems arise if a user does not move through the sequence exactly as planned or if the user does not do so in a single session. For example, a user might get halfway through a process, shut off his or her computer, and go home, hoping to resume the next morning. This is not possible with hidden form elements, because all the form data is lost when the browser is turned off. The same problem occurs if a session key is encoded in the URLs, because this key is lost if the user shuts down the browser. If the user tries to return to the site at a later date, they will be assigned a new session, and will have to start the session afresh.

As a partial solution to this problem, Netscape introduced the HTTP cookie mechanism discussed in the previous chapter. The idea is to have the browser store, on its local hard disk, specific state information sent by the server as part of the HTTP response header. In a sense, this is like storing hidden element data, but outside the document and in such a way that the data can easily be retrieved without bothering the user or modifying the document content. The cookie content is then sent, under appropriate circumstances, to the server as part of the HTTP request header.

We won't go into the details of the cookie mechanism here—this was described in detail in Section 9.12. To summarize briefly, cookie data is sent to a browser using a `Set-Cookie` response header field or fields (the server can send multiple cookies in a single transaction). In turn, the browser returns cookie data to a server using a `cookie` HTTP request header field. For security and privacy reasons, cookies can only be returned to the servers they came from. This helps maintain user privacy by ensuring that the servers at one domain cannot obtain cookie data produced at another.

The big advantage of the cookie approach is that cookie data is saved on disk and remains available even if the browser is stopped and restarted. Thus, if a user quits a transaction halfway through, and then comes back to it the next day, the browser can take the cookie data and return it to the server, telling the server where the user last left off.

Cookies would seem an ideal way of preserving state during a transaction. This would be true—if one could guarantee that they work. However, not all browsers support cookies, and browsers that support cookies let the user *disable* cookie storage. Netscape Navigator, for example, can be configured to prompt the user whenever a server tries to send a cookie, and gives the user the option of refusing the cookie data. Also, a browser can only store a small number of cookies at one time, so it is possible that the browser will automatically delete a cookie to make room for new ones. Thus, although the cookie mechanism can be very useful for preserving state or tracking user sessions, the mechanism is not 100 percent reliable.

10.8 Gateway Program Alternatives

The gateway program approach is very popular: Literally millions of Web sites use gateway programs to provide interactive site components, or use the gateway approach when prototyping new application designs. However, the CGI approach has three inherent limitations:

Lack of speed and scalability. Gateway programs are launched as separate processes, and there is a relative large start-up cost associated with doing so. This is not a problem when the demand for the server or CGI programs is small, but it can be a big problem if the site is used heavily.

Architectural design limitations. The gateway program approach is useful for building small, simple Web-based applications, but is less suited to building complex large-scale applications that require significant software development. In this case, it is often better to use an application development environment that provides many predefined software components that help in the application design process.

Uneasy mix of program code and page design. Programmers design programs, and Web page designers design X/HTML documents and style sheets. Gateway programs mix the two tasks into the same file, making it difficult to cleanly separate these two distinct tasks.

These limitations have led to several alternatives to the gateway program approach. These alternative approaches, such as compiled server modules and server extension frameworks like Java servlets or PHP, generally mimic the CGI mechanisms to get data from the server to the extension packages. Of course, the details are somewhat different, but, in practice, the differences are relatively small. These alternatives are illustrated in Figure 10.14, contrasted with the traditional gateway program approach. We discuss these briefly in the next few sections.

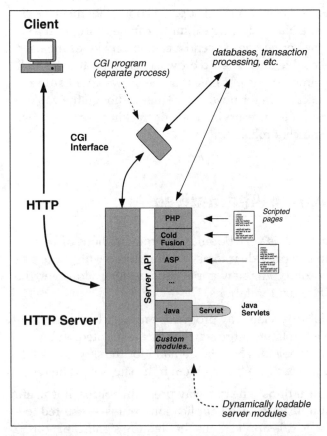

Figure 10.14 Schematic diagram illustrating the data flow between a client, an HTTP server and server-integrated scripting environments (e.g., PHP, ColdFusion, etc.), Java Servlets, or compiled server modules, as discussed in the text.

10.8.1 Server Application Programming Interfaces

Gateway programs are ideal for many problems, because they can be easy to write and are easily added without modifying the HTTP server software. However, flexibility comes at the expense of speed and scalability: Starting up a gateway program can involve significant operating system overhead, which can slow server response, particularly when the demand for a CGI program rises and the system tries to run a number of CGI programs at the same time.

As an alternative, most modern servers support linked-in modules, written in C or other compiled languages, to incorporate gateway-like processing right into the server. To do so, these servers provide a special application programming interface (API) for linking such modules to the underlying server. Unfortunately, the APIs used by each server vendor (iPlanet, Microsoft, Apache, or other) are incompatible, so that modules written for one server are not portable to another. However, this is the approach to use if you want fast server response for processing-intensive operations, such as transaction processing. Indeed, most commerce-grade Web servers from companies such as Microsoft, iPlanet, O'Reilly, Stronghold, and others come already equipped with modules dedicated for such tasks.

Compiled modules may be fast, but they can also be fatal—if a module crashes due to a software error, then the whole server crashes as well, leaving your site out of operation. This does not happen with standard CGI programs, because the CGI program is a separate process: If the CGI program dies, then the user's interaction will fail, but the server will keep running.

For this reason, it is rare today for site developers to actually write their own server modules. Instead, they tend to use special development environments such as servlets, page script parsers, or others. Indeed, the modules that support functions such as Java servlets (see Section 10.8.2), page scripting environments such as PHP, ASP, and so on, are essentially compiled server modules as just described.

Modules for Accelerating Standard CGI Programs

Compiled modules can also help make standard scripted CGI programs faster by providing preloaded environments or libraries for running CGI programs. There are several such modules available, many of which are only available for the Apache Web server. In the case of the Apache server, there are special perl and python acceleration modules that provide preloaded environments for processing perl or python scripts. These modules preload the language interpreters and also preload many of the auxiliary libraries used by standard perl or python gateway programs. Such modules significantly increase the speed with which perl and python CGI scripts load and execute.

The more generic *fastCGI* package provides similar acceleration, but in a language-independent way. However, programs that use fastCGI must be rewritten somewhat to work with the fastCGI programming interface, although the changes are generally modest.

URLs referencing additional information about the fastCGI package and the perl and python accelerator modules for the Apache server are given in the References section at the end of this chapter.

10.8.2 Java Servlets

Java Servlets are a second expansion mechanism, similar in some ways to compiled server modules, but safer and more flexible. With the servlet approach, the Web server is equipped with a Java runtime environment (the code that runs Java programs) that can dynamically load and run Java code written to use a special servlet interface—the code that supports this interface is incorporated into the integrated Java runtime environment.

NOTE This environment is actually provided by a compiled-in module, as described in Section 10.8.1.

The servlet interface effectively connects the Java program to the Web server and lets the servlet program access the same information as a traditional gateway program (the mechanism that passes the data to the servlet is somewhat different and provides some additional functionality not provided by the simpler CGI mechanisms).

Servlets are faster to load and run than traditional gateway programs, because the Java runtime environment is integrated into the Web server and is thus already running. Also, the Java runtime environment is very efficient at running many servlets in parallel, so that the servlet-based systems can scale well when there are many requests for servlets.

Most open source and commercial Web servers provide a servlet interface for writing Java servlets, and this has become, after the traditional CGI approach, one of the more popular ways of adding functionality to Web pages.

10.8.3 Parsed HTML Documents

Neither of the preceding approaches helps to separate the design of the programs needed by a Web application from the design of the Web pages. Separation of this type is possible using a second type of extension mechanism generically referred to as scripted HTML documents. In this model, the X/HTML documents contain regular markup mixed with instructions written in a scripting language. When a Web server retrieves such documents, it passes them through a document-processing engine (essentially another compiled-in server module designed expressly for this purpose) that interprets and executes the script code. The code can contain statements that write markup into the document, allowing for dynamic generation of document content.

There are several different scripted HTML environments, including Apache's parsed HTML, Microsoft's Active Server Pages (ASP), Allaire's ColdFusion, Portable Hypertext Processor (PHP), Java Server Pages (JSP), and more. Section 11.5, and Appendix E on this book's companion Web site, discuss the parsed HTML approach, and Chapter 12 reviews some of the other larger-scale tools. In general, these environments support the CGI mechanisms (or equivalent) for passing data from the Web server to the environment that processes the scripted pages, although some provide enhanced features. The principles, however, remain the same. Indeed, a sound understanding of the basic CGI mechanisms means that you will well understand the data-processing model of all these different environments.

10.9 References

MODULES FOR FASTER CGI PROCESSING

www.fastcgi.com/	FastCGI
http://perl.apache.org/	Perl module (Apache server)
www.msg.com.mx/pyapache/	Python module (Apache server)

CGI Programming Examples and Parsed HTML

Topics/Concepts Covered: Common Gateway Interface (CGI) examples, CGI-based client-pull and server-push animations, CGI programming and security issues, CGI security wrappers, server-side includes (SSI)

The previous chapter described the CGI mechanisms in detail. This chapter begins by looking at some simple CGI program examples that illustrate some practical CGI design issues and the ways in which CGI programs can use HyperText Transfer Protocol (HTTP) headers to control the interaction between client and server. Section 11.2 then looks briefly into the main issues you need to consider (or look out for) when writing CGI programs, while Section 11.3 highlights the main security risks and suggests some tools that can make CGI programs safer. Section 11.4 describes where to obtain CGI programming libraries that can significantly simplify the job of writing complex, large-scale CGI applications.

Section 11.5 presents a brief discussion of server-side includes. This is a feature of many HTTP servers (in particular, Apache-based servers) that allows for *parsable* HyperText Markup Language (HTML) documents that are processed by the server prior to being delivered to a client. These parsed HTML documents can also reference programs on the server. These programs are accessed using the CGI mechanisms, and the output of the programs is included into the HTML documents that reference them.

The next chapter will look at some of the richer Web application development environments that expand upon both the CGI and SSI approaches to allow for easier CGI-like programming and development and richer SSI-like page scripting environments.

11.1 CGI Examples

This section presents some simple CGI programs illustrating some possible uses of the CGI facility. The first subsection describes a simple program that returns a document containing a count of the number of times the page was accessed, and illustrates how extra path information can pass resource location information to a CGI program.

The second subsection looks at two special HTTP extension mechanisms that allow for simple forms of animation based on data streamed to the browser from a Web server. Although these mechanisms are not commonly used today (there are better ways of accomplishing these types of animation), they do help illustrate how CGI programs can create their own HTTP headers, thereby controlling the nature of the communication between the client and server.

11.1.1 A Page Hit Counter

This simple CGI program illustrates one way you can create Web pages containing a "hit" counter—that is, a number listing how many times a page has been retrieved from the server. This program reads in the document to be returned and edits it, replacing a dummy comment string in the document (the string `<!--counter-->`) with the measured count. The count is obtained from a log file that tracks the number of times the file has been accessed. The gateway program opens this log file and increments the counter by 1. The program listing is found in Figure 11.1.

To use this gateway program, you must access a document using a Uniform Resource Locator (URL) of the form

```
http://some.where.edu/cgi-bin/counter.pl/path/file.html
```

where *path/file.html* is the path to the document relative to the root of the server document directory.

The location of the file to be returned is found in the `PATH_TRANSLATED` environment variable; this value is placed into the local variable `&file` at line 8. Line 2 checks to make sure this variable actually exists. If it does not, this means that there was no extra path information in the URL, meaning that the author forgot to reference a file. Lines 8 through 11 process the variable `&path` to extract the path to the directory containing the document being returned (`&path`) as well as the full name and directory of the file being returned

```perl
1   #!/usr/local/bin/perl
2   if (defined(&ENV{"PATH_TRANSLATED"}) ) {
3       &path = &ENV{"PATH_TRANSLATED"} # get file from path info
4   }
5   else {
6       &f_error("No file specified\n");
7   }
8   &file     = &path;              # Path to file to be processed
9   &cnt_file = &path;
10  &cnt_file =~ s/.*\///;          # Extract counter filename string
11  &path     =~ s/\/[\w-.;~]*&/\//; # get path to directory
12
13  &cnt_file = &path.".".&cnt_file; # counter filename=path/filename
14
15  if( !(-e &cnt_file) ) {         # Create count file if it
                                    # doesn't exist
16    open (CNTFILE, "> &cnt_file") | |
17          &f_error ("Unable to create count file\n");
18   print CNTFILE "0";
19   close (CNTFILE);
20  }
21  &loops = 0;                     # try 4 times to lock count file
22  while ( flock(&cnt_file,2) == -1 ) {
23    &loops++;
24    if( &loops > 4) {
25       &cnt = "-1 (Unable to lock counter)\n";
26       goto PROCESS:              # If unable to lock, skip it.
27    }
28       sleep 1;
29  }
30  open(CNTFILE, "+< &cnt_file")   # open the counter file
31          | | &f_error("Unable to open counter file\n");
32  &cnt = <CNTFILE>;               # get the current count
33  &cnt++;                         # increment count by one
34  seek(CNTFILE, 0, 0);            # rewind to start of file
35  print CNTFILE "&cnt";           # write out new count
36  close(CNTFILE);                 # close the count file
37  flock(&cntfile, 8);             # Unlock the count file
38
39  PROCESS:
40  open (FILE, &file)              # Open file to process
41        | | &f_error ("Unable to open file for processing\n");
42  @array= <FILE>;                 # Read in the file
43  close(FILE);
44                                  # Print out the document
```

continues

Figure 11.1 Listing of the Practical Extraction Report Language (perl) gateway program *counter.pl,* which inserts an access count into a designated HTML document. The path to the designated HTML document is passed as *extra path* information in the URL referencing the program. Line numbers (in italics) are added for reference purposes only—they are not present in the original program.

```
45  print "Content-type: text/html\n\n";
46  foreach (@array) {                     # scan for special string:
47      s/<!-- counter -->/ &cnt /i;  # replace it by the count
48      print &_;
49  }
50  # Error Handling Subroutine
51  sub f_error {
52      print "Content-type text/plain\n\n";
53      print "<HTML><HEAD>\n<TITLE>Error In Counter Script</TITLE>";
54      print "\n</HEAD><BODY>\n<h2>Error</h2>\n<P>Error message:
    &_[0]";
55      print "\n<P> Please report this problem to someone.";
56      print "\n</BODY></HTML>";
57      die;
58  }
```

Figure 11.1 *(Continued)*

(&file). The count file (&cnt_file) will have same name as the file, preceded
by a period. Thus, if the file being returned is *home.html*, then the count file
will be named *.home.html*, and will be in the same directory as the file. Therefore, every file has its own distinct count file located in the same directory as
the file itself.

Line 15 checks to see if the count file exists—if it does not, lines 16 through
19 create it and place an initial value of zero inside it.

Lines 22 through 29 attempt to *lock* the file [flock(&cntfile,2)]. Locking the
file means that the running perl program is the *only* program that can modify
the file, and ensures that two requests to the Web server cannot simultaneously try to change it. The program tries four times to lock the file, waiting 1
second between attempts. If it fails, it sets a default value for the string containing the counter value (&cnt) and skips the part of the program that actually reads the count file. If it succeeds in locking the file, it proceeds to the
next phase, beginning at line 30, where the count file is opened and the count
is read, incremented by 1, and rewritten to the file, overwriting the old value.
The file is then closed and the lock is released [flock(&cntfile, 8)], freeing
the file for use by other users.

Line 39 begins the processing of the file returned to the client. The file is
opened at line 40 and read at line 42 into the array @array. Each item in the
array will contain a single line of the file. When finished, the file is closed
(line 43).

Line 45 prints the required content-type header. Lines 46 through 48 print
the data to standard output, replacing every occurrence of the string <!--
counter --> with the counter string (line 47). This is either the counter value
from line 33 or the error string from line 25.

And that is it. The count is inserted, the document is returned, and the counter has been incremented by 1.

There are several limitations to this program. First, it is slower than need be, since it has to check every line in the document for the string `<-- counter -->`. A second problem is associated with file permissions: The server that launches a gateway program usually runs with very limited ability to create and modify files in a user's directory. Thus this gateway program, when launched by the server, will probably not be able to create or modify the count file. If this is the case, the document's author will have to create the count file by hand and change the file characteristics so that the gateway program has permission to modify it. Finally, we note that this program only counts accesses that pass through the gateway program. If the document is accessed via a URL like

```
http://some.where.edu/path/file.html
```

then the access is not counted.

There are several useful features you might also want to add. For example, you might want to exclude your own machine or domain from the counting process, or you may prefer keeping all the count values in a single counter database file as opposed to having one file per document.

These and other variations on page counters are available in a number of counter programs, many of which are far more sophisticated than this example. The references section at the end of the chapter lists some of the CGI program archive sites where you can search for such counter programs.

11.1.2 CGI Animation Techniques

Most modern browsers support mechanisms that allow for slide show–like presentations and for a rudimentary form of "pushed" animation. The animation scheme, called *server-push*, uses a special multipart Multipurpose Internet Mail Extensions (MIME) type to let a server send a client a series of images or documents. These received pages are then displayed by the browser one after the other as they arrive. To use this technique, a Web designer must use a gateway program that sends the data to the client using this special MIME type.

The slide show mechanism, more properly called *client-pull*, uses a nonstandard "`refresh`" HTTP response header that instructs the browser, after a defined delay, to either actively refresh the displayed document or access another document at a specified URL. Again, a gateway program must produce the `Refresh` HTTP header field.

The HTTP refresh header is equivalent to HTML **meta** elements containing `Refresh` header field content (using the **http-equiv** attribute value: please see

Section 3.4.3 of *XHTML 1.0 Language and Design Sourcebook,* and also later in this section). The browser processes **meta** elements that contain refresh information as if the information came from the equivalent HTTP header. Note, however, that this mechanism has some important problems, which we discuss a bit later.

Client-Pull

In *client-pull,* the server sends the client a special HTTP Refresh response header field. The field has the general form

```
Refresh: xx; URL=url_string
```

where *xx* is an integer giving the time, in seconds, that the browser should wait before refreshing the document, and `url_string` is the *full* (not relative) URL that the browser should access when it is time to do the refresh. For example, the header

```
Refresh: 10; URL=http://www.utoronto.ca/home.html
```

tells a browser to wait 10 seconds and then access the indicated URL. The URL portion can be left out, in which case the browser re-accesses the URL it just retrieved. Thus, the header

```
Refresh: 30
```

tells a browser to refresh the currently displayed URL after a 30-second delay. The refresh time can be set to zero, in which case the browser will refresh the display as soon as the currently requested data is fully loaded.

There are several things to note about this procedure. First, this response header field is understood by most, but not all, browsers (it is understood by Netscape Navigator 2 and greater and Internet Explorer 3 and greater); those that do not understand it will simply ignore the header, display the accessed document, and then stop. Second, the Refresh: field must be returned by a gateway program—servers themselves do not return these fields. Third, each request by the client counts as a separate HTTP transaction—in particular, the connection will be broken between requests unless the CGI program is careful to return the correct HTTP response headers that control the keep-alive mechanism.

Client-Pull via meta Elements

As an alternative to using a CGI program, Refresh can be placed inside an HTML document **meta** element. This lets authors add refresh capability into already existing parsed HTML documents (parsed HTML documents are discussed later in this chapter) or build slide shows into a sequence of regular HTML documents, using the URLs in the Refresh fields to reference consecutive pages. The **meta** element equivalent to the general form of the Refresh HTTP response header is

```
<meta http-equiv="Refresh" content="xx; URL=url_string" />
```

so that **meta** elements equivalent to the two examples just given are:

```
<meta http-equiv="Refresh" content="10;
     URL=http://www.utoronto.ca/home.html" />
<meta http-equiv="Refresh" content="30" />
```

Most browsers understand these **meta** elements and interpret their content as HTTP response header fields. This is, of course, only possible with HTML documents; if you are returning other forms of data, such as images, you need to use the gateway program approach.

NOTE PROBLEMS WITH CLIENT-PULL **Each refresh header (or meta) element adds a new document to the browser's history list, and thereby breaks the expected behavior of the browser's "Back" button. Indeed a refresh with a delay time of zero seconds may make it impossible for the user to "back" out to a previous page!**

Server-Push

Server-push is a second and fundamentally different way of creating dynamic documents. When a client accesses a resource delivered using server-push, the client-server connection remains open, and the server sends a sequence of data objects, one after the other, over an open connection. The connection does not close until the sequence is finished. This is done using a special MIME multipart message format, discussed next. There are two advantages to this method. First, it is faster than client-pull, since the browser does not need to recontact the server to get the second (or subsequent) piece of data. Second, the method can be used not just for a document, but also for the images within a document—you can use server-push to download a sequence of images into an `<img src="..." />` element. This allows for embedded animation sequences created by referencing, from an **img** element, a gateway program that delivers a sequence of image files via server-push. The disadvantage is that you absolutely need to write a special-purpose gateway program—unlike the case with client-pull, you cannot implement server-push using **meta** elements.

> **NOTE**   EFFICIENCY OF SERVER-PUSH   **Although faster than client-pull, server-push animation is far less efficient than an animated GIF or Macromedia Flash (or other client-side) approach—you should use the latter whenever possible. Server-push is only appropriate when the animation must be dynamically generated by a gateway program.**

Server-push is implemented using the MIME type *multipart/x-mixed-replace.* By employing this MIME type, a server can deliver a sequence (in principle, an endless sequence) of data files one after the other. This is done by defining a *boundary* string as part of the MIME type header. A boundary string is a string of ASCII characters used to separate each part of a multipart message from the preceding and following parts. The MIME content-type declaration takes the form

```
Content-type: multipart/x-mixed-replace;boundary=String
```

where `String` is a string of ASCII characters used as the separator between the different parts of the message. This string of characters must consist only of letters (a–z, A–Z) and numbers (0–9), and must not appear anywhere within the different parts of the message. This ensures that the software receiving the data will not detect the string within a part of the message and prematurely end the message part. The general form for this MIME message type is shown in Figure 11.2.

Note how the boundaries between different parts of the multipart message are denoted by the string `SpecialAsciiString` preceded by two dashes, that is:

```
--SpecialAsciiString
```

The end of the message is denoted by the same string but with two additional trailing dashes:

```
--SpecialAsciiString--
```

In practice, you can leave out this termination string and send an unending sequence of messages. A user can end this sequence by selecting the browser's "Stop" button, or by explicitly selecting an alternate URL.

The following two gateway program examples illustrate how server-push works.

A Simple Server-Push Shell Script

This simple shell script listed in Figure 11.3 repeatedly returns a document listing the "top" process running on the computer.

This first thing to note is that this is a *non-parsed header* script. This is necessary with server-push as many servers buffer the data returned from a gate-

```
Content-type: multipart/x-mixed-replace;boundary=SpecialAsciiString
                       [blank line, containing a CRLF pair ]
--SpecialAsciiString      [marker denoting boundary between parts]
Content-type: type/subtype
   [blank line, containing a CRLF pair ]
.... content of first chunk ....
.... and more content ....
--SpecialAsciiString
Content-type: type/subtype
   [blank line, containing a CRLF pair ]
.... content of second chunk ....
.... and more content ....
--SpecialAsciiString
Content-type: type/subtype
   [blank line, containing a CRLF pair ]
.... content of third chunk ....
.... and more content ....
--SpecialAsciiString
 .

 .

 . [and so on... any number of parts can be present...]
 .

--SpecialAsciiString-- [The end of the multipart message]
```

Figure 11.2 Structure of a *multipart/x-mixed-replace* MIME message. Here, *SpecialAsciiString* represents the string of ASCII characters used as the separator between message parts, and *type*/*subtype* is the data type of the data being sent. Comments are in italics.

way program and only forward data when the buffer is full or when the gateway program stops running. Here, however, we want each piece of our multipart message to be immediately delivered to the client. We ensure this by using a nonparsed header script, which bypasses the server buffering and dumps data directly down the connection to the client.

Consequently, lines 2 through 5 return all the HTTP (here, HTTP version 1.0) response headers: the status header (response 200, implying success), the date (the format instructions provide a date in the correct format), the server type (obtained from the environment variable), and the content-type declaration for the type multipart/x-mixed-replace. In this example, the multipart boundary string is allpRf5fgFd1dr. Note that there are no space characters in this content-type header. Ordinarily, you can have spaces before and after the semicolons separating the type/subtype from the associated parameters, but this is incorrectly processed by some servers (in particular, early versions of the NCSA HTTP server), so it is safest to remove all optional white space. Finally, line 6 returns a blank line, which indicates the end of the server directives and the start of the data being returned to the client.

```
1   #!/bin/sh
2   echo "HTTP/1.0 200 OK"                    # [ Server
3   date -u '+Date: %A, %d-%b-%y %T GMT'      # Response
4   echo Server: &SERVER_SOFTWARE             # Headers ]
5   echo "Content-type: multipart/x-mixed-replace;boundary=
    allpRf5fgFd1dr"
6   echo ""
7   echo "--allpRf5fgFd1dr"        # [initial boundary for first part]
8   while true
9 do
10    echo "Content-type: text/html"
11    echo ""
12    echo "<html><head>"
13    echo "<title> Top Running Processes </title><head><body>"
14    echo "<h1 align="center"> Top Running Processes at: <br />"
15    date                        # [prints the current time and date]
16    echo "</hr><hr />"
17    echo "<pre>"
18    /usr/local/bin/top -d1  # [Print out "top" running processes]
19    echo "</pre></body></html>"
20    echo echo "--allpRf5fgFd1dr"
21    sleep 10
22 done
```

Figure 11.3 The Bourne shell script *nph-top-list.sh*, which returns, every 10 seconds, a list of the top 10 processes running on the computer. Line numbers are in italics.

Line 7 prints the first boundary marker. This indicates the start of the first part of the message. The script then executes a loop, starting from line 9, which is executed every 10 seconds (see the sleep 10 command at the bottom of the loop). The loop returns a content-type header (here *text/html*) followed by a blank line. The blank line marks the end of the headers for each part and the beginning of the data. This is followed by the HTML document, which includes, inside a **pre** element, the output from the program top. The last thing returned is the boundary marker "--allpRf5fgFd1dr", which tells the client that the message is complete and that it can stop waiting for more data. It also tells the client to keep the connection to the server open in anticipation of the next part of the message.

This program will in principle run forever, sending information every 10 seconds. A remote user can interrupt this process by simply pressing the "Stop" button or by selecting another URL. The server should detect the broken connection and issue a kill signal to the gateway program. Unfortunately, this does not work on some servers, so it is a good idea to have gateway programs check for a broken connection and gracefully quit if this has occurred.

Shell languages, such as the Bourne shell used in this example, are notoriously bad at this—they often "forget" to die—so you should write server-push programs in languages such as perl or C, which properly terminate when the connection breaks. The script in Figure 11.3, for example, does not always terminate when the client breaks the connection. This has, on occasion, left a dozen of these scripts happily running on our server long after the browser that started them has broken the connection to the server.

A C Program for "Pushing" Images

The example C program *nph-doit-2*, shown in Figure 11.4, uses server-push to send a sequence of GIF images. Assume that this CGI program is located in the server's *cgi-bin/* directory. To insert an animated image in an HTML document, you would write the HTML markup

```
<img src="/cgi-bin/nph-doit-2" [... other attributes...] />
```

which assumes that the HTML document and gateway program are on the same server. The client will access the indicated URL to download the requested image. A browser that understands multipart messages will play the image sequence as a simple animation. Browsers that do not understand the multipart MIME type will display nothing, or will display a symbol representing a missing or broken image link.

The first part of the program (between the *GET LIST* and *GOT LIST* comments) gets a list of all the image files in the directory */abs/path/image_dir*, and creates an array (`files[]`) of absolute path file names pointing to these files. The program then writes out the necessary server response headers, as well as the initial multipart headers and message dividers required by the multipart message (just after the *PRINT SERVER RESPONSE HEADERS* comment). The subsequent loop iterates over the different image files, sending them one after the other to the client, each file followed by the required multipart boundary marker (after the *WRITE THE PART BOUNDARY* comment). When finished with the list, the program exits, writes out the final boundary marking the end of the multipart message, and ends the connection.

Because this is a gateway program, you can pass variables to the program using the usual tricks. Thus you can use extra path information in a URL (the `PATH_INFO` environment variable) to pass the location of the image directory to the CGI program, instead of using a hardwired location as done in this example.

Problems with Server-Push and Client-Pull

Both client-pull and server-push are simple but not terribly flexible techniques for automatically updating page content. Client-pull can be mimicked

```
/*
 * doit-2.c
 * Based on doit.c --
 *   Quick hack to play a sequence of GIF files, by Rob McCool.
 *   This code is released into the public domain. Do whatever
 *   you want with it.
 *
 * Doit-2.c Modifications by By Ian Graham, July 23 1998
 * to make it a simpler demonstration example -- or so I thought!
 */

#include <sys/types.h>
#include <unistd.h>
#include <stdlib.h>
#include <fcntl.h>
#include <sys/stat.h>
#include <dirent.h>
#include <stdio.h>

/* Define the server directives and response headers      */
#define HEADER1  "HTTP/1.0 200 OK\r\n"     /* Nph-response header   */
#define HEADER2 \
   "Content-type: multipart/x-mixed-replace;boundary=aRd4xBloobies\r\n"

/* Define the boundary strings, the Content-type header, and the   */
/* path to the directory containing the images      */

#define BOUNDARY     "\r\n--aRd4xBloobies\r\n"
#define END_BOUND    "\r\n--aRd4xBloobies--\r\n\r\n"
#define content      "Content-type: image/gif\r\n\r\n"
#define IMG_DIR      "/abs/path/image_dir"    /*  where the files are*/

int main (int argc, char *argv[])
{
    static char   *file;
    char          *files[1024], *tmp, buf[127];
    caddr_t       fp;
    int           fd, i, ndir=0;
    DIR           *dirp;
    struct dirent *dp;
    struct stat   fi;

    /* Get list of all files in image directory -- we will     */
    /* spit them out in alphabetical order                     */
                                          /* ** GET LIST ** */
    dirp = opendir (IMG_DIR);
```

Figure 11.4 Simple C program *nph-doit-2.c,* for pushing a sequence of images to a client. The files are read from the indicated directory. Commentary not originally in the program listing is in boldface italics.

```
    while ( ((dp = readdir (dirp)) != NULL) && (ndir < 1024) ) {
        if( strncmp (dp->d_name,".", 1)) {
            files [ndir] = malloc(strlen(dp->d_name)+1+strlen(IMG_DIR));
            sprintf(files[ndir], "%s/%s", IMG_DIR, dp->d_name);
            ndir++;
        }
    }
    closedir (dirp);
                                                     /* ** GOT LIST ** */
    /* Write out server directives, and first multipart boundary         */

                                /* ** PRINT SERVER RESPONSE HEADERS  ** */
    if(write(STDOUT_FILENO, HEADER1, strlen(HEADER1)) == -1)    exit (0);
    if(write(STDOUT_FILENO, HEADER2, strlen(HEADER2)) == -1)    exit (0);
    if(write(STDOUT_FILENO, BOUNDARY, strlen (BOUNDARY)) == -1) exit (0);

    /* Now loop over all files, and write to client                      */
    for (i=0; i<ndir; i++) {
        fprintf(stderr, "Doing output loop -- i=%i\n", i);
        sleep(1);
                                        /* ** WRITE PART content-type ***/
        if(write(STDOUT_FILENO, content, strlen(content)) == -1) exit (0);
        if( ( fd=open(files[i],O_RDONLY)) == -1 ) {
            fprintf(stderr,"Unable to open file %s\n", files[i]);
            continue;
        }
        fstat (fd, &fi);                           /* find size of file and */
            tmp=malloc(fi.st_size*sizeof(char)); /*allocate memory for it*/
            read(fd, tmp, fi.st_size);
                                        /* ** WRITE THE IMAGE DATA ** */
            if(write(STDOUT_FILENO, tmp, fi.st_size) == -1) exit(0);
                                    /* ERROR: unable to write image */
            free(tmp);
            close(fd);
                                        /* ** WRITE THE PART BOUNDARY ** */
            if(write(STDOUT_FILENO, BOUNDARY, strlen(BOUNDARY)) == -1) exit
    (0);
                                    /* ERROR unable to write boundary */
    }

    /* Write out the boundary marking the end of the multipart        */
    /* message. Then we are done                                      */

    write(STDOUT_FILENO, END_BOUND, strlen(END_BOUND));
    exit (0);
```

Figure 11.4 *(Continued)*

using a JavaScript program, but with far more flexibility; for example, a JavaScript program could let the user control the delay between pages. Moreover, the client-pull technique "breaks" the browser's "Back" button, since "Back" just returns the user to the previous page, which automatically pulls the next page down again!

Similarly, server-push is a rudimentary way of pushing to the browser data that makes heavy demands on the network (by keeping a connection open for an extended period of time) and on the server (because the CGI program stays running for a long time). Thus most client-side animation is now implemented using animated GIFs, Java applets, Macromedia Shockwave plug-ins, or other approaches.

11.2 CGI Programming Issues

There are many problems that will crop up as you write gateway programs, as is the case with any programming project. This section describes ways to check for four common sources of error that occur when writing gateway programs. Your list might be different, but hopefully this section will help you avoid some common problems!

Check for the correct HTTP method. The environment variable REQUEST_METHOD gives the method being used by the browser to access the script. If the method is incorrect (the request used the GET method, but the program expects POST), the program should return an appropriate error message.

Check for input. The gateway program should always check for the existence of input (if input is expected), either in the QUERY_STRING environment variable or at standard input, depending on the HTTP method. Programs often behave very badly if they attempt to read nonexistent environment variables or an empty standard input stream. If data is missing, the program should return an appropriate error message.

Check for errors in data sent by the browser. Check the input fields for obvious errors, and never trust the data sent by a browser. Innocuous errors, such as an unexpected negative number where a positive one was anticipated, can lead to havoc if you haven't checked for them. Even worse things can happen if the person accessing your CGI program is trying to make things go wrong! Section 11.3 looks into these security problems in more detail.

Remember that browsers parse returned markup. Remember that text returned to a browser inside a **name** or **value** string, or inside a **textarea** region, will be parsed, and that all character and entity references will be converted into the corresponding ISO Latin-1 characters. If you do not want this to happen, you must encode ampersand characters in the original data prior to placing the data in the **form** being sent to the client. This issue was discussed in detail in Section 10.7.2.

11.3 CGI Security Issues

There is always a security risk associated with running a gateway program, since a rogue program can easily corrupt the files located on the server or access restricted information (such as a password file or list of credit card numbers) and send it elsewhere. Some HTTP servers are configured such that executable CGI programs are restricted to special URLs (typically those pointing to the directories */cgi-bin* or */htbin*) and do not permit executable gateway programs in areas where regular documents are kept. The server administrator can then maintain strict control over the installation of gateway programs, and can verify that installed programs are not dangerous to the integrity of the server. However, many servers let any user install and run a CGI program. In either case it is important to know how to design programs that are as safe from hackers as possible.

The details of security management (e.g., who can run CGI programs, restrictions placed on those programs) depend on the server that you are using. In general, most servers allow significant customization of these features. You should check with your server manager—or with your server documentation, if you are the server manager—to determine how your server can be customized.

The next two sections briefly summarize the main issues associated with writing "safe" CGI programs. Much additional information may be found at the World Wide Web Security FAQ at www.w3.org/Security/Faq/www-security-faq.html.

11.3.1 Designing Safe Gateway Programs

Of course, few people set out to write unsafe gateway programs. Nevertheless, it is easy to do so unless you are very careful (and a bit lucky) when writing the programs. Although it is hard to give definitive rules for writing safe programs, here are three points you should particularly consider:

Guard system information. Gateway programs should never return to the client any information about the local system that could compromise system security, such as absolute paths to files, system usernames, password information, and so on. If you must return directory information, provide only a portion of the location relative to a location unknown to outside users—this reveals only limited information about the server's file system structure.

Never trust client data. A gateway program should never trust data sent by a client—the data could be in error, either due to a simple typing mistake or due to an intentional effort on the part of the client to break into your system. As a relatively benign example, you should never blindly trust the e-mail address (either *From:* or *To:*) typed into a fill-in HTML **form**, since you could be mailing data to the wrong user or to a nonexistent mail address.

More importantly, you should be extremely careful about using strings that are derived from user input as arguments to system calls; examples include the C or perl `system()` and `popen()` calls, or the perl or shell `eval` commands. Blindly passing strings to these calls or commands is a classic mistake, since commands executed by these calls can easily delete files, mail your password file to a remote user, and commit other venial sins. If you must execute strings passed by the user, be sure to check them for dangerous commands and to *unescape* special shell characters that can cause fatal problems. The possibly dangerous shell characters are:

`` ` ~ ! # & ^ & * ( ) = | \ { } [ ] ; : ' " < > , . ``

Execute in a secure environment. You can often run a script under a secure, or restricted, shell that takes proactive action to prevent problems.

The next section describes some CGI tools that can help protect you from these sorts of security problems. However, you should still strive to design your own programs to be as secure as possible.

11.3.2 CGI Security Wrappers

One way to make CGI programs safer is to "wrap" them in a security blanket. That is, the Web server, instead of directly launching the CGI program, launches a special security management package that in turn launches the CGI program. The security management package (or *wrapper*) contains special code that performs security checks on the CGI programs, and restricts the types of things the CGI program can do. This doesn't make the CGI programs entirely safe, but it certainly makes them safer than would otherwise be the case.

There are several security wrappers available for Unix-based Web servers. The most common ones are described in the next three sections.

CGIwrap: Security Wrapper   www.unixtools.org/cgiwrap/

CGIwrap, written by Nathan Neulinger, is a gateway program wrapper that causes CGI programs to run with the read, write, and execution permissions of the user who owns the program and not with those of the Web server that launches it. This makes it easier for users to write and run their own CGI programs, with reduced risk that these programs can damage other users' resources. This does not, however, protect users from themselves—they can, if they wish, write CGI programs that delete all their own files!

sbox: CGI Program Security Box   stein.cshl.org/software/sbox/

Like CGIwrap, sbox, written by Lincoln Stein, is a gateway program wrapper that runs CGI programs with the read, write, and execution permissions of the user who owns the program, and not with those of the Web server that launches it. However, sbox provides additional features, such as restrictions on the central processing unit (CPU) time or memory a script can use, that can protect a Web server from inadvertent "denial of service" problems should a script go into an infinite loop and try and gobble up the computer's memory or CPU time. It also supports an optional *chroot* feature. This feature, short for "change root directory," causes a program to run with access restricted to specific directories.

suEXEC   www.apache.org

suEXEC is a CGI security module integrated into the Apache server. This module supports CGI security wrapper functions similar to those provided by CGIwrap. Because it is integrated into the Web server, this module is more flexible than CGIwrap, as you can configure where and how suEXEC should be invoked using the server's configuration files.

11.4 CGI Programming Libraries

Writing many CGI programs from scratch can be quite tedious, as you end up writing a lot of code to handle generic tasks such as decoding the environment variables or standard input data, managing state preservation, or accessing local databases. Fortunately there are several CGI programming libraries that implement these features (and many more) using predefined functions or class libraries.

Most of these resources are language specific, and this short section cannot hope to describe all the tools and libraries available to help with CGI programming. In general, you will want to do some research on your own, looking at programming language-specific sites for useful lists of CGI-related programming resources. The intention here is to briefly describe the most common perl and C language CGI libraries—which will in general be good places to start if you are learning how to write CGI programs. For additional information and resource lists, you should visit the language-specific Web sites listed in the reference section at the end of the chapter.

CGI.pm: Perl 5 CGI Library

www-genome.wi.mit.edu/ftp/pub/
software/WWW/cgi_docs.html

CGI.pm, by Lincoln Stein, is the most complete of the perl 5 CGI programming libraries. There are modules for parsing and processing form data, for generating form-based HTML documents to return to the client, and for error checking and report generation. The package is complicated, complete, and highly recommended. It can be thought of as a more sophisticated (and complicated) successor to the *cgi-lib.pl* package (see later). However, the library is large, and thus can be slow to start up—for smaller, faster perl applications, see *cgi-lite.pm.*

Cgi-lib.pl: Perl 4/5 Library

cgi-lib.berkeley.edu/

Cgi-lib.pl, by Steven Brenner, was one of the first perl libraries for CGI program development. It is simple and compatible with both perl 4 and 5 (although it is rare today to find systems still running perl version 4). There are also modules for constructing standard HTML headers and footers for the returned data. Cgi-lib.pl is simpler than *CGI.pm*, but provides less functionality. It is also smaller and faster than *CGI.pm*, but not as fast as *cgi-lite.pm.*

Cgi-lite.pm:
Perl 5 Library

ftp://ftp.freesoftware.com/pub/perl/CPAN/
modules/by-module/CGI_Lite/CGI_Lite-1.8.tar.gz

Cgi-lite.pm, by Shishir Gundavaram, is a small perl 5 library for processing form data. It is modeled to some degree after *CGI.pm,* but omits many of the advanced *CGI.pm* features. The advantage of *cgi-lite.pm* is speed—since it is much smaller, it is much faster to launch, making it ideal when the CGI program needs to be fast.

Cgic: ANSII C Library

www.boutell.com/cgic/

Cgic, by Thomas Boutell, is a free (noncommercial use only) library of C language routines for parsing and manipulating **form** data. Cgic contains modules for exception and error handling, and for handling standard processing functions, such as bounds checking and multiple-choice selection; it can even check for well-known browser errors. There is also a debugging mode. The package can run under Unix, and also under DOS/Windows 95/98/NT/2000.

11.5 Server-Side Includes

CGI programs allow for programs that dynamically generate entire HTML documents (or other data) for return to a browser. In many cases, however, a complementary approach is easier—namely, allowing for X/HTML documents that can dynamically include generated markup content inside themselves. This is often easier because it separates the job of Web page design from that of programming—the designers can write up the X/HTML pages, while the programmers can write the code that generates the dynamic content needed in those pages. The page designers can then use simple script commands, inside the documents they write, that reference the code written by the programmers.

This approach is employed by a number of sophisticated Web application development environments, such as Microsoft's Active Server Pages (ASP), Allaire's Cold Fusion, the open source PHP package, and Sun's Java Server Pages (JSP). The first mechanism of this type, known as the *server-side include* (SSI) mechanism, was first implemented on the NCSA Web server and is currently supported by the Apache, Netscape/iPlanet, and several other commercial servers. Although the SSI environment is not as rich as the others just mentioned, it does illustrate the main features common to all these approaches. Because of this, and also because it is widely supported, simple to use, and simple to explain, we use SSI in this section to illustrate the overall principles of the parsed HTML document approach to dynamic content generation. The next chapter will briefly review some of the other packages.

With parsed HTML packages such as SSI, the Web server supports a special parser that processes specially marked documents (called *parsable* HTML documents, with SSI often having the file name extension .*shtml*), looking for specially encoded HTML comment strings containing SSI directives. The server replaces these special comments with the output generated by processing the directive. There are several different directives—some that "include" other text or HTML files into the document, and others that can execute server-side programs and include the program output within the document.

Of course, this means that the Web server must specially process each such file, directing the HTML document to a special parser for processing prior to forwarding the data to the client that requested it. As a result, server response will be inherently slower than for static HTML documents. Consequently, dynamic HTML document generation should only be done when the content must be generated dynamically upon almost every request to the server. If, on the other hand, the document content changes on a regular schedule, then it is far more efficient to generate the pages using some sort of document management system that operates independently of the Web server.

The next three sections briefly summarize the SSI command syntax and provide three simple examples illustrating how SSI works. The details of server-side include commands and syntax are documented in Appendix E on this book's companion Web site, and also at the Apache Web site. Please see the reference section at the end of Appendix E for the relevant URLs.

11.5.1 SSI Command Syntax

Server-side include commands are placed inside HTML comment string, using the syntax:

```
<!--#include command -->
```

When parsed by a server supporting this feature, the entire comment string is replaced by the output of *include_command*. Because the command is inside a comment string, this will not cause problems if the document is processed by a server that does not support this feature, or if this feature is disabled. Such servers will simply deliver the document, including the comment line—and the client will treat the string as a comment and will ignore it.

The general form for the include command is

```
<!--#command arg1="value1" arg2="value2" -->
```

where *command* is the name of the command to be executed and *arg1* and *arg2* are arguments passed to the command. The supported arguments depend on the command being referenced. There are eight SSI commands: config, echo, exec, fsize, flastmod, include, printenv, and set. Config configures the way the server parses the document. Include includes another document (*not* a CGI program) at the indicated location, while echo includes the contents of one of the environment variables that are set for parsed documents. Fsize and flastmod are similar to echo; fsize prints out the size of a specified file, while flastmod prints the last modification date of a specified file. Printenv prints out a list of all the variables defined to the parsed HTML page, while set lets the document define special variables used by the parsed document. Finally, exec executes a single-line Bourne shell command or a CGI program. For security reasons, the exec facility can be disabled in the server configuration files, while leaving the other features operational.

Appendix E on the Web site describes these command directives in detail, along with some common language extensions.

11.5.2 A Simple Server-Side Include Example

The following example (shown in Figures 11.5 and 11.6) illustrates the use of server-side includes. The example consists of a main document *stuff.shtml* (in this case the suffix *.shtml* denotes parsable HTML documents) that includes a second parsable document *inc_file.shtml*, and that also executes the CGI program *test_script.cgi*. The listings for these examples are shown in Figure 11.5, while the browser rendering of the document *stuff.shtml* is shown in Figure 11.6.

In this example the document *stuff.shtml* is accessed using the URL:

```
http://www.java.utoronto.ca:8008/stuff.shtml/extra/path?arg1+arg2
```

Note that this passes query strings and extra path information to *stuff.shtml*, as if it were a gateway program (see Chapter 10 for more information about CGI programs and passed variables). All the example documents are designed to print these environment variables. As seen in Figure 11.6, these variables are accessible inside the parsable HTML documents and also inside CGI programs (in the environment variables QUERY_STRING and PATH_INFO) executed from within the parsable document. You can thus access a parsable document and, through it, pass query information to a CGI program just as if you were accessing the CGI program directly.

Figures 11.5 and 11.6 also illustrate the include and echo commands. These are useful for printing information about local files, and can be convenient for dynamically generating listings of resources and related information about those resources. However, you want to do this as sparingly as possible, as every such request slows down the server. For example, it is a waste of server resources to use the LAST_MODIFIED variable to display the last time you edited a simple HTML document, since you could just as easily add this information while editing it.

11.5.3 SSI for Inserting Random HTML Fragments

The most common use for SSI is the insertion of HTML text snippets into an existing HTML document. One common extension of this is to insert a randomly selected HTML text snippet, such as a news article or advertising text. The perl program *rot-new.pl*, listed in Figure 11.7, is a simple CGI program that implements this function.

This program selects a file at random from a specified directory and inserts it inline within the parsed document. Assuming that the program is located in the server's *cgi-bin/* directory, the relevant server-side include instruction is:

```
<!--#exec cgi="/cgi-bin/rot-new.pl" -->
```

1. *stuff.shtml*

```
<html>
<head>
<title> Test of Server-side Includes </title>
</head><body>
<h1> Test of Server-side Includes </h1>
<pre>
Stuff.shtml was last modified: <!--#flastmod virtual="/stuff.shtml"
   -->.
Size of stuff.shtml is:        <!--#fsize file="stuff.shtml" -->.
DOCUMENT_NAME =                 <!--#echo var="DOCUMENT_NAME" -->.
DOCUMENT_URI =                  <!--#echo var="DOCUMENT_URI" -->.
DATE_LOCAL =                    <!--#echo var="DATE_LOCAL" -->.
QUERY_STRING =                  <!--#echo var="QUERY_STRING" -->.
PATH_INFO =                     <!--#echo var="PATH_INFO" -->.
DOCUMENT_PATH_INFO =            <!--#echo var="DOCUMENT_PATH_INFO" -->.
DATE_GMT =                      <!--#echo var="DATE_GMT" -->.
LAST_MODIFIED =                 <!--#echo var="LAST_MODIFIED" -->.
</pre>

<!--#config errmsg="Unable to parse scripts" -->.

<p><em>....now include inc_example.shtml....</em>
</p>
<!--#include file="inc_file.shtml" -->

<p> <em>..... now include test_script.cgi CGI program output......
   </em>
</p>
<!--#exec cgi="/cgi-bin/test_script.cgi" -->
</body> </html>
```

2. *inc_file.shtml*

```
<pre>
Inc_file.shtml last modified: <!--#flastmod virtual="/inc_file.shtml"-
   ->.
Size of inc_file.shtml is:     <!--#fsize file="inc_file.shtml" -->.
DOCUMENT_NAME =                 <!--#echo var="DOCUMENT_NAME" -->.
DOCUMENT_URI =                  <!--#echo var="DOCUMENT_URI" -->.
DATE_LOCAL =                    <!--#echo var="DATE_LOCAL" -->.
QUERY_STRING =                  <!--#echo var="QUERY_STRING" -->.
PATH_INFO                       <!--#echo var="PATH_INFO" -->.
DOCUMENT_PATH_INFO =            <!--#echo var="DOCUMENT_PATH_INFO" -->.
DATE_GMT =                      <!--#echo var="DATE_GMT" -->.
```

continues

Figure 11.5 Example of server-side includes, showing the listings for three example documents. The main file is *stuff.shtml,* which *includes* the file *inc_file.shtml* and also the output of the CGI program *test_script.cgi.* The resulting HTML document, upon accessing the URL http://www.java.utoronto.ca:8008/stuff.shtml/extra/path?arg1+arg2, is shown in Figure 11.6.

```
LAST_MODIFIED =                    <!--#echo var="LAST_MODIFIED" -->.

</pre>
```

3. *test_script.cgi* **(in the cgi-bin directory)**

```
#!/bin/sh
echo "Content-type: text/html"
echo
echo "<pre>"
echo "This is CGI script output."
echo
echo "QUERY_STRING =          \"&QUERY_STRING\"."
echo "PATH_INFO =             \"&PATH_INFO\". "
echo "DOCUMENT_PATH_INFO =    \"&DOCUMENT_PATH_INFO\". "
echo "</pre>"
```

Figure 11.5 *(Continued)*

When the server parses this document, it replaces this string by the output of the program *rot-new.pl.*

The ideas are very simple. At line 8, the program prints a text/html content-type header—this header is required of CGI programs returning data to any-thing—including to a parsed HTML document. The second block, at lines 12 through 14, retrieves a directory listing for the directory */svc/www/InsTest.* This is the directory that contains the insertions. Lines 15 through 17 convert the file names into absolute paths, excluding nondata files (i.e., directories), and store the list of files in the array `@filenames`. The subsequent `if` statement at line 22 checks to see if there are any files in this list (the program exits if there are none). The alternate block of the `if`, beginning at line 25, selects a file name at random (line 28), opens the file (line 29), reads in the file content, and then closes the file (line 31) and prints the content to standard output (line 32). The output is the text included within the HTML document.

11.6 References

CGI REFERENCES, TUTORIALS, AND RESOURCE SITES

web.golux.com/coar/cgi/	CGI specifications (more or less)
www.cgi101.com/class/	CGI tutorial
www.jmarshall.com/easy/cgi/	CGI tutorial
www.cgi-resources.com/	Directory of CGI resources

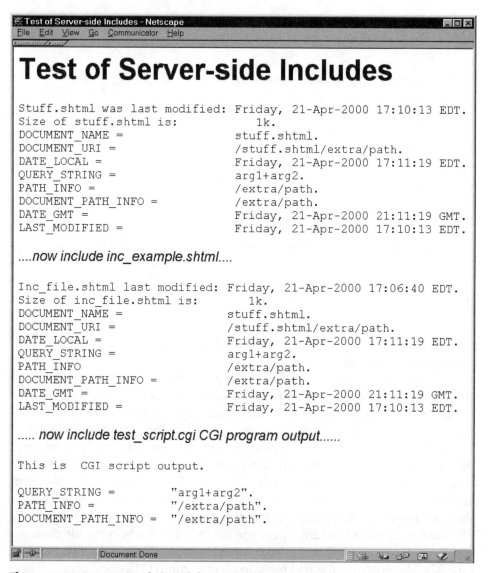

Figure 11.6 Browser rendering of the server-side executable document *stuff.shtml* when accessed using the URL http://www.java.utoronto.ca:8008/stuff.shtml/extra/path?arg1+arg2.

CGI SECURITY

www.irt.org/articles/js184/	Security article
www.w3.org/Security/Faq/www-security-faq.html	Web security FAQ
www.unixtools.org/cgiwrap/	CGIwrap
stein.cshl.org/software/sbox/	sbox
www.apache.org	Apache server/suEXEC

```
1  #!/usr/local/bin/perl
2  # rotator.pl
3  # Author:  Ian Graham
4  #          Information Commons, University of Toronto
5  #          <ian.graham@utoronto.ca>
6  # Version: 1.1.    Date:    April 13 2000
7
8  print "Content-type: text/html\r\n\r\n"; # content-type header
9
10 &include_path="/svc/www/InsTest";   # Directory containing files
11                                      # Second Block: Get listing for
12 if( !opendir(DIR, &include_path)) { # directory containing inserts
13   &f_error("Unable to open notices directory\n",_LINE_, _FILE_); }
14 @tmp = readdir (DIR);               # Read list of filenames; then check
15 foreach (@tmp) {                    # to see they are files, and not dirs
16                                     # (-T tests for "real" files
17 push(@filenames, &include_path."/".&_) if -T &include_path."/".&_;
     }
18 close (DIR);
19 &last_index = &#filenames;    # Get index of last entry
20 &last_index += 1;             # in array of filenames
21
22 if (&last_index < 0) {
23   print " no files to insert ....\n"; die; # no stuff -- do nuthin'
24 }
25 else {                        # If there are files to be
26                               # inserted, select one at random
27   srand(time);                # and print it to stdout.
28   &rand_index = int(rand(&last_index));
29   open(TEMP, &filenames[&rand_index]) ||    # Open selected file --
30     &f_error("Unable to open insertion file.\n", _LINE_,_FILE_);
31   @insertion = <TEMP>; close(TEMP);
32   print @insertion;                # Print contents to output
33 }
34 # ----------- FINISHED --------- FINISHED ------------
35 # Error Handling Subroutine
36
37 sub f_error {                 # What to do if there is an error
38   print "Content-type text/html\n\n";
39   print "Fatal error at line &_[1] in file &_[2].\n";
40   print "Please send mail to: <br />\n";
41   print "<a href=\"mailto:web\@comm.ut.ca\">webm\@comm.ut.ca</a><br
     />\n";
42   print "to inform us of this error. Please, quote the URL\n";
43   print "of the page that gave this error.\n<hr />\n";
44   die "Fatal Error: &_[0] at line &_[1] in file &_[2] \n";
45 }
```

Figure 11.7 Listing for the program *rot-new.pl*, which randomly selects an HTML document segment for insertion within an HTML document. Line numbers (in italics) are added for illustration only, and are not present in the original program. The boldfaced comments are referred to by the text.

CGI PROGRAM ARCHIVE SITES

cgi.resourceindex.com/Programs_and_Scripts/

www.cgiforme.com/

www.oac.uci.edu/indiv/ehood/perlWWW/

www.worldwidemart.com/scripts/ — Matt's script archive

awsd.com/scripts/index.shtml — Darryl's script archive

www.rlaj.com/scripts/ — Ranson's script archive

www.cgi-resources.com/ — Scripts and CGI documentation

LANGUAGE-SPECIFIC INFORMATION/LIBRARIES

www.perl.com — perl information

www.cpan.org — Archive of perl modules/libraries

www.python.org — perl information and libraries

SERVER MODULES FOR FASTER CGI PROCESSING

www.fastcgi.com/ — FastCGI

http://perl.apache.org/ — perl module (Apache server)

www.msg.com.mx/pyapache/ — Python module (Apache server)

CHAPTER 12

Web Application Development Tools

Topics/Concepts Covered: Site management, content management, page scripting environments, Web application servers

The previous 11 chapters reviewed (in some cases in detail) just about every technical issue involved in Web application design and also provided some guidelines to managing the Web application design development process.

However, these sections only alluded to some of the tools available to help build and manage small- and large-scale applications. There are, in fact, many hundreds of commercial and noncommercial (open source) tools available to you. This chapter introduces some of these tools and, more important, tries to highlight the main issues you need to think about when selecting tools or resources so you can make your own reasoned choices. Because management tools are evolving rapidly, it is impossible for any book to be truly up-to-date on specific products. Indeed, new products and services are constantly being launched! One of the most important jobs of a professional Web developer is to be aware of new technologies and services and to be able to analyze the strengths and weaknesses of competing products.

To stay current, you need to read trade magazine articles and surf the Web for information on new products and services. Many trade journals, such as *Information Week* (www.informationweek.com), *PC Week* (recently renamed *eWeek*) (www.zdnet.com/pcweek/), *Network Computing* (www.networkcomputing.com), *Internet World* (www.internetworldnews.com), and others, have regular articles providing comparisons of similar products, high-lighting new technology and business trends, or outlining new Web products and services. Online sites, such as CNET.com, provide similar services in an online format. Although you need to fight your way through the hype and the technical naïveté of some of the writers (who are sometimes writing about technology they do not well understand), these magazines are an excellent way of staying in touch with the latest trends in Internet business models and Web technology. The Web sites are also useful as research tools, and they typically provide searchable indexes of previously published arti-cles or product reviews. Many of these magazines provide free subscriptions to customers who are computer professionals, so the cost of staying current can be quite modest.

12.1 Site Management Tools

directory.google.com/Top/Computers/Software/Internet/Site_Management/
www.dmoz.org/Computers/Software/Internet/Site_Management/

Site management tools are those that can help you manage a deployed site containing largely static Web page collections. There are several management issues to consider, and there are many different tools appropriate to each issue. I won't pretend to tell you which tool is best—indeed, by the time this book is written there will be many new tools to choose from. Instead, I sug-gest some simple tools that I have found useful and try to outline the circum-stance in which the tools are (or are not) appropriate. References to Web sites that provide expanded listings of site management tools are given at the beginning of each section—you can look there for additional information.

You will typically want site management tools for one of three reasons: (1) for your own internal site development, (2) for use in an ongoing site devel-opment project for a client, or (3) as a handoff tool the site owner will use for ongoing maintenance after the site is finished. The tools you use in these three cases will likely be quite different. For your own organization, you may use technically complex tools, since you and/or your staff will be technically proficient and will understand exactly what you are doing. On the other hand, a client will likely be less technically skilled and may need simpler, easier-to-use components.

In most cases you will be considering individual site management tools for small to medium-sized projects. Large projects will often incorporate some sort of content management system (Section 12.2), and such systems gener-ally provide integrated support for things like markup and link validation or site usage analysis.

12.1.1 Markup Validation

www.dmoz.org/Computers/Software/Internet/
Authoring/HTML/Validators_and_Debuggers/

Markup errors are actually the second most common problem (after broken hyperlinks) in a Web site, and they are often the most difficult to spot. This is because markup errors typically show up on only one or two browsers—and invariably not on the browser you or your staff actually use. Thus, it is very useful to have an unbiased tool for checking for page errors, as this can eliminate a lot of tedious work trying to find markup problems.

Moreover, it is easy for small markup problems to creep into Web site pages and cause unforeseen problems in page rendering. This is particularly so if the pages in a site are being regularly edited, as small editing errors can easily break the markup. One way to avoid this is to regularly check the live site for errors in markup using one of the many HTML syntax validation utilities. Some of these are online services—you provide a Web URL and the service retrieves the resource and provides validation (and perhaps other) analysis for the page. Some useful services of this type are as follows:

validator.w3.org/	HTML validator
www.htmlhelp.com/tools/validator/	HTML validator
jigsaw.w3.org/css-validator/	CSS validator
www.netmechanic.com	HTML validation, plus other diagnostics

The last location will also let you arrange for automatic scanning of your entire Web site (for a small fee, of course).

Remote scanning tools are useful for small sites, but typically not for larger ones. With large sites you will most likely want to automatically validate many pages, schedule more frequent validation for pages that change often, or perhaps validate pages before they are published. In this case you will want a tool that you can manage and that can be configured to operate in the desired fashion. The most common tools of this type are as follows:

www.htmlvalidator.com	Windows-based HTML validator
www.jclark.com/sp/	SP: Generic SGML/XML validation tools

The *HTML Validator* tool (a commercial product) is a Windows application that can read in and evaluate local or URL-specified resources. This tool is useful when validating pages before they are published or for quick validation of many documents. However, it is not designed to support automated validation. *SP*, from James Clark, is an open source software library for processing and validating any type of SGML and XML data—this package is actually the back end for many of the online validation services. If you have a qualified *perl* programmer on your team you can easily use this tool to construct your own automated validation tools.

Sometimes, however, validation is overkill, and you simply want to check for the worst errors in the document—once these errors are found and fixed, you can then validate more easily. *HTML tidy* (www.w3.org/People/Raggett/tidy/) is a good example of this type of tool: HTML tidy will read in an HTML document and "tidy it up" by fixing typical markup errors. It can also operate in an XHTML mode, converting existing HTML documents into the newer XHTML format. Other tools, such as *Dr. HTML* (www.w2.imagiware.com/RxHTML/), check for common HTML syntax errors, and some also check for spelling errors. Unfortunately Dr. HTML checks only for accurate U.S. English spelling!

Last, if you want to check that your site is accessible to persons with disabilities, you should use the Bobby Web site, at: www.cast.org/bobby/. This online service site performs accessibility evaluations of Web pages and provides useful feedback to help you better understand important accessibility issues.

12.1.2 Link Checking and Analysis

www.dmoz.org/Computers/Software/Internet/Site_Management/Link_Management/

The most common and annoying problem with a Web site is broken links—and you certainly don't want visitors to your site, or to any site you manage, to encounter them. There are a number of commercial tools that can detect and flag broken links, and you will find good lists of link verification tools listed at the preceding URL. The next few paragraphs describe a few simple tools I have found useful in this regard.

For interactive link verification, *Xenu's Link Sleuth* (http://home.snafu.de/tilman/xenulink.html) is both fast and simple to use. This is a Windows application that starts with a specified page and explores all outbound links up to a specified depth (staying within specified domains). It cannot check **form** elements, nor can it check for accurate fragment identifiers (i.e., for correct links to locations within a document), but in general it is a quick and useful tool for validating links across many hundreds of pages.

The *LinkScan* package from Electronic Software Publishing Corporation (www.elsop.com/linkscan/) is useful for larger-scale projects. This consists of a perl library of utilities for performing a variety of link checking, syntax validation (as described in Section 1.2.1), and other tests of a Web site. Since it is a code library, you can use it to create your own custom validation tools, which makes it useful for building automated link validation systems.

A third option is to outsource link checking to a service that regularly monitors a site for broken links and mails back a summary of observed problems. *LinkAlarm* (www.linkalarm.com/) is an example of such a service, although there are others. This may be a reasonable choice to offer to a client who has a small to medium-sized site that does not change rapidly. This also lets you hand off ongoing site support responsibilities and makes it easier for the owner of the site to take responsibility for site maintenance and management.

On the other hand, this approach is often inappropriate if there is a lot of site content or if the content changes rapidly. In these cases, you may wish to set up your own monitoring services with the ability to quickly check modified pages for errors and to slowly check the entire site (of more slowly changing documents) for broken or obsolete links.

12.1.3 Site Log and Usage Analysis

http://www.dmoz.org/Computers/Software/
Internet/Site_Management/Log_Analysis/

Every Web server maintains a log file that records information about page accesses, and these log files are a treasure trove of useful information about how visitors are using the site. Moreover, many sites must provide regular reports so that the business (or other) case for the site can be justified or evaluated. In either case, you will need suitable tools that can mine the server logs for data and present this data in a useful way.

For simple Web reporting, the open source *Webalizer* package (www .mrunix.net/webalizer/) may be suitable. This produces simple usage summaries showing daily, weekly, and monthly usage rates, usage by domain name of visitors, and so on. There are many other free tools offering similar features; the URL at the beginning of this section mentions most of them.

For larger sites or for richer analysis tools and report generation, you will likely want a commercial tool. There are many, most of which are targeted toward specific markets or uses (general usage summaries, marketing campaign summaries, etc.). WebTrends (www.webtrends.com) is one of the largest players in this field, offering a variety of site analysis products targeted toward different business needs. If you need a product with more flexibility than the freeware products and require elegantly formatted reports tailored for business needs, then you may want to look at the WebTrends products or those offered by competitors such as net.Analysis (www.netgen .com/products/netanalysis/index.shtml) or Marketwave (www.marketwave .com). Again, the URLs at the beginning of this section provide lists of these and other commercial tools.

At the very high end, you may be interested in custom data-mining tools that analyze a mix of server log, cookie-tracked data, personalization profiles, and other data to try to better understand site usage, user patterns, and demographic data sorted by site region. In these cases, you will be looking at pack-

ages such as *Insight* (www.accrue.com/) or *Aria* (www.andromedia
.com/products/aria/index.html). You may also wish to consider dedicated
database analysis systems built using statistical analysis packages (SAS,
www.sas.com or SPSS, www.spss.com, etc.) or data-mining tools.

Note also that some server products (such as Microsoft SiteServer) come
equipped with log and user analysis modules that may perform some, if not
all, of the tasks you need.

If the site has placed advertisements, then there will be additional monitoring constraints imposed by the advertising placement system. In this case
you will need to check with the advertising placement service or system to
find out the requirements they place on your site.

12.1.4 Site Performance Monitoring

www.dmoz.org/Computers/
Software/Internet/Site_Management/Monitoring/
www.softwareqatest.com/qatweb1.html#MONITORING

Once a site is up and running, you will want to make sure it stays up and
continues to run effectively. As noted in Section 6.6 of Chapter 6, there are
three issues you need to consider:

Network performance. It is useful to know when the network connecting
your Web site to the outside world is malfunctioning or has become
overloaded.

Application performance. While a Web site is up, it is important to know
that the servers are running and that the site (or application) is working
properly.

Customer-perceived performance. It is useful to know how outside users
see your site. This is a check, in a rough way, of the preceding two items
plus the performance of other sections of the Internet you may not control. In a fundamental way, however, this is the most important measure-
ment—because if the site doesn't work for customers, the details of
network or application performance do not really matter.

The first two are important for internal monitoring of a site, and they let
you quickly detect and fix internal problems when they occur. Moreover,
long-term monitoring of application performance helps you to understand
the problem areas in your application, and these problem areas will produce
most of the observed problems. Similarly, long-term monitoring of application and network performance will help you understand usage patterns and
the usage growth curve, which is very useful in planning appropriate
upgrades to the network, application servers, or both.

There are many different types of network monitoring tools, and the details of these are beyond the scope of this book. The resource sites listed at the beginning of this section list some such tools, but this issue is better dealt with in collaboration with your network administration experts, who will likely already be using some such tools to manage your network. If you are already outsourcing your network management (for example, if the site is hosted by an ISP), you can contact the service provider and find out what sorts of network monitoring information the company can provide.

Application performance is best monitored using Web site testing tools. If you want to perform only simple tests, then you can write simple script programs that retrieve characteristic pages from the site and that send mail to site administrators when the page retrieval is too slow or fails altogether. There are many perl libraries and utility programs available for developing such tools.

For mission-critical sites and applications, you will want richer tools that can test more thoroughly and trigger more sophisticated alarms when problems are detected—after all, if the server is down because the network is down, then you aren't going to receive e-mail notification of the problem! More-complex tools can page the machine operator, send e-mail, or even phone administrators and play prerecorded messages, thus ensuring that problems are quickly reported and dealt with.

There are many packages that provide this functionality. For example, *Holistix Web Manager* (www.holistix.net/products/webmgr/) can detect a variety of Web server and network-related problems and can page or phone appropriate staff depending on the type of problem it detects. *Topaz ActiveWatch*, from Mercury Interactive (www.mercuryinteractive.com/products/topaz/), provides similar functionality. Most of these products include report generation and site monitoring features that often overlap with the site analysis tools discussed in Section 12.1.3.

Of course, internal network or application performance is not the whole story—it is also important to know how well the outside world can access and use your site, which calls for external monitoring of the site. It is often easiest to outsource this type of monitoring, since it is otherwise expensive to set up monitoring stations at various locations on the Internet. Some examples of companies offering this type of service are AlertSite (alertsite.com), AtWatch (www.atwatch.com), HyperTrak (www.hypertrak.com), SiteAlert (sitealert.computacenter.com), and NetWhistle (www.netwhistle.com). These services typically provide regular reports on perceived site performance and can also be configured to send alerts (by pager, phone, e-mail, or other means) when site performance falls below a predefined level. These service companies also typically offer various levels of performance monitoring, so these services can be affordable for small sites with limited performance monitoring requirements.

12.1.5 Site Load Balancing and Distribution

www.dmoz.org/Computers/Software/
Internet/Site_Management/Mirroring/
www.dmoz.org/Computers/Software/
Internet/Site_Management/Load_Balancing/

With large sites that serve out many millions of pages a day, high quality of service (speed, performance, and reliability) are usually critical business issues for the site. However, with large sites is it almost impossible to guarantee high quality of service without distributing content around the Internet and providing multiple access points to the data. Only in this way can you eliminate network bottlenecks and the possibility of a single point of failure.

With static data you can use mirroring technologies to create distributed copies of your static data at various locations throughout the Internet. By careful use of DNS round-robin (discussed in Chapter 7, Section 7.2.2) or other approaches you can distribute user requests across these multiple servers. This significantly reduces the load on any single server and can significantly improve the quality of service.

There are two ways to provide such mirrored content. Perhaps the simplest is to essentially lease replication or mirroring services from mirroring or content-distribution service providers. The advantage of this approach is that you need maintain only a single Web site. The mirroring service will automatically (after some work configuring the software, of course) mirror content to remote caches and automatically distribute user requests across these caches. There are several companies that provide mirroring services of this type, the best known being Akami (www.akami.com), Sandpiper (www.digisle.com), Inktomi (www.inktomi.com, recently bought out by Vignette), and Mirror Image (www.mirror-image.com). Most of these companies also provide special tools for distributing high-bandwidth services such as streamed media. In many cases these services can be leased on a case-by-case basis, so you can essentially purchase extra bandwidth only when it is needed. You can also use these services to mirror only part of your content—for example, mirroring the static image files while still serving the dynamic content from your own servers.

Alternatively, you can create your own collection of distributed Web servers and replicate the data between those servers. This lets you take ownership of the whole process and is particularly useful if you do not actually manage a single central Web server but instead coordinate multiple servers, each of which has content published to it. The open source *rdist* package (www.magnicomp.com/rdist/rdist.shtml) is a popular tool for managing remote distribution of data files between machines and is a good choice if you have simple replication needs and want to build your own tools for doing so. If your needs are more advanced, then you may want more complex replication packages such as *Global/Site* by F5 Networks (www.f5.com)

or OpenDeploy by Interwoven (www.interwoven.com). On the other hand, if you are running a large site with complex replication needs, you may also be running sophisticated content management tools (see Section 12.2), many of which include replication tools.

If your site has significant interactive content, then the situation is more complicated. This is because most interactive sites interact with both users and back-end databases—and to keep the data coherent across all the sites, you want to make sure that the different replicated sites are all using (and writing to) the same back-end database. For this to work effectively you need to consider the possibility of site replication at the point the back-end software architecture is designed, making sure that the database can maintain coherency across the multiple, replicated copies.

12.1.6 Web Site Backup

If the building burns down, do you have your Web site safely backed up so you can recover it and rebuild it elsewhere? If so, then you probably have a well-defined backup and disaster recovery strategy. And if you don't have a well-defined backup and disaster recovery strategy, then you should think of setting one up. After all, there's no point in setting up a mission-critical Web site (or even one that is not mission-critical) if you have no way to recover from an accidental fire, failure (or bankruptcy) of your service provider, or some other disaster.

In the case of small to medium-sized Web sites you may be hosting the site on a server managed by a service provider, in which case the service provider will hopefully have its own backup and disaster recovery procedures. However, many providers do not guarantee reliable backups or disaster recovery unless it is explicitly written into your contract. Moreover, if the data is critical to your business, you probably want your own backup copy. Otherwise, if the service provider goes bankrupt, then you might find it difficult to get at your data to move it elsewhere.

If this is your situation, contact your service provider and check carefully to ensure that it runs regular backups and can guarantee reliable disaster recovery. You should also talk over ways in which you can obtain your own backup copies of the site. A simple option is to maintain a backup copy of the site on your own computer, from which you can store the size to backup disks (such as zip disks or rewritable CD-ROMs) or to tape. Indeed, it is generally a good idea to do your development work on your own machines, then to upload the production site to the machines managed by your service provider. Your own computers can then keep backup copies of the site, although they will not contain any dynamic data generated by user interaction on the production site.

12.2 Content Management Systems

idm.internet.com/tools/cm/index.html
www.xmlsoftware.com/dms/ (XML-based tools)
www.dmoz.org/Computers/Software/Internet/
Site_Management/Content_Management/

When sites become very large, have lots of regularly updated content, or are maintained on multiple servers, then maintenance often becomes the single largest site management problem. If this is the situation you are looking at, then you may wish to consider constructing and managing the site content using a content management system. Such systems control the publishing of content, protect the content from being altered by unauthorized users, and ensure validity of the content (by validating the markup, validating links, checking spelling, etc.), all under a centrally managed framework. Although such packages can be very expensive, they can be well worth the price if you are managing a very large site and need to establish well-defined long-term management strategies for the site and its content.

Of course, content management systems come with several costs, and you need to be aware of those costs before proceeding. First, many such systems use proprietary technologies for managing the content, which means that it can be difficult (and costly) to migrate from one system to another or to integrate other tools into these systems. Given the rapid rate of technological evolution, it is safest to stick with open standards–based technologies, particularly in this area where there is no dominant company setting de facto industry standards. However, there are currently few open standards that cover site management or publishing, so this is not always easy to do. Some open standards (such as WebDAV, a Web-based standard for managing distributed authoring and versioning of content on Web servers) are now being established, but most are only being integrated into commercial packages.

The second issue is cost. Large-scale content management systems can cost in the hundreds of thousands of dollars or more, so you need a very compelling business case to choose this option. Moreover, such systems will need to be integrated into the work-flow model of the organization that owns and manages the site. This means that, prior to even considering such a system, you should carefully analyze how such a system should be used within the organization so that you can carefully establish requirements for the new system and understand how it will integrate into (or change) the existing work-flow model. Use-case analysis (described briefly in Chapter 5) can be a useful component of this analysis. Given a good understanding of the requirements, you can then determine which of the multitude of commercial products best fit your needs.

Finally, you need to consider training time and cost. Large-scale content management systems are complicated, and you will need to provide training for the staff who will use them. This will involve preparing training materials, delivering courses, and providing ongoing help desk and mentoring support for users.

As a low-cost option for smaller sites, you can consider Web authoring packages such as Macromedia's *Dreamweaver* (www.macromedia.com) or Microsoft's *FrontPage* (www.microsoft.com). In addition to being Web page editors, these tools provide site publishing and some site management features, which can make them a reasonable management option for small sites destined to be maintained by relatively inexperienced Web designers. Note, however, that the publishing and management components of these tools do not easily integrate with the more-complex management systems, although the editing components can generally still be used. These packages do have the advantage of low cost (typically, a few hundred dollars per user to buy the software). However, you will still need to allow for several hours of training time per user if you want your staff to be able to effectively use these packages. Still, the up-front costs are modest compared with those of large-scale management systems.

High-end content management systems generally provide a rich suite of tools for managing content on a Web site or collection of Web sites, including version control, work-flow management, dynamic generation of content pages (such as regularly updated news pages), and content management across multiple distributed servers. Some also provide commonly used dynamic page generation components, such as personalized page views (customized based on user preferences). Most also provide programming APIs or other mechanisms (such as XML data gateways) for integrating content generated by custom applications into the pages delivered by the system. Some example products and their main features are:

BroadVision (www.broadvision.com). Focus is on personalized content for a variety of industry segments (financial, retail, etc.). The company focus is on business-to-customer e-commerce products, of which personalized content is one important component.

DynaBase (www.inso.com). Focus is on managing content as a managed database of XML- or SGML-based data. DynaBase originated as an SGML database system.

Egrail (www.egrail.com). Sells a suite of different content management and personalization tools. Egrail software is built using open source components (Apache server, PHP, MySQL, etc.), which means that this package is less expensive than many others.

NetObjects (www.netobjects.com). Sells a suite of different content management and personalization tools. NetObjects is also one of the few companies to sell products suitable (both in price and performance) for small and medium-sized businesses.

OpenMarket (www.openmarket.com). Sells a set of various content management, personalization, and electronic commerce products.

OpenShare (www.infosquare.com). A low- to medium-end content management application designed for the document management needs of small to medium-sized companies.

Personalization Server (www.atg.com). Focus is on generation of personalized content from existing database resources. The company also sells application server products that can integrate these products with custom applications.

Resolution (www.ncompasslabs.com). A Microsoft-based content management system that incorporates some Windows-specific code to allow "drag-and-drop" publishing.

StoryServer (www.vignette.com). The StorySever product line focuses on content management and site personalization. The next generation of products (the V series) is focused more toward commerce sites and personalization as a tool for building better business relationships.

TeamSite (www.interwoven.com). Emphasis is on work-flow management and version control for the creation and maintenance of content. The company also provides other products for integrating content and for producing personalized content.

Userland (www.userland.com). Sells a content management system that is largely open source—that is, the core database engine is proprietary, but the development environment is essentially open source. The *Manila* product (there are several others) is designed for managing content-rich Web sites such as online magazines or newspapers.

Web Integrity (www.mks.com/products/wi/). A document and script content management system, based on software originally designed for managing software in large-scale software development projects.

There are of course many other products, and the URLs at the beginning of this section are good starting points for information on them. Note that, with all these products, the implementation costs escalate rapidly when you want to include features not supported in the existing tool. Thus, to avoid cost (and schedule) overruns in the implementation phase, it is very important to understand your requirements before you select an appropriate product.

Last, there are some interesting open source products you may wish to consider. Although these generally do not have the same sets of features and performance as the commercial packages, they do hold to open standards, which, in principle, makes them easier to integrate with other products. Also, since they are open source products, your developers will have access to the actual code so that you can actively fix problems or easily add custom functionality. The two best-known products in this category are as follows:

Roxen Internet Software (www.roxen.com). Sells a set of different content management systems written in Java and using open source standards such as XML and XSLT.

Zope, by Digital Creations Inc. (www.zope.com). An interesting mix of a content management system and application server. The system consists of a central object database that manages the content, plus content management tools built on top of the database. The system can be customized using programs written in the Python programming language.

12.2.1 E-Commerce Sites

Most content management packages (including the ones listed previously) are now being designed with a focus on current Web trends—namely on corporate sites wishing to build a compelling electronic commerce presence. Thus, companies like Vignette, BroadVision, and NetObjects provide versions of their products tailored for specific business tasks such as e-business, relationship marketing/personalization, customer support, content management, and so on. In essence, these products integrate automated business process features (such as transaction or account processing or customer support) with a content management core. Nevertheless, this can significantly simplify the task of getting a complex e-commerce site up and running quickly, albeit sometimes at a staggeringly high cost.

Such integrated commerce systems are available from a number of sources, such as Microsoft (*Site Server Commerce Edition*, www.microsoft.com), Vignette (www.vignette.com), BroadVision (www.broadvision.com), BEA Systems (www.bea.com), NetObjects (www.netobjects.com), OpenMarket (www.openmarket.com), Allaire (www.allaire.com), and many others. However, with an existing company, such systems need to be carefully integrated into existing financial or other information systems, which can make them even more complex (and costly) to implement relative to the content management systems just described. In most cases, this will involve extensive customization of the product to integrate it with the existing tools and systems of the company. Thus, most commerce systems are really just Web application servers (discussed in Section 12.4) combined with special programming libraries and tools that provide core e-commerce functions or that help integrate the application into these other existing systems.

12.3 Page Scripting Environments

As discussed in Chapter 10 (Section 10.8) there are basically two ways to add programmed functionality to a Web server. One of these is to actually add programs (gateway programs, Java servlets, or others) to the Web server that are run when the program is referenced by a URL. The program then generates the data (HTML or other) to return to the client that made the request. This approach is very useful if much of the application design involves writing fundamentally new code. However, it does make it difficult to separate the roles of the software designers (who will write the code), and the Web page-, user interface-, and graphic designers who will want to build the markup and other content that make up the pages.

The second approach is to incorporate a special processing environment into the server that can preprocess documents on the server, interpret script code included in the document, and replace the program script lines by content generated by the script. The SSI mechanism described in Section 11.5 of Chapter 11 is a simple example of this approach. This approach is particularly useful if the amount of code needed is small or is simple to implement. Then the Web page, user interface, and graphic designers can design the HTML pages that will make up the site, and the programmers can then update the pages to include the script lines that generate the dynamic content required in the page. This approach becomes less suitable when the HTML documents start to consist of more script code than markup.

These approaches are much more sophisticated than the tools that the server includes, supporting parsed documents that are essentially programs, complete with branching and conditional execution. The corresponding document markup often resembles HTML, but with additional, special-purpose tags reflecting the page processing language or enclosing the instructions processed by the page processor.

There are at least a dozen such products on the market, and probably more. Table 12.1 lists the most common ones and provides a brief description of the main features. Some, such as Microsoft's *Active Server Pages* or Netscape/iPlanet's *Livewire*, come integrated with the Web server. The other packages generally must be purchased and installed as server modules: The companies generally provide easy-to-install modules for most popular Web servers, such as *Apache* (www.apache.org), Microsoft *SiteServer* (www .microsoft.com/siteserver), Netscape/*iPlanet* (www.iplanet.com), O'Reilly *WebSitePro* (www.oreilly.com/catalog/webpro2/), or *StrongHold* (www.c2 .net/products/sh2/). These packages are generally of similar complexity (that is, all are programming environments, so you need to know how to program to use them well), although some have more features than others. In particular, most of these packages have a large set of integrated database

Table 12.1 Commercial and Open Source Web Page Scripting Environments

PRODUCT	AVAILABILITY	STATUS
Active Server pages (ASP)	www.microsoft.com	Commercial (free with base-level Web servers). Scripting language is a version of VBScript. Several companies such as Chili!Soft (www.chilisoft.com) and Halcyon Software (www.halcyonsoft.com) have developed ASP implementations for other platforms such as Linux, Solaris, Apple, and Novell.
ColdFusion	www.allaire.com	Commercial (ranges from $1300 to $5000 depending on platform and features). Uses special markup tags for script instructions. See also Section 12.4.
HTML/OS	www.aestiva.com	Commercial (approximately $800 per server). Scripting language is based on BASIC.
iHTML	www.ihtml.com	Commercial ($150 to $900). Uses special markup tags for script instructions.
Java Server Pages (JSP)	www.javasoft.com/products/jsp/index.html, www.iplanet.com and other servers, and application server development environments	Commercial. Includes Java code (or references to Java Servlets) from within the document. The Apache server project is preparing an open source version (see jakarta.apache.org).
Livewire	www.iplanet.com	Commercial. Server-side JavaScript support is included in most iPlanet servers.
meta-HTML	www.metahtml.com	Free (with license, source code is available). Uses special markup tags for script instructions.
MivaScript	htmlscript.volant.com	Commercial (limited feature-free version, $100 to $900 for various commercial versions). Uses special markup tags for script instructions.
NeoWebScript	www.neosoft.com/neowebscript/	Commercial (free light version, including source code; NeoScript-SA, the advanced version, costs around $30). Scripting language based on *tcl* (dev.scriptics.com/).
PHP	www.php.net	Free (GNU public license). C-like scripting language.
Curl	www.curl.com	Commercial (not yet released). An interesting twist on this class of development environment. Some technical information is found at curl.lcs.mit.edu/curl/.

access commands, allowing for dynamic document generation based on database content.

Similar page-scripted functionality is also possible from standard CGI programs written in perl or python. In these cases, the perl or python program reads a template HTML document and processes the template, producing standard HTML as output. Perl modules appropriate to these tasks are available at the perl CPAN archive (www.cpan.org), and relevant python libraries are available from www.python.org.

In general there are four issues to consider when evaluating such packages as possible tools for developing a Web application:

- Cost
- Platform independence
- Integration with back-end resources such as databases, directory services, or other resources/services required of your application
- Speed and scalability

If cost is a major issue, then you will want to consider the environments that may come integrated with the server, such as ASP (on Microsoft servers) or LiveWire and JSP (integrated with iPlanet servers). On the other hand, PHP is free and available for just about all Web servers and is a compelling alternative if you want to get avoid being restricted to particular Web server software or hardware platforms.

If platform independence is a major concern, then you should consider one of the packages that is not tied to a specific server developer, such as Cold Fusion, iHTML, MivaScript, or PHP. These packages are generally supported on many different machines and operating systems and by many different HTTP servers. This makes it relatively easy to change hardware or software and still reuse the existing Web pages and page scripts.

If your Web application needs to connect to back-end databases, then you must check the packages to find out how well they support the database you will be using. In general, most of these tools provide excellent database connectivity using a variety of database-specific (ODBC, Oracle, Sybase, MySQL) programming interfaces. However, you should always verify that the database you need to use is well supported by the product you select.

Your application may also need to access other resources such as Lightweight Directory Access Protocol (LDAP) servers and mail servers, may need to be able to process other data formats such as XML or PDF, or may need to support complex functions such as user session management. Most scripting packages provide tools for accessing LDAP servers or for processing XML data. However, you should be careful to check with the packages to make sure the special feature you want is supported by the core package or by available extension modules. For example, PHP Version 3 does not itself support session management, although this feature is supported by the freely available PHPLIB extension library. (Session management will be an integral component of PHP version 4.)

The final consideration will be speed and scalability. Obviously, you want the application you develop to work well with the anticipated number of users and to let you expand the application to many more users in the future. In this case, you will need to consider more than just the scripting environment itself—you also need to know how well the Web server will perform as the load increases and whether the server and scripting engine can be replicated across multiple servers for increased performance. Packages such as ColdFusion or JSP can generally satisfy these requirements, although you may need to upgrade to higher-end products (both hardware and software) to get the full range of scalability. However, the other products in this category also tend to scale well in most cases. Unless you are developing a terrifically high-end site that will demand incredible performance, you can safely consider all these tools as possible options.

Many trade magazines or Web sites regularly have articles comparing these different scripting environments or listing other environments that provide similar functionality. Here are some good ones:

http://hotwired.lycos.com/webmonkey/ 99/46/index1a.html?tw=programmin	November 1999 comparisons
www.houseoffusion.com/hof/body/ asp.cfm	Cold Fusion/ASP comparison: January 2000
http://webdeveloper.internet.com/ database/db_connectivity_software.html	Other packages

12.3.1 WebMacro

As mentioned at the beginning of the previous section, page scripting environments are at their best when the document consists mostly of regular markup, with only a small amount of script code. This makes it easier for page designers to design the page, since they don't have to learn how to write complex scripts or share the design works with a programmer. As we all know, programmers—on the average—are poor graphics or page designers, and vice versa. Thus, by separating the two roles as much as possible you can significantly simplify the application development process by letting programmers program and designers design.

The *WebMacro* package, an open source package available from www .webmacro.org, was designed with this model in mind. The are two basic ideas behind WebMacro:

- The detailed functionality of the program components needed in the Web page should be kept outside the page. The current WebMacro implementation codes these components as Java objects, referenced, using the WebMacro language, from within the HTML templates.

■ The WebMacro language should be a minimal macro language that references desired data from the program objects: All the code not directly related to markup generation should be in the program objects themselves.

With current implementations of WebMacro, the Web server first launches a Java servlet, processes the request, reads in and processes the appropriate WebMacro template document, and returns the generated HTML document to the browser. Indeed, a single servlet can then return different pages (by accessing different WebMacro templates) depending on the data it needs to return to the browser.

The advantage is a clean separation of code from markup, which should make the tasks of preparing Web pages and writing code easier since the two jobs can be done separately and often in parallel. In practice, this also means that the programmer must write well-designed code that is easy for the page designer to use. This is also a good thing (although this requirement may slow development in some cases) since it forces the programmer to more carefully think through the implementation details.

The package is still under development, but has already been incorporated into several Web application development environments (e.g., Melati, at www.melati.org, Tigris, at www.tigris.org, and the Apache Turbine project, at java.apache.org/turbine/index.html). There is also an interesting review of WebMacro, comparing it favorably against Java Server Pages, at www.servlets.com/soapbox/problems-jsp.html.

12.4 Web Application Servers

The term *application server* essentially refers to large development suites designed for developing complex Web-based applications. Typically, such suites are designed to integrate with sophisticated back-end databases or applications, to integrate with legacy software, and to be scalable to tens of millions of page views per day—or all of these. If you notice that this description is not very different from the previous descriptions of page scripting environments, then you are correct—the focus of a Web application server is not very different from content management systems or page scripting environments. The difference is that most Web application servers provide a cross section of common Web and application development functionality, including the following:

■ Content management
■ Personalization utilities

- Page scripting languages
- Integrated Web commerce tools
- Support for Java servlets and JavaBeans (a component object model for Java development)
- Support for DCOM (Microsoft's Distributed Component Object Model), CORBA (Common Object Request Broke Architecture), or Java's RMI (Remote Method Invocation) for developing distributed applications

These packages also often come with extensive programming library (API) support for other core functions—for example, transaction processing, connectors to enterprise-class applications such as IBMs IMS Information Management System (www.ibm.com/software/data/ims/), and SAP AG's R/3 (www.sap.com). Indeed, these are industrial-strength software applications, with large price tags and high development costs.

If you are going to be integrating a wide variety of software tools into a Web application, then you will certainly end up wanting to consider a package. However, you should never purchase such a product before you have carefully worked out your requirements for it and have developed an architectural solution for your integrated application design. Projects such as these are generally large and will take an extended time to implement in full.

There are several companies providing products that fall in this category. The following is a short list of some of the better-known suites, with URLs that provide additional information:

Allaire	www.allaire.com
Apple WebObjects	www.apple.com/webobjects/
Art Technology Group (Dynamo App. Server)	www.atg.com
BEA Systems (WebLogic)	weblogic.beasys.com
Bluestone (Sapphire/ Web and XML Suite)	www.bluestone.com/products/ sapphire/
Enhydra	www.enhydra.com (open source)
Haht (HahtSite)	www.haht.com
IBM WebSphere	www-4.ibm.com/software/ webservers/appserv/
iPlanet	www.iplanet.com
Microsoft	www.microsoft.com/siteserver/
NetDynamics	www.netdynamics.com
Open Market	www.openmarket.com/
Oracle	www.oracle.com/appserver/

Silverstream	www.silverstream.com
Zope	www.zope.org (open source)

Note that many of the company names appearing in this list were also mentioned in Section 12.3. Indeed, many application servers are really "script environments on expensive steroids." The previous list simply highlights the more well-known packages in this category. More complete lists of application servers are available at the following:

www.mobileapps.com/WebAppServers.htm

www.omg.org/news/pr99/application_servers.html

dmoz.org/Computers/Software/Internet/Servers/Application/

The following URLs provide some comparisons between the different the different suites and their features:

www.flashline.com/components/appservermatrix.jsp	Java-based suites only
www.techmetrix.com/lab/benchcenter/asdirindex.shtml	
www.techmetrix.com/lab/benchcenter/appserverbench.shtml	
serverwatch.internet.com/appservers.html	
serverwatch.internet.com/articles/ appsvendors/appsvend_1.html	Review article, April 30, 2000
www.interwoven.com/ developer/library/ analyst/forrester.html	A collection of Forrester research articles analyzing content management and application server packages—biased, of course, in favor of Interwoven's products

12.4.1 Avoiding Web Application Servers

Web application servers are sometimes called *middleware* because they reside in the middle, between the front end (the stuff that builds the Web pages or user interfaces) and the back end containing the data or otherwise making up the application's services. The goal of such a three-tier system is to provide a bridge between disparate back-end systems and to provide features (such as load averaging across multiple servers or redundancy for increased reliability) that the back-end products do not provide on their own.

On the other hand, having things in the middle will not magically make an application faster or more reliable. Indeed, adding middleware does exactly the opposite: Adding an additional layer of software will invariably slow an application and introduce new bugs. This is inevitable, since the more software you have, the more the software has to do and the more things there are that can go wrong. Moreover, to develop your local application, your developers will need to learn a whole new system in addition to the existing back-end and front-end components, so development will also be slowed and will introduce additional bugs.

Ideally, then, you should avoid going the application-server route unless you have compelling integration problems you need to solve. Fortunately, most pure Web applications do not integrate disparate back-end products—most simply involve one or more databases (all using the same back-end database system, such as Oracle) and a Web interface–generation system. In this case, middleware should be avoided and you should stick with page scripting environments (or other direct page-generation solutions) that connect directly to the back-end software. In most cases, appropriate back-end software (such as databases) will provide many of the replication or redundant reliability features that you need without a middleware package.

A rather more strenuous (and entertaining) argument of this point is found at photo.net/wtr/application-servers.html.

Index